Financing Education

FINANCING EDUCATION

Overcoming Inefficiency and Inequity

Edited by

Walter W. McMahon and Terry G. Geske

UNIVERSITY OF ILLINOIS PRESS
Urbana   Chicago   London

©1982 by the Board of Trustees of the University of Illinois
Manufactured in the United States of America

This book is printed on acid-free paper.

Library of Congress Cataloging in Publication Data

Main entry under title:

Financing education.

    Includes index.
    1. Education — United States — Finance — Addresses, essays, lectures. 2. Educational equalization — United States — Addresses, essays, lectures.
I. McMahon, Walter W. II. Geske, Terry G., 1941-
LB2825.F515   379.1′21′0973   81-12965
ISBN 0-252-00940-1 (cloth)   AACR2
ISBN 0-252-00941-X (paper)

To our parents
Lucile McMahon
and
Frieda and Garland Geske

Contents

Preface ix

1 Efficiency and Equity Criteria for Educational Budgeting and Finance *Walter W. McMahon* 1

Part I
SOCIAL EFFICIENCY 31

2 Human Capital Approaches in Organizing and Paying for Education *Theodore W. Schultz* 36

3 Household Production of Human Capital: Time Uses of Parents and Children as Inputs *Charles S. Benson* 52

4 Productivity and Cost Effectiveness as Financing Criteria *Richard A. Rossmiller* 78

5 Efficiency in Educational Finance: The Classroom Perspective *J. Alan Thomas, Frances Kemmerer,* and *David H. Monk* 100

6 Measuring Non-monetary Benefits of Education: A Survey *Robert T. Michael* 119

7 The Monetary Returns to Education as Partial Social Efficiency Criteria *Walter W. McMahon* and *Alan P. Wagner* 150

Part II
EQUITY 189

8 Concepts of Equity *Kern Alexander* 193

9 Equity and Higher Education Finance: The Case of Community Colleges *Susan C. Nelson* 215

10 The Search for Equity in School Finance *Stephen J. Carroll* 237

11 Shifting Sources of Financing Education and the
Taxpayer Revolt *John F. Due* 267

Part III
POLICY AND EMERGING PROSPECTS:
COMBINING EFFICIENCY AND EQUITY 287

12 Combining Efficiency and Equity: Optimization of
Resource Allocation in State School Systems
Elchanan Cohn 290

13 State and Federal Pressures for Equity and Efficiency in
Education Financing *Allan Odden* 312

14 Educational Finance: Research Findings and Policy
Implications *Terry G. Geske* 324

Notes on Contributors 347

Index 351

Preface

Greater social efficiency in education is a necessary and important theme in the current environment, and one that does have several very positive aspects. Given the fiscal austerity brought on by declining enrollments, slower economic growth, inflation, and federal budget cuts, all of which are reflected through state and local budget decisions, refinements in the criteria and their use for improving social efficiency in educational planning decisions are needed. By more accurately meeting society's needs and reducing ineffectiveness, social efficiency has the potential of maintaining and improving quality, and of finding additional internal sources of finance for reducing the currently growing inequality of educational opportunity.

Better education through improvements in its social efficiency and equity, as well as through making that which is already good better, is an important goal in itself. But consistent with the suggestion made throughout this volume that greater emphasis be placed on the outcomes (including the ultimate as well as the more immediate), increased efficiency and equity in education also has the even more significant potential of contributing to a more humane form of growth and future well-being in the society at large.

With this theme in mind, leading economists and educators specializing in this field were invited to join in developing original contributions on the major aspects of this efficiency, equity, humane growth quandary. Following Chapter 1, which develops budgeting, planning, and financing criteria related to this conceptual framework, the contributions in Part I address major aspects of social efficiency. These include the lack of adequate incentives for efficiency in the way in which the delivery system is organized and its failure to adequately involve parents (Theodore Schultz), the relation of the parents' socioeconomic status and to the efficiency with which the child's time is utilized for learning in the home (Charles Benson), the use of cost effectiveness analysis and a survey of the current state of the art (Richard Rossmiller), and the relation of individualized instruction to the efficiency with which the child's time is used in the classroom (Alan Thomas et al.). The more eventual outcomes of education are then analyzed by considering recent research measuring the longer-run non-monetary returns (Robert Michael), as well as monetary returns relative to costs specific to each student considered over time as well as by occupational field, degree level, and type of institution (Walter McMahon and Alan Wagner).

In Part II the philosophical, legal, and school finance concepts of equity are explored (Kern Alexander), followed by a discussion of a significant aspect of equity in the financing of post-secondary education (Susan Nelson). Some careful tests of the net effects of much school finance reform are conducted (Stephen Carroll), and tax equity and the implications of the taxpayer's revolt are examined (John Due).

Social efficiency and equity are brought together first at the conceptual level in Part III, within the context of a goal programming model (Elchanan Cohn), and then at the level of actual budget decisions and policy (Allan Odden). The concluding chapter draws together selected findings from all of the studies, developing their interrelationships and some of their implications for social efficiency, equity, and contributions to humane growth.

Financing Education is intended for students, faculty, and policymakers in the economics of education, in school finance, and in the financing of higher education. Those in educational administration who are concerned with the management of retrenchment and who are aware of the important role of innovation and new research in reducing costs, meeting society's needs, and adapting to change should also find it interesting and suggestive. The book is also intended for educational analysts at state-level Offices of Education and state Boards of Higher Education, their counterparts at the federal level, and staff in educational planning and budgeting roles in the other OECD nations and international agencies. For academic use, the book is intended as a supplement to the standard basic texts to add depth and insights from new research in courses in school finance, the economics of education, higher education finance, cost/benefit analysis, and educational planning.

There are other possible uses, for which *Financing Education* was not primarily designed, since some background in educational planning and in economics is assumed. It could be used as a sole text by those with some background, because it develops a conceptual framework in the first chapter and is theme oriented. Given a little background in economics, local school and college administrators and members of school boards and other governing boards who are oriented to the role of innovation, experimentation, and research in seeking fruitful adaptation to change should also find the book interesting.

This book came about in part out of a desire to recognize the lifetime of productive work in the field of school finance by William P. McLure,

Professor of Educational Administration and Director of the Bureau of Educational Research at the University of Illinois. A symposium held at the University of Illinois at Urbana-Champaign to honor Bill at the time of his retirement led to the preliminary versions of most of the articles in this volume. We would like to recognize Bill as a colleague and a friend, and for the inspiration he has contributed to the field over so many years.

We are especially indebted to Myron B. Atkin, Dean of the College of Education at Stanford University, who was Dean of the College of Education at the University of Illinois when this project was initiated, for the support that made the conference possible. We are also indebted to Tom Sergiovanni, Chairman of the Department of Administration, Higher and Continuing Education, and Russell Zwoyer, Associate Dean of the College of Education, for their important roles, and to Vernon Zimmerman, Dean of the College of Commerce, Case Sprenkle, Chairman of the Department of Economics, Joe Burnett, Dean of the College of Education, and to members of the Committee on Interdisciplinary Studies for their support.

A significant contribution to the substance of this volume was made by the discussants and others who participated at the conference and reacted to the papers presented. We acknowledge and thank especially Francine Blau, Associate Professor of Economics, University of Illinois; Howard R. Bowen, R. Stanton Avery Professor of Economics and Education, Claremont Graduate School; David Breneman, Senior Fellow, Brookings Institution; Byron W. Brown, Chairperson, Department of Economics, Michigan State University; Bruce L. Gensemer, Fellow in public finance, the Academy for Contemporary Problems at Columbus; Gilbert Ghez, Associate Professor of Economics, Roosevelt University; G. Alan Hickrod, Professor of Educational Administration, Illinois State University; Roe L. Johns, Professor of Education (emeritus), University of Florida; Jane Leuthold, Associate Professor of Economics, University of Illinois; Sherwin Rosen, Professor of Economics, University of Chicago; Peter S. Stowe, Economist, U.S. Department of Education; and Robert A. Wallhaus, Deputy Director, Illinois Board of Higher Education.

We would also like to express our appreciation to the personnel in the Word Processing Center of the College of Education, particularly to June Chambliss, Cathy Armetta, and Nancy Schum, for their indispensable help during the typing of the manuscript.

Finally, we greatly appreciate the significant help given by our wives, Carolyn and Kathy. Their assistance with drafts of the manuscript and their support and continuing encouragement were vital in bringing this book to fruition.

Urbana, Illinois Walter W. McMahon
  Terry G. Geske

CHAPTER 1

Efficiency and Equity Criteria for Educational Budgeting and Finance

WALTER W. McMAHON

There are new and increased incentives for finding ways to improve efficiency and equity in education. As costs rise and all education budgets grow tighter, there is an increasing struggle to find resources that can be put to more efficient uses to maintain quality and innovation, while also assuring equitable access to all education. This concern with inefficiency (when resources are wasted) and with inequities (such as continuing inequality of educational opportunity) is intensified by the fact that new sources of inefficiency and inequity are constantly created by declining enrollments, by shifting job markets, and by inflation. Slower growth and inflation simultaneously contribute to political budget restrictions and the fiscal austerity affecting many aspects of education.

Yet there are important payoffs from reducing these growing problems of inefficiency and inequity. Potential gains include finding ineffectively utilized resources that can be used to improve the quality of education and to arrest the growing inequality of educational opportunity. Better education is an important end in itself, but better education also has a strategic role in that it can contribute to humane growth in the entire society.

One response is for education to ignore these problems. Under pressure, some systems have resisted innovation, slid toward lower high school graduation requirements in the basic disciplines (see Kirst, 1981, pp. 14-18), and maintained low-quality entrenched courses that are popular because of lower grading standards for college admissions. Another response is to assert that any attempts to evaluate the efficiency or the ultimate benefits of educational programs risk using imperfect measures or ignoring some benefits, so it is better to keep the criteria hidden and implicit. In offering partial criteria, this chapter and other parts of this book are not suggesting that measurement is essential to the successful application of logical criteria. To omit qualitative appraisals of potential benefits that cannot now be measured, given the current state of the art, would merely favor blind applications. Instead, the criteria offered are more like early warning systems. When used judiciously, they are better than doing nothing, which can perpetuate both waste and inequity.

Inefficiency and inequity currently permeate much of primary, secondary, and higher education. Buildings, administrative staff, and teachers are underutilized as enrollments decline, and this creates potential for inefficiency, waste, and lower productivity. Another symptom of social inefficiency, or inefficiency from society's point of view, occurs because many children are not learning the basics of reading, writing, and mathematics. This lack of knowledge limits their capacities in other subjects, their achievement if admitted to college, and their lifetime potential. Problems with efficiency also arise when, in the face of enrollment drops, lower-quality curricula become very costly and yet are preserved. Another example of social inefficiency is seen, in the opinion of most people, when the allocation of scarce educational resources results in large surpluses of educational outcomes that have limited practical, esthetic, or humanitarian uses--such as costly Ph.D.'s in fields which are already very low paid and overcrowded, offering extremely limited job prospects.

A particularly important source of inequity, also endemic to the system, involves the distribution of educational benefits, among pupils. Wide differences in benefits are traceable to differences in per-pupil expenditure among states, among school districts, and within districts--differences on the order of five to one in most states. Such variations arise because of the differences in wealth of the parents and the neighborhoods. Wealthier districts can afford to purchase teachers with more graduate training, more experience, and better verbal skills, as well as better staff support for children;[1] children born in poor neighborhoods may not receive the same educational opportunity. This reduces the latter's chances for access to college, leads to greater inequity in the eventual distribution of income, and diminishes chances for these children in life. Of course, programs to correct this are costly, but they may also be cost effective. Inequities in the distribution of benefits among the young also have implications for the distribution of income later in life and for distributive justice in society.

When it is efficient and equitable, education brings about three kinds of returns that together comprise humane growth--a growth of actual earnings, a growth of non-monetary returns, and a more equitable distribution of income. Education's potential contribution to the first component, economic growth, has taken on increased interest in a world deeply concerned about the slowdown in productivity growth and anxious to find less energy-intensive means of bringing new technology to bear on production. The second, consisting of non-market, non-monetary returns to education during leisure hours, is an important aspect of improvement in the quality of human life. Finally, improvements in the equity with which education is distributed among pupils has an important bearing on the equity with which full income is distributed later in life, reducing the need for income redistribution later by the current methods involving more costly tax and welfare programs.

The Theme

The theme of this chapter, and of this book, illustrated in the foregoing examples, is that improved social efficiency and equity in the entire educational process will contribute to better education for all, and through this to humane growth in the society. Defined in this way, the educational process is not limited to the classroom; it also includes the home, the neighborhood, and learning on the job. While school and college budgets cannot control these environments, some elements within them can be influenced and need to be included in the planning process if the budgeted activities are to be socially efficient. The goal of better education for all, furthermore, refers to finding the best resource allocations that can be made toward this end assuming *limited resources*. This and the following chapters consider possibilities for improvement either of efficiency or of equity toward achieving the best and most equitably distributed education possible under tight budgets.

This chapter explains and seeks some improvements in the criteria for achieving greater efficiency and equity in education. Social efficiency and equity criteria are poorly defined; those criteria that have been operationalized are poorly understood, and hence often are not applied effectively. The problems, however, are difficult, major ones. Agreement does not exist among key leaders on what educational outcomes are most desirable. Whatever consensus does exist is often understated. There also are no workable ways to define, much less to accurately measure, some of the benefits of education.

Both expenditure and tax-side decisions involve efficiency and equity. Both are part of financing education, and both are considered in the chapters that follow. A budgeting decision, made at the federal, state, or district level can be viewed as the source of finance from the perspective of the next-lower level of education; the educational services provided also affect the financial resources that can be raised. Analyzing the expenditure decisions in the budget as well as the traditional tax-side decisions is in line not only with the more recent trends in research in public finance, but also with the growing popular concern with efficiency (and equity) of resource use. Each and every education budget decision at every level implicitly involves the potential benefits, or effects, in relation to costs. Furthermore, a budget decision can be regarded as the educational plan for the following year--that is, as educational planning implemented within a shorter-run situation, especially if there is an appropriate integration between educational planning and the budget. Regarded in this way, financing education deals with the heart of the process of securing efficiency and equity in the acquisition and use of resources.

Criteria for Social Efficiency and Equity

Pareto efficiency is defined as improvements in how resources are used to embody knowledge, skills, and values in persons ("production efficiency"), or to provide education in the kinds and amounts that society needs ("exchange efficiency") so that some people are made better off, but no one is made worse off.[2] Equity, in contrast, deals with a different question--the question of the justice with which the benefits of education, or taxation or other burdens, are distributed. The achievement of equity is defined in the purest sense as concerned with the redistribution of resources where some gain and some lose. If all possible improvements in efficiency have been made so that there are no untapped resources available, and if justice in the initial distribution has not been achieved, to improve equity would require a redistribution of the educational benefits (cr tax burdens). This process makes some better off, but some worse off, albeit in the interest of greater distributive justice.

Efficiency and Equity in Education

Efficiency typically means a potential for increases in the desired outcomes of education without increases in the quantities of resources used. Efficiency does not mean simple across-the-board budget reductions, or across-the-board increases in the number of pupils per teacher, for such a "speed up" leaves the pupils (and the teachers) worse off. Efficiency does mean maintaining all outcomes of education while reducing waste or using existing resources more appropriately, perhaps through the application of new knowledge or technology to the learning process. The released resources can be used to make some pupils, teachers, or taxpayers better off, and no one need be worse off.

Budget changes that redistribute educational benefits among young people involve interpersonal comparisons. The amount of satisfaction gained by some must be assessed in relation to the amount lost by others before a judgment can be made about whether or not social welfare has been increased. Although typical of most practical situations, these equity judgments lie beyond the realm of pure economics. The basis of the equity judgment lies instead in philosophy, ethics, and to some extent in legal interpretations.

Combining Efficiency and Equity

Efficiency and equity are regarded by many as in conflict--that is, the trade-off for an increase in equity is a loss in efficiency and higher costs. Put the other way around, the trade-off for increasing the efficiency with which pupils learn is restricted access to educational programs. Such trade-offs do exist, of course, and are an important feature of most educational systems. Nevertheless, there are situations in which improvements in the social efficiency of education and improvements in distributive justice can be made simultaneously. In a situation where improvements can be made in both without making anybody worse off in any absolute sense, less political opposition to such changes can be expected; we can also be more certain that such changes involve moves toward a truly better solution. We therefore will devote considerable attention to defining criteria to guide budget (and tax) decisions toward finding resource reallocations of this type.

Figure 1 provides a useful frame of reference for relating contributions on efficiency or equity to the common goal of the best and most equitable distribution of educational benefits attainable under tight budgets. The horizontal axis represents the benefits or lifetime satisfactions from education received by Individual A, whereas the vertical axis represents the lifetime satisfactions from education received by Individual B.

Increases in social welfare, as they relate to the distribution of these benefits from education among children, can be expressed in a social

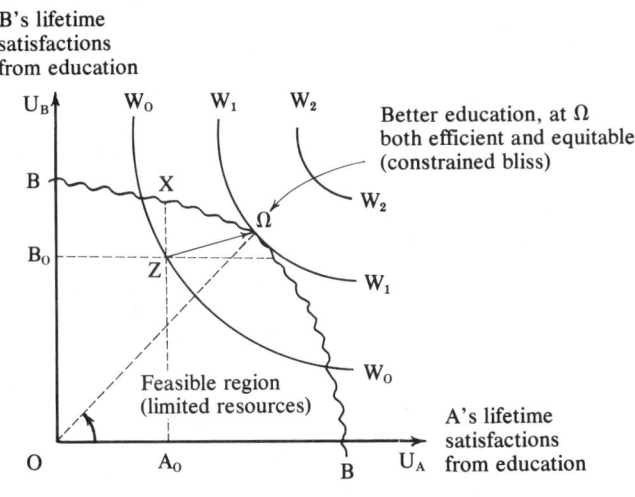

Figure 1.

welfare function illustrated by the contour lines labeled WW in Figure 1, as well as in later figures (e.g., Bator 1969: 509-10). This objective function can be thought of as a utility function expressing the preferences of the school principal or college administrator, which avoids the technical difficulties that sometimes arise in the voting-type methods considered by Arrow (1951). Ideally, it is the objective function of an omniscient ethical observer, in the sense that it does require that a clear ethic be drawn (or chosen from the hierarchy to be discussed below) from outside the analysis presented here, and from the fields of ethics, philosophy, and law as mentioned above. In practical applications, it should not be necessary for the economist or educational finance specialist to be given the objectives in a polished formal manner. Instead, as emphasized by Eckstein (1961: 455) and others, he must interpret the desires of the policy people whom he is serving, and then express them in an analytical form as an objective function. He can then seek to maximize this function subject to the relevant economic and institutional constraints, as is illustrated in Figure 1, where moves toward better education for both are up $Z\Omega$ and to the right, toward an area defined by contour line $W_1 W_1$. But movements toward better education for both A and B are constrained by the limits imposed by the real resources that are available--the maximum efficiency frontier represented by the line BB.

Individuals A and B are also typical of two groups, Group A children may be from a poor neighborhood and receive fewer benefits from education than Group B children at the starting position, point Z (i.e., $A_0 < B_0$.[3] The objective is to use the untapped resources that exist at point Z (due to social inefficiency) in such a way that budget and other planning decisions are made to improve the quality of education received by both A *and* B, as well as the equity with which it is distributed. The goal is the best and most equitably distributed education attainable within the resources available. That goal is achieved at Ω, the point of constrained bliss.

Humane Growth Criteria. A move from Z to X increases efficiency (no one is worse off). A move from X to Ω increases equity (the benefits are more equitably distributed). A move directly from Z to Ω contributes simultaneously to efficiency and to equity, leaving both A and B better off. The latter move is consistent with humane growth--both within education and in the society at large. We shall offer humane growth criteria that should be useful in identifying moves of this type in practical educational planning at the primary, secondary, and college levels.

But first, what is wrong with changes in educational planning and budgets designed exclusively to increase efficiency, or to only increase equity? Nothing, if they are designed so that the benefits exceed the costs. Pure equity moves in educational finance reform, such as those from

X to Ω in Figure 1, redistribute in a way that hurts someone, and therefore generate opposition. A group containing people like Individual B in Figure 1, who is receiving a better education to start with at point X, is left worse off. Those involved with Group B will complain, and others can be expected to join their cause, arguing that the quality of education received by this group is being sacrificed for something inferior at Ω. The achievement of greater distributive justice in this case is impeded by the inability to be sure that the gains to Group A exceed the damage to Group B. As national, state, and institutional budgets for education are affected by slower growth, improvements in equity and access cannot be financed with new resources and must increasingly be financed by internal budget reallocations like X to Ω. Such reallocations generate conflict and thereby doom many educational finance reform efforts.

Pure efficiency moves also have pitfalls. They can help to locate and use untapped resources, but if done only for an elite few, the cost is greater relative inequity for others. For example, an efficiency move in Figure 1 such as that from Z to X uses untapped resources to improve B's benefits. But the change results in even less equality of educational opportunity and equity than had existed before.

To avoid these dilemmas, humane growth criteria which combine both efficiency and equity considerations are proposed. These criteria are to be used to seek out those reallocations of resources when making short- and longer-run budget decisions that either (1) *improve efficiency without reducing equity*, or (2) *increase equity without reducing efficiency*. Both of these criteria combine improvements in efficiency with improvements in equity such as those from Z to Ω in Figure 1. Full application of these humane growth criteria somewhat overrestricts the decision space; in many practical situations there will be at least some adverse side effects on either efficiency or equity. But the literature to date has tended to emphasize the conflict and trade-offs between efficiency and equity so heavily that perhaps we are justified in making a more vigorous effort to find those situations where simultaneous improvements in both can be made. Further operational concepts and measures of efficiency, equity, and humane growth are needed for the practical application of these criteria and will be considered below.

The resources necessary for better education can come from growth in the real financial resources available to education. This is equivalent to a shift outward in the constraint line (BB in Figure 1). But these additional new real resources are increasingly unavailable. Instead, educational planners must often allow inflation to act as an across-the-board tax on the units they administer, and then they must carefully distribute nominal increments to a few selected productive programs. In this sense, most current budgeting and educational planning is really internal reallocation.

Since this has become so common, a premium is placed on knowing where to "allow" budgets to be eroded due to inefficiency, and on knowing where the potential for improvements in efficiency is greatest.

Efficiency Criteria

Efficiency has two major aspects. *Production efficiency* refers to the efficiency with which inputs of time and resources are combined in the educational process to secure desired outcomes. *Exchange efficiency* refers to the efficiency with which appropriate educational outcomes are matched with the citizens' educational needs.

Production Efficiency: Technical, Price, and Economic Efficiency

Production efficiency, which is concerned with which classroom and which home and neighborhood factors contribute most to learning, is developed in Figure 2a with two inputs, and in Figure 2b with two outputs, based on a simplified educational production function.[4] For the two-input case, isoquant $Q_0 Q_0$ illustrates combinations of student time and teacher time used to produce one unit of educational output. This trade-off along $Q_0 Q_0$, with possible improvements in the technical efficiency with which student time is used (Z to C), is also illustrated in Chapter 5, where more individualized instruction is found to elicit more student "time on task." The isoquant in Figure 2a is a unit isoquant (with the index of output and all inputs divided by the output index), so that all output dots above $Q_0 Q_0$ are less efficient production points. *Technical efficiency* exists when, from point Z, any point down on $Q_0 Q_0$ is reached. This requires a reallocation of available resources in such a way that technical efficiency is maximized, such as when teacher verbal skills are used to explain things clearly. *Price efficiency* involves considering the relative costs of the resources used--as opposed to technical efficiency, which ignores the costs. In this illustration, the costs of teacher time in terms of the salaries required to hire teachers with the necessary skills, as well as the costs of student time (as measured by foregone learning or foregone earnings), must be brought together with production-function information in a cost effectiveness analysis before the most price-efficient combination of these resources can be found. A movement from Z to B constitutes an improvement in technical efficiency; a movement from B to δ_1 constitutes an improvement price efficiency. Only at δ_1, which combines both, is full *economic efficiency* achieved.

Production efficiency in education also involves the choice of optimum outputs among various alternatives, as illustrated in Figure 2b. There is more than one output in education at both the intermediate and final-

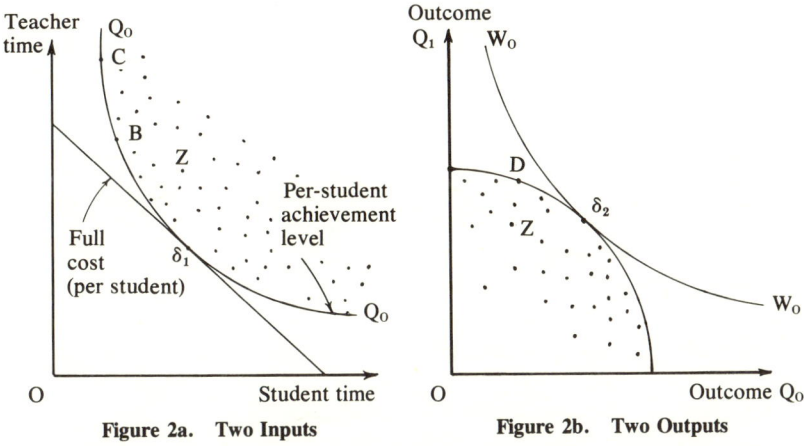

Figure 2a. Two Inputs   Figure 2b. Two Outputs

good levels; as a result, there is both the difficulty and the need to ascertain society's output goals and the weight to be assigned to each. Within higher education, for example, there are instruction, research, and public service; at all levels one may make breakdowns by curricular areas and by cognitive and non-cognitive outcomes, as well as by the subdivisions of each, that are the focus of curriculum specialists and of educational evaluators. Intermediate instructional outcomes such as student achievement contribute to the ultimate outcomes (or benefits) such as lifetime earnings and non-monetary returns.

Figure 2b illustrates a choice in the use of resources, with inefficient points (e.g., Z) below the production frontier so that a movement from point Z to point D constitutes achievement of *technical efficiency*. There is no pure price efficiency, since outputs are not sold for a price on the market; but an analogous concept, called *allocative efficiency*, relates to the attainment of that best mix of educational goals. It is given in this case by a beneficient educational administrator's utility function $W_0 W_0$, representing his best effort to ascertain society's true longer run objectives for education. That these goals are normally not made very explicit limits the possibilities for cost effectiveness in education. Nevertheless, a movement from point D to point δ_2 constitutes an improvement in allocative efficiency. To make such moves requires careful ascertainment of the educational policymaker's goals, and of society's goals as expressed through school boards, legislatures, Congress, and public opinion polls.

Cost effectiveness decisions such as the resource allocation and curriculum choice decisions illustrated in Figures 2a and 2b are made every day by vice-chancellors for academic affairs, department heads, school district superintendents, principals, and students. But their cost effectiveness analysis is normally implicit rather than explicit, and it does not go by such a formal name. More explicit formal attempts at cost effectiveness analysis and at goal programming are considered in Chapters 4 and 12. Effective informal use of the framework above, together with the production function information that underlies it, is possible, however. It only requires that a careful attempt be made to consider costs in relation to outcomes. The user also should at least try to place socially acceptable weights on the probable longer-run outcomes of each educational process.

Exchange Efficiency: Technical, Allocative, and Economic Efficiency

Exchange efficiency, in contrast to production efficiency, deals with the exchange or delivery of a given amount of educational services to families. It involves changes in the structure of the educational program, or the number of students in each field, until there is a better fit with the students' and the society's needs. The total return possible from education, as was indicated by line BB in Figure 1, depends in part upon how efficiently the outcomes of the educational system are designed to meet true individual and social needs.

Human capital skills cannot be exchanged among students, since human capital is embodied in individuals. Exchange efficiency can be improved, meeting private and social needs more adequately, as students are allocated efficiently among classes and institutions, as special education programs try to match offerings with needs and abilities, and as informed choices of institutions and majors are exercised by college students. Exchange efficiency is sometimes impeded by budgeting and other decisions such as those that restrict entry in medicine (following debatable studies popular with the profession that suggest that a surplus is being trained without explicit reference to the expected future monetary returns in relation to the educational costs). Similarly, if exchange inefficiency is to be reduced, local schools should train more apprentices for entry into crafts such as plumbing, where craftsmen are in short supply and unions try to limit entry. Exchange inefficiency is also evident when widely different monetary rates of return to education are found to persist in different college-related occupations.

On the other hand, the development of community colleges and of the federal Basic Economic Opportunity Grant programs have encouraged exchange efficiency (in addition to equity) by facilitating freer choice by students, both among curricula and among institutions. Students are reasonably knowledgeable about their longer-run best interests. But low academic standards for high school graduation, combined with easily accessible low-quality courses with easier grading standards, continue to persist, together with unreasonable barriers to entry in some college curricula. These barriers are enforced by overly restrictive budgets and other types of quotas, even where returns are high in relation to the costs. Coupled with over-enrollment and budgets adequate to support low entrance standards in less-needed fields, they promote unwise choices by students and social inefficiency.

An Efficiency Criteria Hierarchy

Overall efficiency criteria are needed for determining whether each practical budget decision in the financing of education will or will not improve economic efficiency.[5] The following efficiency criteria hierarchy is suggested, ranked from the lowest to the highest. Because each stage is a partial criterion, only by going the full distance to include some qualitative evaluation of all of the private and social benefits and their relative weights can full social efficiency be attained.

1). *Accountability Tests.* Lower-level or elementary efficiency criteria consist of normal financial accounting controls and accountability checks on whether processes that are financed are being performed by the unit. If the services are not delivered, even basic efficiency is unlikely to be achieved. But these criteria alone fail to analyze the production effectiveness of what is done, much less to analyze whether it is cost effective. Competency testing goes somewhat further in that it tries to measure at least some outputs, rather than measuring only inputs.

2). *Production Function Analysis* is an effort to determine what is effective in producing the desired educational outcomes. It can range from trial and error (What works?) to the production function relationships of the types discussed in Chapters 3, 4, 5, and 12. Such knowledge of what does and does not contribute to learning helps schools and colleges to be efficient by developing productive activities and avoiding unproductive ones.[6] Although necessary for efficiency, action using these relationships from production function studies still is not sufficient to attain the highest level of economic efficiency; the latter also requires consideration of the costs of the inputs involved and the relative value of the outputs.

3). *Cost Effectiveness Analysis* considers costs in relation to the quantities of output obtained, and in this sense goes beyond simple accountability tests or production function relationships. Cost effectiveness analysis normally uses the prices of all of the inputs, although sometimes some costs are omitted, such as the cost of student time. Frequently, only intermediate outputs such as instructional units are analyzed, whereas longer-run outcomes such as the current and future demands for graduates in the field are ignored. However, even with these limitations, if the decisionmaker's goals are well conceived, cost effectiveness ratios can be helpful guides to increased efficiency. One example might be the comparisons now being made of the cost effectiveness of producing instructional units of comparable quality at different colleges or schools within each state. With statewide retrenchment, state agencies are discovering that those institutions that lose enrollment first also lose the advantages of scale and become very costly per student.

4). *Cost/Benefit Analysis.* Costs are considered in relation to the expected value of outputs, which cost effectiveness analysis does not do, and either benefit/cost ratios or rates of return (a form of benefit/cost ratios) are calculated. The main problem is that, as developed thus far, the measurement of expected future benefits is usually limited to monetary earnings because they are most easily measurable, although full costs are normally considered. There is also the need to predict expected future job-market trends and their implications for earnings, although there is evidence that the returns expected by students at least in the medium-term future, and the expected rates of return based on these, are reasonably accurate.[7] Differences in the actual monetary rates of return to education over time, by type of occupation and by type of institution, do tend to persist however and are suggestive, as are the expected rates of return that also help to anticipate major trends. These differences are developed further in Chapter 7.

One criterion is to suggest that, where expected rates of return are high in relation to alternatives, the program should be expanded, assuming that all of the non-monetary returns and social benefits can reasonably be assumed to be positive, or at least zero. A second criterion is to attempt to adjust the monetary rates of return by including, judgmentally, specific non-monetary private returns of such types as those surveyed by Robert Michael in Chapter 6. They should, in principle, be included in the final qualitative judgment made about total benefits.

5). *Cost/Benefit Analysis with Social Benefits Included.* The highest-level efficiency criterion from the point of view of society as a whole must consider the full social costs as well as the full expected social benefits when calculating more comprehensive rates of return or other benefit/cost ratios. The student needs to think only about the private benefits and costs, to himself and his family, in making his investment decision. Educational administrators, and school boards, boards of higher education, and legislative bodies whose responsibility is to think about all persons in their jurisdiction should consider the full benefits, including the benefits of research to future generations, and the spillover benefits from education to employability, to reduced crime and welfare costs, and to democracy. A partly social benefit that has become more pertinent recently, due to the widespread concern with the showdown in economic growth, is the larger contribution education could make to productivity if curricula were organized more efficiently to this end. In Japan and Russia, for example, much more high school science and math is required; more college students are trained in areas related to economic productivity, such as engineering and science; there are higher literacy rates, and lower dropout rates. Other important social benefits of education were stressed by Thomas Jefferson, who urged that Virginia support public education as the key to securing effective individual participation in the democratic process, and hence as the key to the preservation of our freedoms. These types of social benefits are undoubtedly the hardest to measure, but they can nevertheless be observed and are real.

Use of Social Efficiency Criteria

Detailed measurement is not essential to the successful application of these efficiency criteria. They are continually being applied implicitly at all levels, without much measurement or use of their formal names. However, more conscious consideration of the costs in relation to effectiveness and longer-run benefits can only help to improve efficiency. The use of the criteria, with or without formal measurement, involves considering a) effectiveness in relation to cost, or b) longer-range monetary and psychic benefits in relation to cost, and ultimately c) qualitative judgments that conceptually seek to add up the monetary, psychic, and social benefits to obtain full ultimate benefits in relation to cost as a basis for decisions, all the while seeking to avoid reducing equity.

Many indexes are used by educational evaluators that could become a part of cost effectiveness tests if they related outcomes to cost. The cost per instructional unit in the same discipline across institutions is one common example. University departments also have research outputs, which (in experimental studies) are conceived of in terms of the cost per refereed publication or weighted "research unit." Research effectiveness is evaluated internally by committees on program evaluation, promotion committees, and research-support committees; the recommendations of these committees then are related to costs before final decisions are made. There are also, in principle, "public service units" resulting from a separate third output. Another commonly specified index of instructional effectiveness is a measure of the increments to scores on standard achievement tests covering basic skills, science, social sciences, and the humanities. When a sufficiently comprehensive index of effectiveness is specified, such as these test score increments, the cost per unit in principle can be estimated, and social efficiency can be increased by gradually transferring resources from the less cost effective approaches to the more cost effective ones.

By moving toward more comprehensive concepts of the longer-run monetary and psychic benefits of education, or "full earnings" used in benefit/cost criteria, further improvements in social efficiency can be achieved. This assumes that some estimate can be made of the value of the psychic benefits, or that they are positive, resulting in an index that is more comprehensive than the index of effectiveness. Then total rates of return can be estimated that do provide some guidance--although they still must be supplemented with medium-term (3-5 year) projections, and with qualitative judgments about the social benefits of each program. The result is a higher-order criterion for increasing social efficiency by allowing those programs to gradually contract where the expected adjusted total rates of return are lowest, and by allocating more resources to the expansion of those programs where the expected adjusted total rates of return are highest.

Equity

The poor quality of the education and the poor results being achieved in the urban ghettos and other poor neighborhoods in the United States is a national and international disgrace. It leaves a heritage of costs and inequity for the future--overloading the welfare system, filling up the jails, contributing to low productivity growth, and limiting the earning capacity and life chances of many. These costs and inequities are passed along from one generation to the next.

Concern with equity among all children at each age (child equity) and with equity among taxpayers (tax equity) has dominated the literature in school finance, whereas the literature on financing post-secondary education has tended to focus more specifically either on efficiency or on equity. The attention given to efficiency and its combination with equity, as demonstrated in this book, therefore represents a considerable departure.

Improvements in efficiency can be a source for financing improvements in equity from internal sources--an important fact in this era of tight budgets. Furthermore, some inequity is due to inefficiency in the schools in poor neighborhoods. How much inequity is due to such inefficiency is hard to say, but improvements in the social efficiency of these schools would simultaneously increase equity.

The persistence of child inequity is suggested by indexes of inequality (or dispersion) of expenditure per pupil among schools and among districts--inequality so vast that expenditure as noted by Jay Chambers in Windham (1979: 81) was twenty-three times higher in rich districts than in poor districts in Texas, Wyoming, and South Dakota, for example. Using the longest span of time series that has been analyzed thus far, Alan

Hickrod (1981) has found that the effect of district power equalizer formulas such as the one resulting from school finance reform in 1973 in Illinois plus the inflation of the late 1970's and 1980's narrowed the inequalities only for the first four years, and since then the inequalities have steadily widened. Inflation increases local property values more in property-rich districts, thus increasing local property assessments, the inequality of local property tax receipts, and child inequity. Unless initiatives are taken by state governors and other key policymakers to support school finance reforms in response to the strains of inflation, continuing property taxpayer revolts are sure to result. However, the spending and tax limitation lobby is now guarding against the state-level budget increases that have sometimes been a by-product of the school finance reform efforts.

In urban ghettos, the problems with child inequity have not been overcome by federal categorical programs such as Head Start, Title I, or Community Development (housing) programs, which now are being reduced by federal budget cuts. However, successful experiments are underway, such as the one in District 13 (Beasley) of south Chicago which requires contracts with parents to see that homework is completed, bedtime is enforced, and TV time is limited. The impressive results are consistent with the research results reported by Benson in Chapter 3. He finds that poor parents are just as concerned about their children and spend just as much time guiding their children as do higher SES parents. To relate Benson's findings to improved child equity and school achievement, need-based education grants to parents could require learning contracts involving a parental commitment to see that homework is done (using Benson's findings) while facilitating more parental involvement and choice among schools as discussed by Schultz in Chapter 2. The federally sponsored 842 equity studies are also significant, but have not yet led to comprehensive state-level reforms. As yet, no president or political party has come forth with a comprehensive approach to the underlying school efficiency and school financing problems troubling low-income, high unemployment neighborhoods nationwide.

In post-secondary education, the problems associated with child inequity and tax inequity have eased somewhat, due in part to the creation of community colleges. Community college programs have improved access and reduced inequity for those who had previously been excluded from higher education. Similarly, the careful calibration of financial need as determined by the federal Basic Economic Opportunity Grants (Pell Grants) significantly reduces inequity among young people. Colleges still inherit problems caused by inequity in the financing of the common schools, but college-age students have a somewhat freer choice, even though they are increasingly dependent on their parents' incomes following the large federal cuts in the student loan program. In the Hansen-Weisbrod (1969) study, the inequity on the tax side which they also cite has been reduced somewhat as more states exempt food from the state sales tax, and as public institutions are now pressed harder to raise their tuition in the high-cost, high-return programs, (such as medicine).

These equity features of the U.S. system of higher education finance have not permeated European or other countries nearly so extensively, and equity problems in higher education persist elsewhere. In the United States, however, the child equity problems appear to be considerably more acute than in Europe at the primary and secondary level, with adverse spillover effects on the colleges and on society.

Types of Equity

Equity is defined as involving a redistribution of resources (or of costs) designed to achieve the community's philosophical and ethical standards of fairness. This was illustrated in Figure 1 as a redistributive move from point X to point Ω, the latter representing society's judgment of an ethical and equitable distribution of benefits (or of costs) between A and B, and hence the point of constrained bliss. Such redistributive moves can be designed to achieve either 1) *horizontal equity*, generally held to require equal treatment of equals (and accepted as having this meaning here); or 2) *intergenerational equity*, in-between horizontal and vertical equity, and a case of considerable importance in education; or 3) *vertical equity*, requiring unequal treatment of unequals, in ways to be discussed. A fully equitable solution (such as at point Ω) would require that horizontal, intergenerational, and vertical equity be achieved. These concepts of equity can be applied to equity among all students in each age bracket, whether in school or not. We will refer to this as *child equity*. They can also be applied to equity among teachers, administrators, and other staff members; we will refer to this as *staff equity*. Equity among taxpayers or others who bear the costs of education we will refer to as *tax equity*. Staff equity, while important, is not dealt with in this book because it raises different issues of personnel administration, morale, and productivity, and different complementarities and trade-offs between equity and efficiency.

Horizontal Equity

The above definitions of horizontal and vertical equity are standard, but stressing the distinction will make it clear that some measures of equity now in use introduce elements of both. The most practical measure of horizontal equity is *real current expenditure per child*. This needs to be defined further, and modified with considerations relating to intergenerational equity, but the latter gets into the equalization of ultimate outcomes and vertical equity criteria that follow. The initial (and probably most important) criterion is that, if there is equal real current expenditure per pupil among groups of young persons with essentially comparable abilities, there is horizontal equity. Measures of the degree of inequity or inequality include the full range, restricted range (95th to 5th percentile range), variance, coefficient of variation, mean deviation, and the Gini coefficient. The Atkinson (1970) index merits special attention, since it is capable of weighting the ends of the distribution to include vertical equity, and the bottom 10 percent or so is of special political and practical interest.

Expenditures should refer to current expenditures, not including the more erratic capital outlays. From the point of view of economic logic, these expenditures should also include an element for the current cost of capital, reflecting bond interest and other current imputed costs of the capital invested in buildings. For measures of horizontal equity, expenditure per child furthermore must be compared for like groups--groups with comparable proportions of disadvantaged pupils, or of high-ability pupils. Within or among educational systems, pure horizontal equity tests would involve comparing expenditure per pupil in one primary school with that in other primary schools, high schools with high schools, comprehensive districts with comprehensive districts, college discipline with college discipline, etc.[8] The weights often applied to different pupils at different levels to reflect differences in per-pupil costs do involve a cost benefit criterion, but they also involve a vertical equity principle.

Measurement of horizontal equity using expenditure per pupil should, in principle, be in real terms in order to remove the effects of geographical price-level differences--particularly in relation to teacher and staff salaries, which account for 70-80 percent of most educational costs. Geographical differences in the cost of living affect the salaries that districts must pay to attract teachers of comparable quality. The result would be toward equalization of the real resources purchased, and hence of the quality of education provided. This can be done by dividing expenditures by a cost of education or cost-of-living index. Cost-of-living indexes are correlated with the prices of the other things schools buy; they are now available for all states. By relatively simple methods reported in McMahon and Melton (1977, 1978), they can be extended for counties and school districts in any state.

Operational measures of horizontal equity among taxpayers logically focus on the tax rate paid by individuals. Since individuals ultimately pay all taxes, they are the ultimate object of any concern with equity, expressed in relation to their ability to pay. The most basic operational criterion for horizontal equity among taxpayers is equal tax rates for all who are essentially equal with respect to real income and wealth. This basic criterion has been reinterpreted in many school finance laws to equal property tax rates across districts as a measure of effort and tax equity. But this criterion ignores the point that equity refers to *people,* and not to districts; it also ignores differences in income which are an important source of differences in the ability to pay and in property tax rates. There is the further problem that proportional property tax rates, when combined with typical assessment procedures, result in a regressive tax incidence--at least unless combined with circuit-breakers that exempt low-income persons. School districts are normally given real property as their legal tax handle, but taxes are paid out of income and are ultimately paid by individuals in relation to their properly measured ability to pay. When these facts are ignored, horizontal inequity among individual taxpayers results.

Intergenerational Equity

When equity concepts are applied to the *outcomes* of education, however, they go beyond equality of opportunity and horizontal equity, since students' academic abilities and parental abilities to pay are in fact unequal. Student abilities, parental education, and family wealth all contribute to the skills and knowledge accumulated, or to human capital formation, from a human capital perspective. These skills and knowledge, or the credentials that measure and advertise them, contribute to higher earnings later in the life cycle of the student. An interesting alternative outcome to be considered, therefore, is the expected lifetime "full earnings" of the student, defined here as the student's earnings from his labor plus his or her non-monetary returns from education during leisure hours. To achieve a degree of vertical equity among those ultimate outcomes would be to seek to avoid burdening children with the "sins" of their parents (as does fiscal neutrality). That is, vertical equity reduces the intergenerational transmission of inequality.

This choice situation is illustrated in Figure 3. Here children with lower-income parents (and/or with lower academic ability) are confined to transformation curve $Y_0 Y_0$. They have lower future full earnings at $E_0 (< E_1)$, and are less well off at Ω_0 on $W_0 W_0$ than those with higher lifetime returns at Ω_1.

Hundreds of research studies of earnings functions have developed ever-expanding evidence to the effect that improvements in the quantity and quality of schooling significantly increases earnings later (e.g., Jacob Mincer in Windham 1979: 1-31; Psacharopoulos 1972; Appendix B to Chapter 7). Other factors that also contribute to inequality in earnings are emphasized by the dual labor market hypothesis and the screening hypothesis, although both seize on factors that are correlated with and considerably overlap measures of the quantity and quality of schooling.[9] The radical approach also emphasizes factors that overlap measures of

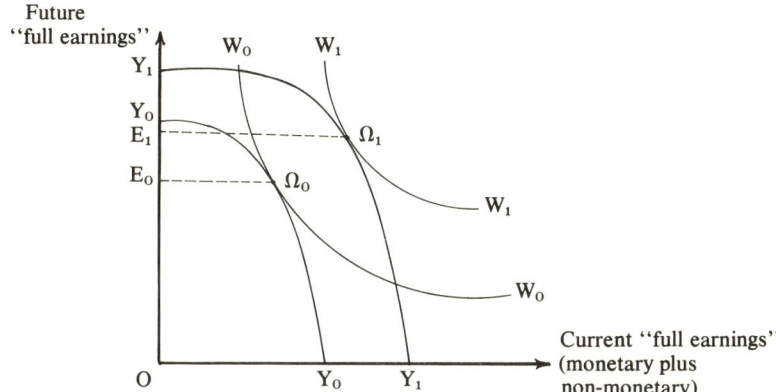

Figure 3. Intertemporal Choice and Intergenerational Equity

education, such as social class. Class reflects family income, which in turn is well known to be a key determinant of the quality and number of years of education received. Things other than education have some effects on earnings, of course, including monopoly rents, screening, and chance events as surveyed by Sahota (1978). Earnings inequality also is not the same as income inequality, since income includes rent, interest, profits, and inheritance as additional major sources of property income inequality.

Since the quantity and quality of education affect earnings later in life, vertical equity decisions that seek to achieve equity in *ultimate outcomes* need to consider eventual earnings and non-monetary returns to education. That is, the choice of an equity principle (discussed below) for the treatment of children whose parents are unequal and the recognition of its effect on the intergenerational transmission of inequality are important dimensions of all vertical equity criteria.

Fiscal neutrality now also can be interpreted as an intergenerational equity concept, like equality of educational opportunity, in the sense that both seek to break the link between the parents' wealth and the student's future. Neither, however, undertakes to correct for initial disadvantages that may come from limited learning opportunities in the student's home and neighborhood.

Vertical Equity

The concept of equal treatment of equals appears to be relatively widely accepted. Therefore the choice of an equity principle narrows down to the choice of a principle to apply to intergenerational equity and to vertical equity, both of which are concerned with the unequal treatment of unequals. In the vertical equity hierarchy presented below, these principles range all the way from commutative equity (which would leave undisturbed the inequalities produced by inheritance and by markets) to positivism (which would be sharply redistributive, to correct for initial disadvantages).

On the tax side, this vertical equity hierarchy is perhaps most closely analogous to regressive, proportional, or progressive tax rates. Corresponding on the benefit side are regressive, proportional, or progressive rates of benefit. The latter corresponds most directly to positivism in equity as developed by the philosopher John Rawls (1977), since it involves the effort to correct social wrongs borne by the child but for which he is not responsible.

An Equity Criteria Hierarchy

Choosing an equity principle from the equity criteria hierarchy that follows, and determining which is the highest and which the lowest level, depends upon the philosophical and ethical views of the community, sometimes as reflected through the courts and legislature. If an acceptable improvement in equity can be made without a reduction in efficiency, a contribution can be made to *humane* growth in the society later.

1) *Commutative Equity*. This first level of equity implies that the state leaves undisturbed the results of the marketplace. In its most extreme form, it leaves little room for public schools at the local level, because tax-supported schools do redistribute benefits among families. Most practical positions of commutive equity advocate localizing school finance, rather than doing away with public schools.[10] Presumably private scholarship funds would be used only to attract the most able students, and student need would not be considered. This libertarian or laissez-faire approach implies emphasis on pure competition and opposition to monopoly, including steps to reduce both private and public monopolies, allowing competition to eliminate the inefficient units. The problem is that the commutative equity criterion allows persistence of unlimited differences in wealth among parents and unlimited differences in expenditure per child. It permits considerable intergenerational transmission of inequality.

2) *Fiscal Neutrality*. At this second level of equity, the state seeks to achieve a degree of equity through transfer payments so that local school districts, community colleges, or individual students (in the case of need-based education grants) are treated as though they had access to an equivalent amount of wealth per student. After attainment of an equal fiscal base (which seldom is attained, under current practices), unlimited variation in local effort would be permitted, as would unlimited variation in expenditure per pupil. State school finance systems in practice generally go beyond commutative equity and travel part of the distance toward

fiscal neutrality. Similarly, the financing of higher education goes beyond commutative equity through the use of grants and aids based on need, such as private scholarships, low-interest loans, work-study programs, state scholarship commission grants, and federal BEOG grants. But higher education also falls short of fiscal neutrality, for parental income is still a very important determinant of the quantity and quality of the college education received. The achievement of fiscal neutrality should move the current system toward greater horizontal equity, toward a higher level of vertical tax and student equity, and toward less intergenerational transmission of inequality.

3) *Proportionality*. This requires equal effective tax rates in relation to ability to pay, and benefits that are proportional to need on the expenditure side. Among students who are unequal, a clear definition of proportional vertical equity is difficult to achieve, because it is hard to measure need from smallest to greatest. But proportional vertical equity does imply that a larger percentage of total expenditure per student will go to the disadvantaged students through special education programs. This degree of rectification presumably would not preclude the more able from moving ahead more quickly, or from completing advanced degrees more frequently. This level of equity most closely corresponds to equality of educational opportunity. It still allows for differences in total expenditure based on differences in tastes among families (given that some are myopic and others are more farsighted), as well as on differences in innate ability. This level would severely reduce but not eliminate intergenerational transmission of inequality of earnings.

4) *Positivism*. The fourth-level equity criterion implies progressive rates on both the tax and the benefit sides. This is Rawlsian equity, designed to have a corrective effect on the current income distribution and to assist the least advantaged. Positivist equity could be illustrated by full financing by the state of high-cost special education programs for handicapped or disadvantaged children, large Pell grants for the poor, and affirmative action. Finally, this level of positivism also implies a correction for those individual cases where parents and students have myopic tastes. Hence positivism provides for intergenerational equity should the parents' welfare function be too shortsighted (and hence $W_0 W_0$ too close to the horizontal axis in Figure 3 above). This fourth and final level of equity thereby implies elimination of the intergenerational transmission of inequality, and attainment of intergenerational distributive justice among peers.

Maximum Social Benefit

Finally, there is the "equal sacrifice" equal benefit doctrine, with its long tradition in public finance (e.g., Edgeworth 1925: 100ff.). Only when the common assumptions of diminishing marginal utility of income and benefits are made, does it become the economists' counterpart of Rawls's positivism.[11] It says that to minimize the aggregate sacrifice borne by taxpayers, and to maximize the aggregate benefits from education received by children, "equal sacrifice" must be interpreted as equal *marginal* sacrifice, and "equal benefit" must be interpreted as equal *marginal* benefit. To equalize real costs and real benefits *at the margin* requires progressive tax and benefit rates--or positivism.[12]

The courts have sometimes taken a positivist stance, such as in *Levittown* v. *Nyquist* (State Supreme Court of New York 1978). A modified stance along these lines is developed further in Chapter 8 by Alexander.

Operational measures of vertical equity among children are somewhat difficult to develop, because they require difficult judgments about the value of the benefit of education (or intensity of the need for it) among children who are unequal. It is easier on the tax side, where the operational measure is merely the tax rate, once the ability to pay has been measured properly (as discussed above). The benefit rate among unequals can be approximated, however, by calculating the percent of real current expenditure spent per member of the special population, and asking whether it is larger than, equal to, or less than the percent spent per member of the regular student population. An equal percent would correspond approximately to fiscal neutrality or to equal educational opportunity, whereas a larger percent spent per pupil on disadvantaged or handicapped students would indicate a progressive rate structure of the type required by a positivist equity principle.

Humane Growth Criteria

The contributions of education and of academic research to humane societal growth include their contributions to full earnings, as well as their contributions to non-monetary and social benefits (which are important to both national growth and the quality of human life) and their contributions to distributive justice.

Efficiency and Equity as Joint Products

The challenge is to bring together efficiency criteria and equity criteria, especially by locating the more limited situations in which they are joint products. The successively more comprehensive criteria for efficiency, equity, and humane growth are listed below. Together with the operational measures for most (discussed above), they can be applied judgmentally by both small unit and larger area administrators and educational planners. Further measurement is not always practical (especially at small unit levels), so it is important to draw on existing research studies.

An Efficiency Criteria Hierarchy

1. Accountability
2. Production function relationships
3. Cost/effectiveness criteria
4. Cost/monetary benefit criteria
5. Cost/"full" earnings criteria
6. Cost/"full" private and social benefit criteria

An Equity Criteria Hierarchy

1. Commutative equity
2. Fiscal neutrality
3. Proportional equity
4. Positivism

Humane Growth Criteria

1. Improvements in efficiency, with no reduction in equity
2. Improvements in equity, with no reduction in efficiency
3. Improvements in both efficiency and equity

Choice of one of these humane growth criteria for practical application will restrict policy changes to that area where efficiency and equity are complementary. This is illustrated again in Figure 4 (from Figure 1) as the shaded area $ZX'\Omega$. To summarize, starting at point Z, improvements in efficiency consistent with humane growth criterion #1 above would limit budget changes to those above line $Z\Omega$ and to the right of line ZX so that

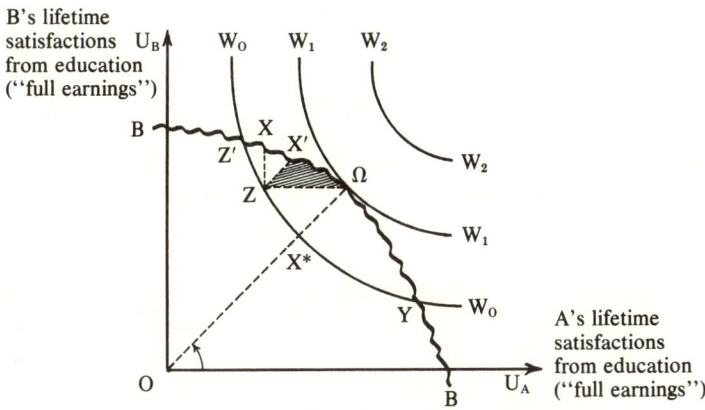

Figure 4. Humane Growth Criteria ($ZX'\Omega$)

neither A or B are made worse off (the criterion for Pareto efficiency). To avoid reducing equity, however, the region is further limited under equity criterion #3 to the shaded area to the right of line ZX'. Using humane growth criterion #2 above, improvements in equity would occur when moving to the right from line ZX', but parallel to line $Z\Omega$ to avoid reductions in efficiency. A joint improvement in both equity and efficiency occurs in any move upward from point Z and to the right of ZX'.

Efficiency and Equity Trade-Offs

To go beyond this gets into the delicate trade-off between inefficiency and equity. Atkinson's (1970) equality measure defines equality in such a way that the measure of inequality (in contrast to the Gini coefficient) is specifically related to the Welfare Function, $W_0 W_0$ in Figure 4. To simplify, if point Z' is the current distribution of full lifetime earnings from education between A and B, Atkinson would merely define equivalent earnings as any other point along $W_0 W_0$. Noting that these equivalent earnings are equally distributed at point X^*, and average actual benefit is approximately at Ω, Atkinson's measure of inequality is $A = \frac{OX^*}{O\Omega}$. That is, the distance ΩX^* measures the efficiency loss in total benefits from education due to the greater inequality and child inequity at point Z'.

This is a theoretical framework for widening the range of budget decisions beyond those where there is a joint gain in efficiency and equity. The humane growth criteria 1-3 limit the region for planning, budgeting, and financing decisions to area $Z\Omega X'$, where little opposition can be expected because nobody is made worse off--efficiency and equity are both increased. But opposition will arise as budget decisions move into the trade-offs in region $ZX'Z'$, where there are gains in efficiency at the cost of increasing the existing inequity, or into region $Z\Omega Y$, where the students from the best neighborhoods become the worse off.

An operational measure may now be obtained, however, for these trade-offs between efficiency and equity. It requires the choice of an equity principle from the equity criteria hierarchy above, and a substitution of this choice into the equation that gives the general shape and position of the welfare function $W_0 W_0$ in Figure 4. (See note 13.) The combination is a significant step, somewhat unique in education, to obtain a measure of the cost of the inequity (at Z') in terms of an efficiency loss $(X^*\Omega)$. If commutative equity is chosen, $W_0 W_0$ is flat, and the inequity that exists is valued at zero. A change in the distribution of benefits that shifts some per-pupil expenditure from group B toward group A would result in no gain (no move upward toward W_1). If fiscal neutrality or proportional equity (i.e., equality of educational opportunity) is chosen, $W_0 W_0$ would be more convex to the origin, and there would be a larger gain measured in efficiency--terms (i.e., $X^*\Omega > 0$) by changing the distribution of educational benefits among children from Z', where they are unequal, to Ω, where they are more equal. If positivism is chosen, there is an even more convex welfare function in Figure 4 and a still larger welfare gain (in efficiency terms) through redistributing the benefits to correct for initial inequities.[13]

These trade-offs still incur opposition on behalf of the group who are made worse off, so emphasizing the humane growth criteria wherever possible holds the greatest promise.[14] The trade-offs between efficiency and equity cannot be completely avoided. However, in education there are likely to be many more situations where improvements in equity simultaneously *increase* efficiency (and vice versa) than is typical of the rest of the economy. The reason is that among working-age adults, redistribution of earnings reduces work incentives, whereas redistribution of educational benefits to achieve greater equality of educational opportunity may actually *increase* the work incentives of these young persons over their life cycles, without reducing the future work incentives of others. This is partly because there is some evidence of diminishing returns in the high-expenditure-per-child school and college districts; smaller percentages of their budgets are spent on instruction as cited by Carroll (Chapter 10) and Geske (Chapter 14). Most important, as children from low-income neighborhoods benefit from better preparation, the incentive effect is not negative as it is in the case of welfare payments.

Conclusion

There are strong nationwide pressures to increase social efficiency in the schools and colleges. These pressures arise from the squeeze caused by rising energy costs and inflation, declining enrollments, and slower economic growth. All of these phenomena are reflected in the federal budget cuts, tax and expenditure limitation movement, and budgets determined through the political process, and all necessitate internal reallocation. If equity is to be maintained, much less improved, it will be necessary to more actively seek internal sources of funds.

The main efforts to improve efficiency must come at the local level where the final allocative decisions are made. They require clear incentives to achieve efficiency, and criteria that can be applied informally and judgmentally. State and federal levels have a role--states can reduce the budgets for programs that are not cost effective or socially efficient, and they can increase the incentives for local efficiency by avoiding cost-plus arrangements in the design of categorical programs. State and federal policies might facilitate competition and increased parental involvement as means of policing the system (and getting homework done by students) where possible. But beyond this, it is likely to be counterproductive if state and federal agencies require too much paperwork or intervene directly in the management of schools and colleges.

In the effort to improve equity, there are also important local school board and college trustee and staff planning roles, especially in moderating the strong effects of neighborhood wealth disparities on the quality of the schools. But given the wide disparities in local wealth among districts, states, and those seeking access to college, there is a necessary state and federal role. Again, however, equity criteria and measurements are required as informal judgments are made about equity as a part of each decision.

It would be a mistake to underestimate the inefficiency, waste, and inequity in the system. However, it should be clear that we believe the United States has basically good schools and colleges; what is needed is more and still better education, not poorer quality or reduced access. There are unnoticed sources of waste in schools and colleges, including temporarily unutilized cash balances that are not drawing interest, underutilized classroom buildings, underutilized staff as enrollments decline, protectionist admission requirements in fields where there are inflationary pressures and shortages, low secondary-school requirements in mathematics and science, higher dropout rates than in Japan, the USSR, and other rapidly growing nations, high school graduates with insufficient basic skills, and high levels of subsidy and low admission standards in fields where there are oversupplies. Furthermore, inequity persists, as evidenced by the poor education found in urban ghettos and the unequal educational opportunities available to children in the poorest neighborhoods and states.

This chapter has sought to present an overview of the state of the art with respect to the criteria currently available. The operational measures for the "full" private-plus-social projected rates of return are still not sufficiently comprehensive, and the selection of an equity principle requires that delicate ethical judgments be made. But these limitations are not sufficient for ignoring what does exist. Some analysis and data can be quite informative, helping to isolate the missing elements needed in each final judgment, and to make what is already good better. Such a combination of efficiency and equity considerations, and their use along with the humane growth criteria that are suggested, have implications not only for better education, but for the longer-run welfare of society as a whole.[15]

NOTES

1. See Jay Chambers (in Windham 1979: 95, 101) for effects of community income differences on teachers' salaries and for information on the positive relationship between salaries and teacher traits such as years

of schooling, years of experience, verbal ability, and teacher education in basic disciplines.

2. This Pareto criterion is the central criterion for efficiency moves in welfare theory. The subsidiary Hicks-Kaldor compensation principle allows for compensation to be provided to disadvantaged parties (e.g., college students whose programs have been eliminated by the state, or teachers whose teaching loads have been significantly increased). But "hold harmless" clauses reduce to the more central Pareto criterion when the compensation is actually paid (as it often is, to facilitate the change), since after the payment of compensation no one is worse off. The broader definition of economic efficiency relative to Pareto efficiency, which includes trade-offs with equity, is considered in the section on "Humane Growth Criteria" and in Figure 4.

3. Technically, A and B are individuals throughout, but it will be more interesting to think of them as representative of groups of "poor" and "rich" children of young adults. Without assuming additivity of utility, what is said for two individuals here is easily generalizable to three or more.

4. Many persons in educational evaluation are concerned with situations where there are more than two educational outcomes (outputs), and/or more than two inputs. We seek here to reduce the situation to its essentials, however, so what is said here for two outcomes (outputs) can be generalized to refer to three or more. Generalizations are developed in Henderson and Quandt (1971: 58-91), and a survey of recent work with educational production functions is offered by L. Lau (in Windham 1979: Ch. 2) and by E. Cohn (1979: Ch. 8).

5. Public administrators experience political pressures to minimize the tax costs while simultaneously maintaining or increasing the benefits. If they fail, they risk being replaced; this prospect provides incentives for efficiency in public institutions. The point is developed further in the literature on budget determination through voting; see Bowen (1948: 188), Downs (1957), and McMahon (1970, 1971).

6. A review of educational production functions which summarizes the empirical evidence to date, as well as providing an exposition of their basic theoretical elements and the problems in their application, is provided by Lawrence J. Lau (in Windham 1979: 33-70).

7. See evidence on the accuracy of expected earnings (McMahon and Wagner 1981), as well as on female response to these expectations (Ferber and McMahon 1979), for example.

8. For some applications of horizontal equity measures, see Odden, Berne, and Strefel (1979: 18-84). The five least equitable states by most of the measures reported are Virginia, New York, Wyoming, Georgia, and Pennsylvania. Implications of the choice among measures are considered by Berne (1978).

9. Evidence of a positive relationship between education, earnings, and job performance is developed by Layard and Psacharopoulos (1974), Wise (1975), and Wolpin (1977). The screening hypothesis (or signaling argument) continues to be defended by Lazear (1977).

10. Because wealthier taxpaying districts (neighborhoods) will not voluntarily redistribute much to poor districts (neighborhoods), much decentralization of finance eliminates all redistribution.

11. Specifically, one must assume that the marginal utility of each dollar of income declines as income increases, and that the marginal benefit of each dollar's worth of education provided to a child diminishes as the amount of education provided increases. The latter is more debatable when we compare students who differ with respect to their parental incomes and academic ability. On efficiency grounds, for example, the more able can learn more from one additional year of education and expenditure than can the less able students. But then, one additional dollar of income may mean more to the less able students later in life.

12. The fact that the interpersonal comparisons of utility involved rest on philosophical and ethical grounds, and not on economic grounds, has been mentioned previously.

13. The level of $W_0 W_0$ in Figure 1 can be described by

$$W_0 = \frac{1}{\alpha} y_A^\alpha + \frac{1}{\alpha} y_B^\alpha, \quad 0 < \alpha < 1$$

where y_A and y_B equals the real expenditure per pupil on A and B. This then requires that an equity principle be chosen from among those presented in the equity hierarchy above to specify the alpha weights. If $\alpha = 1$, social welfare is the simple sum of the real expenditures for A and B. This would correspond to commutative equity, because the distribution of expenditure between A and B makes no difference. As $\alpha = 0$, $W_0 = \log y_A + \log y_B$, and a given number of dollars can accomplish a larger proportional increase if used to benefit the student who is currently worse off. This advantage in the use of marginal dollars would continue until benefits are equal, which means that the logarithmic form corresponds to the equality of educational opportunity equity criterion #2. Rawlsian positivism arises as y_A and y_B are redefined as outcomes (e.g., lifetime full earnings) or as $\alpha = -D$, with increasing degrees of corrective action for the disadvantaged. It then is possible to measure the cost of the loss in equity from redistribution of the benefits using the above equation to compute the change in W_0 when y_B increases and y_A decreases for comparison to the gains from the improvement in efficiency, to see if there is a net gain.

14. It is not uncommon to seek near-consensus on changes, since then the interpersonal comparisons of utility that are involved, and the choice of an equity principle, do not have to be defended in every situation.

15. I am indebted to Terry G. Geske, Keith Hartley, Mark Blaug, an anonymous referee, and Carolyn H. McMahon for helpful comments on this article.

REFERENCES

Arrow, Kenneth. 1951. *Social choice and individual values.* New York: John Wiley and Sons.

Atkinson, Tony. 1970. On the measurement of inequality. *Journal of Economic Theory* 2: 244-63.

Bator, Francis. 1969. The simple analytics of welfare maximization. *American Economic Review* 62 (March): 22-59. Reprinted in D. R. Kamerschen, *Readings in microeconomics.* New York: John Wiley and Sons, 1969.

Berne, Robert. 1978. Alternative equity and equality measures: does the measure make a difference? *Selected studies in school finance,* ed. Esther Tron. Washington, D.C.: U.S. Office of Education.
Bowen, Howard R. 1948. *Toward social economy.* New York: Rinehart.
Cohn, Elchanan. 1979. *The economics of education.* Cambridge: Ballinger.
Downs, Anthony. 1957. *An economic theory of democracy.* New York: Harper & Bros.
Eckstein, Otto. 1961. A survey of the theory of public expenditure criteria. Pp. 439-504 in *Public finances: needs, sources, and utilization.* Princeton: Princeton University Press.
Edgeworth, F. Y. 1925. *Papers relating to political economy,* II. London: Macmillan.
Ferber, Marianne A., and McMahon, Walter W. 1979. Women's expected earnings and their investment in higher education. *Journal of Human Resources* 14 (Summer): 405-20.
Hansen, W. L., and Weisbrod, B. 1969. The distribution of costs and direct benefits of public higher education. *Journal of Human Resources* 4 (Spring): 176-91.
Heckman, James. 1976. A life cycle model of earnings, learning, and consumption. *Journal of Political Economy* 84, part 2 (August).
Henderson, James M., and Quandt, Richard E. 1971. *Microeconomic theory, a mathematical approach.* 2nd ed. New York: McGraw-Hill.
Hickrod, G. Alan; Chaudhari, Ramesh B.; and Hubbard, Ben C. 1981. *Reformation and counterreformation in Illinois school finance: 1973-1981.* Center for the Study of Educational Finance, College of Education, Illinois State University, Normal, June 1981.
Kirst, Michael W. 1981. Curriculum: a key to improving academic standards. Faculty Working Paper, College of Education, Stanford University, May 1981.
Layard, Richard, and Psacharopoulos, G. 1974. The screening hypothesis and returns to education. *Journal of Political Economy* 82 (September-October): 985-98.
Lazear, E. 1977. Academic achievement and job performance: note. *American Economic Review* 67 (March): 252-54.
McMahon, Walter W. 1970. An economic analysis of the major determinants of expenditures on public primary and secondary education. *Review of Economics and Statistics* (August).
———. 1971. Cyclical growth of public expenditure. *Public Finance* 26, 1 (September).
———, and Melton, C. 1978. Measuring cost of living variation. *Industrial Relations* 17, 3 (October): 324-32.
———. 1977. A cost of living index for Illinois counties and school districts. Pp. 67-113 in *Perspectives on Illinois school finance.* Springfield, Ill.: State Board of Education. November.
McMahon, Walter W., and Wagner, A. 1981. Expected returns to investment in higher education. *Journal of Human Resources* 16, 2.
Odden, Alan; Berne, Robert; and Strefel, L. 1979. *Equity in school finance.* Report No. F79-9. Denver: Education Commission of the States.

Psacharopoulos, George. 1972. *The returns to education*. Amsterdam: Elsevier.
Rawls, John. 1977. *A theory of justice*. Cambridge: Harvard University Press.
Sahota, Gian S. 1978. Theories of personal income distribution: a survey. *Journal of Economic Literature* 16, 1 (March): 1-55.
Schultz, T. W. 1974. *Economics of the family*. Chicago: University of Chicago Press.
Windham, Douglas M., ed. 1979. *Economic dimensions of education*. Washington: Report of a Committee of the National Academy of Education.
Wise, D. A. 1975. Academic achievement and job performance. *American Economic Review* 65 (June): 35-66.
Wolpin, K. I. 1977. Education and screening. *American Economic Review* 67 (December): 949-58.

PART I

Social Efficiency

The returns to education, including increased earnings, leisure-time satisfactions, and contributions to the preservation of our freedoms, are returns to a stock of human capital skills and knowledge acquired by individuals largely through deliberate investment of their own time in learning. These inputs of human time, and achieving greater efficiency in the use of those inputs, are an important focus of the contributions in Part I. These time inputs are often overlooked in studies of how resources are used to achieve more learning without increased costs, and yet they are influenced--to be sure, in differing degrees--by the choices of what is financed and are a vital part of the human capital formation process. The chapters in Part I seek ways of achieving greater social efficiency in the use of resources devoted to education.

There is extensive economic literature on the benefits and costs of education in the United States (Cohn 1979). In the last two decades economic analytic techniques, such as benefit/cost analyses and cost effectiveness studies, have been used with increasing frequency to address efficiency concerns in education. These economic tools have proved useful in analyzing investment decisions with regard to educaton in general, as well as within specific educational institutions.

From an economic perspective, additional investment in formal schooling should be encouraged only where the full rate of return from the investment exceeds the rate of return available from other alternatives such as investments in physical capital, financial assets, or on-the-job training. Similarly, if care is taken to make provision for the non-monetary returns and social benefits, relative rates of return may be used to guide investment decisions for different types of schooling, such as preschool, primary, secondary, vocational, or types of higher education.

The research on human capital formation has been basically concerned with conceptualizing and measuring the benefits of education, both to the individual and to society. Theodore Schultz (1963: Ch. 3; 1971: Ch. 12) has continually emphasized the value of education and has categorized a number of educational benefits, including the social benefits from research, as well as the benefits accruing from the strong relationship between education and economic growth. Furthermore, Schultz has noted that education serves to identify and nurture potential student talent, while also increasing the ability of individuals to adapt to a changing job market.

Initially, research on the benefits of education focused almost exclusively on the direct monetary returns from investments in education. Studies typically defind the returns to education solely in terms of the amount education adds to lifetime income, using different methods involving the shape of age-earning profiles, earnings differentials, and the discounted present value of lifetime income differentials. These studies investigating the relationship between education and earnings have tried to sort out the confounding effects of innate ability, on-the-job training, family background, and quality of schooling (Welch 1974). Recent research is confronting the more difficult task of attempting to quantify the non-monetary benefits associated with education.

Increasingly, educational organizations are being required to consider the quality of their outputs, and to consider the relationship between those outputs and the costs involved. Declining enrollments in secondary and higher education are forcing program reevaluation and creating strong incentives to cut back high-cost and less basic fringe programs. Therefore, controlling for quality by determining which institutions and which programs are high cost are questions very much on the minds of legislators and of state boards of higher education and state school boards, as well as of education staff these days. Cost comparisons, costs in relation to effectiveness, and the cost effectiveness criteria to be applied become crucial in finding the sources of waste so that, in view of the limited resources, educationally sound programs can be financed and preserved.

From another perspective, the sheer magnitude of educational costs and the large fraction of those costs borne by the taxpayer ensure that concerns with costs and with cost effectiveness will remain a major public policy issue for the foreseeable future. The public and policymakers alike are concerned about the productivity of educational institutions and are asking, "What are we getting for our money?" And a lot of money it is: education accounts for about 12 percent of the Gross National Product, an amount, as estimated by Cohn (1979: Ch. 4), that increased from $18 billion in 1950 to $230 billion in 1977, and to $376 billion in 1982, by projection of Cohn's estimate. A portion of this amount is the cost of the students' time as measured by their foregone earnings. Demands for accountability, for competency testing programs, and for tax expenditure limitation provisions are all intended to force more efficient uses of school resources.

In Chapter 2, Theodore W. Schultz suggests that current organizational, financial, and administrative arrangements in public education, particularly in large urban school systems, promote substantial inefficiencies that significantly undermine effective investment in human capital. This unsatisfactory condition has been brought about because the parental role in determining the quality of their children's education has been sharply reduced over the years, and because, among schools in large, monolithic school systems, there is little competition to provide the necessary incentives for greater efficiency. This change or shift in the locus of educational decision-making has concentrated authority in the hands of professional educators and government agencies and has removed the consumers (parents) from their capacity to police the system. Schultz wants to stimulate more competition among the schools in order to increase the amount of learning that takes place, and thereby to encourage greater efficiency.

One reviewer of this paper, Jane Leuthold, raised a question about how equity among children could be maintained, given the proposals for decentralization that are being advanced. The disparities in local wealth would dominate per-child expenditures, and racial segregation would prevail unless practical measures were proposed to deal with these side effects of decentralization. Although this trade-off with equity can be identified, it can be put aside until later in this book (see Parts II and III) in the interest of considering ways to increase efficiency. More competition among schools (presumably with techniques to phase out inefficient units, and federally supported, efficiency-oriented research, such as in agriculture), more parental concern through more direct involvement, and the other suggestions to promote efficiency made by Theodore Schultz merit serious consideration.

Chapter 3, by Charles S. Benson, deals with the broader social efficiency with which the skills and knowledge that are the focus of the educational system are acquired--the important matter of the uses of time by parents and students in the home, and neighborhood effects on the educational achievement of students. Benson analyzes data on the amount of time used by parents at different SES levels in controlling their children, taking them to the library, and in doing homework with them, as well as examining some of the effects of the neighborhood, all aspects of a broader educational production function. Francine Blau, a referee for this paper, suggested that we remain alert to the effects of differences in the quality of parental time inputs among families at different SES levels, of different market incentives in the neighborhood, and of role models at different SES levels as they relate to school achievement.

In Chapter 4, Richard A. Rossmiller examines the methodological approaches used in school effects research and cost effectiveness criteria, critically surveying several studies which have concentrated on the allocation of resources within school systems. Rossmiller stresses the importance of the teacher in the educational production process and suggests that research which has focused on how the various inputs are transformed into outputs has rendered useful insights. Recent research conducted at the individual school or classroom level has focused on process-related variables, such as the use of student and staff time, certain characteristics of students and teachers, and various instructional strategies; that research is beginning to provide clues about how school resources might be organized more efficiently. Robert Wallhaus reviewed this paper and pointed out some of the uses of cost effectiveness analysis by the state board of higher education staff today, including a new trend toward use of the more limited concept of average unit cost for instruction at each institution to allocate funds on a statewide basis among institutions.

In the next chapter, J. Alan Thomas, Frances Kemmerer, and David H. Monk focus on the technical efficiency of time-allocation decisions made by teachers and students in the classroom. Viewing classrooms as structures wherein production-type decisions are made about the use of purchased resources and students' time, these researchers hypothesize that classrooms containing high-SES students will be structured differently from classrooms with low-SES students. After stratifying for high-SES vs. low-SES classrooms, they report on the percentage of classroom time allotted to a variety of instructional formats and examine the relationship between these instructional formats and the proportion of total observations during which students were actively "on task." Byron Brown, commenting on this paper, suggested that this type of research represents an effort to find student learning curves, or the educational production function, that applies under different modes of instruction.

Chapter 6, by Robert T. Michael, focuses on the non-market benefits of schooling. If education increases the efficiency of work time, it is only reasonable to assume that it also increases the efficiency and the productivity of consumption time. Michael deals with the non-market returns to education (arising largely during non-market consumption-time hours) that are a part of "full" earnings, because those returns must be a part of "full" benefit/cost judgmental comparisons. He reviews several studies that explore the relationship between schooling and investment in various forms of human capital, including the effect of education on the efficiency of additional schooling itself. Research investigating the effects of education on household productivity in capital markets and consumer markets is summarized, and research suggesting strong positive effects of schooling on health is discussed. In addition, the chapter examines another important line of research concerned with the impact of schooling on the family: the formation of the family, the relationships among the adults, and the well-being of the children.

Sherwin Rosen, who commented on Michael's paper, raises a question involving technological neutrality, which would assume that the schooling effects on productivity are the same for both labor and nonlabor market activity. If schooling is considered in terms of expanding a person's consumption possibilities, does the efficiency gain associated with education become available in equal proportion in *all* consumption-time activities, as well as in market sector activities? If so, the valuation of non-monetary benefits becomes a relatively straightforward exercise. Michael suggests that, in this case, the estimated monetary rates of return to education would be almost doubled.

Chapter 7, by Walter W. McMahon and Alan P. Wagner, asks, "Are the monetary benefits derived from higher education alone worth the cost involved?" In addressing this question they focus on the monetary rates of return over time to higher education, and they present measures of the efficiency gain to investment at each type of institution, at each of four degree levels, and in each of a score of major fields of study and employment. Their chapter explains the method of computing rates of return, reflecting a view of the entire life-cycle that minimizes the impact of transitory fluctuations in the starting salaries for college graduates. Based on longer-run rates of return, the authors suggest that the rates of returns to investment in higher education have not shown clear evidence of a significant declining trend, at least up through 1980, and that they have also compared favorably with rates of return to financial assets during this same period. This chapter provides new evidence by using microeconomic data to compute different rates of return among institutions based on very specific differences in costs, and it indicates that there are wide differences in many of the rates of return among occupational fields that also appear to persist over time.

REFERENCES

Cohn, Elchanan. 1979. *The economics of education.* Rev. ed. Cambridge: Ballinger.
Schultz, Theodore W. 1963. *The economic value of education,* New York: Columbia University Press.
―――. 1971. *Investment in human capital.* New York: Free Press.
Welch, Finis. 1974. Relationship between income and schooling. In *Review of research in education 2,* ed. Fred N. Kerlinger and John B. Carroll. Itasca, Ill.: F. B. Peacock.

CHAPTER 2

Human Capital Approaches in Organizing and Paying for Education

THEODORE W. SCHULTZ

The overarching question before us is, To what extent does human capital theory tell us how to finance education?

The theory treats education as a private stock of human capital that is acquired normally during one's youth. The acquisition of an education has the attributes of undertaking an investment. It calls for the commitment of private resources including the value of the time of youth, and of the time that parents devote to the schooling and education of their children. The returns to the investment in education are private returns, subject to risk and uncertainty that are borne privately. Human capital theory tells us a good deal about the economics of time allocation, and about the pervasive effects of education on the value of our own time, on earnings, on consumption activities, on marriage, on health, on self-esteem, on ability to reason, and on a wide array of personal satisfactions. The theory is also useful in determining the effects of education on the distribution of personal income and on the intergenerational transmission of inequality (Tomes 1981).

Human capital theory, however, does not tell us the optimum scale of schools and school systems; nor does it tell us what is an equitable distribution of personal income and an equitable distribution of educational opportunities. It is not about to solve the problem of weak and distorted incentives that teachers face. It has not (although it should have, by now) led to studies of the adverse effects of the declining authority of parents in school decisions that pertain to the quantity and quality of the schooling available to their children. Last but not least, human capital theory remains silent on the politics of education.

Clearly, education is in trouble. In diagnosing the causes of this trouble, a short-term view will not suffice. To take our bearing calls for an historical perspective. Without history, current events and problems produce much pessimism. Past achievements not only give us courage, but also give us clues as to what has gone wrong in recent years.

Overview of the Returns to Education

Education, including university research, over the years has contributed substantially to the productivity of the economy and to welfare. The remarkable rise in earnings is an important part of the story. The total compensation in real terms per hour for manufacturing workers, who are the largest part of the labor force, increased over fivefold between 1900 and 1975 (Schultz 1977a). The dynamics of productivity have been such that the rates of return to education have tended to exceed the rates of return to physical capital. In response to this difference in returns, the growth in stock of human capital, consisting largely of education, has been higher than the growth of physical capital. The share of income accruing to property has declined from about 45 to 20 percent, whereas the share accruing to labor, broadly defined to include all human services of the market sector, has risen from 55 to 80 percent. Meanwhile, the inequality in the distribution of personal income has declined somewhat, as a consequence of the changes in factor shares.

All of these achievements, however, omit the non-market contributions of education in household production, in caring for children, in acquiring and maintaining the health of family members, in being more efficient in purchasing consumer goods and services, in evaluating the quality of education that children receive, and (most important) in determining social competence and the quality of the style of living. None of these non-market values is included in the monetary rates of return to education that are derived from market-sector activities.

There's Trouble in Metropolis

Keeping these achievements firmly in mind, how do we account for the present trouble throughout much of education? There is a woeful inadequacy in the schooling of many elementary and high school students. High school grades have become increasingly unreliable (Walsh 1979); college freshman have high school grades higher than ever, whereas their college test scores are declining (Astin, King, and Richardson 1979).

The quality of instruction in many colleges is declining, and college grades have become inflated. A *Science* editorial asks, "Can Meritocracy in Academe Be Saved?" (Palmer 1979). Universities are being seriously impaired by increasing government intervention and sanctions. Universities are not defending their true function; they have, in the words of Edward Shils, become too fond of Caesar (Shils 1979).

More Efficient Schools Are a Major Means in Achieving More Child Equity and Learning

Inefficiency is at the heart in what has gone wrong in the public schools. Many of the school systems in our major cities are performing badly. Teachers face distorted incentives. The schooling of the children is inadequate. Federally mandated educational reforms are enforced by placing children in jeopardy. Parents know that the quality of their children's schooling is bad, but they can do little about it except change their place of residence, or opt for private schools and pay both school taxes and tuition. Clearly, in terms of quality many American children are undereducated.

The complementarity between efficiency and equity in elementary and secondary schooling is being overlooked in the quest for equity. An optimum level of efficiency in our big school systems would, in all probability, contribute more to the cause of equity than any of the many school reforms now being imposed on our schools.

Public finance is also in trouble. The convenience of deficit financing is no longer assured. Furthermore (and a serious issue for school finance), property taxes are being "frozen" or sharply reduced, as has already occurred in California. To the extent that local schools still have some political autonomy, that autonomy is a function of revenue from local property taxes. Moreover, the economics of property taxation is being replaced by the politics of property taxation. In the case of real estate taxes, once their effects are accounted for in the capitalization of land values, the rents paid for the services of the land is in general altered very little. Yet publicly we are bent on reducing taxes on real estate, the land component in homes, and on land generally, although the prices of land have risen substantially more than the rate of inflation.

The value of education is not in doubt. The art of financing education is available. There is much confusion, however, in using what is known about the value of education and about financing education in solving the present acute problems in primary, secondary, and higher education. There is a lack of agreement with respect to these problems. Until we identify them clearly and precisely, the prospects of solving them are bleak. Although the concepts of efficiency and equity are relevant for this purpose, they are not sufficient.

We need to ask, Has education become all too dependent on public funds? Public funds are not free; they are not unencumbered; they are not an unmixed blessing. The allocation of public funds to support education obviously is not a minor problem. The public control of how these funds are used is clearly a critical issue. Public funds are also unstable; when they increase rapidly, the boom in education results in distortions.

Sudden richness has its price. (The oil-producing nations are finding it hard to live with their sudden boom in wealth.) When public funds are cut, the educational enterprise is in difficulty. Nor is it clear that more funds would remedy the Big School Disease. Unless there are changes in the way these funds are used, more funds per se would not correct the lack of teachers' incentives to improve their own performance. They also would not reduce the burden placed on school children by our various endeavors to mandate social reforms via education. More federal and state funds could further reduce the decision-making authority of parents pertaining to educational activities.

Education as Human Capital and Its Attributes

Education is a personal, acquired ability. It is unique in the sense that once you have it, no one can take it from you. Nor can you get rid of it! We call this acquired ability *capital* because it renders valuable services and it entails investment. We call it *human capital* because it is embodied in human beings. We are well aware of the fact that no individual can sell his own stock of educational capital. He cannot sell himself, because that would be slavery. Nor can he transfer his stock of education to someone else. It is his stock of human capital to keep and use as long as he lives. Physical capital, which still dominates our thinking, differs markedly in some important respects. Private ownership of physical capital is governed by property rights. Such property can be sold; it can be transferred as a gift to other individuals and to corporate bodies. Factories, equipment, homes, and inventories can be destroyed. Private property is subject to annual taxation, to inheritance taxation, and it may be confiscated by governments. During World War II the stock of human capital in Germany and Japan, despite casualties, was much less impaired than was the stock of physical capital. Refugees take their stock of human capital with them when they flee for safety. Walls are built to make it impossible for people to flee; out-migration can be controlled and even prohibited. Nevertheless, in the extreme, governments cannot confiscate human capital, although they can destroy its value.

The services of human and physical capital have many economic attributes in common when we consider the contributions of these services in production and consumption. At many points in ongoing economic activities they are complementary; they may also be substitutes for each other. Highly skilled labor is essential in many modern types of economic activity--for example, in producing and operating computers. Physical capital is often a substitute for labor; tractors reduce the farm labor that is required. Large modern tractors, however, require highly skilled operators. The complementarity and substitution between human and physical capital in household production and consumption are, in principle, similar to that in production in the market sector.

That small corps of economists concerned about human capital have been all too silent on the political implications of their contributions. Studies of the effects of the brain drain on the country of exit and on the receiving country are an exception, although policy still remains indifferent to these studies. Americans proclaim their liberal values and democratic institutions, and human values are deemed to be fundamental. Consistent with these values, our government does not build walls to keep educated people from leaving the United States. But, inconsistent with these values, we erect fences to keep people out, and we mandate fancy selective quotas on immigration. We are occasionally liberal in allowing particular refugees to enter. Public policy that minimizes the authority of parents in determining the quality of the schooling their children receive is clearly inconsistent with these liberal values.

Within the private market sector, which still accounts for most of the formation of physical capital, individual entrepreneurs decide the specifications of the investment they will undertake and the amount that they will invest. Would that it were so in our large urban school systems. Parents who have children in these schools can do very little, through their private endeavors, to help determine the specifications of the schooling their children receive. This state of affairs is all the more incongruous in light of the impressive secular rise in the education of parents. Parents, of course, have the option of moving from the city into the suburbs, and many are doing so. To contemplate the possibility that all parents of the million elementary and high school students in the New York City public school system could move into the suburbs, is to contemplate a theoretical nightmare.

My plan is of three parts. First, I examine some of the reasons for this unsatisfactory condition. I then consider its effects. The last part of the article is devoted to concluding observations. The thrust of my argument is that the stock of educational capital now being acquired is far less than optimal, both in quantity and in quality, because of what has been done to the organization of education.

Why Has This Unsatisfactory Condition Occurred?

This condition is largely a consequence of the ever deeper wedge that is separating education from the self-interest of parents and students. This separation is most acute in elementary and secondary schools, especially in the big school systems. The educational investment that matters is in the acquired ability of children and youth. Parents and their children have much at stake in this educational capital. Although their self-interest is fundamental to the success of organized education, it is ever more excluded because of the way in which education is financed, organized, and administered. Why has this exclusion of the self-interests of parents and their children occurred?

As intellectuals who specialize in education, and as a nation, we have invented four presumably good reasons for reducing the authority of parents. The first pertains to the technical attributes of schooling. The technology of schooling is now largely determined by professional educators and school administrators. Even classroom teachers are deemed to be unqualified on this matter. Parents, regardless of how well they may be educated, are also deemed not to be competent about what their children should be doing in school. They are merely informed of what has already been decided--and even that is largely a matter of public relations.

Second, the political belief is that big school systems have a comparative advantage in providing the essential components of quality instruction. Some professional educators share this belief.

The third reason for reduced parental authority arises out of the long-standing concern of most educational finance experts to achieve equality in per-pupil expenditures. The method of achieving this objective has undoubtedly contributed much to the centralization of educational decisions. The source of funds for education has been shifted ever more from local to state and federal sources. In 1929-30, about 83 percent of U.S. public elementary and secondary school revenue came from local sources, and almost none came from the federal government. By 1977-78, local revenue had declined to slightly less than 48 percent; federal funds accounted for 8 percent, and state funds for 44 percent of the revenue. The control of education has shifted accordingly. This situation should have been anticipated, knowing as we do that he who pays the piper calls the tune. It is a critical error to overlook this centralizing control effect, although some approaches could hold this process of centralization in abeyance (for example, general-purpose grants could be enacted that would foreclose central control). Clearly, this theory has not been applied, as is evident from the strong tendency of the federal and state governments to mandate how schools are to be administered.

There once was a time when parents administered each school. They built the schoolhouse, hired the teacher, levied the taxes on themselves to pay the teacher and all other costs. Gradually, over time, the management of schools shifted to school superintendents and school boards, and then to citywide administrators. They, in turn, became beholden to state superintendents of education, and now they and all others are subject to the regulations of the Department of Education.

The fourth reason for this shift in control has become, in recent years, even more compelling than any of the first three reasons. It is a consequence of our political commitment to bringing about particular social reforms. Education is deemed to be one of the major instruments in achieving these reforms. In terms of accountability, *all* parts of our educational system are required by law to be active reforms agents. The social objectives of these reforms are consistent with widely held values of our society. Moreover, the attainment of some of these objectives is long overdue. The unsettled questions are: Is education an effective instrument for achieving these reforms? Are the changes in educational administration and in the programs that have been mandated appropriate means for attaining the social objectives? To what extent is the quality of education altered by these means? I shall leave these questions until later.

Parents have, as I have argued, a larger stake in the education of their children than anyone else has in the investment in this form of human capital. Our educational system, however, has measurably reduced effective parental authority in determining the quality of their children's education. I have featured the following reasons why this has occurred: 1) the technology of schooling, which is determined by professional educators and administrators, has reduced the role of parents; 2) the administration of large school systems is not capable of delegating any meaningful authority to parents; 3) the political process of achieving equity for children in school finance has led to the centralization of education; and 4) laws that require schools to serve as active agents of social reform have further impaired the authority of parents in determining the quality of schooling that their children receive.

What Are the Consequences?

To the extent that parents and teachers are bound to the existing school organization and to the way it is financed and controlled, what can they do to improve the stock of human capital that children acquire from their schooling? Consider the mammoth school system of New York City. What can parents of any of the one million children enrolled in public elementary and secondary schools, and any one of the more than fifty thousand classroom teachers, actually *do* individually to improve this school system? Frank J. Macchiarola, who has been appointed chancellor to administer the New York City school system, is by all accounts an exceedingly competent public administrator. But what can he do to make that system perform? The answers are obvious, it seems to me: little can be done by any one individual, given the financial structure, the public sources of control, and the inordinate size of the system.

My stress is on the shifts in the loci of decisions in education, which entail a basic transformation of public education. The authority of parents and teachers has dwindled. School administrators, in turn, have become beholden to superior public bodies. The decision-making authority of colleges and universities has also been reduced. Pervasive intervention by federal agencies is seriously impairing the true functions of higher education and of university research. In short, because of the authority now vested in city, state, and federal agencies, the decisions throughout the educational establishment are vastly overcentralized and exceedingly harmful.

I shall concentrate on two sets of effects of these shifts in authority, namely 1) the effects on teachers' behavior, and 2) the effects on parents.

Schoolteachers

Teachers have been much maligned during recent years. It is said they are not concerned about the educational achievements of their students. In the large school systems they have established strong teachers' unions, through which they bargain for "less instructional time, less extracurriculum involvement, greater reliance upon union contracts as the standards of professional responsibility,"[1] better facilities, more fringe benefits, and promotion and school assignment formulas that will serve their self-interest. Some are said to show little or no interest in improving the quality of their teaching. My argument is that most of these attitudes of schoolteachers should have been anticipated, in view of the way schools are organized and administered. The curriculum is not for them to decide, nor is the content of the courses to be taught and the plans to be followed. The promotion and the permissible discipline of students are not determined by the teacher. These decisions require the specialized talents of professional educators; the role of the lonely teacher in these decisions is small indeed. The critical fact is that the incentives to become an excellent teacher have become weak, ambiguous, and badly distorted. In assessing the performance of teachers, it is a dictum of economics that incentives matter. Schoolteachers are responding to the much-circumscribed opportunities open to them. They are not robots but human agents who perceive, interpret, and act in accordance with the worthwhile options available.

I do not condone the poor performance of many teachers in the big school systems. Like organized construction workers, organized teachers exact a high toll. Rather, my argument is that these teachers are responding to the organization and administration of these over-large systems. It certainly is true that teachers did not create them; professional educators, public finance experts, and the politics of education are the architects of these highly inefficient school systems.

The one-teacher school has become a curiosity. In my youth, there were more of them than of all other public schools combined. When they became an endangered species, there was no protection. Professional educators promoted consolidation, and they succeeded politically. Ever more consolidation became a compelling objective. Since 1931-32, the number of school districts has been reduced from 127,000 to 16,000. Public elementary schools have diminished from 233,000 to 63,000, whereas nonpublic elementary schools have increased from 9,000 to 14,000. The percentage increase in enrollment since 1931-32 in these two classes of elementary schools has been the same.

As of 1976, 188 public school systems each had enrollments of 25,000 or more children. They accounted for 28 percent of all public school children, and they averaged over 66,000 per school system. The saddest part of this story is in the size of the school systems in the 20 largest American cities for which data are readily available.[2] Nor have colleges and universities been immune to this big-system disease--as of 1976, forty U.S. college and university campuses had enrollments of over 25,000 students.[3]

Although the volume of rhetoric on efficiency in education is very large, the number of competent studies of efficiency in education is minuscule. In determining the efficiency of any school system in producing educational services, we must ascertain the economics of the scale of that system. The costs of the services that enter into education and the value of the services that are produced depend in no small part on the scale of the educational enterprise. The analytical task is not easy because of the jointedness of the services that enter, namely, those of the parents, students, teachers, the community and transportation, and the interactions between them; because of jointedness of the services that are produced, mainly the wide array of abilities that the student acquires, along with the interactions between these abilities; and because the size of the school system both affects and is affected by the input and output services. There are all too few such studies.

The scale that we have is rarely the optimum scale. Although I do not believe the ideology that small is necessarily beautiful (because it can be expensive), the apparent political belief that *bigger is better* must be challenged. I find the review of the sparse literature and the conclusions of Sher and Tompkins (1976) a useful contribution. They find untenable the premise that supports the widely accepted view that bigger is better.

Parents in Bondage

As a people, we profess liberal values that call for the protection of the individual's freedom of choice in a democratic society. In practice, we have evolved a public school system that has acquired the economic attributes of a company store. Parents are bound by residence to the school district in which they live, and they are tied for reasons of finance to the school system of that district. Like serfs in old Russia, parents can purchase their freedom, but the price is very high. To enroll their children in a private school requires double payments--namely, in taxes that are used to support public schools, and in the high tuition of the private school. Not all private schools are free of religious and racial overtones or readily accessible. As long as public schools in different locations vary in quality, and as long as families are permitted to change their residence and these differences in quality are not eroded by public interventions, families can and do pay the price of moving. The movement out of the large cities into the adjacent suburbs is clear evidence that this change in residence occurs. Taking up residence in a suburb does not give assurance, however, that the children will not be bused back into the schools of the city system.

On the role of parents and of students in public education, there is frequent reference in the literature on education to the concepts of participation and involvement. These concepts, however, appear to have no precise operational specifications. I have found few suggestions for delegating to parents a modicum of authority over any part of the school's affairs. Moreover, such a delegation of power would violate the legal authority under which public schools operate and are administered.[4] It is in this important sense that public school systems have the economic attributes of a monopoly, more so than a private company store. Because school attendance is compulsory, children and parents must endure it, however bad it may be, unless they can afford the cost of changing their place of residence or make double payments by opting for a private school.

To approach public education as I have begs two questions. 1) Are parents competent to determine the quality of schooling? 2) Are they willing privately to promulgate reforms that the politics of education have mandated? It is to be regretted that the old controversy on the competence of parents on matters pertaining to education is no longer with us. Professional educators, with the support of experts in public finance and government, have won the decision. The tacit verdict is that parents are not sufficiently competent to judge technical requirements, classroom efficiency, and the quality of schooling that their children obtain. Assuming that parents are not qualified makes it both necessary and convenient to keep them tied to the public school where they reside and to treat them as robots. Nor should it come as a surprise that a formidable array of special interests within and outside these school systems have acquired a strong, vested self-interest in maintaining the existing public elementary and secondary school monopoly.

The baneful notion that parents as a class are neither qualified nor responsible agents when it comes to the schooling of their children must be challenged. It is inconsistent with the economic behavior of parents, jointly and as individuals, in many other activities. The implications of human capital theory and the appeal to evidence to determine the validity of these implications tell us that parents are competent, calculating human agents--in household production, in the marriage market, in the behavior of women in deciding between household work and work in the labor force, in the substitution of quality for quantity of children, in investing in health and schooling of children, and in still other activities. Several years ago I challenged the then widely held view that the lowly cultivators in low-income countries were creatures of habit who were, it was said, indifferent to any and all new technical and economic opportunities that could improve their lot (Schultz 1964). No doubt the Green Revolution and related events since the early 1960's undermined that erroneous view of the economic behavior of cultivators. Furthermore, parents in low-income countries are not indifferent to opportunities to improve the health of and to acquire more schooling for their children. Difficult as it is, in view of their meager incomes, they make what are for them real sacrifices on behalf of their children. What has been overlooked is evidence which clearly shows a strong private demand on the part of parents in a goodly number of low-income countries for health services and schooling for their children. Their actual investment in population quality is one of the remarkable achievements of many of these countries during recent decades (Schultz 1979).

There is all too much economic evidence in the now available human capital studies and in the health and schooling achievements in low-income countries for economists to continue to remain silent on the implicit proposition on which the organization of the public school systems rests--that is, that parents are not qualified to determine the quality of schooling appropriate for their children. The notion that parents in this country, who are in general better educated than any earlier generation of parents, are incompetent in this regard is patently false.

The question pertaining to social reforms is beset with difficulties. That there is a public interest in various social reforms is not in doubt. Public policies to reduce the inequality in the personal distribution of income were authorized back in 1913 by a constitutional amendment legalizing the progressive income tax. Public transfers of income to various low-income people have become very large. There is a clear and cogent public interest in protecting civil rights and in eliminating various forms of discrimination in order to equalize the opportunities of disadvantaged racial and ethnic groups and of women. One of the major difficulties is a consequence of the side effects of some of the public programs mandated to achieve these social reforms. Whereas some of these programs have proven to be appropriate and effective (for example, civil rights protection for blacks in the South has enabled them to exercise their right to vote), other public programs appear not to be achieving their social objectives. Some of them may even be counterproductive. It is my contention that various public social reform programs now being imposed on school systems and institutions of higher education *are*, in effect, counterproductive. They fail to achieve their objectives because enough parents[5] perceive that particular programs actually reduce the quality of the education their children receive. Inasmuch as most parents place a high value on educational quality, they strongly resist these particular programs, which are mandated primarily by the Department of Education. While one might infer that these parents are opposed to the social objectives that have called forth these programs, the validity of this inference is hard to assess. An alternative inference is that many parents believe these programs are counterproductive, and they will not sacrifice the education of their children in order to accommodate them. There is, however, a more serious issue, which can be stated very bluntly: Will society long condone having children used as hostages to obtain policy compliance? The harassment of school superintendents by withholding federal and state funds and by taking them into court is tolerable. So is the mandated assignment of teachers. But to place children in jeopardy as a means to achieve whatever the objectives are is not tolerable in a civilized society.

Conclusion

To attract attention I should have argued that there is too much education, using as my title "Educational Obesity in the United States." I know full well that my argument, which is to the contrary, pleases no one who has a vested interest in the existing organization and administration of public education. In my view, whatever the causes, many graduates are *under*educated. Although the extent of this undereducation is hard to measure, there are many indications that it is pervasive and serious. This failure on the part of our public schools is one reason why I am critical of Richard Freeman's *Overeducated American*[6] thesis. His thesis is also vulnerable because of his omission of several important factors in analyzing the supply and demand for college-educated individuals. The recent poor performance of the U.S. economy and its effects on this demand is not caused by an oversupply of college-educated people. A reduction in the supply of such individuals would not reduce the rate of inflation; nor would it increase the productivity of the economy--as I have argued in my "Education in an Unstable Economy" (Schultz 1977b). Meanwhile, in an important paper Smith and Welch (1978) argue that "at best Freeman exaggerates the case for an oversupply of college-educated manpower and

Although it is useful to look for various trade-offs between efficiency and equity, it is more important not to overlook the complementarity between efficiency and equity in the case of elementary and secondary schooling. Efficiency in this context would reduce very substantially the inequity that now prevails, because it is generally true that the children of the most disadvantaged families are shortchanged most seriously by the existing inefficiency of our school systems. School reforms that would bring about an at least approximately optimum level of efficiency in schools would probably contribute more to the cause of equity than any of the various trade-off schemes.

I have advanced the proposition that the larger the school system, the greater the inefficiency. This proposition implies that to keep on looking for inefficiencies in the smaller schools is to be blind to the fact that large school systems are bedeviled by all manner of inefficiencies that account for so much of the inequity in schooling. This blindness is now evident when the better small schools are closed in order to adjust to the decline in school enrollment.

Our big school systems were not created in response to the demands of schoolteachers or parents. I contend that professional educators, public school finance experts, and the politics of education are the architects of these inefficient school systems. The schoolteachers who are employed in them are frustrated by weak and distorted incentives and by centralized management. Parents are tied by virtue of their places of residence; their alternative options are very costly. The authority of parents as individuals with respect to quality of schooling that their children receive is minimal.

Human capital studies strongly support my contention that parents are competent, calculating economic agents. Their behavior in acquiring and utilizing various forms of human capital, including the education of their children, implies that they have a strong preference for quality schooling. However, their preferences in this connection are thwarted by our big school systems.

The inefficiency on which I have concentrated is predominantly a consequence of the monopoly that is vested in the public schools. They are effectively sheltered from competition--presumably because it is deemed to be in the public interest. There is obviously a public interest in education; the question is, Would competition impair the essential public interest in education? The experience in higher education indicates that the answer is No. I doubt that anyone would argue that the 65 private universities and the still remaining 1,266 other four-year private institutions of higher education[7] do not serve the public interest. Private colleges and universities provide some useful competition. It will require competition to compel public elementary and secondary schools to reduce their inefficiency and thereby contribute substantially to equity, which is surely in the public interest.

The politics of education, however, are strongly influenced by organized groups who have a vested interest in keeping competition out of the schooling sector. It may be the better part of valor to remain silent when it comes to the politics of education. Nevertheless, the public-interest stakes are high enough to warrant speaking out on this issue. Meanwhile, we await a new generation of architects to devise educational policies that will give parents and their children meaningful options in acquiring quality schooling. The economic requirements are, in principle, very simple: competition would bring about greater efficiency; parents and students would demand quality education; and public funds could be allocated to them, leaving them free to choose their schools with no strings attached except that such funds be used for schooling.[8] Our G.I. educational subsidies gave proof that this principle is also applicable to higher education.

What are the prospects? The politics of education in Washington, in the states, and in specific school systems are not immune to change. Our political institutions tend to respond (albeit with a lag) to the changes in public demand for both quantity and quality of education. On this score an optimistic long view is warranted. But our inability as economists or educators to comprehend the serious limitations of the existing organization, administration, and public finance of education lends support to a pessimistic view. I hope we learn from the troubles of our schools that it will be necessary to improve the range of choices available to parents and children. My plea is that we not continue to protect our vested interest in the *status quo* of our public schools by arguing that all children must be protected from their incompetent and malevolent parents, whereas in fact only a very small fraction of parents are of this type. Schools must not be active agents of social reform, if such reforms have adverse effects on the quality of the schooling that children receive. And competition in the domain of schooling is not fundamentally bad.[9]

NOTES

1. Macchiarola 1979: 11. In the first seven pages *accountability* is stressed fourteen times; also featured is "the immense and far-flung bureaucracy," "proliferation of fraudulent academic courses," the "situation of waste," "society has turned against children," "we are sorely mistaken if we believe that increased funding provides a solution to the problem of lack of commitment," the "rip-off" by bus contractors, and "the management task is enormous." (I would have said *impossible*.)

2. See, e.g., *Digest of Education Statistics 1977-78*, Table 36.

3. See, e.g., *Digest of Education Statistics 1977-78*, Table 78.

4. See, e.g., Mann 1976.
5. It is all too convenient to believe that only the high-income families are concerned about quality in this context. Although the controversy continues, an increasing body of evidence (which federal agencies are bent on discrediting) implies that school busing has not provided quality schooling for blacks. Moreover, an increasing number of black families are perceiving that this is the case.
6. Richard B. Freeman has been in the forefront in making the case that the U.S. population has become overeducated. In 1975 his assessment was put forth with a question mark in "Over Investment in College Training?" His book, *The Overeducated American*, appeared in 1976, and he has extended this assessment in "The Declining Economic Value of Higher Education and the American Social System." On the supply response of college students which began as his Ph.D. research, Freeman (1971) made a major contribution, which he then extended and published as *The Labor Market for College-Trained Manpower*. The supply response of college-educated blacks in the Carnegie Commission's *Black Elite: The Market for Highly Educated Black Americans*, is also cogent and a real contribution.
7. See, e.g., *Digest of Education Statistics 1977-78*, Table 108 (the statistics are for 1976-77.) See also *A Classification of Institutions of Higher Education, 1973*, Table 1.
8. I am not featuring the voucher proposal at this point, despite its many merits, for reasons: 1) there are also alternative approaches, and 2) before any such proposals will be taken seriously in the politics of education, the underlying basis for the inefficiency and inequity of education must be fully comprehended.
9. I am indebted to Walter W. McMahon and Terry G. Geske for their helpful suggestions.

REFERENCES

Astin, Alexander W.; King, Margo R.; and Richardson, Gerald T. 1979. *The American freshman: norms for Fall, 1978*. Los Angeles: Graduate School of Education, University of California.

Carnegie Commission on Higher Education 1977. *Black elite: the new market for highly educated black Americans*. New York: McGraw-Hill.

A classification of institutions of higher education. 1973. Technical Report, Carnegie Commission on Higher Education. Berkeley, Calif.

Digest of educational statistics, 1977-78. Washington, D.C.: National Center for Education Statistics, Department of Health, Education and Welfare.

Freeman, Richard B. 1971. *The labor market for college-trained manpower*. Cambridge: Harvard University Press.

———. 1975. Over investment in college training? *Journal of Human Resources* 10, 3 (Summer): 287-311.

———. 1976. *The declining economic value of higher education and the American social system*. New York: Aspen Institute of Humanistic Studies.

———. 1976. *The overeducated American*. New York: Academic Press.

Macchiarola, Frank J. 1979. *Mid-year report of the chancellor of the schools for New York City Board of Education.* January.
Mann, Dale. 1976. *The politics of administrative representation.* Lexington, Mass.: D. C. Heath.
Palmer, John D. 1979. Can meritocracy in academe be saved? *Science* 203, 4386 (March 23): 1199.
Schultz, Theodore W. 1964. *Transforming traditional agriculture.* New Haven: Yale University Press. Reprinted, New York: Arno Press.
———. 1977a. On the economics of the increases in the value of human time over time. *Proceedings.* Fifth World Congress, International Economics Association.
———. 1977b. Education in an unstable economy. Human Capital Paper No. 77:1, University of Chicago.
———. 1979. *Investment in population quality throughout low income countries.* New York: United Nations Fund for Population Activities.
Sher, Jonathan P., and Tompkins, Rachel B. 1976. Economy, efficiency and equality. Washington, D. C.: National Institute of Education, Department of Health, Education and Welfare. July.
Shils, Edward. 1979. The conflict of God and Caesar. Jefferson Lecture, University of Chicago. April.
Smith, James P., and Welch, Finis. 1978. The overeducated American? A review article. Report no. P-6253. Santa Monica, Calif.: Rand Corporation.
Tomes, Nigel. 1981. The family, inheritance, and the intergenerational transmission of inequality. *Journal of Political Economy* 89, 5:928-58.
Walsh, John. 1979. Does high school grade inflation mask a more alarming trend? *Science* 203, 4384 (March 9): 982.

CHAPTER 3

Household Production of Human Capital: Time Uses of Parents and Children as Inputs

CHARLES S. BENSON

One of the most robust findings in social science is the existence of a close association between the socioeconomic status of students' families and the educational attainment of the students themselves. The best-known research on the topic, the Coleman Report (1966), launched a series of studies of "educational production functions." Though the statistical techniques employed by researchers in the last few years are considerably more advanced than those used by Coleman, these more sophisticated studies confirm the basic finding that SES "determines" educational attainment.

It is a curiosity in educational policy that policymakers at both federal and state levels attribute power to reform in the distribution of educational resources that Coleman's (and subsequent) evidence would appear to deny. So far at least, Coleman is winning. Neither federally financed compensatory education nor the rather ambitious efforts of a large number of states to reduce the effect of disparities in locally taxable wealth on school district expenditures have served to remove the baleful influence (certain success stories excepted) of family background on student performance.[1]

The Nature of the Relationship between Social Class of Child and School Achievement

In recent times Theodore Schultz (1971) has drawn our attention to the creation and valuation of human capital. The school is seen, in human capital theory, as a major agency in the development of skills and aptitudes. But we recognize as well that families create human capital, and we may also postulate that human capital production may be affected by interactions between school and family as well as among school, family, and neighborhood. Indeed, one may also imagine that the family's-and-the-child's view of the expected future place of the child in the social order may influence production of human capital.

In short, educational policy deserves clarification of a major point: *How* does SES impinge upon student achievement? I suggest for purposes of discussion that there are four broad mechanisms, not mutually exclusive.

The Parent-Dominant Model

This is the most straightforward and simple path of explanation. First, some parents have more time than others to give to their children. Second, some parents use time available for children in ways that are more effective in supporting school achievement. For example, effective parents might read together with their children, visit libraries with them, help with homework, regulate meal and bed times, and control TV watching.

We might then presume that higher-SES parents have more time available for their children, or for whatever reasons use available time in ways more supportive of school achievement than lower-SES families, or both. The policy to flow from this model logically would be directed to parental behavior. That is, we would train and induce lower-SES parents to emulate higher-SES parents in promoting school achievement. A harsher policy would be to disqualify parents who do not spend enough time in supporting school achievement, or who spend that time foolishly, from the privilege (or responsibility) of raising their children.

The School-Dominant Model

On the other hand, it might be that school personnel willingly or unwillingly thwart the efforts of low-SES families that have strong tastes for education. In that case, policy directed toward changing the behavior of the low-SES parent toward his/her child could be to no avail. The school-dominant model appears to occupy a central place in the writings of John U. Ogbu (1978: 133).[2] Ogbu maintains that teachers often are hostile to youth from low-SES families, and that they are unwilling to listen when these parents try to explain why their children's school performance is not up to standard. Parents, according to Ogbu, are forced by teachers to adopt mannerisms and to pretend to attitudes that the teacher assumes to be typical of "low-class" people.

Alternatively, one may imagine that some teachers, from feelings of either fear or compassion, are excessively permissive toward low-SES children. Such a child may remain blissfully unaware that he/she is failing to meet acceptable standards of learning.

The policy implications of the school-dominant model suggest that, for modifications of behavior of low-SES parents to be successful in promoting educational attainment of children, modifications in the attitudes and behavior of teachers are required as well. This is somewhat different from the standard compensatory education approach of using money to hire more staff and supplies, i.e., to assume that the quantity more than the composition of educational resources will make the difference. It follows that conventional practices in measuring school quality by dollar expenditure per student may simply be missing the point. Schools may have powerful effects on children's development even though educational production function studies attribute little power to school variables as ordinarily identified. But we should also admit that money may become important after some kind of "takeoff point" in students' performance is reached, i.e., beyond a threshold of student achievement and commitment to learning.

The Neighborhood-Dominant Model

It is unrealistic to assume that attitudes and actions are confined within the single family. In upper-SES neighborhoods the child of the uncaring family may do well in school because he is surrounded by children whose parents have the time to provide supporting services for their children and who have positive attitudes toward the usefulness of education when one enters the market place. Positive reinforcement from the majority of families in the neighborhood would "spill over" into the home of the family that chose not to pay much attention to its children.

Just the opposite might happen in low-SES neighborhoods. The "spill-over" from families that either were unwilling or unable to give educational support to their children could nullify the efforts of the families who manage to act in a supportive way.

Education production functions studies have stressed the importance of the influence of a child's classmates--in particular, the SES characteristics of those classmates--on the given child's school performance. Suggested here is a much broader possibility that inter-family spillovers occur during *all or most of the given child's waking hours*. Spillovers that take place out of school hours and during the summer might even cancel the effects of changing the SES composition of a classroom (through a policy, say, of social class integration).

Household spillovers to affect consumption patterns have been discussed in economic literature by Thorstein Veblen (1899), James Duesenberry (1949), J. D. Galbraith (1958), and most recently, Tibor Scitovsky (1975). I suggest here that household externalities can affect household production as well as household consumption--specifically, the production of human capital.

The point being made here is more inclusive than the assertion that classroom performance is affected by one's peers, to use the terminology of educational production function studies. The peer group, or set of classmates, can be altered for a given child by busing and other means to achieve social class integration (or segregation). A child ordinarily is in touch with such "peers" during class hours only. Influences in the neighborhood, on the other hand, impinge on the child during the remainder of his waking hours. That remainder constitutes the larger part of the child's life.

The policy implications of this model would probably stress an expanded provision of out-of-school activities, an essential component of which would be the attempt to develop favorable attitudes toward working hard in school. In other words, one would seek to neutralize the negative spillover of attitudes and actions that occurs in low-income neighborhoods.

The Class-Dominant Model

This model is basically an extension of the neighborhood-dominant model. It suggests that even a unified neighborhood approach toward encouraging educational excellence in low-SES neighborhoods is likely to be of little avail, as long as our society is characterized by high rates of youth unemployment, the predominance of secondary labor market jobs in inner cities, and a very unequal distribution of income in general. It is virtually impossible to convince low-income youth that education has a meaning *for them* in the market place. Further, the absence of close contact with or knowledge of quality jobs, through older friends and siblings, creates lack of information about the intellectual skills demanded by such work.

This model may be seen as an outcome of the writings of such authors as Samuel Bowles and Herbert Gintis (1976), Martin Carnoy and Henry Levin (1976) and Michael Katz (1968). They suggest that the educational system serves the capitalist economy by channeling persons into the work hierarchy in accordance with their class, encouraging docility, submissiveness, and punctuality in lower-class youth and encouraging creativity, imagination, and leadership in the progeny of the upper classes. The educational system fosters the belief that "what you get is what you deserve," thus reducing the possibility of violent conflict between the haves and the have nots. In this model the teacher is the prime agent of the sorting process, though just why the teacher so often and so willingly accepts this role is not wholly clear.

On the other hand, John Ogbu holds that poor work prospects directly damage the student and his peers; thus the teacher need not assume primary responsibility as agent of the screening process. Citing an impressive amount of evidence, Ogbu concludes that "although blacks (to cite a minority group adversely affected by poverty) say they desire education and although they try in many ways to change the education system so that their children will receive better education, black students neither make sufficient efforts in their studies nor match their aspirations with accomplishments. This lack of serious effort has developed partly because they see their future opportunities for employment limited by the job ceiling" (Ogbu 1979: 188).[3]

Policy to flow from the class-dominant theory could hardly be confined to revising of education programs or changing parental behavior. At the least, it would also include such measures as industrial siting controls and subsidies for youth employment. At the most, it would call for structural changes in our economy. It would recognize 1) that most people pursue education in order to get a good job; 2) that there aren't going to be good jobs available for a substantial proportion of youth growing up in low-SES neighborhoods; and 3) accordingly, that the incentives of low-SES youth to invest in their futures are constantly being eroded. Measures should then be taken to compensate such youth for the failures of our industrial order; these should be less isolating than our present welfare system.

Two References from the Time Budget Literature

Which of the above models is/are appropriate to explain the association between SES of students' families and their school attainments? The research on which I offer a preliminary report is based on time budget studies. Most authors of the extensive set of studies in that subfield are either economists or sociologists. Yoram Ben-Porath, Joseph Hunt, James Heckman, Claire Vickery, William Garner, Alan Gustman, Alan Thomas, James Morgan, Russell Hill, Frank Stafford, Alice Rossi, Peter Lindert, and Reuben Gronau have used time data in the analysis of family activities, school activities, or both. Space does not permit a review of that literature, though I have attempted such elsewhere (Benson 1980). Here I shall note two illustrative references only.

In a paper entitled "Child Endowments, and the Quantity and Quality of Children," Gary Becker and Nigel Tomes (1976) argue that children should allocate time to schooling on the basis 1) of the discounted value of the return in wages per unit of educational capital and 2) the marginal productivity of the student's time in increasing his stock of educational capital. Students who can look forward to good jobs should work hard at school; others could presumably find a better use for their time. Fast learners should spend a lot of time on schoolwork and school-related activities; slow learners might as well not. Furthermore, parents will seek to equalize the marginal productivity of their own time in supporting the school progress of each child—that is, the last hour of parents' input on Child K yields the same increment of learning as the last hour of parental input on Child J, etc. Assuming the productivity ratios decline smoothly for successive additions of parental time, it is likely that faster learners will receive more parental inputs of time than slow learners (Becker and Tomes 1976: 11-13).

Implicit in the Becker-Tomes argument is the assertion that school attainment is a function of time inputs of the student and his/her parents. Presumably these time inputs would be directed in part toward homework and in part toward school-related activities such as reading in a library or examining objects in a museum.

The second reference to the time budget literature is made with regard to the work of Arlene Leibowitz. In an article entitled "Parental Inputs and Children's Achievement," Leibowitz (1977: 247-50) reported a negative relationship between family size and children's language development, and a positive relationship between the mother's schooling and her child's test score. Yet the significance of mother's education dropped substantially when mother-child activities were entered into the regression analysis. Leibowitz concluded: "The effect of maternal education on verbal development may be attributed at least partly to the allocative effect. That is, more educated mothers are more likely to engage in those specific activities that promote verbal abilities. Thus, when measures of those specific activities are entered into the regression, the coefficient of maternal schooling becomes no longer significantly different from zero. Reading with children appears to be the activity that most promotes verbal skills, and TV viewing appears to be the activity most detrimental to those skills." Leibowitz, hence, indicates that school achievement is affected not only by the amounts of time that parents devote to their children, but also by the types of parent-child interaction.

Some Questions and a Hypothesis

Recalling Coleman's finding that household SES and children's achievement are closely related, we can pose from the Becker/Tomes/Leibowitz research the following questions for further empirical analysis: 1) Does the availability of parents' time for children vary systematically by SES? 2) Do patterns of parent-child interaction vary systematically by SES? 3) Controlling for SES, do the amounts of time available and the patterns of parent-child interaction appear to have significant associations with school achievement of children?

From these questions we pose the hypothesis shown in Figure 1. The points to be tested deal with the propensity of parents in different SES categories to contribute time in support of their children's school performance, *and* with the distribution of school performance by SES category. The arrows in Figure 1 are intended to suggest that more high-SES families will be found in cell 1 than in cells 2 or 3; that middle-SES families

SES \ Parental Time	High Input	Medium Input	Low Input
High	1^{+++}	2^{++}	3^{+}
Middle	4^{++}	5^{+}	6^{-}
Low	7^{-}	8^{--}	9^{---}

KEY: $+++$ = many high achievers relative to low
  $++$ = moderately large number of high achievers relative to low
  $+$ = slight majority of high achievers
  $-$ = slight majority of low achievers
  $--$ = moderately large number of low achievers relative to high
  $---$ = many low achievers relative to high

Figure 1. Hypotheses on Parental Time Inputs and Relative School Achievement, by SES Category

will be distributed rather evenly among cells 4, 5, and 6; and that low-SES families will be found in greater relative numbers in cell 9 than in 8 or 7. Thus, the first hypothesis is that time commitment of parents to children is an increasing function of SES.

The second hypothesis is that school achievement is jointly determined by time commitment of parents and by SES, as indicated by the plus and minus signs in the cells. These hypotheses are obviously related to the four SES achievement models discussed above. If our data indicate that parental time inputs are the strong factor in explaining school achievement, then the case for Model 1, the parent-dominant model, is enhanced. On the other hand, if data on parental time contributions explain relatively little of the SES-achievement connection, then one might be inclined to consider one or more of the other models.

The Data Base

The sample on which we report here is a stratified random sample of sixth graders in the Oakland, California, public schools. In the Spring of 1976, 764 students were interviewed and a parent (ordinarily the mother) was asked to fill out a questionnaire. The questions asked of both child and parent covered a broad range of subjects, but the central focus was on a description of the out-of-school activities of the child and the involvement of the parent in those activities.

Sample response was excellent. Extraordinary care was taken in the training of interviewers and in monitoring the process of data collection.

24.2 percent of the respondents were white and 59.8 percent black. Reported family incomes were as follows:

Less than $3,000	47	(6.1%)
$ 3,000 - 4,999	86	(11.2%)
$ 5,000 - 7,999	82	(10.7%)
$ 8,000 - 9,999	78	(10.2%)
$ 10,000 -14,999	122	(16.0%)
$ 15,000 -19,999	110	(14.4%)
$ 20,000 -24,999	73	(9.6%)
$ 25,000 -29,999	48	(6.3%)
Greater than $30,000	64	(8.4%)
Uncodable	54	(7.1%)

Parents' educational levels (highest) were reported as follows:

Eighth grade or less	80	(10.5%)
Some high school	122	(16.0%)
High school graduates	203	(26.6%)
Some college	170	(22.3%)
College graduate	74	(9.7%)
Graduate of professional school	85	(11.1%)
Uncodable	30	(3.9%)

In due course, the Children's Time Study Project, University of California, Berkeley, will publish the detailed results of this survey. Here I confine myself to time availability of parents, joint parent-child uses of time (in some cases as reported by both parent and child for the same set of activities), and the association of the above to student achievement. The measure of student achievement is the California Test of Basic Skills. Only achievement in English is reported; the results for mathematics are similar.

SES categories are based on both income and education, specifically:

High SES (N = 175) Income ⩾ $20,000
                    Education ⩾ High school graduate
Middle SES (N = 251) Income = $10,000 - 19,999
                     Education = all categories
Low SES (N = 278)   Income ⩽ $10,000
                    Education ⩽ some college

Students' achievement categories on California Test of Basic Skills were established as follows:

High — greater than 1 standard deviation above mean
(N = 88)

Normal — the range from 1 standard deviation below mean to 1 standard deviation above, inclusive (N = 397)

Low — less than 1 standard deviation below mean (N = 79)

The distribution of students in the achievement categories is as follows:

ACHIEVEMENT	SES Low	Middle	High
Low	51	23	5
Normal	174	145	78
High	10	46	32
Excluded from test	43	37	60

Indexes of Time Activities of Children and Parents

Eight indexes of time availability and time use have been prepared. These are as follows.

1) *Parents' Household Time Availability*. This is an index constructed as a sum of the free time of parents. Two-parent families, especially those in which one parent works less than fulltime, tend to rank higher than single-parent families in this index. A negative adjustment is made if the work schedules are such that no parent is at home when the child comes home from school. This recognizes that there is, in most families, a "prime time" for child-parent interaction.

2) *Mother's Household Time Availability*. This is a similar index, but only the mother's time is entered.

3) *Cultural Activity Index* (as reported by the parent). This index is constructed from variables of parents' working with children on hobbies, going to an event at the child's school, going with the child to a library, museum, play, or concert, and trying to find an organized activity or lesson(s) for the child.

4) *Cultural Ability Index* (as reported by the child). This index includes the child's going to church with a parent, going to a library with a parent, doing homework, engaging in hobbies, or playing games with a parent, going to museums, the zoo, the aquarium, the planetarium, Lawrence Hall of Science, and the redwood forests.

5) *Household Time Index* (as reported by the parent). This is based on parent-child activity in working around the house or yard, going together to a restaurant or coffee shop, shopping for groceries, visiting relatives or friends, going to movies or sports events, going to a park, and going on a family vacation.

6) *Household Time Index* (as reported by the child). This covers the activities of the child with parent in doing the things listed in 5, above. In addition, the index includes the variable of eating dinner with parents, watching TV with parents, and whether TV is on during dinner (negative).

7) *Parent Involvement Index*. This index reflects the parents' willingness to spend time in supporting the child by getting involved with other parents and teachers. It includes belonging to the PTA, serving as room mother or doing regular volunteer work in the child's school, or serving as a leader or volunteer with any organized activities for children (e.g., Scouts, church group, Little League).

8) *Parent Control-Time Index*. This index reflects the willingness of the parent to give time to controlling the activities and personal habits of children. It includes regularity of bedtime, whether the child is supposed to be in the house at a regular time for dinner on school days, whether the child is allowed to play outside on school nights, and whether the parent exerts guidance over the child's "free time."

The association of these eight time indexes with the SES index is reported below, as are the associations of the time indexes with school achievement by SES group. Also shown are the above associations with the single variable of the parents' helping the child with homework (as reported by the child).

Socioeconomic Status and Achievement Categories Further Considered

Here I have sought to provide a certain degree of separation in the SES and achievement categories. Considering SES, we now know that household income, while central to analysis, has become a somewhat ambiguous variable. If both parents work fulltime in low-quality jobs, the income of the household may be reasonably high, even though the educational background of the parents is minimal. On the other hand, a highly educated single parent may have a rather low income. Income and education variables must be considered jointly in studying the association of SES with school achievement. Accordingly, we have defined high SES as high income *and* an educational level of high school graduate or more. Low SES likewise is low income *and* an educational level of less than college graduate.

With regard to achievement, we are plagued with two problems: 1) in any given year, certain children are not tested, and 2) the same child may show variations from one test period to the next. I thus choose to establish categories of high and low achievers as falling outside the range of one standard deviation from the mean. A student in the high group should be a genuine high achiever, not an accidental one; likewise for the low group.

Some Preliminary Results

I shall present results here first in the form of contingency tables. This allows us to see the extent to which the time use indexes follow an SES pattern. Second, use of contingency tables allows us to examine whether high, normal, or low achievers display different patterns of time use *in their actual numbers*, after we control for SES categories.

Table 1 shows that nonwork time availability of parents is a positive function of SES. Approximately 68 percent of high-SES families fall into the two higher time availability categories (3 and 4), while only 28.5 percent of low-SES families are found in these same categories. The relationship between time availability and SES is significant at the .01 level.

Table 1. Availability of Parents' Time to Children, by Socioeconomic Status
($N = 672$)

Parents' time availability		Low	SES Middle	High
Low	1	86(33.6)	65(26.5)	21(12.3)
	2	97(37.9)	38(15.5)	34(19.9)
	3	22(8.6)	68(27.8)	82(48.0)
High	4	51(19.9)	74(30.2)	34(19.9)

Figures in parentheses = percentages arrayed vertically
$X_6^2 = 115.520; p < .01$
Source: Children's Time Study, Oakland Survey (1976)

Table 2 indicates time availability of mothers alone. Here the SES relationship is also highly significant, but the direction of the relationship is reversed. That is, higher-SES mothers have less time available for their children, on the average, than do low-SES mothers.

The fact that availability of both parents' time is positively related to SES while that of mothers is negatively related is explained by three conditions. 1) There are relatively more single-parent families in low than in high SES groups. 2) In Oakland, at least, many higher-income families have both parents working fulltime outside the home. 3) Many of the low-SES families include mothers who fall into the unemployed category.

Tables 3 and 4, dealing with parent-child cultural activities, may properly be viewed together. Whether reported by parent or by child, both

Table 2. Availability of Mothers' Time to Children,
by Socioeconomic Status
(N = 678)

Mothers' time availability		SES Low	Middle	High
Low	1	81(30.9)	111(45.3)	94(55.0)
	2	41(15.6)	47(19.2)	30(17.5)
High	3	140(53.4)	87(35.5)	47(27.5)

Figures in parentheses = percentages arrayed vertically
$X_4^2 = 35.514; p < .01$
Source: Children's Time Study, Oakland Survey (1976)

Table 3. Parent-Child Cultural Activity Index, Based
on Parents' Statements, by Socioeconomic Status
(N = 704)

Cultural activity index (from parent)		SES Low	Middle	High
Low	1	55(19.8)	34(13.5)	18(10.3)
	2	84(30.2)	59(23.5)	41(23.4)
	3	61(21.9)	71(28.3)	55(31.4)
	4	39(14.0)	55(21.9)	37(21.1)
High	5	39(14.0)	32(12.7)	24(13.7)

Figures in parentheses = percentages arrayed vertically
$X_8^2 = 19.455; p < .02$
Source: Children's Time Study, Oakland Survey (1976)

indicate a positive relationship between degree of cultural activity and SES. In both instances, the relationship is statistically significant. It is worth noting, however, that many families appear not to conform to the relationship. Thirty-nine low-SES families (14.0%) fall into the highest cultural activity category (as reported by parents in Table 3) and fifty-nine high-SES families (33.7%) fall into the lowest two categories.

Likewise, in Table 5 and 6, we find a positive relationship between household time and SES. In higher-SES families parents spend more time

Table 4. Parent-Child Cultural Activity Index, Based
on Children's Statements, by Socioeconomic Status
($N = 704$)

Cultural activity index (from child)		SES Low	SES Middle	SES High
Low	1	70(25.2)	37(14.7)	16(9.1)
	2	51(18.3)	27(10.8)	16(9.1)
	3	49(17.6)	46(18.3)	24(13.7)
	4	65(23.4)	61(24.3)	41(23.4)
	5	32(11.5)	57(22.7)	53(30.3)
High	6	11(4.0)	23(9.2)	25(14.3)

Figures in parentheses = percentages arrayed vertically
$X^2_{10} = 61.719; p < .01$
Source: Children's Time Study, Oakland Survey (1976)

Table 5. Parent-Child Household Activity Index, Based on
Parents' Statements, by Socioeconomic Status
($N = 704$)

Household activity index (from parents)		SES Low	SES Middle	SES High
Low	1	49(17.6)	25(10.0)	10(5.7)
	2	51(18.3)	28(11.2)	18(10.3)
	3	45(16.2)	43(17.1)	25(14.3)
	4	46(16.5)	41(16.3)	37(21.1)
	5	42(15.1)	53(21.1)	39(22.3)
High	6	45(16.2)	61(24.3)	46(26.3)

Figures in parentheses = percentages arrayed vertically
$X^2_{10} = 33.425; p < .01$
Source: Children's Time Study, Oakland Survey (1976)

Table 6. Parent-Child Household Activity Index, Based on Children's Statements, by Socioeconomic Status
(N = 704)

Household activity index (from child)		SES Low	SES Middle	SES High
Low	1	30(10.8)	29(11.6)	15(8.6)
	2	27(9.7)	30(12.0)	16(9.1)
	3	56(20.1)	37(14.7)	20(11.4)
	4	49(17.6)	39(15.5)	28(16.0)
	5	53(19.9)	29(11.6)	27(15.4)
	6	31(11.2)	28(11.2)	21(12.0)
	7	24(8.6)	42(16.7)	34(19.4)
High	8	8(2.9)	17(6.8)	14(8.0)

Figures in parentheses = percentages arrayed vertically
$X^2_{14} = 29.377$; $p < .02$
Source: Children's Time Study, Oakland Survey (1976)

with children in going to restaurants, coffee shops, movies, parks, etc., and engaging themselves jointly in various kinds of household duties. Again, there are numbers of exceptions to the general relationship. Forty-five low-SES families (16.2%), as reported by parents, were in the highest time category (Table 5) and twenty-eight high-SES families (16%) were in the two lowest time use categories. As reported by children (Table 6), thirty low-SES families (11.5%) were in the two highest categories (on a scale of 8) and thirty-one high-SES families (17.7%) were in the two lowest. Because SES dominates time use in the sorts of activities we are describing, we might say that there are upper-class and lower-class patterns of time use. However, we should also note that numbers of low-SES families behave toward their children like high-SES families do, and vice versa.

Table 7 shows parental involvement in children's activities in school and in formally-organized activities outside school. The association of parental involvement with family SES is extremely strong, though it should still be noted that sixty-eight low-SES families (24.4%) were in the highest two involvement categories. There is a special irony here: to serve as a volunteer in a school or in a child's program is more typically an

Table 7. Parental Involvement Index, by Socioeconomic Status
(N = 704)

Parental Involvement		SES Low	Middle	High
Low	1	52(18.7)	29(11.6)	11(6.3)
	2	89(32.0)	59(23.5)	27(15.4)
	3	69(24.8)	70(27.9)	40(22.9)
	4	46(16.5)	48(19.1)	49(28.0)
High	5	22(7.9)	45(17.9)	48(27.4)

Figures in parentheses = percentages arrayed vertically
$X_8^2 = 59.475; p < .01$
Source: Children's Time Study, Oakland Survey (1976)

activity of mothers than of fathers, and we have seen that low-SES mothers have more time available for children than do high-SES mothers. Yet, *the high-SES mothers* do a relatively larger share of the volunteer work.

Table 8 refers to parents' efforts to control the lives of their children, that is, to inculcate regularity and "good work habits." Strikingly enough, there is *no statistically significant relationship* between SES and parental control time. One might expect, for example, that successful families would attempt to instill a kind of puritan ethic in their progeny, or, alternatively, that low-SES families would see strictness toward children as being especially important. Neither condition expresses itself strongly in the data.

Table 9 shows results on parents' helping with homework. As with parental control time, there is no statistically significant relationship between SES and the inclination of parents to assist their children with school assignments.

Now let us turn to the relationship between patterns of time use and school achievement, controlling for SES. Tables 10-12 offer the only instances in which time availability and time use indexes hold a statistically significant relationship to achievement, as measured by the English component of the California Test of Basic Skills, even at the .10 level. Parents' time is positively related to achievement at the .10 level in the high-SES category. Mother's time availability is significantly related to achievement at the .01 level in the high-SES group, but the relationship is negative—the more of mother's time that is available, the *lower* is the child's school achievement. These results should not be interpreted liter-

Charles S. Benson 67

Table 8. Parental Time Control Index, by Socioeconomic Status
(N = 704)

		SES		
Parental control time index		Low	Middle	High
Low	1	55(19.8)	54(21.5)	34(19.4)
	2	56(20.1)	50(19.9)	36(20.6)
	3	61(21.9)	66(26.3)	30(17.1)
	4	52(18.7)	38(15.1)	25(14.3)
High	5	54(19.4)	43(17.1)	50(28.6)

Figures in parentheses = percentages arrayed vertically
$X_8^2 = 12.759$; not significant
Source: Children's Time Study, Oakland Survey (1976)

Table 9. Parent-Child School Homework Activity,
by Socioeconomic Status
(N = 680)

	SES		
Did parent(s) help child with homework?	Low	Middle	High
Yes	125(47.7)	128(52.5)	89(51.1)
No	137(52.3)	116(47.5)	85(48.9)

Figures in parentheses = percentages arrayed vertically
$X_2^2 = 1.208$; not significant
Source: Children's Time Study, Oakland Survey (1976)

ally to mean that the time a mother spends with her children diminishes their school performance. We have no longitudinal data to report. It is entirely possible, for example, that mother's time spent with children under age three is positively associated with later school success, but we have no means to assess that kind of relationship in the present study.

The cultural time index, as reported by the parent (though not as reported by the child), is significantly related to achievement at the .10 level in high-SES families and at the .05 level for middle-SES ones. In terms of bivariate analysis, there are no other significant relationships. So far, then, the harvest of results on achievement is meager.

Table 13 shows the distribution for parental help with homework. No relations are significant. This table could mean that some parents use

Table 10. Student Achievement as Related to Availability of Parents' Time, by Socioeconomic Status

Students	Availability of parents' time to children				
	Low 1	(N = 171) 2	3	High 4	
High achievers	1(3.1)	5(15.6)	22(68.7)	4(12.5)	High SES
Normal achievers	15(18.5)	16(19.8)	35(43.2)	15(18.5)	X_6^2 = 11.409;
Excluded from test	5(8.6)	13(22.4)	25(43.1)	15(25.9)	p<.10
	Low 1	(N = 245) 2	3	High 4	
High achievers	14(31.1)	6(13.3)	10(22.2)	15(33.3)	Middle SES
Normal achievers	35(24.6)	25(17.6)	42(29.6)	40(28.2)	X_6^2 = 4.490;
Low achievers	8(34.8)	5(21.7)	3(13.0)	7(30.4)	not significant
Excluded from test	8(22.9)	2(5.7)	13(37.1)	12(34.3)	
	Low 1	(N = 256) 2	3	High 4	
Normal achievers	65(38.5)	60(35.5)	14(8.3)	30(17.8)	Low SES
Low achievers	11(22.4)	21(42.9)	6(12.2)	11(22.4)	X_6^2 = 6.960;
Excluded from test	10(26.3)	16(42.1)	2(5.3)	10(26.3)	not significant

Figures in Parentheses = percentages arrayed horizontally
Source: Children's Time Study, Oakland Survey (1976)

helping with homework as positive reinforcement toward school progress of higher-achieving children, and that an approximately equal number of parents come to help with homework when they see that a child is having trouble keeping up with his/her classmates.

Let us consider the bivariate results in terms of the three questions raised earlier. 1) Are there differences in availability of time by SES? Yes, but the signs are contrary for parent' and mother's time. 2) Are there differences in uses of time by SES categories? Yes, on the average, for cultural time, household time, and parental involvement. In these aspects of family life, higher-SES parents are able and willing to give more of themselves to their children than are lower-SES parents. But no, on the average, for parents' efforts to exert control over their children and to

Table 11. Student Achievement as Related to Availability of Mother's Time, by Socioeconomic Status

Students	Availability of mother's time to children			
	($N = 171$)			
	Low 1	2	High 3	
High achievers	17(53.1)	10(31.2)	5(15.6)	High SES
Normal achievers	54(65.9)	9(11.0)	19(23.2)	$X_4^2 = 15.172$;
Excluded from test	23(40.4)	11(19.3)	23(40.4)	p<.01
	($N = 245$)			
	Low 1	2	High 3	
High achievers	19(42.2)	10(22.2)	16(35.6)	
Normal achievers	69(48.9)	24(17.0)	48(34.0)	Middle SES
Low achievers	13(56.5)	0(0)	10(43.5)	$X_4^2 = 4.490$;
Excluded from test	10(27.8)	13(36.1)	13(36.1)	not significant
	($N = 262$)			
	Low 1	2	High 3	
Normal achievers	56(32.4)	31(17.9)	86(49.7)	Low SES
Low achievers	12(24.5)	7(14.3)	30(61.2)	$X_4^2 = 4.459$;
Excluded from test	13(32.5)	3(7.5)	24(60.0)	not significant

Figures in parentheses = percentages arrayed horizontally
Source: Children's Time Study, Oakland Survey (1976)

help them with homework. 3) Controlling for SES, are there associations between values of these indexes of time use and the placement of children in achievement categories? Essentially, no.

Bivariate analysis, especially that which is based on composite indexes, has its limitations. To supplement the results shown above, I offer results from some basic multiple regression work. Taking CTBS English score as the dependent variable, I chose two SES variables, income and education, and a set of dummy time variables as independent. The time variables are described in Table 14, the correlation matrix. I sought to choose variables

Table 12. Student Achievement as Related to Parent-Child Cultural Activity Index (Reported by Parent), by Socioeconomic Status

Students	Cultural activity index					
	Low 1	2	3	4	High 5	
	(N = 175)					
High achievers	2(6.3)	3(9.4)	13(40.6)	8(25.0)	6(18.7)	High SES
Normal achievers	9(10.8)	28(33.7)	25(30.1)	15(18.1)	6(7.2)	$X_8^2 = 14.961$;
Excluded from test	7(11.7)	10(16.7)	17(28.3)	14(23.3)	12(20.0)	$p < .10$
	(N = 251)					
	Low 1	2	3	4	High 5	
High achievers	4(8.7)	6(13.0)	15(32.6)	18(39.1)	3(6.5)	Middle SES
Normal achievers	21(14.5)	37(25.5)	44(30.3)	25(17.2)	18(12.4)	$X_8^2 = 18.084$;
Low achievers	3(13.0)	6(26.1)	6(26.1)	2(8.7)	6(26.1)	$p < .05$
Excluded from test	6(16.2)	10(27.0)	6(16.2)	10(27.0)	5(13.5)	
	(N = 278)					
	Low 1	2	3	4	High 5	
Normal achievers	34(18.5)	53(28.8)	45(24.5)	26(14.1)	26(14.1)	Low SES
Low achievers	13(25.5)	15(29.4)	9(17.6)	8(15.7)	6(11.8)	$X_8^2 = 4.065$;
Excluded from test	8(18.6)	16(37.2)	7(16.3)	5(11.6)	7(16.3)	not significant

Figures in parentheses = percentages arrayed horizontally
Source: Children's Time Study, Oakland Survey (1976)

Table 13. Student Achievement as Related to Parents' Helping with Homework, by Socioeconomic Status

Students	Parent(s) helps with homework		
	($N = 174$)		
	Helps	Does not help	
High achievers	16(50.0)	16(50.0)	High SES
Normal achievers	45(54.9)	37(45.1)	$X_2^2 = .956$;
Excluded from test	28(46.7)	32(53.3)	not significant
	($N = 244$)		
	Helps	Does not help	
High achievers	18(40.0)	27(60.0)	Middle SES
Normal achievers	72(51.1)	69(48.9)	$X_2^2 = 4.192$;
Low achievers	14(66.7)	7(33.3)	not significant
Excluded from test	24(64.9)	13(35.1)	
	($N = 262$)		
	Helps	Does not help	
Normal achievers	83(48.0)	90(52.0)	Low SES
Low achievers	23(48.9)	24(51.1)	$X_2^2 = 0.136$;
Excluded from test	19(45.2)	23(54.8)	not significant

Figures in parentheses = percentages arrayed horizontally
Source: Children's Time Study, Oakland Survey (1976)

that, on a priori grounds, might have an important relationship to achievement. For example, if the mother is home after school, she has time to nurture the child; if the family uses the library, it clearly has an interest in written materials; if the family goes out to dinner together, it displays a degree of "warmth," or mutual concern.

Table 15 indicates that for the total sample, using all eight independent variables, R^2 is significant at the .01 level. The two coefficients on SES are significant, and so are the coefficients on "library" and "restaurant." Splitting the regressions into SES categories and dropping SES coefficients from the equation, we find that the value of R^2 for the high-SES group is significant at the .05 level and the value of R^2 for the middle SES group is significant at the .01 level. No coefficients are significant in the case of the low-SES category. Except for "mother home" and possibly homework (high SES only), the signs are all in the expected direction.

Table 14. Correlation Matrix: School Achievement and Time Variables

	Grades	Income	Education	Mother at home	Library	Restaurant	Room mother	Dinner	Homework
Grades	1.000	.373	.332	-.066	.144	.235	.117	.136	.037
Income	.373	1.000	.415	-.161	.011	.239	.134	.126	-.027
Education	.332	.415	1.000	-.182	.044	.255	.184	.043	-.088
Mother at home	-.066	-.161	-.182	1.000	.059	-.094	.174	.016	-.049
Library	.144	.011	.044	.059	1.000	.095	.126	.085	.039
Restaurant	.235	.239	.255	-.094	.095	1.000	.094	.069	.044
Room mother	.117	.134	.184	.174	.126	.094	1.000	.062	-.124
Dinner	.136	.126	.043	.016	.085	.069	.062	1.000	.017
Homework	.037	-.027	-.088	-.049	.039	.044	-.124	.017	1.000

Grades = English score on California Test of Basic Skills
Income = Reported family income
Education = Educational level of adult respondent (ordinarily the mother)
Mother at home = Dummy variable; whether mother is home in the afternoon
Library = Dummy variable; whether child has gone to a library with an adult in last month
Restaurant = Dummy variable; whether child has gone to a restaurant or coffee shop with an adult in last month
Room mother = Dummy variable; whether parent has ever served as volunteer room mother in the child's school
Dinner = Dummy variable; whether child has a definite time for dinner
Homework = Dummy variable; whether parent regularly helps child with homework
Source: Children's Time Study, Oakland Survey (1976)

Table 15. Regression Results of Time Use Variables on Student Achievement

	Total Sample (N = 540)	High SES (N = 114)	Middle SES (N = 206)	Low SES (N = 220)
Mean of CTBS English score	63.369	76.261	69.000	53.353
Constant	26.983	69.091	48.750	45.923
Family income	2.709**(.455)			
Parents' education	3.629**(.821)			
Mother home after school	.551(1.906)	-3.133(4.650)	-1.568(3.640)	-2.988(2.591)
Child to library with adult	5.719**(2.010)	13.690**(5.247)	4.117(3.677)	2.126(2.850)
Child to restaurant with adult	5.348**(2.046)	11.430*(5.446)	10.662**(4.128)	4.202(2.476)
Mother is room mother	1.082(1.915)	1.324(4.572)	6.183(3.645)	.260(2.562)
Child has definite dinner hour	3.564(1.826)	2.021(4.504)	4.678(3.457)	3.949(2.505)
Parent helps with homework	2.510(1.817)	-3.886(4.345)	4.264(3.443)	3.179(2.446)
R^2	.463	.323	.288	.227
S.E.E.	20.909	22.494	24.399	17.926
F Ratio for regression	18.357**	2.078*	3.004**	1.929

Figures in parentheses are standard errors of coefficients
* $< .05$
** $< .01$

Source: Children's Time Study, Oakland Survey (1976)

What is interesting is the relative power, statistical significance aside, of the involvement ("room mother"), control ("regular dinner times"), and homework variables in the middle-SES group. Provisionally, the data seem consistent with the following broad observations. 1) High-SES children are likely to do well in school in any case, but intellectual stimulation and family warmth help them do even better. 2) For families in the middle SES--that is, at or beyond a "takeoff point" in family development--family warmth, involvement, and control count substantially in raising their children's achievement. 3) In low-SES categories, the family is relatively impotent, although warmth, control, and assisting with homework help somewhat.

Observations and Qualifications

The relationship between parental inputs and school achievement is complex. We should not be inclined to accept easy hypotheses that changes in parental behavior in the single household will alter achievement standards of the children of that household drastically, because other conditions in the child's life also appear to be important.

Power of parental action may be different in the different social classes. To illustrate: in the high-SES category, only 5 of 115 children who took the CTBS scored less than one standard deviation below the mean. Yet substantial numbers of high-SES parents appear to take minimal action to support the school progress of their children. Let us recall the various models to explain the relation of SES to achievement: parent dominant, school dominant, neighborhood dominant, and class dominant. Even assuming that some high-SES parents play a neutral or negative role in helping their children, the other models, nevertheless, are all positive. The high-SES child is easily understood and accepted in school; the child's friends and their families support school achievement generally, and certainly the child, his/her friends, and the adults of his/her acquaintance believe in the pay-off of educational accomplishment.

Consider now the lower-SES group. Only 10 of 235 who took CTBS scored higher than one standard deviation above the mean, even though substantial numbers of low-SES parents appear to take strong action to support the school achievement of their children. What goes wrong? It is entirely possible that the three models of schools, neighborhoods, and class operate in a negative way for lower-SES children, cancelling the efforts of the conscientious parents. The teachers may be too suspicious, too fearful, or too tender (or all of the above?); the neighborhood may provide spillovers that denigrate individual accomplishment, and the marketplace may signal that ordinary standards of achievement count for little in getting and keeping a good job.

The above comments are intended to suggest that parental action in high- and low-SES circles lack great power, either to prevent a high-SES child from doing rather well in school, or to help a low-SES child find him/herself in a high-achievement category. What of the middle group? Here it would appear that parental actions *do* have power, at least relative to the other SES categories. In the middle-SES group there are large numbers of families who are rising and large numbers who are falling in the social order. One's prospects are much less clear than in the high or low groups. Likewise, the effects of school, neighborhood, and class (meaning assessment of the worth of educational accomplishment) on the child are themselves problematical. The parent in this confused situation becomes the more dominant force in determining his or her children's achievement. When the parent helps, the child is likely to rise; when the parent fails to help, the child is likely to fall. Our data are consistent with the idea that parental action is the strongest, relatively speaking, in the middle-SES group.

Some people have found my conclusions pessimistic, especially regarding the possibilities of single low-SES families building better lives for themselves. I hold, the contrary, that my conclusions, in their particular context, are optimistic. Oakland has been a depressed industrial city for most of the post-World War II period. It contains, nevertheless, a prosperous middle and upper-middle class. A substantial number of persons in these classes are from minority groups; many have risen in affluence in a very short time. Yet, their children do passing well in school, just as if they were "to the manor born." By the end of the century it is easier to imagine changes in our economic system to relieve the oppressive burden of poverty on families than it is to imagine the kind of restructuring of family behavior that acceptance of the parent-dominant hypothesis would imply.

The premise of the educational component of the war on poverty is as follows. If we put extra resources in schools for low-income children, these children will do better in school and as a consequence, once grown, will break out of the vicious cycle of poverty. What I suggest is different: alleviate poverty, and school failure will disappear. If this premise were accepted, we could remove from our thoughts the ideas that feckless families are the cause of our social difficulties and that we could change the behavior of low-SES families by example and exhortation.

Now, briefly, for some qualifications of our results. The data lack a control for ability, in terms of either I.Q. or prior achievement. We made no attempt to measure quality of time in parent-child interaction. We do not report yet on school effects, though we expect to do so later. Finally, these data refer to parent-child time use. Forthcoming research findings will include data on time uses of children alone and with other children, on TV use, and on attitudes of parents and children.[4]

NOTES

1. See Jencks (1979: Ch. 3). For a somewhat contrary view, see Summers and Wolfe (1977) and Summers (1979: Tables 1 and 2).
2. Ogbu (1978) notes: "My research in Stockton reveals two . . . aspects of the problem connected with teacher attitudes and expectations. The first has to do with the kind of relationship between teachers and parents that prevents a mutual understanding of children's academic problems and what to do about them; the second has to do with teachers' evaluations of children's classroom performance which, among other things, prevents children from learning how their efforts are related to rewards in the form of marks and consequently prevents them from acquiring the good study or work habits necessary for maximizing both efforts and rewards." A similar point of view is presented in Sowell (1972: The importance of the "school effect" is further developed in Rutter et al. (1979).
3. Essentially the same line of argument is taken in De Lone (1979).
4. I wish to make the following acknowledgments of aid in the preparation of this paper. Elliott Medrich, project director of the Children's Time Study Project, is responsible for the collection of data on which the paper is based. Other present and former members of the Project also provided valuable insights, namely, Mary Berg, Stuart Buckley, Shan Hernandez, Mary Milos, Anthony Rodriquez, and Victor Rubin. Lena Johnson is responsible for the computer programming. Outside the Project, I received additional assistance from Francine Blau, Jacqueline Fralley, Joan Haller, Christine Harris, E. Gareth Hoachlander, Terry Geske, Walter McMahon, Dorothy Merrick, Ina Spinka, David Stern, and Diana Thomason. None of the above is responsible for any errors.

REFERENCES

Becker, Gary S., and Tomes, Nigel. 1976. Child endowments, and the quantity and quality of children. Stanford: National Bureau of Economic Research, Working Paper no. 123.

Benson, Charles S. 1980. Time and how it is spent. In Charles S. Benson et al., eds., *Education finance and organization: research perspectives for the future*. Washington: U.S. Government Printing Office.

Bowles, S., and Gintis, H. 1976. *Schooling in capitalist America: educational reform and the contradictions of economic life*. New York: Basic Books.

Carnoy, Martin, and Levin, Henry M. 1976. *The limits of educational reform*. New York: David McKay.

Coleman, James S., et al. 1966. *Equality of educational opportunity*. Washington: U.S. Government Printing Office.

De Lone, Richard H. 1979. *Small futures: children, inequality, and the limits of liberal reform*. New York: Harcourt Brace Jovanovich.

Duesenberry, James S. 1949. *Income, savings and the theory of consumer behavior*. Cambridge: Harvard University Press.

Galbraith, J. K. 1958. *The affluent society*. Boston: Houghton Mifflin.

Jencks, Christopher. 1979. *Who gets ahead? The determinants of economic success in America*. New York: Basic Books.

Katz, Michael B. 1968. *The irony of early school reform*. Cambridge: Harvard University Press.
Leibowitz, Arlene. 1977. Parental inputs and children's achievement. *Journal of Human Resources* 12, 2 (Spring): 247-50.
Ogbu, John U. 1978. *Minority education and caste: the American system in cross-cultural perspective*. New York: Academic Press.
Rutter, Michael, et al. 1979. *Fifteen thousand hours: secondary schools and their effects on children*. Cambridge: Harvard University Press.
Schultz, Theodore S. 1971. *Investment in human capital*. New York: Free Press.
Scitovsky, Tibor. 1975. The place of economic welfare in human welfare. *Quarterly Review of Economics and Business* 3, 3 (Autumn).
Sowell, Thomas. 1972. *Black education: myths and tragedies*. New York: David McKay.
Summers, Anita A. 1979. What helps fourth grade students read? A pupil-classroom-program-specific investigation. Philadelphia: Federal Reserve Bank of Philadelphia, Research Paper No. 40.
―――― and Wolfe, Barbara L. 1977. Do schools make a difference? *American Economic Review* 67 (September): 639-52.
Veblen, Thorstein. 1899. *The theory of the leisure class*. New York: Viking.

CHAPTER 4

Productivity and Cost Effectiveness as Financing Criteria

RICHARD A. ROSSMILLER

Because productivity is widely regarded as a means to achieve desirable goals in our society, the notion that more of any product or service might be obtained from a given set of resources by alternating the way they are deployed is intuitively appealing to most people. Persistent increases in output per worker have often been singled out as the most important reason for the growth in America's standard of living during the past century. Enormous increases in output per worker in agriculture, for example, often are cited as evidence of the dramatic gains in productivity which have been achieved largely through improvements in technology.

Education--or more accurately, formal schooling--has never been acclaimed for its rising productivity, at least when one uses the conventional measure of output per worker. While more people are being educated to higher levels today than ever before, at least in terms of average years of schooling completed, this important aspect of human capital formation has been accomplished primarily by applying more resources rather than by using existing resources more efficiently. Although the amount of human capital formed per pupil may well have increased, as judged by conventional measures, schooling seems to be *less* efficient today than ever before. Pupil-teacher and pupil-professional staff ratios currently are at or near their lowest levels in history, making it appear that output per worker, when taken with declining test scores, has actually been declining in schools (Haggerty 1973). The well-publicized declines in scores on college entrance examinations as well as on other standardized tests commonly used in elementary and secondary schools make it difficult to sustain a claim that the quality of schooling has increased in concert with the decrease in pupil-teacher ratios. While the richer mix of staff personnel in schools today can be rationalized in various ways--for example, the expansion of resource-intensive special programs for handicapped and disadvantaged students, and attempts to individualize and personalize instruction for all students--the fact remains that inputs to education as measured by resources per pupil in real terms have tended to expand over the years. The years of education embodied in the population has continued to increase, but this increase in human capital appears to account for only part of the greater resource inputs.

The recent emphasis on accountability has given rise to frantic efforts on the part of educators to be accountable. Their responses have ranged from advocating competency-based education (implying that previous efforts have been incompetency based) to implementing private-sector management systems such as Management by Objectives (MBO). Several analytic techniques and procedures borrowed from management science have been applied to education in recent years in an attempt to demonstrate a concern for accountability--and perhaps even to become more efficient. Planning-programming-budgeting (PPB), scheduling using program evaluation review techniques (PERT), cost/benefit analysis, input-output analysis, and cost effectiveness analysis are among the analytic techniques and procedures that educators have tried to apply to the practical problems confronting them.

In this article I shall outline some of the models and methods which have been employed in studies of school productivity, review briefly some of the recent contributions to production function and cost effectiveness techniques, and discuss some problems and prospects for research directed toward increasing the productivity of schooling.

Studies of School Productivity

Following the well-known early studies of cost-quality relationships by Mort and his associates (Mort, Reusser, and Polly, 1960: 77-125), many more studies of school productivity have been completed during the past twenty-five years.[1] It is convenient to classify these studies as falling into two broad categories, educational production function studies and cost effectiveness studies.

Models and Methods

Most of the production function studies and cost effectiveness studies to be reviewed used an educational production function model as the basis for the analyses. Production function analysis stems from economics and is based on the assumption that the productivity of an enterprise can be analyzed by treating the outputs as a function of various combinations of resource inputs. An equation that describes the transformation of a set of resource inputs into the desired outputs is known as a production function (Cohn, 1979: 171-74). The following equation from Levin (1974) can serve as a prototype, representing a generalized educational production function:

(1) $A_{it} = g(F_{i(t)}, S_{i(t)}, P_{i(t)}, I_{i(t)})$

where

A_{it} = the educational outcomes for the ith student at time t
$F_{i(t)}$ = the student's family background characteristics cumulative to time t
$S_{i(t)}$ = school inputs relevant to the ith student cumulative to time t
$P_{i(t)}$ = fellow student or neighborhood characteristics cumulative to time t
$I_{i(t)}$ = the initial or innate endowments of the ith student at time t

Newer studies, which use longitudinal data and match children to teachers, estimate a prototype model of the following general form:

(2) $A_t = a + bA_{t-1} + cD + dF_t + fP_t + gS_t + hT_t + e_t$

where

A_t = human capital (typically measured in terms of academic achievement) at the end of a particular school year (t)
A_{t-1} = human capital (academic achievement) at the end of the previous school year (t-1)
D = a vector of the child's demographic characteristics
F_t = a vector of family characteristics in year t
P_t = a vector of schoolmate and/or neighborhood characteristics in year t
S_t = a vector of school characteristics in year t (excluding teacher attributes)
T_t = a vector of teacher attributes in year t
e_t = an error term that is assumed to be normally distributed with zero mean and constant variance (Murnane and Phillips 1979: 2-3).

Since equation (2) specifies a student's achievement at the end of a particular school year, and controls for the student's achievement at the end of the previous school year, as well as for a set of characteristics likely to affect the student's achievement during the course of the particular year under study, it also provides a model suitable for cost effectiveness studies. The factor cost of the variables included in the equation can be determined, and alternative combinations of these variables could be related to different levels of achievement. It must be noted, however, that most cost effectiveness studies have dealt with a much more restricted set of independent variables.

Educational Production Function Analyses

One of the first production function analyses of the type described above was reported by Mollenkopf and Melville (1956), who surveyed over 9,000 ninth-grade students and over 8,000 twelfth-grade students. Student scores on aptitude and achievement tests served as dependent measures, and the researchers had thirty-four independent variables reflecting the quantity and quality of school inputs. Using stepwise multiple regression techniques, the researchers found significant relationships between the student achievement measures and expenditure per pupil for instruction, number of special staff personnel, average class size, and pupil-teacher ratio.

Thomas (1962) estimated a production function of the second type above, using information obtained from Project TALENT and 1960 census data to examine the impact on student achievement of home, school, and community variables in a national sample of high school. He found significant relationships between student achievement and three input variables: 1) beginning teacher salaries, 2) number of volumes in the school library, and 3) teacher experience.

The Equality of Educational Opportunity (EEO) study, better known as the Coleman Report (Coleman et al. 1966), is the largest production function study of the nation's schools undertaken to date. Input measures consisted of ninety-three variables grouped into four major blocks (home background, teacher characteristics, student body, and school facility and curriculum variables). Scores on standardized achievement tests served as output measures. Home background factors were the strongest predictors of student achievement, and student body characteristics were next in importance. Of the school-related variables, those measuring teacher characteristics were the most useful.

The analytic procedures used in the EEO study have been criticized severely, and subsets of the EEO data base have been analyzed and reanalyzed by a number of researchers. Hanushek (1968), for example, developed a model to estimate educational production functions for black and white sixth-graders in northern metropolitan schools. He found that the verbal ability and years of experience of teachers were significantly related to their students' achievement. The work of Bowles (1970), using a subset of the EEO data consisting of twelfth-grade black male students, reaffirmed the importance of teacher characteristics and suggested that school inputs, such as the average amount of time a teacher spent in guidance activities and the number of days a school was in session during the year, also were important. Bowles argued that student characteristics such as attitude and motivation can be viewed as either inputs or outputs and developed a simultaneous equations model to determine the relative effects of these variables.

Katzman (1968), using data from elementary schools in a northern city, examined the importance of home background and school variables in explaining change in student achievement between second and sixth grade. He found a significant relationship between gains in reading scores of students and the percentage of students in noncrowded classrooms (a measure of pupil-teacher ratio in individual classrooms), the number of students in the school attendance area, and the percentage of teachers with one to ten years of teaching experience.

The relationship of school inputs to school performance in urban and non-urban New York school districts was investigated by Kiesling (1969). He used a set of seventeen independent variables, with sixth-grade achievement into five subgroups based on the family breadwinner's occupation, and it was found that this occupational index was significantly related to student achievement for all subgroups in both urban and non-urban categories. Per-pupil expenditures in urban districts were negatively related to student achievement, but they had no significant effect in the nonurban districts.

Cohn and Millman (1975) estimated a simultaneous equations model for fifty-three Pennsylvania high schools for which twelve output measures and more than fifty input measures were available. Inputs included socioeconomic, school (both teacher-related and others), and non-school (environmental) variables. Several manipulable inputs were significant predictors of the outputs, among them teaching load (negative), average teacher salaries (positive), increased use of paraprofessionals (negative), and curriculum units per grade (negative). The socioeconomic variables were not found to be significant predictors of school outputs in this study.

Summers and Wolfe (1975) used data on about 2,000 individual students at various grade levels in 150 Philadelphia schools to relate the achievement growth of individual pupils between the end of the third and sixth grades, the sixth and eighth grades, and the ninth and twelfth grades to socioeconomic factors and specific school resources. The results of their analyses revealed that school inputs (e.g., teachers and school size) and school climate (e.g., racial composition, achievement mixture, and disruptive incidences) did influence student achievement. All types of elementary students learned more in schools in which 40-60 percent of the student body was black and in schools with a larger percentage of high achievers. Elementary school students did better in smaller classes and with teachers who were graduates of higher-rated colleges. Junior high school students learned more in schools which were part of an elementary school and in schools in which there were more high achievers. The students also did better with teachers who graduated from higher-rated colleges and with mathematics teachers who were trained in the post-Sputnik, new math era. Senior high school students displayed higher achievement in smaller schools and in schools with fewer dropouts. Summers and Wolfe also found that specific types of students were helped even more if particular types of resources were made available. Black

Richard A. Rossmiller 83

students, for example, appeared to do better in the smaller elementary schools and in junior high schools with larger black populations. Low-achieving elementary students did better with relatively less experienced teachers, in smaller classes, and in schools with more high achievers.

Murnane (1975) also used data on individual students to investigate the impact of school resources, especially teachers, on the cognitive achievement of inner-city children in New Haven, Connecticut. The data covered a two-year period (second and third grades) for one group of children and a one-year period (third grade) for another group. Murnane discovered important differences in the amount of learning that occurred in different classrooms *within* the same school as well as *among* different schools. Differences in the quality of classroom environments were found to have a greater effect on student achievement in mathematics than in reading. Black teachers with less than six years of experience were more effective in teaching reading to black children than were white teachers with similar teaching experience. A high rate of student turnover had an adverse effect on the reading achievement of children, particularly those who were high achievers.

Murnane and Phillips (1979) used data on individual students and teachers in inner-city elementary schools in a large midwestern city to investigate the extent to which the variables typically used in educational production function research and variables typically used in process-product research explained differences in the effectiveness of teachers in improving the vocabulary skills of inner-city black children at four grade levels. Variables describing teacher behavior and teacher characteristics were both found to be important in predicting teacher effectiveness. Murnane and Phillips found support for the hypothesis that direct instruction (i.e., a businesslike orientation on the part of the teacher, creation of a learning environment that maximizes the amount of time students spent actually working at learning tasks, and a structured curriculum emphasizing feedback) is effective in teaching elementary school children from low socioeconomic backgrounds. Although the relationship was not linear, years of teaching experience was the single teacher characteristic consistently found to be related to teaching effectiveness. The researchers cautioned that considerable variation existed across grade levels in the specific teaching techniques that were related to teaching effectiveness, and they suggested that experienced and more able teachers are particularly effective because they are most successful in finding techniques that provide a good match of the teacher's skills and personality with the curriculum, the available materials, and the needs of the children in the class.

I have studied the relationships between a set of school input and instructional process variables and reading achievement, mathematics achievement, and self-concept of students at the intermediate level in elementary schools using the system of Individually Guided Education (Rossmiller 1978). Several variables were consistently related to student achievement in reading and/or mathematics: 1) enrollment of teachers in a degree program (reading and mathematics achievement); 2) years of teaching experience (reading); 3) sex of the teacher (mathematics); 4) social maturity of students (reading); 5) social confidence of students (mathematics); 6) teacher's perception of the principal's leadership (reading and mathematics); 7) job satisfaction expressed by teachers (reading); and 8) teacher involvement in decision-making (mathematics). A set of twelve independent variables was identified that accounted for 78 percent of the variance in reading achievement. A similar set of twelve variables was found that accounted for 71 percent of the variance in mathematics achievement. All of the variables included in these two sets were susceptible to some degree of control by teachers and administrators. Strong positive relationships were found between cognitive outcomes (reading and mathematics achievement) and affective outcomes (e.g., social maturity and social confidence).

Cost Effectiveness Studies

Cost effectiveness studies, while related to production function studies, tend to be more narrowly focused. Cost effectiveness analysis may be used to assess the relative effectiveness of a program over time, or to compare the relative effectiveness of alternative ways of accomplishing the same objectives. A few studies will suggest some of the results of cost effectiveness analysis in education.

Levin (1970) applied cost effectiveness analysis to the problem of teacher recruitment and retention. Teacher salaries typically account for by far the largest portion of a school's operating budget and thus merit close attention. Levin used data from the EEO study to investigate the relationship of a teacher's verbal ability and teaching experience to the verbal performance of his/her sixth-grade students as measured by a standardized test of verbal ability. He estimated that each additional unit of teacher verbal score raised the verbal score of white students an average of .179 points and the verbal scores of black students by an average of .175 points. Each additional year of teacher experience, on the other hand, was associated with an average increase of .06 points for white students and .108 for black students. Levin estimated the teachers in the sample were, on the average, receiving about $79 more for each additional year of teaching experience and about $24 more for each additional point of verbal score. Bringing the cost and achievement data together, he concluded that hiring teachers of high verbal ability would be five to ten times more effective per dollar of expenditure in increasing students' verbal achievement scores than would hiring more experienced teachers.

Kiesling (1972) used a 6 percent sample of Title I projects (which included 10 percent of the EASA Title I students enrolled in the second, third, fourth and fifth grades) to estimate the relationship between selected educational inputs and the reading performance of children enrolled in these projects in California. He found that the number of minutes of instruction by reading specialists was most consistently related to reading gains by pupils, and that the relationship was particularly strong in the third grade. Translating these findings into cost terms, Kiesling estimated that an expenditure of $300 per pupil for reading specialists would provide an additional 0.3 increase in the amount of instruction, per month, and that this amount of additional instruction per pupil would produce a gain in learning rate of 0.7 units per month.

Blaschke and Sweeney (1974) reported on the cost effectiveness of compensatory reading programs in Michigan. The study focused on twenty-five high-achieving schools and twenty-three low-achieving schools, classified on the basis of 1972-73 Title I evaluation reports filed by Michigan school districts. Individual schools were classified as either high- or low-achieving on the basis of their average grade equivalent gain score divided by the number of months between the pre- and post-test. The COST-ED Model developed by Education Turnkey Systems was used in the analysis of costs, with each program viewed as consisting of one activity in which students were directly involved (classroom reading activities) and four supportive activities in which students were not directly involved (planning, training, decision-making, and administration). Blaschke and Sweeney reported, "Some schools in Michigan do make a difference ... the characteristics of these schools are in many instances very significant ... the factors which appear to describe, if not make, the difference between effective and non-effective 'comp-ed' programs are for the most part 'controllable' by local district staff, and usually those at the building level" (1974: 61). Among the significant factors they identified were 1) the role of the school principal, including how principals allocated their time and delegated decision making authority to teachers; 2) the role of teachers, including their involvement in decision-making and the amount of time they allocated to instructional management activities; 3) the nature and extent of coordination among members of the teaching staff, especially between regular teachers and compensatory education teachers; and 4) the amount of time allocated to planning by the compensatory education director and teachers. With regard to resource allocation, Blaschke and Sweeney noted, "The factors or variables which characterize the differences cost few additional marginal dollars; rather, they reflect different time usage patterns of building staff" (1974: 62-63).

Wolfe (1976) used data obtained from the individual records of 627 students enrolled in Philadelphia's schools over a three-year period (1967/

68-1970/71) and cost information based on the 1975/76 school year to analyze the cost effectiveness of various ways of reducing school expenditures. Utilizing a production function relationship between school inputs and outputs, she examined how resources might be reallocated more efficiently if the current budget level were maintained, and how resources might be allocated if an across-the-board budget reduction of $30 per pupil were required. Wolfe concluded:

(1) The systematic evaluation of inputs in relation to outputs, combined with cost figures, can increase the effectiveness of educational dollars.... (2) the cost per pupil is not directly tied to pupil achievement growth. Current resources can be used more effectively by reallocation. Different expenditure patterns yield very different results. (3) A systematic budget cut yields more satisfactory results than an across-the-board cut. (4) Even in terms of budget cuts it may be best to increase expenditures on certain resources, i.e., smaller classes for low achievers, more experienced teachers for high achievers, and compensate with larger cuts elsewhere to maximize the output of the school system. [1976: 18-19]

Charp and Sebastian (1978) evaluated the cost effectiveness of a combined computer-assisted instruction/computer-managed instruction (CAI/CMI) system. Based on other research concerning the effectiveness of CAI/CMI systems, as well as small-scale comparative studies of matched groups of pupils in Philadelphia, they concluded that CAI/CMI systems were at least comparable in effectiveness to teachers operating alone, i.e., without computer assistance. Their analysis indicated that a CAI/CMI system could reduce program cost by an average of 10 cents per pupil hour as a result of increasing the effective class size (and thus the pupil/teacher ratio). The savings would be accomplished by having a teacher, a teacher aide, and the CAI/CMI system handle the instruction formerly provided by two full time teachers.

Detailed Analyses of the Complex Educational Production Process

Although the production function model has been used extensively in research on school productivity during the past ten years as indicated above, the model does not yield much information about *how* resource inputs are converted to educational outcomes. Several writers have constructed models which draw upon general systems theory to describe the educational production process in greater detail. For example, Abt (1969), Alkin (1970), and Kim and Harris (1976) have outlined models of this type.

Rossmiller and Geske (1977) have also outlined a general systems theory framework for economic analysis of schooling in which the school is viewed as a system amenable to economic analysis. The model (Figure 1)

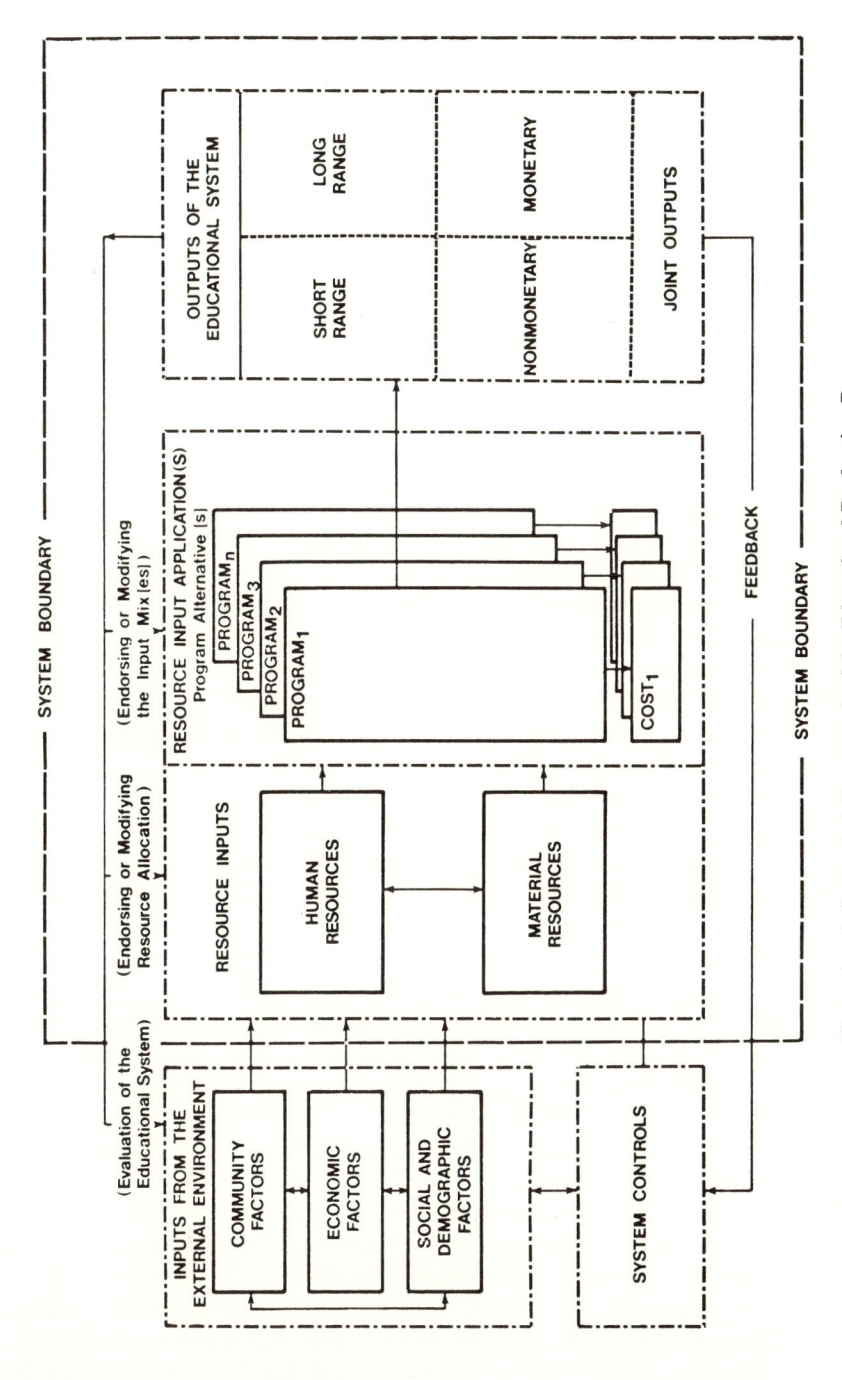

Figure 1. A Conceptual Framework of the Educational Production Process under School Conditions (Rossmiller and Geske 1977)

includes four major components: 1) inputs to the system, including policies which constrain and/or control the system's operation; 2) the formal educational system and the processes associated with that system; 3) outputs of formal schooling; and 4) feedback. It can be applied to the analysis of production processes either within the classroom, within the school, school district, or even within the state. The model follows the various *resources* which are provided to the formal educational system from the community in which it is embedded through the process which occurs within the school to the outcomes of schooling. It may be useful to discuss in greater detail the four major components of the model.

Expectations and preferences held by members of the school community affect both a community's inputs to its school and the priorities assigned to objectives, i.e., the outcomes of schooling that are the most valued as was discussed in Chapter 1. The economic base of a community largely determines its ability to finance education. In most states the level of funding of schools is strongly influenced by the economic resources of the community and its willingness to support education. Factors such as household income levels, manufacturing activity, and retail sales are important determinants of a community's economic base.

The second major component of the model consists of two major elements--resource inputs and resource applications. The resource inputs include human resources and material resources (school buildings, equipment, books, etc.). The human capital students bring to school is an important human resource input used in further learning, and without deficiencies in student knowledge there would be no need for schools. Personnel employed by the school are another important resource, and one over which school managers can exercise some control.

Determining the way in which the available resources can most effectively be applied is the most important managerial task confronting school administrators and teachers. It is at this stage of the model that school resources are combined to produce the educational program. From the resources that are provided, educators must determine appropriate instructional strategies and choose the most effective mix of resources, considering the attributes of the individual students as well as instructional content and instructional process variables.

The third major component of the conceptual framework encompasses the outputs of the educational system. These may be classified in various ways--short range and long range, cognitive and affective, monetary or non-monetary, etc. The outcomes of schooling may be manifested in many ways. Some outcomes can be ascertained through standardized achievement tests or tests of basic knowledge; other outcomes are best assessed by observing a student's performance of certain tasks requiring intellectual and/or motor skills. Still others may be assessed through anecdotal records and observations of students both within and outside the school. There should be a direct connection between the objectives established for the school and the performance measures used to assess educational outputs. If schools are to be held accountable for accomplishment of certain objectives, the measures by which they are judged must accurately reflect the established objectives. Thus measures in addition to scores on standardized tests *must* be utilized, if the outputs of the schooling process are to be evaluated adequately and fairly.

The fourth major component of the model is the feedback loop. Feedback results from comparing the system's outputs with its objectives. Through decisions based on a comparison of outputs and objectives, resource allocations can most effectively be altered or modified to achieve a better match between objectives and results. Feedback can provide a basis for altering the allocation of resources within the educational system itself, or it can result in modifying the resources made available to the system from its external environment. Dissatisfaction with the output of the system may, for example, result in a decision to make more (or less) resources available to a school. Similarly, feedback may alter the nature of the instructional process within a given curricular area by instituting changes in time allocation, grouping procedures, or staffing patterns. The feedback component ties the system together and ensures that it remains dynamic.

What Have We Learned?

The results of studies reviewed in the preceding sections demonstrate the complexity of the process of formal schooling. A school does not exist in a vacuum; it exists within a community with distinct social, cultural, and economic characteristics. A school is affected by the human resources it draws from this milieu and, in turn, effects the community through the human resources if forms. The process of human resource formation which occurs within schools is complex and dynamic. Despite the complexity of the process, the following regularities can be discerned.

1) Money is a necessary, but not a sufficient, resource input in the educational production process. Although early studies found statistically significant correlations between a school's expenditure level and the achievement of students, the correlations were never particularly high. More recent work has uncovered significant relationships between some of the resource inputs that money can buy and student achievement. However, it is evident from the research that expenditure level alone does not control the difference in student achievement. Equally important is the way in which school resources are deployed to meet the specific needs of individual students.

2) Teachers are a particularly important resource input in the educational production process. Researchers have consistently found teacher-related variables (e.g., years of teaching experience) to be related significantly to student achievement. More recent studies that have focused more closely on the process of schooling have found variables such as the recency of the teacher's professional training, the extent to which teachers are involved in decision-making, and the instructional strategies and techniques employed by teachers to be related significantly to student achievement.

3) The social, cultural, and economic milieu in which a school or classroom exists establishes parameters which influence the outcomes of schooling. A number of variables which reflect various aspects of the school's milieu (e.g., occupational status of the head of the household, student turnover, racial composition of the student body) have been found to influence student achievement. In Chapter 3, Benson also finds strong neighborhood effects. How these environmental influences are exerted and how they might be turned to advantage in the formation of human resources is not yet clear.

4) The *process* of schooling is emerging as a potentially useful focus of inquiry. As noted by Thomas in Chapter 5, and in the studies summarized here, the way resources are deployed in a school is of singular importance in the achievement of students. The way the time of students and teachers is utilized, the way paraprofessionals are used, and the matching of instructional strategies and tactics to the nature and needs of students are illustrative of the process-related variables that have been shown to be related to student achievement.

Problems and Prospects

Given the results of the work on school productivity conducted to date, what can be said concerning productivity and cost effectiveness as financing criteria? In addressing this question, one must distinguish between applications at the state and school district levels and at the individual school level. One must also distinguish between activities for which there is a single, clearly identified output criterion and activities for which there are multiple objectives with no clear consensus concerning the priority to be accorded each objective.

At the state and school district level, the application of cost effectiveness techniques may improve productivity in such ancillary services as transportation, feeding, and housing of students. The output criterion in such activities is relatively clear cut: transporting a given number of students at the lowest cost per mile, or preparing palatable and nutritious meals at the lowest cost per serving. Cost/benefit techniques may be used to help inform decisions concerning the relative economic merits of allocating resources to various levels or types of education. For example, cost/benefit analysis might be used to compare the costs and economic benefits of educational programs designed to enable handicapped children to live independently with the costs and benefits of providing institutional care for such children.

Turning to those aspects of schooling in which multiple objectives are the norm, one must be considerably less sanguine. The raison d être of schools, the educational program, is characterized by multiple objectives, an absence of consensus concerning priorities, and relatively ambiguous output criteria. Given the current state of the art, it is difficult to justify the application of cost effectiveness criteria alone to determine the amount of state funds that should be allocated to local school districts to support their educational programs. They must be augmented with judgments about the relative desirability of outputs, as emphasized earlier. Furthermore, we simply do not know enough about relationships between resource inputs and the outputs of schooling to make this a sufficiently solid single base for public policy determination. That is, it is impossible to guarantee that a given set of resources will produce a specified amount of student achievement, however defined, for any identifiable population of students.

At the school and classroom level the results of the research are suggestive but not definitive. The variables that have been found to be related most consistently to student achievement measures are those related to teachers. Not only are variables such as teacher experience important, but there is reason to believe that teachers with certain attributes are more effective with some pupils than with others (Summers and Wolfe 1975: Murnane 1975: Murnane and Phillips 1979). At best, however, the research base provides leads which principals and teachers might consider in their staffing and programming decisions. The research in the area is promising, perhaps even tantalizing, but again more work is needed before it can provide a firm foundation for policy decisions at the school or classroom level.

Efficiency versus Equity and Choice

Three value preferences shape the thinking of those who are concerned about the public financing of education--equity, efficiency, and choice. Writers have paid their respects to the virtue of equity in school finance programs for decades, typically in terms of equality of educational opportunity for pupils and equitable treatment of taxpayers (Cubberley 1906; Updegraff and King 1922; Strayer and Haig 1923). For various reasons (the explication of which are beyond the scope of this paper) equity has proven to be an elusive goal--so elusive, in fact, that those frustrated by the lack of equity in existing systems of school finance finally resorted to the courts. Litigation contesting the constitutionality of existing state school finance programs has been a cornerstone of the school finance reform movement of the late 1960's and the 1970's on the well-founded assumption that justice is more likely to be attained through the judicial process than through the legislative process.

Efficiency has been recognized as a valuable aspect of school finance for nearly as long as equity. Callahan (1962) discussed in some detail attempts by administrators in the early 1900's to make schools more efficient by applying business techniques to the problems of school management. The late 1960's witnessed a renewed interest in efficiency in schools, with the impetus coming primarily from public policymakers in response to rising school costs and growing competition for public sector resources.

A third value which emphasizes choice in education has recently attracted renewed attention. Although the right to choose to educate one's children in a private school has always existed and is constitutionally protected, the argument that public funds should be available to subsidize the education of children in an elementary or secondary school of their parents' choice is of relatively recent origin. This approach, of course, is characteristic of federal higher education subsidy programs, such as the various GI Bills, in which grants are paid directly to those who qualify in order to help them subsidize their education at the college or university of their choice. The case for educational choice has been put forth by T. W. Schultz in Chapter 2, as well as by Coons and Sugarman (1978).

The values inherent in the equity and efficiency goals are likely to conflict. Not infrequently, equity can only be achieved at the expense of efficiency, and efficiency can only be maximized by sacrificing some degree of equity, although instances where efficiency and equity sometimes can be joint products are explored by McMahon in Chapter 1 and by Geske in Chapter 14. How the third value of choice will interact with the values of equity and efficiency remains to be seen.

The point of this discussion is simple: Efficiency is only one of several competing values. Public policymakers and school administrators seldom are afforded the luxury of basing their decisions on a single criterion. They operate in a world of conflicting values where the choice is more likely to be one of satisficing than maximizing. They frequently deal in trade-offs, since explicit weights are not available among these competing values.

Defining the "Black Box"

All of the models used in studies of the productivity of schooling are based, either explicitly or implicitly, on general systems theory. Few researchers, however, have given adequate attention to *how* the transformation of resource inputs to school outputs is accomplished. In systems terms, they have paid little heed to what occurs within the "black box."

One difficulty is that of distinguishing between "education" and "schooling," a distinction which is not always clear in the literature. I prefer to define "education" as all of the experiences which result in learning on the part of an individual. And I use the term "learning "to subsume knowledge, skills, attitudes, behaviors, and any other outcome that one might reasonably wish to include. Obviously, a great deal of what I have defined as learning does not result from "schooling," which I define as all of the formal, structured, purposeful activities which are conducted under the auspices of the social institution called a school. I emphasize this distinction because investigators have not always been entirely clear with regard to whether they were studying education or schooling. We need to define our black boxes with greater precision--to specify clearly the system we are studying. As long as one investigator's endogenous variables are another investigator's exogenous variables, it will be difficult to make sense of the results.

Most of the early production function studies defined the black box as a school system or a school; relatively few investigators have defined the black box at the classroom level (as has J. Alan Thomas in this volume). Yet it is at the level of the classroom or individual student that the interface between the potential learner and the instruments of learning occurs. If there is indeed a definable technology of schooling, it exists at the level of the instructional group. We need research which focuses explicitly on the way resource inputs are used at the learning interface--the use of time by instructional personnel and students, and the nature of their interactions; the nature and amount of instructional materials and how they are employed; the grouping patterns, assessment procedures, and other classroom management techniques; the alternative teaching strategies used to accomplish specified instructional objectives.

Although it is heartening to know that variables such as expenditure per pupil and years of experience of teachers are correlated with student achievement test scores at statistically significant levels, this kind of information is more useful to state and federal policymakers, regional planners, and district-level personnel than it is at the school or classroom level. Such information is not very useful to principals and teachers confronted with the question of how best to use the resources at their command, or, as mentioned by T. W. Schultz in Chapter 2, that they could enlist. Research which focuses on instructional groups may produce findings that will help school and classroom managers do a better job of using the resources they can influence.

Models, Methods, and Variables

As noted earlier, a great deal of the research on school productivity has used a production function model. Several writers have criticized the use of this type of model and have identified some of its shortcomings (Levin 1974, 1976; Hanushek 1978). They point out that the term "production function" has a specialized meaning to economists, and they claim that a production function approach is inappropriate for studying the relationship between input variables such as teacher characteristics and output variables such as student achievement. The critics note that the basic assumptions which underlie the production function model may not be met in schools. Schools are not under great pressure to operate at the most efficient point (even if that point were known), although they are under pressure to expand their output within the limits of their resources. Unlike the inefficient private sector operation, which may be forced out of business unless it operates efficiently, schools are more likely to go out of business as a result of declining enrollments than as a result of inefficiency. Empirical studies based on the production function model reflect what is actually occurring with regard to the use of the resource inputs under study, not what could or should be accomplished if they were operating at the most efficient mix of resource inputs.

Brown and Saks (1975) have argued that the typical production function model alone is not appropriate for studies of schooling because schools strive not only to increase average output but also to affect the distribution of student outputs. They proposed supplementing the production process with a welfare function in which it is assumed that schools attempt to maximize "welfare," which is affected by both the average student outcome and by the distribution of student outcomes. Using data from the Michigan Assessment Survey for 1971, they were able to show that all of the school inputs they studied were related to school output when both the average outcome and the distribution of outcomes were considered.

Researchers using the production function model must cope with another difficulty: the fact that the shape of education production functions is not known. In most studies a linear relationship has been assumed. There is room for doubt, however, as to whether the relationships under study are linear, and there is reason to suspect that (at least for some variables) the relationship is log-linear, which allows substitution among the inputs. Additional research using a wider spectrum of inputs for the variables under study may shed more light on the shape of the production function.

The fact that schooling is not a single-product industry also poses problems for the production function approach. There is general agreement that schooling produces multiple outcomes and that several outcomes are produced simultaneously. Furthermore, high intercorrelations among the variables (multicolinearity) has been a persistent problem with both input and output variables. My own research (Rossmiller 1978) revealed a very high correlation between affective outcomes (student self-concepts) and cognitive outcomes (student achievement in reading and mathematics). Given the fact that the multiple outcomes of schooling are produced simultaneously, simultaneous-equation methods appear more appropriate than single-equation procedures. Elchanan Cohn (in this volume) and Boardman, Davis, and Sanday (1977) have proposed and demonstrated the application of simultaneous-equation procedures in studies of school productivity.

It is likely that not a single educational production function is applicable to all schools. Even if schools have identical objectives (which is seldom the case), the variability in student inputs alone provides reason for questioning whether there exists a single education production function. The existing research sheds little light on this question. The utility of the production function model ultimately will depend upon the extent to which reasonably precise production functions can be specified for clearly defined groups of students.

Another persistent problem is that of separating nonschool learning from that which occurs in school. From a human capital viewpoint, education may be regarded as a form of household production. Previous research demonstrates that what children bring to school--knowledge, skills, attitudes, etc.--affects what they take from school. That is, learning acquired in the home, from peers, from social and other organizations, and the like varies from pupil to pupil. Benson's chapter in this volume provides an excellent example of research to test these effects. Public schools cannot exercise control over the quality of their student inputs. The innate endowments possessed by children differ; consequently, students cannot be treated as identical, interchangeable units. They must be viewed as unique individuals, and each student varies with regard to the amount of learning he or she obtains *outside* the formal schooling process. It is important to know the amount of knowledge or skill a pupil brings to the learning activity if measures of gain are to be employed. The more precisely inputs to the schooling process can be measured, the more likely that reasonably precise estimates of the impact of input and process variables can be made.

Relatively little research has been done with regard to the effect of process variables on school outcomes with inputs controlled. The recent work of Murnane and Phillips (1979) and of Thomas (in this volume) utilizing both production function and process-product approaches indicates that further research which attempts to relate input variables to the way in which these variables are used at the instructional interface may help us understand better the transformation of inputs into educational outcomes.

The ways in which time is used by both students and teachers has received increasing attention, and deservedly so. While time may be regarded as a gross input to the schooling process, the way time is utilized in the instructional process is important. Time is a key variable, for example, in the human capital conceptual model of the learning process, as well as in work by Harnischfeger and Wiley (1976) and in that of Garner (1978) demonstrating the importance of considering out-of-school time (homework) in determining the total time allocated to a given body of subject matter. Future studies can profitably consider the various ways in which time is utilized and their effect on school productivity.

The problems of measuring school outcomes extend to the priorities which are to be assigned to specific educational objectives, or to social benefits, spillovers, or externalities. For example, while nearly everyone agrees that schools should turn out "good citizens," it is very difficult to obtain consensus on operational measures that indicate whether or not a student is learning to be a "good citizen." One can anticipate that specific goals will vary among school districts, and even among schools within a district, depending upon the nature of the student population and the aspirations and expectations of the community served by the school. Even if consensus concerning the general goals of education can be attained, the priority attached to each goal and the specific instructional objectives established for various goals may differ quite widely. Caution must be exercised in aggregating data; if one school's priorities and objectives differ from those of another school, there is no reason to believe a priori that their inputs or processes are comparable.

The outcomes of schooling may be demonstrated in many ways. Students may establish that they have accomplished educational objectives by demonstrating through behavior and performance the possesssion of certain values, attitudes, and motivations; expressing through their actions a sense of cultural appreciation or a sense of social responsibility; or demonstrating their ability to learn independently. Some outcomes of schooling can best be ascertained through standardized achievement tests or tests of basic knowledge; other outcomes are best assessed by observing a student's performance of certain tasks requiring intellectual and/or motor skills. Still others are best assessed through anecdotal records and observations of students both within and outside the school. It is essential that there be a direct connection between the objectives established for the school or student and the performance measures used to assess educational outputs. Measures in addition to performance on standardized tests must be utilized if the outputs of schooling are to be evaluated adequately and fairly.

In conclusion, a realistic assessment indicates that school productivity studies have not fully achieved the expectations of their early proponents. Certainly the technical systems approach so widely advocated in the early 1970's has not proven to be a panacea for problems of efficiency and productivity. The results have served to underline the complexity of the human learning process. Research which will add to our knowledge of the interrelationships and interactions between resource inputs and variables measuring educational outcomes is necessary if we hope to achieve greater efficiency in the use of resources and greater equality of outcomes for students. In an era of declining enrollments, continuing inflation, and dwindling resources, continuing research on educational productivity is essential.[2]

NOTES

1. In the space available it is not possible to review all of the school productivity studies. I have elected to stress studies at the elementary and secondary school levels, primarily because they are more numerous and the methodology has been developed more fully than in higher education. The reader interested in more comprehensive reviews including higher education is referred to Wallhaus (1975), Rossmiller and Geske (1977), Brudner (1978), or Cohn (1979: 163-206).

2. I wish to acknowledge useful comments and criticisms from Walter McMahon, Terry Geske, and Robert Wallhaus.

REFERENCES

Abt, Clark C. 1969. Design for an education system cost-effectiveness model. Pp. 65-91 in *Efficiency in resource utilization in education*. Paris: Organization for Economic Cooperation and Development.

Alkin, Marvin C. 1970. Evaluating the cost-effectiveness of instructional programs. Pp. 221-38 in *The evaluation of instruction: issues and problems*, ed. M. C. Wittrock and D. E. Wiley. New York: Holt, Rinehart and Winston.

Blaschke, Charles L., and Sweeney, J. M. 1974. *Report on preliminary results of the cost-effectiveness study of Michigan compensatory education programs*. Washington: Education Turnkey Systems.

Boardman, A. E.; Davis, O. A.; and Sanday, P. R. 1977. A simultaneous equations model of the educational process. *Journal of Public Economics* 7 (February): 23-49.

Bowles, Samuel S. 1970. Toward an educational production function. Pp. 11-16 in *Education, income, and human capital*, ed. W. Lee Hansen. New York: National Bureau of Economic Research.

Brown, Byron W., and Saks, Daniel H. 1975. The production and distribution of cognitive skills within schools. *Journal of Political Economy* 83 (3): 571-93.

Brudner, Harvey J. 1978. *Gedanken* experiments in educational cost effectiveness. *The Journal: Technological Horizons in Education* 5 (2): 32-37, 50, 51.
Callahan, Raymond E. 1962. *Education and the cult of efficiency*. Chicago: University of Chicago Press.
Charp, Sylvia, and Sebastian, Robert N. 1978. Cost-effectiveness considerations in the use of a combined CAI/CMI system. *The Journal: Technological Horizons in Education* 5 (2): 42–46.
Cohn, Elchanan. 1979. *The economics of education*. Rev. ed. Cambridge: Ballinger.
———, and Millman, S. D. 1975. *Input-output analysis in public education*. Cambridge: Ballinger.
Coleman, James S.; Campbell, E. Q.; Hobson, D. J.; McPartland, J.; Mood, A. M.; Weinfeld, F.; and York, R. L. 1966. *Equality of educational opportunity*. Washington: U.S. Department of Health, Education and Welfare.
Coons, John E., and Sugarman, Stephen D. 1978. *Education by choice: the case for family control*. Berkeley: University of California Press.
Cubberley, Elwood P. 1906. *School funds and their apportionment*. New York: Columbia University, Teachers College.
Garms, Walter I.; Guthrie, James W.; and Pierce, Lawrence C. 1978. *School finance: the economics and politics of public education*. Englewood Cliffs, N.J.: Prentice-Hall.
Garner, William T. 1978. Linking school resources to educational outcomes: the role of homework. *Horace Mann-Lincoln Institute Research Bulletin* 19 (1).
Geske, Terry G. 1979. Some observations on cost-effectiveness analysis in education. *Journal of Education Finance* 4 (Spring): 451-68.
Haggerty, Patrick E. 1973. Research and development, educational productivity and the American economy. *Educational Researcher* 2 (September): 4-10.
Hanushek, Eric A. 1968. The education of blacks and whites. Ph.D. dissertation, Massachusetts Institute of Technology.
———. 1978. A reader's guide to educational production functions. Paper prepared for N.I.E. Invitational Conference on School Organization and Effects, San Diego.
Harnischfeger, Annegret, and Wiley, David E. 1976. The teaching-learning process in elementary schools: a synoptic view. *Curriculum Inquiry* 6 (1): 5-43.
Katzman, Martin T. 1968. Distribution and production in a big city elementary school system. *Yale Economic Essays* 8 (Spring): 201-56.
Kiesling, H. J. 1969. The relationship of school inputs to public school performance in New York State. Report No. 4211. Santa Monica, Calif.: Rand Corporation.
———. 1972. Some estimates for the cost-effectiveness of educational inputs for reading performance of disadvantaged children in California Title 1 projects. Report No. ED 068616. Washington: Educational Resources Information Center.
Kim, Jin E., and Harris, R. C. 1976. *A cost-effectiveness model for secondary vocational programs*. Bloomington: School of Education, Indiana University.

Levin, Henry M. 1970. A cost-effectiveness analysis of teacher selection. *Journal of Human Resources* 5 (1): 24-33.
——. 1974. Measuring efficiency in educational production. *Public Finance Quarterly* 2 (January): 3-24.
——. 1976. Concepts of economic efficiency and educational production. Pp. 149-91 in *Education as an industry*, ed. J. Froomkin, D. Jamison, and R. Raduer. Cambridge: Ballinger.
Mollenkopf, W. G., and Melville, D. S. 1956. A study of secondary school characteristics as related to test scores. Report No. RB-56-6. Princeton: Educational Testing Service.
Mort, Paul R.; Reusser, Walter C.; and Polley, John W. 1960. *Public school finance*. New York: McGraw-Hill.
Murnane, Richard J. 1975. *The impact of school resources on the learning of inner city children*. Cambridge: Ballinger.
——, and Phillips, Barbara R. 1979. Effective teachers of inner city children: who they are and what they do. Institution for Social and Policy Studies, Yale University.
Rossmiller, Richard A. 1978. *Input-output relationships in IGE schools*. Technical Report No. 451. Madison: Wisconsin Research and Development Center for Individualized Schooling.
——, and Geske, Terry G. 1977. *Economic analysis of education: a conceptual framework*. Theoretical Paper No. 68. Madison: Wisconsin Research and Development Center for Individualized Schooling.
Strayer, George D., and Haig, Robert M. 1923. *Financing of education in the state of New York*. New York: Macmillan.
Summers, Anita A., and Wolfe, Barbara L. 1975. Which school resources help learning? Efficiency and equity in Philadelphia public schools. *Business Review* (Federal Reserve Bank of Philadelphia) (February): 4-28.
Thomas, J. Alan. 1962. Efficiency in education: A study of the relationship between selected inputs and mean test scores in a sample of senior high schools. Ph.D. dissertation, Stanford University.
Updegraff, Harlan, and King, Leroy A. 1922. *Survey of the fiscal policies of the state of Pennsylvania in the field of education*. Philadelphia: University of Pennsylvania.
Wallhaus, Robert A., ed. 1975. *Measuring and increasing academic productivity*. San Francisco: Jossey-Bass.
Wolfe, Barbara. 1976. *A cost-effectiveness analysis of reductions in school expenditures: an application of an educational production function*. Madison: Institute for Research on Poverty, University of Wisconsin.

CHAPTER 5

Efficiency in Educational Finance: The Classroom Perspective

J. ALAN THOMAS, FRANCES KEMMERER, AND DAVID H. MONK

A much-debated public policy issue in recent years has been how best to reduce expenditure inequalities among school districts for elementary and secondary education. A number of state legislatures have passed new laws which are designed to respond to or forestall court decisions requiring that existing expenditure differences among school districts be reduced, or at least that the relationship between educational expenditures and local property valuations be weakened.[1]

State-level actions to equalize expenditures have required new state aid formulas, increases in state appropriations for schooling, and limitations on local school districts' access to the property tax base as a source of revenue for schools (see Odden 1978: 29-43). While these changes may have increased equality among taxpayers living in different jurisdictions, provided economic benefits through an infusion of state funds to economically depressed communities, and partially equalized teachers' salaries, they may not have substantially reduced interdistrict variations in educational outcomes. For this and other reasons, a renewed interest in issues of equity and efficiency appears to be justified.

The school finance literature reflects a preoccupation with issues of equity or equality and has little to say about efficiency. One reason for this one-sided emphasis is that, while equality is often measured in terms of inputs, the measurement of efficiency requires that attention be paid to outcomes as well. Efficiency may be easier to deal with in higher education, where outcomes are often expressed as increments in lifetime earning, than in elementary and secondary schooling, where the link between schooling and later economic success is more difficult to establish.

Economists have written extensively about the conflict between the objectives of efficiency and equity in the provision of higher education.

However, as suggested in the latter part of Chapter 1, there is some evidence that equity and efficiency are not always competing goals in elementary and secondary schooling. Bloom's (1976: 161-67) research suggests that the mastery learning approach may result in a decrease in variance in the time required by students to attain mastery in succeeding units, thus ensuring greater equity. Mastery learning may also lead to a decrease in the time taken by individual students to achieve the mastery of subsequent units, thus resulting in greater efficiency (Bloom 1976: 187-88). This example of complementarity between efficiency and equity may be generalized to other attempts to bring about improvements in learning among young children. Compensatory education programs, especially in the earlier grades, are designed to enhance learning efficiency by helping students improve their reading and computational skills. Since these programs are largely directed toward low-income, educationally disadvantaged children, they also promote equity.

For the most part, issues of equity and efficiency in education have been addressed through macro-level policies, while research into the relationship between financial resources and educational outcomes has typically utilized data aggregated to the school or district level. We propose that, in the analysis of equity and efficiency in education, greater attention also be paid to the arenas in which learning takes place, especially homes and classrooms. We argue that equity and efficiency in education are affected by individual decisions made by teachers, students, and parents, as well as by legislators, courts, and administrators.

Resource Allocation in Education

Levels of Decision-Making

The allocation of resources is a central function of the decision-making systems which are designed to facilitate learning. These systems are complex for several reasons. First, decisions are made at several levels; resources are allocated by state, federal, and local governments, as well as in administrative offices, schools, classrooms, and homes. Second, financing and budgeting decisions made at one level affect and are affected by decisions made at other levels. Third, each level of decision-making is characterized by a unique set of actors and a specific definition of the resource set.

The size of the school budget is determined by financial decisions made by legislators and taxpayers, and this total amount of money available affects the quality and amount of teacher services, space, materials, books, and equipment which may be purchased for the school year. Budget decisions made by superintendents and principals determine the allocation of resources among schools, curricular areas, and classrooms.

In addition, these officials are responsible for policies which result in the assignment of teachers, teacher aides, and specialists to particular students. The amount and quality of purchased resources in the classroom in turn affect the manner in which teachers structure learning activities. Classroom structures and processes then affect the amount of time students are willing to spend on learning. Thus decisions made at one level define the constraints and opportunities for decision-making at other levels.

This broad view of decision-making is not universally accepted, and scholars who examine one level of decisions are seldom in communication with those who work at other levels. For example, those who study classroom processes and those who study state school finance systems work largely in isolation from one another, although both are concerned with the allocation of resources. The closest extant approach to studying educational systems at several levels is the work of some production function researchers who examine the relationship between inputs and educational outputs; some of the work in this area has utilized both individual-level and classroom-level data (see Summers and Wolfe 1975). But production function research seldom deals explicitly with the classroom processes through which resources are transformed into learning.

Students' Time as a Valued Resource

The relationship between decisions made in homes and classrooms and those made at higher levels of government is not self-evident and is partially dependent on the importance of student's time. Because time has alternate uses the time of students, even at an early age, has value and is analogous to purchased resources. Furthermore, within broad limits such as those established by compulsory education laws, students have considerable discretion over the amount of time they allocate to education-related activities.

There is, of course, general agreement among economists that the time of older students is valuable and should be included as a cost of schooling because, by being in school, students forego the opportunity to earn money in the labor market (see Schultz 1961: 46-88). However, since in our society, the monetary opportunity costs of the time of young children are negligible, economists have seldom extended their analyses to include the time of elementary school students. Other arguments, however, support the view that the time of young students has value. The first of these is the "foregone learning" argument,[2] which states that when students spend their time studying a given subject, using a given curriculum (such as New Math), or employing a given technology (such as library research), they forego the benefits associated with alternative subjects, curricula, or technologies. The value of students' time is therefore determined by the learning which is foregone when the best alternative is sacrificed. This alternative varies among students, since talents differ. For example, a student who excels in piano-playing may begrudge the time he spends doing homework in mathematics because he is foregoing the opportunity to spend the same time practicing the piano.

A second reason why the time of students at all ages has value is that students possess knowledge and skills which were developed through prior investments. This argument is based on human capital theory. Differences among students in time value (or differences for a given student across subject areas) may partially reflect differences in prior investments.

The third argument which logically follows the second is that a student's time has value because he or she has the knowledge and skills which are required to produce additional learning. Differences among students in the value of their time may simultaneously reflect differences in previous investments and differences in the amount of time taken to master a new unit of learning. Regardless of whether these differences in time value reflect inherent aptitudes (if these exist), motivation, or previous investment, the differences may be defined as learning productivity or the amount of time taken by a student to produce a given amount and kind of learning (see Carroll 1971: 29-45). Time value (or aptitude) differs among students and for the same student among subject areas.

Student Decision-Making, Equity, and Efficiency

The degree to which equity and efficiency in the production of learning are attained is related to 1) the amount of time supplied by students to learning and 2) students' aptitudes. Looking first at the *quantity* of time, students who frequently choose to absent themselves from school, who pay little attention in class, who avoid involvement in learning-related activities at home, or who leave school at an early age have less exposure to education than those who are usually present, pay attention in class, study at home, and remain in school for a longer total period. These variations in the supply of time by students are not necessarily related to such school finance variables as the distribution of funds across budgetary items; however, the time supplied by students may affect learning to as great a degree as do expenditures of money and stocks of goods and services,[3] and differences in efficiency across students, classrooms, schools, or school districts may result partly from differences in the time which is supplied to learning in homes and classrooms by individual students or groups of students.[4] Such classroom-level resources as the availability of competent teachers, attractive homes and classrooms, well-stocked libraries, and academically oriented peers may motivate students to spend more time on their studies. Some students and parents may compensate for inadequate school programs by utilizing educational television, or by using hired tutors; in these cases, resources supplied by parents and students may act as substitutes for school resources, rather than as complementary inputs.

Progress toward equity and efficiency goals may also be affected by differences in ability among individuals within a classroom, or across aggregates of individuals at the classroom and school level. Where students are able to produce a given increment in learning in a relatively short time span, they will use less teacher's time and other resources to produce a certain amount of learning. If all students are exposed to a subject for the same amount of time, inequalities in measured outcomes will result among individuals and aggregates of students with different levels of ability. Efficiency will also be affected, since a given financial investment will produce more or less learning (for individuals or in group average) according to the quality of time which students supply. This phenomenon explains and justifies investments in students' learning skills through remedial or compensatory programs which constitute investments in "learning to learn".

A Theory of Classroom Structure

Classrooms and homes constitute the primary settings within which learning takes place. Within classrooms, a variety of structured activities may be observed. These activities may be analyzed from several perspectives; our approach is to view classrooms as the context within which purchased resources are combined in varying proportions with students' time. In this section we discuss the situational factors which affect resource combinations in classrooms.

We define an instructional setting as a unique combination of student's time with purchased resources. Teacher's and student's time are considered to be the most valuable of all resources used in the production of learning; they therefore constitute the basic ingredients of technologies in classrooms. Elementary school classrooms include a variety of technologies which comprise, in their totality, a technological structure. The structure of a classroom is determined rather early in the school year; since it is based on relatively constant combinations of space and time, it usually remains stable over the entire year. For reasons which Thomas has discussed elsewhere (Thomas 1977: 75-88), the structuring of a classroom may also be affected by the characteristics of residents of the attendance area.

Assumptions

1) The basic units of the classroom structure are activities located within modules which are bounded by space and time. Each classroom contains a fixed amount of space; within this setting, teachers may use file

cabinets, tables and desks, rugs and blackboards to rearrange the classroom into working areas (see Prohansky and Wolfe, 1974). Analogously, teachers divide the total time available into subunits within which curricula and activities are located.

2) A given level of learning can be brought about through the use of more than one combination of inputs. Students may, under some circumstances, supply additional time to compensate for a shortage of purchased resources; in other cases (as in crash programs in foreign languages for diplomats) a high level of purchased inputs may make possible a reduction in the amount of students' time required to bring about a desired level of educational outcomes.

3) Our analysis is based on the assumptions that additional resources will in general produce additional learning, and that, beyond a certain point, increments of any single input produce successively decreasing marginal increments in outcomes.

Substitution among Inputs

We now present our analysis of input substitution in classrooms. Figure 1 represents the various possible trade-offs between different amounts of student's and teacher's time. It is the same as Figure 2a in Chapter 1 in that it considers the aspect of the education production function that relates two inputs (including teachers' time, which is a purchased input, and students' time) to the output (or outcome), new learning. The three curves in Figure 1 are called insoquants; isoquants I, II,

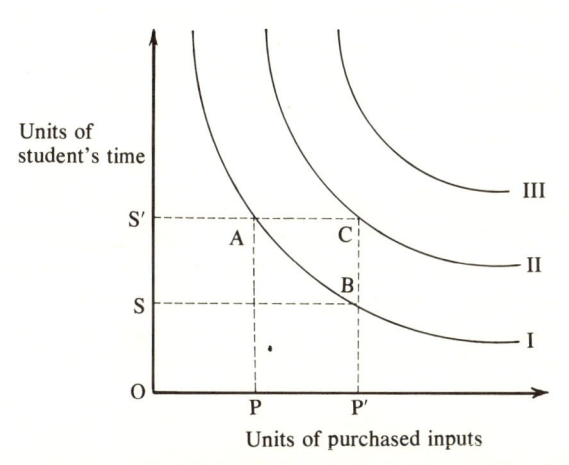

Figure 1. Trade-Offs between Student's Time and Purchased Inputs

and III represent successively higher levels of student attainment. It is assumed that each isoquant joins points which represent unique combinations of student's time with purchased inputs which result in a given level of outcome.[5]

In addition to displaying the combinations of inputs which can be used in obtaining a given level of outcome, the diagram also illustrates the potential for reaching higher levels of outcomes through the use of additional inputs. For example, level I may be reached through a combination of OS' units of student's time and OP units of purchased resources, or through using more purchased resources (OP') and less student's time (OS). Reaching level II requires more of either or both inputs, for example, OS' student's time and OP' purchased inputs.

Two factors which affect the input combinations and attainable output levels are the availability of purchased inputs and student's time. If a school district has a shortage of funds, it may reduce the purchased inputs available to individual students by (for example) using larger classes. Students may ensure attaining a desired level of performance by devoting more out-of-school time to their studies. Similarly, college students may compensate for the disadvantage of large lecture classes by spending more time in libraries. If purchased resources are plentiful and classes small, and if there is no incentive for them to reach more than the minimum performance level, students may reduce their time investment by foregoing homework; if the incentive to reach a higher level of performance is sufficient, students may supplement even small classes and bountiful school inputs with homework and a high degree of involvement in school.

Because of the interaction between purchased resources and student's ability, resources may be scarce in even the wealthier school districts. Even in well-equipped and well-staffed classrooms, teachers who attempt to accommodate instructional procedures to different student ability levels are faced with problems of inadequate resources. For example, if three students in a given class are falling behind in their work and another is capable of doing much more difficult work than the class as a whole, all four may profit from tutoring, while the remainder of the class may benefit from teacher-led discussions. Well-financed school systems of sufficient size sometimes deal with this problem by providing tutorial instruction outside the regular classroom, both for the gifted and for those suffering from learning disabilities.

Effect of Ability on Input Substitution

We define student ability as the amount of time it takes a student to attain a given level of performance (as in Carroll 1971: 31-32). This concept of student ability meshes quite well with our discussion of students' time as an input, and the relationship between students' time, purchased inputs, and performance level becomes one of considerable interest.

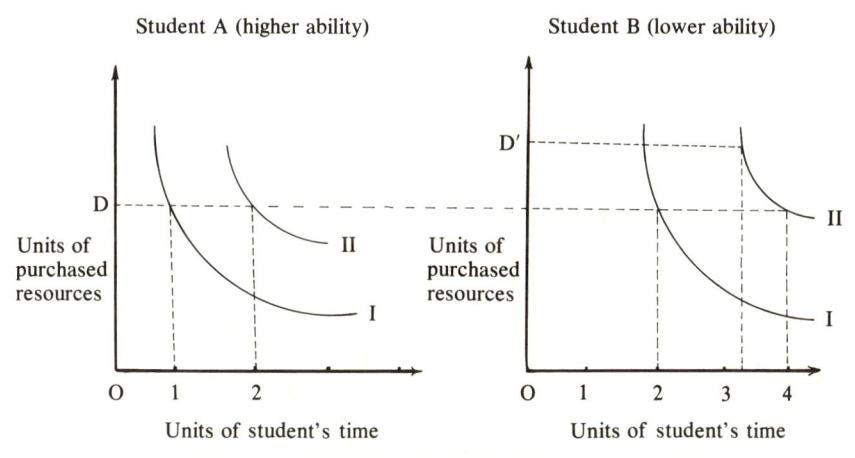

J. Alan Thomas, Frances Kemmerer, and David H. Monk   107

Figure 2. Trade-Offs between Inputs Provided by and for Students of Unequal Ability

Figure 2 displays the types of trade-offs which can be made between student's time and purchased inputs when two students of unequal ability are involved. Student A, who has greater ability, can attain performance level I more quickly than can B. Thus, for OD purchased resources, Student A requires an investment of one unit of his time; B requires a larger investment, of two time units, in order to reach level I. With the same amount of purchased resources, A could reach level II by increasing his time commitment to two units, while B would require an even larger amount of time--namely, four units. Reducing the purchased inputs which are provided would still further increase the time investments necessary for A and B to reach either level I or level II.

If the incentive to move from achievement level I to II is sufficient, both students might invest more of their time by doing homework or by being involved in class. Parents might encourage students to do homework under parental supervision, as a way of helping them to improve their grades. Teachers might find it necessary to provide more of their own time and other purchased resources to Student B than to A, in order to bring the slower student to a desired performance level.[6] For example, if OD' units of purchased resources are used, B reaches level II with an investment of only three units of his own time. Under mastery learning, B would be assigned the additional teacher time and other resources in the necessary skill areas to permit him to achieve at level II, A's level. This improvement in B's skills will cause the value of a unit of B's time to approach the value of a unit of A's time and hence move toward equalizing *outcomes*, a Rawlsian positivist position as discussed in Chapter 1 and by Kern Alexander later in this book.

An additional aspect of resource allocation which has important fiscal and budgetary implications is the manner in which student's time is combined with *material* resources such as books, programmed materials, audiovisual aids, and *human* resources such as teacher's time. It is possible to represent this type of trade-off in a manner similar to that used above. However, additional complications are introduced when students' ability is taken into account, since the most able students are probably better able than students of lower ability levels to utilize material resources, such as the library, as a substitute for teacher's time. Windham has observed that one way to take individual differences into consideration may be to assign the most competent students to library research while the slower children are given intensive teaching in small groups or even in tutoring situations.[7] It should be noted that this procedure would result in more costly resources being provided to the slower students, since human resources are more costly, on an hourly basis, than material resources. This procedure does not imply that the teacher embraces an egalitarian philosophy, but merely that she utilizes appropriate technologies to enhance the learning of both "slow" and "fast" students.

The Empirical Results

This section describes the methods used to collect data to test some propositions drawn from the resource allocation theory, and also presents some results. Data were gathered at the school district, school, classroom, student, and home levels in a total of 58 classrooms in 19 school districts. The classrooms were selected from within school districts chosen by a stratified random process which was based on three SES levels and two district expenditure levels. Within each district, a school and classrooms were selected (two in each school in 1978, and four in each school in 1979). Within each class, eight students whose parents had signed consent slips were selected for close observation; parents of these students were interviewed in the home. Data were gathered for 58 classrooms, 233 students, and 233 homes.

Classroom observations were carried out by trained observers who spent two or three weeks in each classroom, one observer per classroom in 1978 and two in 1979. Fifth-grade classes were selected throughout; mathematics and social studies (or in some cases, a substitute for social studies) were the subjects chosen for observation. Instruments were developed to record classroom observations; an interview protocol was used to obtain information about human and material resources available for the promotion of learning in homes, and about the manner in which students spend their time out of school. Classroom observations focused on the availability of resources, the structuring of activities (including the use of teacher's and student's time), and the subject matter and curricular materials which formed the basis of classroom instructional activities.

The Structuring of Classroom Activities

Considerable research points to the existence of a correlation between student's achievement and socioeconomic status (see e.g., Coleman 1966). If students in high-SES classrooms possess, on the average, a high level of aptitude (or of embodied human capital), educators may recognize the high value of student's time by combining it with expensive purchased resources so as to economize on students' time. In low-SES classrooms, on the other hand, there may be a tendency to regard students' time as having less value, to combine it with less costly resources, and to use technologies which are wasteful of students' time.

Table 1 reports on the percentage of time allotted to different instructional formats in twenty-two classrooms stratified by SES and by subject matter. The listing of formats proceeds from those which are teacher centered, and progresses toward those which are more flexible, individualized, and involve a degree of student control over the content and pace of instruction.

Table 1 roughly confirms our expectations about the distribution of services across classrooms serving different social class groups. In general, low- and middle-SES classrooms were characterized by a larger proportion of teacher-centered whole-class instruction than classrooms serving a high-SES population. On the other hand, instruction in small groups, individualized seatwork, and tutoring are most characteristic of classrooms serving high-SES students, and were not observed at all in low-SES classrooms. This analysis of data from the pilot study did not, however, reveal a clear pattern of differences among different SES levels in the proportion of time allocated to seatwork.

The Allocation of Teacher Time among Students within Classrooms

Observers of classroom practice have long known that teachers allocate their time unequally among students. This study attempted to develop a methodology for measuring the flow of teacher time to individual students, and to test a model which is intended to explain differences in the amount of teacher's time that different students receive.

The theoretical and empirical work of Brown and Saks (1975: 571-93; 1979: 53-118) deals in part with issues of resource allocation among students or categories of students at the level of the classroom or the school district. They proposed that the manner in which school districts or teachers allocate resources among students may reflect either elitist or egalitarian values. The resource allocation procedures of the elitist school districts and teachers would favor the most competent students, while

Table 1. Percent of Time Allocated to a Variety of Instructional Formats Controlling for SES, and for Subject Matter

Instructional Format	Low SES Math (N = 3)	Low SES Second subject (N = 3)	Middle SES Math (N = 4)	Middle SES Second subject (N = 4)	High SES Math (N = 4)	High SES Second subject (N = 4)
Whole group						
(1) Lecture	7.0	6.6	10.4	8.1	2.4	6.7
(2) Recitation	23.7	15.1	9.6	34.2	8.9	7.6
Small group				3.3		9.5
Seatwork	17.8	29.5	42.3	13.8	29.5	17.7
Individualized seatwork	1.9		4.1	2.7	14.0	16.1
Tutoring			1.0		5.9	
Audiovisual		6.9			1.3	17.8
Other less common technologies	49.6	41.9	32.6	37.9	38.0	24.6
Total	100.0	100.0	100.0	100.0	100.0	100.0

districts and teachers with egalitarian values would distribute disproportionately more resources to the least competent in an effort to reduce differences in performance.

The within-classroom differences in resource flows may, however, reflect students' characteristics in classrooms, as well as the values of teachers. For example, in classrooms where students' ability levels are heterogeneous, teachers may group students by ability levels, in order to reduce the range of abilities they must deal with at any given time. Other teachers may prefer to deal with individual differences by using "individualized instruction" methodologies. Our data suggest that individualized and differentiated technologies result in a greater variance in the resources students receive than does the traditional "whole class" form of instruction.

Differences in resource flows may, therefore, be influenced by differences in ability among students in a given classroom. If an entire class is given the same assignment, some students will finish before others. When this pattern is repeated, a number of results may be observed. One is that the faster students waste time waiting for the others to catch up. There is also considerable potential for classroom disruption when a portion of the class is without work while the remainder is completing an assignment. While the "egalitarian" teacher may regard a waste of time by the better students as a necessary by-product of the commitment to equality, parents may complain, and teachers may be uncomfortable when a large amount of time is wasted by any group of students. Many teachers provide students with a list of assignments when they finish early. Preparing this seatwork, monitoring its performance, and ensuring that students who complete one task proceed to a new one requires teachers' time and often additional materials as well. Hence, an additional flow of resources to brighter students may reflect the realities of classroom instruction rather than a commitment to elitism.

Issues in the Measurement of Resource Flows to Students

Measuring resource flows to students is at least as difficult as explaining why differences in resource flows exist. Four key issues must be resolved before the measurement of resource flows to students can proceed. The most difficult conceptual problem in measuring the flow of resources to individual students lies in the fact that students are usually taught in groups. Hence, a given set of inputs, including the time of the teachers, is being used to provide simultaneous instruction to more than one student. This situation, where more than one outcome is produced by a single set of inputs, corresponds to what economists call jointness in production. If all students in a group are receiving the same benefits and if the fact that one student is benefiting from instruction does not subtract from the benefits received from the others, education takes on some of the characteristics of what economists call a "public good." In the extreme case of jointness, *all* students are receiving the full cost of teacher's time and other inputs, and hence all are treated in an identical manner. If this is the case, the size of the instructional group is immaterial to the measurement of resource flows.

This argument is flawed if the teacher's services are utilized in an unequal manner by different students. For example, when a teacher speaks at the level of the average student, above-average students may be bored, while slower students may find the presentation unintelligible. An alternative assumption to that of jointness is the assumption of "separability" according to which the teachers' services are divided among students so that the services used by one student or group of students decreases the value of resources received by others. In this case, the resources received by a student are inversely proportional to the size of the group since in smaller classes a given amount of resources is divided among fewer students.

The second issue is how to assign a cost to teacher's time. Because our study included teachers in different school districts as well as in different classrooms in a given district, we were reluctant to base our measures of resource flows on the salaries of the specific teachers involved. Such a procedure would provide a measure of resource costs at the classroom level but it would not correctly reflect salary differences among districts, since the salary of a specific teacher reflects her own training and experience as well as district salary policy. A second possibility was to use the average teacher's salary in the school district as a measure of the value of teacher's time; this measure assumes that the teachers included in the study were representative of all teachers in the district. A third alternative was to use a measure of the drawing power of the district for teachers; in this case, the beginning salaries paid to teachers with the bachelor's degree were used on the assumption that these salaries may also provide an indication of the quality of new teachers attracted to a district. Since none of the three assumptions is clearly superior to the others, all three can be used in a sensitivity analysis.

The third issue is related to the question of how to divide the cost of teachers' time among simultaneous activities. Teachers may, for example, provide instruction for one group of students while simultaneously supervising the behavior of a second group. The best approach appears to be to distinguish between the cost of time spent instructing and the cost of time spent supervising student behavior. Specifically, the cost of supervising student behavior was assumed to approach the cost of services provided by teacher aides who typically supervise the behavior of students but who are often prohibited (sometimes by contract) from conducting lessons. On the basis of this assumption, when a teacher's attention is divided between the instruction of one group and the supervision of a second group, the division of the cost of the teacher's time between the groups would correspond to the ratio of the cost of the time of teacher aides to the cost of the teacher's time.[8]

A final and even more intriguing issue concerns the role of student involvement in the flow of resources. Can resources be said to flow to a student when he or she is "off task"? As in the other cases, we used both assumptions--first, that resource flows exist only when students are actually "on task," and second, that resources flow to students regardless of whether the latter are involved in the assigned work. Sensitivity analysis can then be used to assess the effect of student engagement or nonengagement on the determinants of resource flows.

Student Involvement in Learning

Table 2 reports the percentage of total observations during which the students in our sample were actively engaged in the assigned task. There are substantial differences across subjects, instructional formats, and SES categories. The column means indicate that the low- and high-SES classes showed a higher proportion of involvement than the middle-SES classrooms. The table shows the proportion of involvement to be relatively low for seatwork, and relatively high for audiovisual instruction and tutoring. In the middle-SES classrooms, engagement is low for both lecturing and recitation. While the data on which Tables 1 and 2 are based were obtained from the pilot study and the number of observed instances in each category was small, the tables suggest that SES differences across classrooms and format differences within classrooms may be related to the time given by individual students to the instructional task.

Table 2. Proportion of Total Observations during Which Students Were Engaged in the Assigned Task by Specific Instructional Format for Each SES Level and Each Subject

Instructional Format	Low SES Math ($N = 3$)	Low SES Second subject ($N = 3$)	Middle SES Math ($N = 4$)	Middle SES Second subject ($N = 4$)	High SES Math ($N = 4$)	High SES Second subject ($N = 4$)
Whole group						
(1) Lecture	.8845	.9100	.6736	.4645	.8958	.7359
(2) Recitation	.7791	.7657	.6860	.7842	.8361	.8269
Small group				.7083		.8873
Seatwork	.7506	.8169	.7982	.7639	.7507	.7378
Individualized seatwork	.8464		.8009	.8704	.6972	.6750
Tutoring					.8906	
Audiovisual		.8546				.9262

Examining the different amounts of teacher's time that students receive involves examining differences in the manner in which classroom structure mediates between the total resources available and the amount of these resources which each student receives. It also requires examining differences among students within classrooms in the amount of resources which they receive.

In both the inter- and intra-classroom analysis, the key issues concern the nature of instructional groups and the division of teacher's time between direct instruction and indirect supervision of student's seatwork. Table 2 also suggests that some classrooms are characterized by the allocation of substantial periods of time to small group instruction and individual tutoring, while other classrooms focus on whole-class instruction. There are also differences across classrooms in the time devoted to seatwork, as opposed to direct instruction.

Differences among classrooms in available resources may influence the manner in which their activities are structured, while intra-class differences reflect the proportion of the total time during which individual students are involved in small-group and individualized instruction (as opposed to whole-class involvement). The analysis that follows begins to identify and determine the effect of variables designed to predict individual-level resource flows and the nature of resource flows in classrooms.

Table 3 reports on the relationship between classroom structure and certain antecedent variables for each subject in the twenty-six classrooms involved in the study. This table suggests a positive relationship between the social class of residents of the classroom attendance area and the proportion of time spent in small-group instruction and seatwork. On the other hand, there is a *negative* relationship between social class and the mean proportion of time devoted to whole-class instruction. This reinforces our findings (reported in Table 1) that high-SES classrooms tend to be characterized by a relatively small amount of whole-class instruction and a relatively large proportion of small-group instruction. The above findings hold true for both mathematics and the second subject.

Student characteristics are also good predictors of classroom structure. Both the mean and the standard deviation of reading and mathematics scores are highly correlated with the mean proportion of time spent on small-group and (negatively) whole-group instruction in mathematics. The mean of test scores is a better predictor of the use of seatwork in mathematics classes than is the standard deviation, but both statistics are good predictors of the use of small-group instruction. This finding suggests that teachers are sensitive to both the level and variability of student ability in deciding whether to use whole-group and small-group instruction in mathematics.

Table 3. Zero-order Correlations between the Incidence of Whole Class, Small Group, and Supervised Seatwork and District and Classroom Characteristics

	Math classes (N = 13)			Second-subject classes (N = 13)		
	Whole class	Small group	Seatwork	Whole class	Small group	Seatwork
DISTRICT CHARACTERISTICS						
Median family income	-.44	.23	.45	-.52	.68	.49
Median education level	-.44	.33	.39	-.43	.50	.41
Per-pupil expenditures	-.28	.09	.32	-.56	.59	.54
CLASSROOM CHARACTERISTICS						
Reading comprehension						
Mean	-.53	.48	.43	-.06	.47	.02
Standard deviation	-.18	.47	-.02	.15	.15	-.17
Math concepts						
Mean	-.39	.29	.35	-.08	.44	.04
Standard deviation	-.45	.58	.27	-.01	.30	-.01
Math problems						
Mean	-.52	.47	.42	-.03	.60	-.03
Standard deviation	-.35	.55	.15	.49	-.23	-.49
Occupational status						
Mean	-.46	.32	.43	-.35	.74	.30
Standard deviation	.05	.13	-.13	.19	-.11	-.19

Summary

The main thrust of proposed changes in methods of financing education has been toward equalizing monetary inputs and examining the cost implications of variations in the educational program. Some researchers, unhappy with input measures as indicators of educational opportunity, have attempted to estimate the effect of various school-level and socioeconomic variables on measures of educational attainment.

This research proposed three modifications of the production function approach. 1) Student time, which is partially under the control of the students themselves, constitutes a potentially important resource. It incorporates the effects of prior investment, and its quality is an important determinant of achievement. 2) While the factory analogy leads to the asumption that procedures determine outcomes, it seems likely that, just as children affect the behavior of parents, students affect the procedures used by teachers. In particular the mean, variation, and skewedness of the distribution of ability in classrooms may partially determine the manner in which teachers organize their students for instruction. 3) Policy-related research in education must be informed by a knowledge of the technologies on which the production of learning depends. Since educational structures or technologies are developed in classrooms, classroom-level research is needed to identify the determinants of classroom structure and the effects of structure on student behavior.

The work has important implications for equality and efficiency in the production of education. Differences in student performance result not only from differences in the availability of purchased resources among classrooms and districts, but also from differences within classrooms in the flow of resources to individual students. Decisions made by students, parents, and teachers influence the degree of equity which exists in the distribution of the benefits of education. Similarly, while macro-level approaches to the study of educational efficiency (for example, accountability systems) emphasize decisions made by administrators, school boards, and legislators, many of the decisions which actually determine efficiency are made by individuals in homes and classrooms. A knowledge of these micro-level relationships can be used in developing policies and incentive systems which, in combination with appropriate macro-level decisions, can result in a more equitable and efficient educational system.[9]

NOTES

1. For discussions of school finance reform, see Levin (1976) and Pincus (1976).

2. This idea, and many others in this paper, originated in earlier discussions with Mary Jean Bowman.

3. Bloom (1976: 187) writes, "Anderson reports a correlation of .66 (.75 corrected) between time-on-task and final achievement."
4. Here efficiency is defined as the relationship between stated outcomes and financial cost. If the opportunity cost of the student's time is also included, the statement may no longer be true.
5. The slope of the curve at each point represents the ratio of the marginal products of the two types of input.
6. Bloom (1976) reported that Arlin found that "the non-mastery student needed more than twice as long (2.2) to reach the criterion as did mastery students."
7. Comment made in a discussion with Douglas M. Windham.
8. This procedure was suggested in a letter written to the principal author by Lee Hanson, Department of Economics, University of Wisconsin.
9. The authors extend special thanks to Susan S. Stodolsky, who directed the empirical phase of the 1979 study, and to David Rogosa, who is providing valuable assistance in the statistical analysis of the data. We also thank our colleagues in the Educational Finance and Productivity Center, University of Chicago, for their criticism and advice. Teresa Ferguson and Robert Wimpelberg provided us with invaluable assistance as project coordinators. We also extend our thanks to our staff of observer-interviewers, and to the teachers, school principals, and superintendents who provided support and cooperation in the fieldwork. Robyn Beatty deserves special thanks for her work in preparing the manuscript.

REFERENCES

Bloom, Benjamin S. 1976. *Human characteristics and school learning*. New York: McGraw-Hill.
Brown, Byron W., and Saks, Daniel H. 1975. The production and distribution of cognitive skills within schools. *Journal of Political Economy* 83, 3 (May/June).
———. 1979. Production technologies and resource allocations within classrooms and schools: theory and measurement. In *The analysis of educational productivity, I: issues in microanalysis*, ed. Robert Dreeben and J. Alan Thomas. Cambridge: Ballinger.
Carroll, John B. 1971. Problems of measurement related to the concept of learning for mastery. In *Mastery learning: theory and practice*, ed. James H. Block. New York: Holt, Rinehart and Winston.
Coleman, James S. 1966. *Equality of educational opportunity*. Washington, D.C.: Department of Health, Education and Welfare.
Levin, Betsy, ed. 1974. *Future directions for school finance reform*. Lexington, Mass.: Heath.
Odden, Allan. 1978. School finance reform: emerging issues and needed research. Pp. 29-43 in *Dilemmas in school finance*, ed. J. Alan Thomas and Robert Wimpelberg. Chicago: Midwest Administration Center, University of Chicago.
Pincus, John, ed. 1974. *School finance in transition*. Cambridge: Ballinger.
Prohansky, Etta, and Wolfe, Maxine. 1974. The physical setting and open education. *School Review* 82 (4): 557-74.

Schultz, Theodore W. 1961. Education and economic growth. In *Social forces influencing American education*, Sixtieth Yearbook of the National Society for the Study of Education, ed. Nelson B. Henry. Chicago: University of Chicago Press.

Summers, Anita A., and Wolfe, Barbara L. 1975. *Equality of educational opportunity quantified: a production function approach*. Philadelphia: Department of Research, Federal Reserve Bank of Philadelphia.

Thomas, J. Alan. 1977. *Final report to the National Institute of Education*. Project Number 4-0794, Grant No. NIE G-74-0037.

CHAPTER 6

Measuring Non-monetary Benefits of Education: A Survey

ROBERT T. MICHAEL

"The direction in which education starts a man
will determine his future life."
Plato

Since at least the time of Plato we have been told that education yields benefits throughout life. Interest in scientific inquiry regarding the economic attractiveness of formal schooling was greatly encouraged by Theodore W. Schultz's essays two decades ago (Schultz 1961, 1963). Studies had previously explored both the logic and the magnitude of schooling's payoff, in the form of higher earnings (e.g., Adam Smith's compensating wage differentials and Friedman and Kuznets's inquiry into the income of professionals), but Schultz's essays emphasized that the benefits from education were not to be found exclusively in the form of higher market earnings. There were "consumption benefits" as well.

The insightful and socially influential research on investments in education begun in the early 1960's with the work of Schultz and Becker (1964) and Mincer (1958, 1962) focused on the labor market returns to schooling. That analysis and the subsequent literature that investigated relations over the life cycle among formal schooling, on-the-job training, labor earnings, labor supply, and the resulting distribution of labor earnings represent probably the most widespread, sustained, and successful research venture by economists in the past few decades.

Research interest in the "consumption benefits" to which Schultz referred did not enjoy the same success. In 1967 he surveyed studies in the field and lamented, "All these studies omit the consumption value of education.... It is a serious omission.... The available estimates of earnings from education in this respect all underestimate the real value of education" (Schultz 1967: 300).

Over the past decade research on the consumption benefits of education has made progress in conceptualizing these benefits and in measuring their magnitude. Its success, however, has been limited. This

119

area has not attracted widespread research interest. Findings have often come as side issues in papers directed toward other topics. There are, I suggest, three reasons for this.

First, there is a strong collective judgement that while "consumption benefits" from schooling may exist, relative to the money income effects of schooling, they are probably small and surely of little importance. This intuition is prompted by economists' general inclination to focus on phenomena which have rather easily observable monetary value. This money illusion is reflected in our national income accounts, in our research, and thus in our awareness and our collective intuition.

Second, the prevailing paradigm used in modeling the consumption benefits of schooling has not excited the intellectual interest of a large number of researchers. The impressive ingenuity of researchers in estimating such seemingly immeasurable concepts as utility-based marginal rates of substitution suggests that where there is a will there is an estimate. This ingenuity has not often been applied to the consumption benefits of education, implying to me the lack of a sufficient analytical stimulus. (By contrast, Becker's brilliantly simple statement of the investment model of schooling in Chapter 2 of *Human Capital* is itself probably responsible for a significant portion of the research on the economics of education.)

Finally, because of the intrinsic difficulty in obtaining information about household non-market behavior (as emphasized so delightfully in Mitchell [1937]), the available data for analysis of consumption benefits of schooling are not abundant; because of the lack of research attention given to the topic, the nature of relevant data is not sufficiently clear. Thus it is not surprising that a researcher choosing a project on the returns to education would select a study of earnings differentials by schooling levels—rather than choosing a project with a far less obvious product, and with probably lower-quality data, a less well accepted and less well articulated model, and less apparent public interest.

Lest I discourage you from reading further, there have been important and interesting findings which are discussed below. Moreover, there are grounds for expecting greater interest and product related to this topic in the future. Since diminishing returns apply to research areas as surely as they apply elsewhere, the relative attractiveness of research on *non-monetary* returns to schooling must be rising. More important, there is increasing public interest and intellectual concern about non-market production as evidenced by research on a broader set of national income accounts, by the social indicators "movement," "quality of life" studies, etc. For men (if not for women) over the past several decades the fraction of the lifetime spent in the labor market has been declining,[1] so the non-labor-market effects of schooling are becoming relatively more important. Data, too, are becoming less of an obstacle to research on non-market behavior—

the detailed spending information of the 1972-73 Consumer Expenditure Survey and the Michigan Time Use Survey represent exciting new sources of information. Finally, the success of research over the past few years on non-earnings effects of schooling, though limited, is sufficient to prompt the realistic expectation of a substantial payoff from additional research.

It should be stressed that the survey undertaken here is almost exclusively a survey of recent economic research, while the topic of effects of schooling on behavior and attitudes has long been a research focus in other disciplines, such as social and developmental psychology and in sociology. The interested reader is encouraged to see Feldman and Newcomb's *Impact of College on Students* (1969) for a wide compendium of non-economic research, and to look also at two more recent volumes, *A Degree and What Else* by Withey (1971) and *The Enduring Effects of Education* by Hyman, Wright, and Reed (1975). For an excellent and wide-ranging recent review of knowledge on the private and social consequences of higher education, see Bowen's *Investment in Learning* (1977).

Categories of Non-monetary Benefits

There are at least three quite distinct notions of non-monetary benefits of schooling found in the literature. (The Appendix delineates these potential benefits.)

Schooling affects the non-wage dimensions of labor market remuneration. The return to investments in schooling through the labor market may not be fully reflected in money wages because of differences in fringe benefits and working conditions. This rather obvious extension of the earnings function literature has been given surprisingly little attention. With recent data sets, however, work has begun, and it now represents one of the most fruitful areas for future research. Duncan's (1976) study of non-pecuniary benefits represents an exciting step forward; likewise Freeman's (1978) study of fringe benefit differences by unionization is an important example of this new line of research. The use of hedonic prices to value and incorporate attributes of working conditions constitutes another direction of this research. In one such study, Lucas (1977) estimates that the omission of job attributes causes an understatement of the returns to schooling of from 10 to 40 percent. Additionally, labor market effects of schooling, such as the widely cited lower level and shorter duration of unemployment and greater earning stability, are usually not adequately represented in the labor market earnings literature. These characteristics of employment represent, however, a part of the labor market benefits of schooling. These non-wage-rate effects are too often ignored in cost/benefit analyses of schooling investments; this article will, unfortunately, continue that tradition and discuss these labor market benefits no further.[2]

Schooling has pure consumption effects (see Appendix, section 2). Schooling may yield benefits for the same reason attending a sports event or reading a book yields benefits--the activity of schooling is itself enjoyable. Few studies address this consumption effect directly. Lazear (1977) represents one of the only exceptions of which I am aware. Indirectly, of course, all studies of demand systems which include expenditures on "schooling" as a part of the total consumption expenditure are treating schooling on a par with all other durable and nondurable goods and market services, but these studies do not attempt to reconcile the consumption and investment motives for schooling. This survey does not summarize these studies.

Schooling affects productivity in activities outside the labor market (see Appendix, section 3). At a minimum one might think that whatever it is about schooling that raises productivity in the labor market also affects productivity in some other formal or informal markets. If schooling enhances labor market productivity by affecting skills per se (e.g., in making decisions, in communicating, in organizing daily activities), then it is intuitively likely that these skills affect productivity in the capital market (e.g., in deciding to or from whom, for how long and under what arrangements to lend or borrow funds) or in making consumer choices in durable goods markets. If instead schooling affects productivity in labor markets by affecting job opportunities through the signal content about worker quality, then in other "markets" in which the individual must sell himself or herself these same (privately) beneficial signals may be given by schooling level. Examples include the informal "markets" in which social contacts are made e.g., clubs, mate selection, neighborhood friendships. More generally, if there are "allocative" skills acquired from schooling, they might be expected to affect productivity in activities outside any market. The household production function approach to consumption behavior is frequently used in modeling these effects, as in Michael (1972) or as described in the context of environmental variables in Michael and Becker (1973).

There is a degree of arbitrariness between the pure consumption benefits and the non-labor-market productivity benefits of schooling, especially if one thinks of the former as having a durable element. Whether the enhanced enjoyment of an art museum which results from an art appreciation course taken years before is a durable consumption benefit or a non-market productivity effect does not seem worthy of much debate. A related methodological point is important, however. If schooling alters tastes--i.e., changes the utility function per se--then it is not feasible to sign (let alone quantify) the change as a benefit (or a cost) of schooling; whereas if the utility function is not affected and only the amount of some commodity is altered, then (in principle, at least) the change may be quantified in a dollar metric (see Becker and Stigler 1977).

Schooling and Non-Labor-Market Productivity

The central question addressed by the studies detailed below is whether there is evidence of this third type of non-monetary benefit from schooling, a productivity effect of schooling in activities outside the labor market.

Measuring these non-labor-market productivity effects is difficult. In labor market studies one can use wage rates as a measure of productivity,[3] but it is seldom possible to obtain either direct or indirect measures of productivity outside the labor market. A measure analogous to a wage rate is almost never available, and one seldom has direct measures of both total inputs and output. Instead, the research strategy involves measuring the effect of schooling on either the output of some activity or the time or goods input into some activity alone, while imposing sufficient restrictions to permit inference about the effects on productivity.

Given that schooling affects labor market wages, it is essential to control for wage effects on non-labor-market output in order to make inferences about non-labor-market productivity. Wage changes imply income effects and, in general, shadow price effects on demand for output. Only when these effects are held constant can one infer something about productivity from a relationship between schooling and output: if output rises with schooling level, holding constant the price and income effects of a higher wage rate, that rise in output can be interpreted as a response to a decline in its price or a rise in the productivity of producing that output. Using changes in inputs such as time spent in an activity to infer productivity effects also requires controlling for the shadow price and income effects. In addition, information on the price elasticity of the demand for the output and the substitutability among inputs must be known before one can infer how schooling affects productivity from information on its effect on the derived demand for an input.

Beyond the question of evidence of a productivity effect of schooling outside the labor market, there is a further question of whether the productivity effects in any of these non-labor market activities are as large (in percentage terms) as the measured effect in the labor market. If the productivity effect is equally large in two activities, then schooling is said to be technologically neutral between these two. In the extreme case, if schooling enhances productivity in all activities by an equal percentage-- i.e., if schooling is completely neutral in its effect on the productivity of time--then the benefits of schooling could be measured by the change in the wage rate multiplied by the sum of working and non-market time, whereas it is usually measured by the change in the wage rate multiplied by only working time. In reality, such technological neutrality across all activities for all levels of schooling seems unlikely. Certain kinds of schooling are surely biased toward labor market activities, while other kinds of schooling are designed to enhance non-labor-market skills. Neutrality would provide analytical and computational convenience and is often invoked because of these properties. But, as suggested below, there is practically no direct evidence that supports the assumption of neutrality.

Schooling and Human Capital Investments

Formal schooling may affect productivity in producing human capital itself. There have been several studies that suggest this phenomena with respect to investments in additional schooling, on-the-job training, health, and migration.

Schooling

Regarding the plausible notion that schooling enhances productivity in producing knowledge or "productive capacity," the important life-cycle model of earnings by Ben-Porath (1967) assumed technological neutrality in the effect of schooling on the productivity of time in two activities: on time used in the labor market, and on time used to produce human capital through schooling. This neutrality assumption--often referred to as "Ben-Porath neutrality"--was introduced for its analytical simplification. It implies that the ratio of the opportunity cost of time spent in school (the wage rate for a working person) to the marginal product of time spent in school (in producing human capital) is unaffected by the amount of schooling one has. Hence, for a working person, the cost of producing human capital is not affected by the amount of human capital one already has. Also, in making a decision at some age about the optimal human capital investment at that age, the neutrality assumption implies that it is irrelevant how time will be allocated between working in the market and studying in school in subsequent periods.

In a companion study, Ben-Porath (1970) develops a "test" of the neutrality assumption, inferring its presence or absence from the observed decline in investment in human capital as workers age. Ben-Porath argues that, if neutrality holds (and of course some other assumptions), the only rationale for declining investment is the finiteness of life. His evidence rejects neutrality, implying that human capital raises productivity in working more than it raises productivity in producing human capital. Ben-Porath does not address the subsequent issue of interest here. If it is not neutral, how "non-neutral" is it? Does the evidence suggest that human capital has any effect on efficiency in producing more human capital?

Mincer's (1970) comment on the second Ben-Porath paper suggests the answer to this second question is: Yes. Indeed, Mincer suggests that although

Ben-Porath's test shows a more rapid decline in investment than neutrality would imply, "perhaps not enough" of a discrepancy is found "to reject the null hypothesis--particularly in view of the few degrees of freedom" (Mincer 1970: 149). So, while schooling may not be neutral in its effect on productivity in the labor market and in subsequent training, the non-neutrality may not be large; schooling appears to have a non-labor-market productivity effect in producing more schooling human capital.

However, Rosen (1977) makes a fundamental criticism of the Ben-Porath "test." Rosen stresses that the test uses data generated by a method inconsistent with an optimizing investment model and suggests that the empirical exercise simply reproduced the assumptions that underlay the data. (See Rosen 1977: 21-22, 34.)

A more recent extension and empirical exploration of Ben-Porath neutrality is found in Heckman (1976). Using a life-cycle utility maximization framework (as distinct from the life-cycle income maximization framework in Ben-Porath [1967]), Heckman extends the assumption of technological neutrality to include three uses of time: working, learning, and consuming. Here, as schooling rises, the productivity of time in all three activities rises proportionately, so there is no induced substitution of goods for consumption time as wages rise with job skills over the lifetime. Thus, the optimal accumulation of human capital is not only independent of how one expects to allocate subsequent time between learning and earning, but is also independent of the portion of time spent in consuming (i.e., in "leisure" activities).

Heckman does not test this expanded neutrality assumption directly but nests it with a sizable number of other assumptions, including functional form assumptions. He concludes that his model, including the expanded neutrality assumption, fits life-cycle earnings data relatively well, and that it is also consistent with life-cycle consumption expenditure patterns.

Despite considerable ingenuity, the literature on life-cycle models of schooling investment contains no direct evidence and at best only suggestive indirect evidence of a non-monetary benefit of schooling via improved proficiency in learning. What evidence there is is couched in terms of neutrality with the effect on labor market productivity and is motivated largely by the analytical convenience that "neutrality" affords. Moreover, these life-cycle models lump schooling and post-school job training together. But as Ben-Porath comments (1970: 143), even within the formal schooling system lower levels of schooling tend to emphasize skills useful for further learning, while "terminal" schooling degrees tend to focus on skills which more exclusively influence job market productivity. This heterogeneity in schooling should affect whether or not it is neutral. Clearly, further work is required before we can have confidence in the evidence that schooling enhances productivity in subsequent schooling; even more evidence is needed to warrant a conclusion that this effect is as large as the effect on labor market productivity.

Health

Schooling may affect productivity in producing other forms of human capital as well. Research by Grossman (1972a,b, 1976) regarding schooling's effects on investment in health offers the best direct evidence of a non-market productivity benefit from schooling.

Numerous studies have shown that schooling is highly correlated with good health. Grossman (1976) substantially refines that evidence, investigating the effect of schooling on health using a recursive model with information about an individual's health status as a teenager, his level of schooling, and his health status at about age forty-six. Using a somewhat controversial scaling of health (which Grossman derives from the relationships between qualitative health status and observed work weeks lost due to ill health), a scaling (in logs) in which "poor" health equals 0.0 and "fair," "good," and "excellent" health are scaled 2.3, 3.3 and 4.5, respectively, Grossman finds that schooling raises health by 3.5 percent (holding nothing but age constant) or raises health by 1.2 percent (holding constant age, wage rates, health status as a teenager, background characteristics, measured ability, property income, job satisfaction, an index of obesity, and wife's schooling). Based on an investment demand function for health, these results suggest that "schooling raises productivity in the production of health by 2.4 percent at a minimum." (1976: 179). This productivity effect in the production of health may be compared to an effect on hourly wages (hence, presumably, labor market productivity) of about 5.5 percent (based on the same data set, the NBER-TH sample). Grossman contends, "The non-market productivity effect of schooling ... is approximately 40 percent (2.4 ÷ 5.5) as large as the market productivity effect" (1976: 179). This relative effect is in the same order of magnitude as Michael's estimate discussed below, even though Grossman's data include only men with at least twelve years of schooling, so the effects of lower levels of schooling--which might be relatively less labor market oriented--are not captured in Grossman's results.

Several other of Grossman's results deserve mention. Wife's schooling appears to have an even greater effect on husband's health than does his own schooling.[4] Grossman argues convincingly that the result is *not* primarily a reflection of selective mating (i.e., that healthier men marry women with more schooling). Grossman points out that several of his control variables--wife's schooling, job satisfaction, and the obesity index (actually a variable reflecting deviation from ideal weight for a given physical height)--are themselves influenced by the man's schooling level if, as hypothesized, schooling enhances non-market as well as market productivity. From auxiliary regressions on each of these three variables, together with their effects on health, Grossman computes the "indirect" effect of schooling on health via its effect on wife's schooling (+), job satisfaction (+), and obesity (-), which altogether adds 0.7 percent as the indirect effect, in comparison to the direct net effect of schooling on health of 1.2 percent.

The sensitivity of Grossman's qualitative results to his scaling of the health variable is investigated by estimating an OLS regression and a logistic function on a dichotomous variable indicating "excellent" health. The signs and statistical significances of the variables here mirror those found with the scaled variables, giving further credibility to the results summarized above. The results suggest that, holding constant teenage health status, measured ability (which itself is positively related to health), background variables, etc., each additional year of post-high school education raises the probability of excellent health by about 1 percent.

Finally, Grossman is able to identify in the sample observations those who died during a fourteen-year period while the cohort aged from about thirty-two to forty-six. The mortality rate among this relatively highly educated (and healthy) sample was 2.8, compared to a U.S. population rate of 4.3 for a comparable age and time interval. Moreover, in studying which of the sample members died during that time interval, logistic functions suggested that, *ceteris paribus*, each additional year of schooling lowered the probability of death by 0.4 percent.

While Grossman's study represents the most compelling evidence on the relationship between schooling and health, it by no means is the only evidence. For example, work disability, as reported in the 1970 Census 5 percent sample, shows a striking negative relationship with schooling, controlled for age, race, and sex—but not for wage rates, unfortunately (see Lando 1975).

Migration

One of the oft-cited findings in the literature on determinants of migration is that the more educated are more likely to migrate a longer distance when they move. (See, for example, Schwartz [1971] and Greenwood's survey [1975: 407]). To investigate the reason for the schooling difference in migration behavior, Schwartz (1971) uses net and gross migration flows by age and schooling level from the 1960 census to perform a test of the "efficiency of migration." He concludes that the data support an "information hypothesis which states that the level of information (about the economic attractiveness of locations) is an increasing function of the level of education" (1971: 205).

More recently, Schwartz (1976) offers an explanation for the observed differences by education level in net and gross flows and in distance traveled.[5] Schwartz contends that his model, which utilizes the known shape of age-earnings functions by schooling level, "can explain all the empirically observed relations of migration measures ... and education. No other assumptions ... are needed" (1976: 718). He states, "I cannot and do not claim that the efficiency assumption ... is wrong. Rather I claim that some of the empirical phenomena need human capital arguments to explain them and that the rest are easily explained by the same arguments ... no direct study sheds light on the alternative hypothesis" of increased search efficiency with schooling (Schwartz 1976: 703). Occam's razor is here, as elsewhere, a compelling argument. But several nontrivial assumptions are built into Schwartz's 1976 model, and the empirical tests are not of a detailed nature. The issue at this point remains open.

Recent studies use household micro data (as distinct from aggregate migration flows) to study migration behavior, but here too the evidence on the search efficiency hypothesis seems mixed. DaVanzo's is typical of the better work done in this area. DaVanzo (1976) uses the five-year panel from the Michigan Income Dynamics data to study geographic migration and finds essentially no education effect--but her regressions include several occupation, wage, income, and prior migration variables. A part of the explanation for the lack of the usually observed education effect is found in a more recent DaVanzo study which uses the eight-year MID panel (DaVanzo 1978). Here she distinguishes among movers who return to their original destination, movers who move again to a new location (SMSA and non-metro-state economic areas), and movers who do not move again. Using a polytomous logit model, holding unemployment and housing tenure in the original and current location constant, and holding the distance of the initial move constant, DaVanzo finds that the more educated are *less* likely to engage in a return move after a short (one-year) stay but are relatively *more* likely to move on after a one-year period. After a longer tenure in the new location, the schooling coefficient falls essentially to zero. The schooling effect in short duration moves also disappears when occupation and a poverty index are included. Thus, much of this observed education effect is probably actually an income effect. DaVanzo suggests, not inappropriately but with little direct supporting evidence, that on the basis of these recent results "one plausible interpretation here is that the less-education migrant processes information less effectively, implying that the initial migration decision is more likely to have been based on limited or faulty information" (1978: 9). So the efficiency hypothesis in migration behavior is not fully discredited; but neither is there yet a definitive test of its validity or magnitude, or much evidence which unambiguously lends it support.

Comment

Amounts of human capital in various forms--schooling, on-the-job training, health, migration--tend to be positively correlated across individuals. This positive correlation between, say, schooling and health does not necessarily imply anything about the non-labor market productivity of schooling. The correlation can be explained by either a third factor or by complementarity. The third-factor explanation might be best understood in the context of an optimal investment model of the kind proposed by Becker (1967). That is, the costs of investment funds differ among people and are probably highly correlated across types of human capital investment; this induces a positive correlation in investments across individuals. Likewise, differences among people in time horizons and in the relative attractiveness of risky human capital investments can also induce the positive correlation in types of human capital investments. Regarding complementarity, the returns on some forms of human capital (e.g., job training) are necessarily linked to the magnitude of the stock holdings of other types of human capital investments (e.g., health, which increases the number of potential work days each year by reducing illness and which lengthens the potential work life by reducing mortality). So forms of human capital are likely to be technical complements, in the sense that the marginal products of some are positively related to the levels of others.

Most of the studies cited above go beyond this demand-induced positive correlation between forms of human capital. They purport to show an effect of schooling on the productivity of time in producing human capital. To do so requires controlling for the common determinants of investment in human capital. Even if many of these common determinants are controlled for, any unmeasured characteristic of the individual which affects the general attractiveness of human capital investments can induce a positive correlation between forms of investment. It seems likely that schooling level, used as an exogenous variable in a relationship of investment in some form of human capital, might proxy these unmeasured third factors. If so, a causal interpretation from schooling to other investment would not be appropriate. Grossman's recursive scheme is probably the best evidence here of an effect of schooling on a human capital investment activity. If there were simply some omitted or unmeasurable variable which induced a positive correlation between health and schooling, then prior health should also proxy that phenomenon. So in Grossman's equation on current health regressed on prior health, schooling, measured ability, etc., the robust finding of a strong positive effect of schooling is noteworthy evidence of a nonmarket effect of schooling on health.

Schooling and Asset Management

The capital market is another arena in which allocative decisions play an important role and in which schooling may affect productivity. As Ehrlich and Ben-Zion (1976) point out, the management of one's assets (and debts) requires time. Presumably the proficiency and amount of time input should influence the yield on assets (and cost of debt). In discussing the life-cycle pattern of time allocated to the labor market and allocated to asset management, they employ a Ben-Porath neutrality assumption that human capital affects productivity of time in labor markets and in asset management proportionally (1976: 576). While they show evidence that the average propensity to save is relatively high among occupations in which specific skills in asset management are likely to be great (1976: 581), they stop short of any empirical analysis of the impact of schooling on the return on invested assets or on the corresponding incentive to save.

One suggestive piece of evidence on productivity in asset management is found in Solmon's (1975) analysis of data from a 1959 survey of members of Consumers Union, a sample of some 6,000 relatively well educated, higher-income and presumably relatively well informed consumer units. The respondents were asked a question about their judgment as to the best investment hedges against inflation. The answers were qualitatively judged in terms of their "accuracy"; answers of fixed-dollar assets and avoiding debt were judged "incorrect," and answers of purchase of real or financial assets were judged "correct." In regressions on this qualitative variable, education had the strongest effect (more educated answering correctly), while level of family income and a professional or business occupation dummy also showed a significant partial correlation with the "correct" answer (1975: 282). More than 45 percent of the interpretable responses by consumers with twelve or fewer years of schooling chose the "incorrect" inflation hedge, while less than 15 percent of those with sixteen or more years of schooling chose incorrectly. Correspondingly, less than half of the twelve-or-less group selected stocks or real estate as an appropriate hedge, while over 80 percent of the group with sixteen or more years of schooling did so.

Of course, more educated consumers can expect to have more income and thus to have a larger level of savings, so they would have greater incentive to invest in asset management skills. Even if the costs of acquiring those skills were equal among consumers, the benefits would be greater for those with greater saving; hence investment in asset management skills would be higher among the more educated. The importance of controlling for the effect of schooling on wages and income is clearly seen here. Solmon's regression holds family income, age, and certain occupations constant when looking at the effect of schooling in a measure of investment knowledge, so it may be reflecting a real productivity effect. Yet here, as elsewhere in this research area, one has the impression that a rather low burden of proof regarding a nonmarket productivity effect is imposed on the evidence, either because of the analytical simplicity afforded by the technological neutrality assumptions about schooling-productivity effects or because of the intuitive plausibility of the arguments.

Schooling and Consumption Behavior

In General

Most of one's lifetime is not spent in the labor or capital market. Productivity in other activities in which one engages--in consumer markets, home and leisure activities, etc.--has a profound effect on the level of real consumption. Several studies of effects of schooling in one or another aspect of productivity in consumption have been undertaken within the past decade; the most directly focused and most comprehensive study of which I am aware is Michael (1972). Here a model is proposed, based on the household production function approach to consumer behavior, in which empirical evidence of an inferential nature is adduced showing an effect of schooling on real income through non-market productivity.

The logic which underlies this test of the schooling effect is that, abstracting the effect of schooling on wages or money income, *if* schooling enhances nonmarket productivity, then 1) it thereby raises real income; and 2) thus it induces shifts in spending patterns among consumption items, shifts which reflect that increase in real income. So if schooling has a non-labor-market productivity effect, consumers with higher levels of schooling will have--and will behave as if they have--more real income (over and above the higher money wage income which they may also have). If schooling has a different quantitative effect on productivity in different non-market activities, then schooling will alter relative prices as well as real income through the non-market sector. An important simplifying assumption necessary for the empirical analysis which Michael undertakes is that schooling is technologically neutral in the non-market sector--affecting productivity in all non-market production activities by the same proportion, thereby assuming away potential relative price effects. With that neutrality assumption, the methodology for estimating the effect of schooling on non-market productivity is, in essence, to exploit the following chain differentiation:

$$\left.\frac{dX}{dS}\right|_{\text{money income}} = \left.\frac{dX}{dI} \cdot \frac{dI}{dS}\right|_{\text{money income}}$$

where S is the schooling level, X is the consumption expenditure on some items, and I is the real income which is a positive function of both money income and non-market productivity. By estimating from expenditure data the two terms $dX/dS\,|_{\text{money income}}$ (which is the effect of schooling on the expenditure) and dX/dI (which is the effect of income on the expenditure) one can calculate the remaining term $dI/dS\,|_{\text{money income}}$, which is the measure of the effect of schooling on real income through non-market productivity, the "consumption income effect."

The empirical estimation itself is somewhat more complex because it is essential to hold money income--preferably permanent money income--fixed. Furthermore, each consumption item (food, clothing, etc.) on which expenditure information is used yields a separate estimate of the analytically interesting term, the "consumption income effect." Michael (1972) uses a number of alternative schemes to deal with the over identification and concludes that, on the basis of several different levels of aggregation of the consumption bundle and two distinct national data sets (the BLS Consumer Expenditure Surveys of 1950 and 1960-61), the consumption income effect is positive. Estimated values in elasticity form range from 0.05 to 0.75, with a best-guess point estimate of 0.5. By comparison, the schooling elasticitiy of money income is estimated to be 0.8, so by this reckoning the effect of schooling is only about 60 percent (.5 ÷ .8) as great in non-market activities as in the labor market. Schooling is technologically biased toward the labor market, but nonetheless has a substantial non-market productivity effect.

In Particular

Several studies of specific consumption activities shed light on schooling's effects. Decisions regarding consumer purchases represent an area in which skills of acquiring, assimilating, and acting upon information play an important role. Differences in these skills by schooling level seem likely and are frequently assumed to exist. There is substantial evidence that new products are often adopted relatively quickly by the more educated, which is often taken as an indication of this skill difference.

But here, as in the investment areas discussed above, it is important to distinguish between a behavioral response to an economic incentive and a productivity effect. We know that the more educated person has higher real money income, and hence has greater incentive (at constant cost) to acquire information about consumer goods markets for all normal goods (see Stigler [1961] and Mincer [1963]). If variety of goods is itself a "normal" good, then new products and varieties of goods and services will be adopted by the more educated simply because the more educated are wealthier. The economic incentive to know about these new products will be greater for the more educated wealthier consumer. (In the Consumers

Union panel data referred to above, 60 percent had at least sixteen years of schooling, compared to only about 10 percent of the U.S. households in total [Juster 1975: 401]. The more educated have *an incentive* to be relatively well informed.) So, whether it involves videotape machines, vasectomies, or credit cards, the finding that the more educated adopt a new product more readily is not surprising, nor does it necessarily reflect a differential productivity effect of schooling. Higher income which accompanies schooling may induce the observed behavior.

There are studies, however, which attempt to standardize for this differential incentive to acquire information in the consumer behavior area. Bank credit cards were first introduced in the early 1950's but were not in widespread use until after installment repayment was introduced on card balances in 1959. In a study by Mandell (1972) using data from the 1970 and 1971 Surveys of Consumer Finance, 50 percent of the consumer units reported that they used some form of credit card (bank, gas, department store, or travel and entertainment card). Use rose with income and with education level. As household head's education level rose from 0-5, 9-11, 12, 16, to 17+, the percentage using any card rose from 15, 40, 54, 81, to 83 percent, respectively, with the biggest increments for bank credit card use: 4, 11, 17, 33, to 36 percent respectively (Mandell 1972: 14-23). While a thorough control for income was not used, Mandell does report the education effect partitioned by income. Of those with income under $7,500, only 20 percent of those with less than twelve years of schooling and 40 percent of those with twelve or more years of schooling used credit cards; among those with incomes over $7,500, the comparable percentages were 55 and 78. So there it at least suggestive evidence here that the effect of education on credit card use is not altogether explained by differences in income. However, Mandell notes that it was common practice for credit card companies to encourage credit card use by college graduates via solicitation. This surely undermines an interpretation of more informed choice by the more educated; it also raises interesting questions about the supply side of consumer markets.

A number of surveys of fertility control behavior have shown that more educated women are more likely to use contraception, to adopt contraception at an earlier birth interval, and to have fewer "unwanted" births or less "unplanned" fertility. (Michael [1975]: 349-55 summarizes several such studies.) Here again the differences in incentives to avoid undesired pregnancies may explain much of this result, since the wife's time value is positively related to education and the cost of a child is positively related to wife's time value. One study which investigates this relationship between schooling level and contraception, holding constant several of these incentive effects, is Michael (1973).

Contraceptives marketed by the mid-1960's in the U.S. varied considerably in their efficacy in reducing the risk of conception. The best available techniques--the oral contraceptive (pill) and IUD--exhibited in actual use a substantially lower monthly risk of conception than more traditional techniques.[6] Michael (1973) studied the relationship between schooling level and contraceptive technique used by women in specific birth intervals, using the 1965 National Fertility Survey. Each technique was scaled according to its average measured use effectiveness, and the regression analysis involved regressing the monthly probability of conception (based on the contraceptive the woman used in that birth interval) on her schooling level and her intended or desired level of fertility, holding constant her age, birth interval, race, and religion (Catholic/non-Catholic). The control for intended fertility eliminates the differential incentive to contracept by level of schooling, which is related to different levels of desired fertility; it does not, however, eliminate any differential incentive related to the difference in *net* loss from an unwanted conception, if such a differential exists. Table 1 reflects the nature of the findings for white, non-Catholic women ages 30-34, expressed here as the difference in expected time to

Table 1. Differences in expected time to conception (in years) by schooling levels, for all women and for contraceptors only (for non-Catholic white women age 30-34; *third birth interval*)

	Contraceptors and non-Contraceptors	Contraceptors only
Sample size	330	242
Sample average time to conception	1.3 years	5.1 years
From regression with wife's schooling		
High school minus grade school	0.9 years**	1.5 years**
College minus high school	0.2	0.8*
From regression with husband's schooling		
High school minus grade school	1.2**	1.1**
College minus high school	0.1	0.9**
From regression with both spouses' schooling		
Wife's high school-grade school	0.5*	1.0
college-high school	0.3	0.3
Husband's high school-grade school	1.0**	0.8
college-high school	0.2	0.8*

**implies the coefficient's t-value > 2.0; * implies its t-value > 1.7
Source: computed from Michael (1973), Table 7, p. S158.

conception at different schooling levels.[7] Among all (contracepting and non-contracepting) women, the high school-educated women had a 0.9 year longer expected waiting time to conception than the grade school-educated women--the high school women were using contraceptive techniques which were, on average, that much more efficient. Likewise, the college-educated women had a 0.2 year longer expected waiting time than the high school-educated women. Excluding the non-contraceptors and thus excluding the difference attributable to the decision to use or not to use any contraception, column 2 of the table shows that again the high school-educated women faced a lower risk of conception--a 1.5 year longer expected time to conception--and the college-educated woman faced 0.8 year longer expected time to conception than the high school-educated woman.

As the regressions on which these estimates are based hold constant the desired fertility, much of the effect of income and time value differences on incentives to contracept are held constant. The assumption of a linear schooling effect which has the same gradient for all desired fertility levels seems excessively strict and should have been tested with interaction terms. Nevertheless, these results are among the stronger direct findings of a non-market productivity effect of schooling.

Another study which focuses on non-market benefits from schooling through consumption behavior is Hettich's (1972) essay. Hettich points out that if more educated consumers are more efficient in market search, they will reap a benefit in the form of lower prices for goods of a given quality or higher-quality purchases at given prices. Hettich performs an intriguing empirical exercise which is little more than illustrative, but is worthy of note. Using the annual buying guide of *Consumers Report*, the price differences for different brands of a given "quality" for many consumer goods are calculated. The price reduction realized by buying the least-expensive brand compared to the average-priced brand for that quality is averaged (unweighted) across goods for each Consumers Union "quality" level. These price differences range from 15 to 30 percent for different qualities, so the "informed" consumer can realize a substantial savings. With quite ad hoc assumptions about differences in search behavior by education level and average propensities to consume, these potential "savings" are attributed to schooling and added to the nominal income increments from schooling, raising estimated rates of return to college-level schooling from 14.5 percent to about 16.0 percent. While the estimates themselves are only suggestive, Hettich's imaginative effort should serve to encourage work on the effects of schooling in search behavior in consumer goods markets.[8]

Schooling and Intra-Family Behavior

In the preceding sections we considered evidence regarding the influence of schooling on non-labor-market productivity in investment and consumption activities. The impact of schooling within the family--in terms of the determination of the family structure per se, the interpersonal effects of the schooling level of one adult on the behavior or opportunity set of another, and the interpersonal effects of the schooling level of one generation on the behavior or opportunities of another--constitutes a separate, potentially important avenue of influence. Here too, for purposes of this paper, we wish to put aside the direct and indirect effects of schooling through labor market productivity or earnings and consider what evidence there is of non-monetary benefits from schooling.

The partitioning of effects into labor market and non-labor-market effects is even less clear in this line of research than in others. Many of the non-market effects may be interpreted as simply second-order or indirect effects of the primary influence of schooling on wage rates and, thereby, on labor supply. Indeed, optimization models of efficient use of time emphasize that, at the margin, the value or productivity of time is related across all uses of time (ignoring corner solutions, and given other usual assumptions). So if schooling affects the market wage rate, there will likely be repercussions on the amounts of time spent and on the productivity of time spent in other activities. These results of induced substitution and wealth effects are not what we have in mind in asking about non-monetary benefits from schooling. Nevertheless, they may be what we observe, unless they are intentionally and adequately controlled for.

Family Formation

Marital sorting is a good example of this difficulty. It is generally the case that the correlation between spouses in their education levels is at least +0.4 if the sample has not been censored on schooling level in some way. Long before social scientists thought to document the fact, it was well known by young people (and their parents) that going to school is a good investment in securing a desirable mate. As in the earnings-function literature, it really does not matter (for the private gains) whether schooling helps one attract a better mate by changing the content of what one has to offer, or by signaling to prospective mates the content which was there originally but not costless to discern. A more desirable mate--or the competitive advantage to attract one if you choose to--is surely one of the non-monetary benefits of schooling.

It can be argued that this positive correlation of own schooling and the schooling level of one's mate (which presumably is positively associated with the mate's overall desirability) is analytically on a par with the positive correlation of own schooling and earnings. In each of these two markets, investments in schooling pay a dividend. But does this imply anything about the effect of schooling on productivity in the marriage market (in either securing or in searching) over and above the indirect effect of schooling on labor market wages and hence on one's competitive position in the marriage market?[9] Perhaps the answer is implied by a revealed preference argument. In times past, when women had relatively little expectation of labor market careers, they still attended school. They, *not* their less-schooled counterparts, secured relatively highly schooled husbands. Why did these women succeed in attracting the highly schooled husbands? Physical proximity to these men or the signal content regarding the woman's parental wealth may be sufficient explanation; but it might also imply that these more desirable (higher earnings capacity) men felt the schooling augmented (or signaled) a higher non-labor-market productivity in the women. So long as the men (who were the market earners) did not select their mates solely on grounds of these women's market earning potentials, there is evidence here of *some* non-labor-market benefit from schooling. We cannot be sure whether it is a "direct effect" in the marriage market or, for women, an indirect effect though augmented (or signaled) non-market productivity, just as we can't distinguish the marriage market and labor market effects for men. (Of course, as women's market career orientation has risen, the sex role distinction utilized here has been attenuated, if not eliminated.)

If schooling facilitates a more nearly optimal sorting of men and women in the marriage market, then there are subsequent benefits in the form of 1) more stable marriages (see Becker, Landes, and Michael 1977: 1166-69) and so presumably more productive or privately beneficial marriages; and 2) if that optimal sorting increases positive assortative mating by inheritable IQ, geneticists tell us the genetic variance in IQ in the population will be greater, raising the proportion of the population in the upper tail of the distribution. (The lower tail is affected by another phenomenon.) Jensen (1969) indicates that, assuming an IQ assortative mating correlation of +0.6 and an inheritability of IQ of 0.8, there are about "twenty times as many persons above an IQ of 160 as we would find if there were no assortative mating for intelligence" (Jensen 1969: 37). That this represents a social benefit seems obvious; it is also a private benefit if the probability of parenting a genius is a "good." The measurement of non-monetary benefits of schooling here are not easily calculable, but they may be substantial both privately and socially if schooling facilitates positive assortative mating by intelligence.

Among Adults

Within the family one benefit of schooling on which correlational evidence exists is the impact of wife's schooling on husband's earnings. (Again, here the taxonomical distinction is blurred between labor market effects and non-labor-market effects.) Benham (1974) shows that wife's schooling raises husband's annual and weekly earnings by roughly half as much as does his own schooling. (His schooling raises his earnings about 7 percent; hers raises his earnings about 3.5 percent.) The effect here may be marriage market selectivity or non-market productivity. (See Welch [1974] for some suggestive evidence that at least a large part of the effect is selectivity.) There would be a social as well as private benefit if this finding were the result of non-market effects of the more educated wife on her husband's market skills, market-oriented motivation, or health (and thus earnings), while there would be only a private benefit (through competition in the marriage market) if it results exclusively from selectivity. In light of Benham's (and Welch's) statistical findings it is somewhat surprising that we do not find wife's education included (perhaps interacted with marital status) in more of the large earnings function estimates in the literature.

Similarly, there is evidence that wife's schooling increases the health level of her husband, holding constant his schooling, his prior health, age, wage, etc. (See Grossman [1976: 176, 189] as discussed above.) As health level as a teenager is held constant in Grossman's analysis, the selectivity interpretation seems less compelling here. Women appear to spend more on medical care than men. One explanation currently under study (Sindelar 1979) is that women provide their families with medical attention, so if there is non-market production of health with the wife (or more generally, any other family member) contributing to the production by other family members, the positive schooling effect of wife on husband's health may be reflecting differential productivity. I am aware of no study in which the effects of husband's schooling on wife's health have been investigated.

Between Generations

A related area in which considerable work has been done in recent years is the influence of family background variables--including parental schooling levels--on success, measured most often in terms of earnings. Parental schooling level affects positively the schooling level of offspring, even holding constant measures of the family income, and often measures of ability. There is, however, considerable inconsistency in the evidence about whether parental schooling affects earnings over and above its indirect effects through family income, offspring's schooling, and measured ability.

Several studies suggest that the effect of parental schooling on earnings, *ceteris paribus*, is statistically insignificant. Griliches (1976: 81-82) uses the young men's cohort from the NLS data and finds an insignificant effect. Sewell and Hauser (1975) use a survey of Wisconsin high school graduates of 1957, resurveyed in 1964 with additional information on 1957-67 earnings and income from state and federal (SSA) tax sources, and find insignificant effects of father's education on earnings in 1957 (1975: 73) or on earnings in 1966 (1975: 3). Leibowitz (1974b: 445-46) uses the high-ability sample of men from the Terman longitudinal study and finds an insignificant effect of mother's and of father's education on earnings in 1940 (at about age thirty) and by 1960 (at about age fifty), but a statistically significant effect of mother's schooling on earnings measured in 1950 (a 2.6 percent increase in earnings per year of mother's schooling). Finally, Taubman (1975: 58-63) uses the longitudinal NBER-TH sample and finds mother's schooling (or father-in-law's schooling!) a significant determinant, and father's (or mother-in-law's) schooling an insignificant determinant of 1955 earnings (when these men are about age thirty-three). Taubman finds all four "parental" schooling levels significantly related to earnings by 1969 (around age forty-seven).

Without attempting to reconcile these representative findings of the direct effect of schooling on the earnings of sons (I am unaware of any such studies for daughters), there is surely evidence that the schooling of parents influences the earnings of their children through indirect routes-- through an effect on the schooling level of their children, holding constant parental income. (For evidence for both sons and daughters, see Leibowitz's study of Terman data [1974b: 442, 443]. For evidence from a father-son sample from the NLS, see Parsons [1975]; and see Leibowitz's survey essay [1977]). This is a "non-monetary" effect of schooling, an effect over and above the effect on one's own earning potential.

The potential second-generation effect of schooling investment on earnings has led Lazear (1978) to question whether this effect is sufficiently large to justify social subsidies to schooling for one generation in behalf of the potential earnings of their offspring. Using the Michigan Dynamics panel (an eight-year panel) Lazear concludes that for whites there is no appreciable "underinvestment" in schooling by parents, but for blacks there is about a 2.3 year underinvestment in schooling by parents, who, in Lazear's scheme, ignore part of the payoff in the form of a lower cost of education to their sons--a sort of Ben-Porath technological effect one generation removed.[10]

A related line of research looks at the effects of parental schooling on measures of health status of children. Edwards and Grossman (1979) use the extensive Health Examination Survey of children ages six to eleven to attempt to disentangle the effects of genetic endowment and home environment on child health. With birth weight, mother's age at birth, congenital abnormalities, other proxies for genetic endowment, and family income held constant, parents' schooling is found to have positive and statistically significant effects on many measures of health in childhood and adolescence. Children and teenagers of more educated mothers have better oral health, are less likely to be obese, and are less likely to have anemia than children of less educated mothers. Father's schooling is less highly correlated with these measures of child health than is mother's schooling. The latter findings are important, because equal effects would be expected if the schooling variables were simply proxies for unmeasured genetic endowments.

Finally, there is a growing body of literature which addresses the question of the determinants and consequences of the time parents spend with their children. Here the role of the parent's schooling level is of central interest. In some studies schooling is used as a proxy for mother's time value, but the finding that mother's schooling is *positively* (not negatively) related to time spent with children is often explained by suggesting a technologically biased effect of a woman's schooling on productivity in parenting. If schooling raises productivity of time spent with her children *more* than it raises the productivity of time in the labor market, then the induced substitution effect will be toward more, not less, time spent with children. (Unless family income is held constant, the positive effect of schooling may also be reflecting a positive income effect on child care.)

A thorough discussion of these time allocation results is not presented here. Indirect evidence that more educated women spend relatively more time with their children (based on changes in their labor supply) is found in Leibowitz (1974). (See also Smith [1977]). More direct evidence, in the form of time budget data, shows that more educated women spend more time with their children (and per child) in physical and other care (Leibowitz [1974a]: 187-94). Gronau's (1976) findings for Israeli women show decreasing total time spent in work at home but increasing time spent in child care (insignificantly) with higher schooling levels.[11] Hill and Stafford (1974: 330-31) have more direct evidence that women of higher socioeconomic status spend significantly more time with preschool children than those of low SES. Finally, the most detailed and potentially useful information on time spent with children is from the new Michigan Time Use Survey. Hill and Stafford (1977) show with these data that more educated mothers spend more time with their children, but one of the most important categories of time use in terms of the mother's educational difference is time spent transporting children from place to place ("college educated women spend 30-40 minutes per week in child related travel, high school ... 20 minutes ... and ... grade school almost no time in child related travel" [1977: 16]). As Hill and Stafford suggest, this difference may reflect a difference in the provision of developmentally appropriate experiences or a suburban residence--two phenomena that we may wish to distinguish. In either case, identifying income, parental time value, and non-market productivity effects of schooling in a revealing manner is a major challenge which still lies ahead.

Conclusion

This survey has focused on economic research on only one type of potential non-monetary benefit of schooling, productivity in activities outside the labor market. Many studies that show behavioral correlates of schooling have not been surveyed here. These include relationships between schooling and criminal behavior (Ehrlich 1975), schooling and political behavior (Stapleton 1978), and schooling and religious behavior (Feldman and Newcomb 1969), and others. (See the essays in Withey [1971] and the discussion in Bowen [1977].)

Even within the narrow focus of this survey there is a wide variety of findings. These include several pieces of evidence that support the hypothesis that schooling raises productivity in non-labor-market activities and thereby provides non-monetary benefits. To characterize the nature of the evidence, it is more than suggestive but far from overwhelming in either its breadth or its precision of estimation.

Unless the well-documented effects of schooling on wages (and therefore on money income and relative shadow prices) are controlled for, one cannot draw inferences about productivity from correlations between schooling and measures of output or inputs. Even when these wage effects are adequately controlled, the inferences of changes in productivity are only valid in the context of an analytical model of production and assuming no systematic changes in preferences.

Several suggestions for further study have been made throughout this survey, and one will be stressed here. Investments in schooling are probably no more homogeneous than investments in corporate stocks and bonds. For some purposes it is convenient and sufficient to assume homogeneity in each of these investments; for other purposes attention must be paid to heterogeneity and the composition of the investment portfolio. If we are to make progress in identifying the impact of schooling on productive activities outside labor markets, we must begin to distinguish among types of schooling, including grade levels and types of curricula. We should see if data tell us it is permissible to lump grade school years and high school and college years together as a continuous accumulation; we should see if traditional college curricula and the recently expanding adult education curricula have discernibly different magnitudes of non-monetary benefits. If the degree of heterogeneity is substantial, then types of schooling will differ in their payoff in various market and non-market activities. As the proportion of one's lifetime spent in the labor market, in schooling, in convalescing, in childrearing, and in various other activities changes through time and over the lifetime, the economic incentives to hold one schooling investment portfolio or another will differ. I hope that, by the time someone next surveys this research area, there will be progress to report on this issue, as well as continued progress on the general topic.[12]

APPENDIX

Let the individual's utility function be $U = u(Z_1, Z_2, ..., Z_n)$ where the Z's are non-transferable non-market commodities produced by the individual according to the set of production functions: $Z_i = f_i(X_i, t_i)$, using market goods and services X_i and own non-market time t_i. The maximization of utility is constrained by the set of household production functions and a money income and time budget constraint, $wt_w + V = \Sigma X_i P_i$ and $T = t_w + \Sigma t_i$ respectively, with the usual definitions of wage rates w, time spent in the labor market t_w, property income V, the price of market goods P_i, and total time T.

In a single period framework, the constrained maximand is then

$$L = u(f_1(X_1, t_1), f_2(X_2, t_2), ..., f_n(X_n, t_n)) - \lambda (wT + V - \sum_i (P_i X_i + wt_i))$$

where λ is interpreted as the marginal utility of income. Differentiation of this now-familiar Lagrangian yields the individual's demand system.

1. If schooling affects only the individual's wage rate, we would modify L by writing w(s) and by adding money and time cost of school terms $P_s X_s + w(s)t_s$ (assuming the wage rate reflects the opportunity cost of schooling time). Then the first-order differentiation with respect to s yields

$$\frac{\partial w}{\partial s}(t_w) - \Pi_s = 0$$

where $\Pi_s = P_s(\partial X_s/\partial s) + w(\partial t_s/\partial s)$, the marginal cost of s. In equilibrium, the marginal cost equals the marginal benefit of s where the benefit is defined in terms of increased earnings.

2. If schooling also yields utility directly, then the utility function would include an additional term Z_s or simply s, and the first-order condition for the optimal amount of schooling would be

$$\frac{\frac{\partial u}{\partial s}}{\lambda} + \frac{\partial w}{\partial s}(t_w) - \Pi_s = 0$$

The benefits would include the dollar value of the consumption of s as well as its effect on earnings as a part of the total marginal benefit.

3. If schooling affected the yield on assets, then replace V by V(s) in the Lagrangian and an additional benefit term $\partial V/\partial s$ is added to the first-order condition. Likewise, if schooling affects the productivity of the non-market production functions f_i, then one would add to the marginal benefits this nonmarket productivity effect

$$\sum_i \frac{\partial u}{\partial Z_i} \frac{\partial Z_i}{\partial s} \Big/ \lambda.$$

Finally, if through market search s affected the market prices paid for goods and services, then $P_i(s)$ (including $P_s(s)$), so one final set of terms would be added: $\sum_i (\partial P_i/\partial s) X_i$. The first-order condition would then, in total, be

$$\frac{\sum\limits_{i}^{n} \frac{\partial u}{\partial Z_i} \frac{\partial Z_i}{\partial s}}{\lambda} + \frac{\frac{\partial u}{\partial s}}{\lambda} + \frac{\partial w}{\partial s}(t_w) + \frac{\partial V}{\partial s} + \sum\limits_{i} \frac{\partial P_i}{\partial s} X_i - \Pi_s = 0$$

| The dollar value of the increment in non-market production | The dollar value of the enjoyment of schooling per se | The incremental labor earnings | The incremental non-wage income | The effect on market prices (these terms would be negative if the effect is beneficial) | Marginal cost of s |

NOTES

1. Age at school completion has been rising and age at retirement falling, so the fraction of the lifetime spent in relatively fulltime labor market activities has declined. Also, average number of hours of work per week and weeks of work per year have declined. Of course, for married women these reductions have been offset by rising labor force participation rates, so the decline may be restricted to men.

2. Appendix, section 1, reflects the market wage effect of schooling where the non-monetary wage effect can be considered an issue in measuring the "wage" rate. Incidentally, the fringe benefits which are not paid on an hourly basis--benefits such as stock options or medical insurance premiums paid to employees who work in excess of, say, halftime--affect the total labor market remuneration but not the marginal remuneration, and hence may not affect the opportunity cost of time within a broad range of hours of work. I am not aware of any work done on this aspect of these non-wage payments.

3. Of course, even in labor market studies of schooling effects, other factors that affect productivity must be held constant and forces which cause wage rates to diverge from marginal value products must also be properly accounted for (i.e., such forces as monopoly/monopsony power, non-pecuniary dimensions of work, job-specific human capital investments, certain long-term contractual arrangements).

4. This effect exists despite the fact that her time value is not held constant in the regression. The finding may, in part, be due to the lower level of schooling of the wives in the sample. (There was no sample censoring on wife's schooling level.)

5. The propensity to migrate rises with education for a given age because the opportunity cost of migrating is linked to job experience. At a given age the more educated person has spent fewer years on the job and hence has lower opportunity costs of moving. The distance migrated rises with education, both because workers with more schooling have higher time costs of searching and seek to diminish waiting time by expanding the area of search, and because employers search in a wider area for jobs requiring more education.

6. If a woman is subject to a monthly risk of conception of p for a long time interval, she can expect to get pregnant in $1/p$ months, or in $1/(p \cdot 12)$ years. Based on actual measured use effectiveness, the risks associated with pill-IUD, condom-diaphragm, jellies-foams, rhythm-douche, and no contraception, expressed in expected time to conception in years: 83 years, 7 years, 5 years, 2.5 years, and 0.4 years, respectively.

7. The regression was run for each birth interval separately, for non-Catholic white and black women separately, and by age interval separately. The dependent variable was p_i, the monthly birth probability for the contraceptive technique used by a woman i in that interval. The independent variables were her education level expressed as two dummy variables DHS_i and $DCOL_i$ defined as equal to 1 if she had nine or more years of schooling and thirteen or more years of schooling, respectively. A third independent variable, N_i^*, was the total number of children the ith woman intended to have. In a separate regression the two school dummies were replaced by comparable variables reflecting the husband's education

level (DHSH$_i$ and DCOLH$_i$). In a third regression all four schooling dummies were used together with N_i^*. The effects shown in the table here convert the observed linear effects of the schooling dummies on p_i into their implied (nonlinear) effects on waiting time to conception, centered around the sample mean. For example, the coefficient on DHS$_i$ in the first regression was -.0427--the high school-educated woman has on average a monthly probability of conception 4.27 percentage points lower than the grade school-educated woman. Thus centered on the mean probability of .0654, that coefficient implies .0654+(.5)(.0427) = .08675 (or 0.96 years) compared to .0654-(.5) (.0427) = .04405 (or 1.89 years), or a difference in expected waiting time of 1.89 - 0.96 = 0.93 years, as shown in the table.

8. For further discussion and references to studies on the effects of education on "practical competence" for living, see Bowen 1977: Ch. 6, 7).

9. Of course, one could make the same logical argument in reverse-- schooling's direct effect is in securing a "better" mate who then contributes to one's earning capacity. But this we could test (and presumably reject) by looking at the effect of schooling on earnings for single men and women.

10. Lazear's estimates are intended to identify not the whole second-generation effect, but only the part apparently ignored by the parent--the part of the externality that is not internalized by the parent.

11. Gronau's comparable study of time allocation of American women yields little information on this issue. He is unable to specify whether child care is contained in the "work at home" or in the "leisure" component of time use (1977).

12. I wish to thank William Johnson, Sherwin Rosen, and Sharon Scott for helpful comments on an earlier draft of this paper.

REFERENCES

Becker, Gary S. 1964. *Human capital*. New York: Columbia University Press for NBER.

———. 1967. *Human capital and the personal distribution of income: an analytical approach*. Woytinsky Lecture, University of Michigan. (Also in Becker, *Human capital*, 2nd ed. [1975].)

———; Landes, Elisabeth M.; and Michael, Robert T. 1977. Economics of marital instability. *Journal of Political Economy* 85, 6 (December): 1141-87.

Becker, Gary S., and Stigler, George J. 1977. De gustibus non est disputandum. *American Economic Review* 67, 2 (March): 76-90.

Benham, Lee. 1974. Benefits of women's education within marriage. Pp. 375-89 in *Economics of the family: marriage, children and human capital*, ed. Theodore W. Schultz. Chicago: University of Chicago Press for NBER.

Ben-Porath, Yoram. 1967. The production of human capital and the life cycle of earnings. *Journal of Political Economy* 75, 1, part 1 (August): 352-65.

———. 1970. The production of human capital over time. Pp. 129-47 in *Education, income and human capital*, ed. W. Lee Hansen. New York: Columbia University Press for NBER.
Bowen, Howard R. 1977. *Investment in learning*. San Francisco: Jossey-Bass.
DaVanzo, Julie. 1976. Why families move: a model of the geographic mobility of married couples. Rand Publication #12-1972-DOL. September.
———. 1978. Repeat migration in the U.S.: who moves back and who moves on? Draft of Rand Publication #P-5961. June.
Duncan, Greg J. 1976. Earnings functions and nonpecuniary benefits. *Journal of Human Resources* 11, 4 (Fall): 462-83.
Edwards, Linda N., and Grossman, Michael. 1979. Children's health and the family. Mimeo.
Ehrlich, Isaac, and Ben-Zion, Uri. 1976. Asset management, allocation of time, and returns to savings. *Economic Inquiry* 14, 4 (December): 558-86.
Feldman, Kenneth A., and Newcomb, Theodore M. 1969. *The impact of college on students*. 2 vols. San Francisco: Jossey-Bass.
Freeman, R. B. 1978. The effect of trade unionism on fringe benefits. NBER Working Paper #292. October.
Greenwood, M. J. 1975. Research on internal migration in the U.S.: a survey. *Journal of Economic Literature* 3, 2 (June).
Griliches, Zvi. 1976. Wages of very young men. *Journal of Political Economy* 84, 4, part 2 (August): S69-86.
Gronau, Reuben. 1976. The allocation of time of Israeli women. *Journal of Political Economy* 84, 4, part 2 (August).
———. 1977. Leisure, home production, and work—the theory of the allocation of time revisited. *Journal of Political Economy* 85, 6 (December).
Grossman, Michael. 1972a. On the concept of health capital and the demand for health. *Journal of Political Economy* 80, 2 (March/April): 223-55.
———. 1972b. *The demand for health: a theoretical and empirical investigation*. New York: Columbia University Press for NBER.
———. 1976. The correlation between health and schooling. Pp. 147-211 in *Household production and consumption*, ed. Nestor E. Terleckyj. New York: Columbia University Press for NBER.
Heckman, James J. 1976. A life-cycle model of earnings, learning and consumption. *Journal of Political Economy* 84, 4, part 2 (August): S11-44.
Hettich, Walter. 1972. Consumption benefits from education. In *Canadian higher education in the seventies*, ed. Sylvia Ostry. Economic Council of Canada.
Hill, C. Russell, and Stafford, Frank P. 1974. Allocation of time to preschool children and educational opportunity. *Journal of Human Resources* 9, 3 (Summer).
———. 1977. Parental care of children: time diary estimates of quantity, predictability and variety. Mimeo.
Hyman, Herbert H.; Wright, Charles R.; and Reed, John Shelton. 1975. *The enduring effects of education*. Chicago: University of Chicago Press.

Jensen, Arthur. 1969. How much can we boost I.Q. and achievement? *Harvard Economic Review* 39 (Winter): 1-123.
Juster, F. Thomas. 1975. Appendix A: basic data. Pp. 397-404 in *Education, income and behavior*, ed. F. Thomas Juster. New York: McGraw-Hill for Carnegie Foundation and NBER.
Lando, Mordechai. 1975. The interaction between health and education. *Social Security Bulletin* 38, 12 (December): 16-22.
Lazear, Edward P. 1977. Education: consumption or production? *Journal of Political Economy* 85, 3 (June): 569-98.
―――. 1978. Intergenerational externalities. University of Chicago. Mimeo.
Leibowitz, Arleen. 1974a. Education and the allocation of women's time. Pp. 171-98 in *Education, income and human behavior*, ed. F. Thomas Juster. New York: McGraw-Hill for Carnegie Foundation and NBER.
―――. 1974b. Home investments in children. Pp. 432-52 in *Economics of the family: marriage, children and human capital*, ed. Theodore W. Schultz. Chicago: University of Chicago Press for NBER.
―――. 1977. Family background and economic success: a review of the evidence. Pp. 9-34 in *Kinometrics: determinants of socioeconomic success within and between families*, ed. Paul Taubman. Amsterdam: North Holland.
Lucas, Robert E. B.1977. Hedonic wage equations and psychic wages in the returns to schooling. *American Economic Review* 61, 4 (September): 549-58.
Machlup, Fritz. 1962. *The production and distribution of knowledge in the United States*. Princeton: Princeton University Press.
Mandell, Lewis. 1972. *Credit card use in the United States*. Ann Arbor: Institute for Social Research, University of Michigan.
Michael, Robert T. 1972. *The effect of education on efficiency in consumption*. New York: Columbia University Press for NBER.
―――. 1973. Education and the derived demand for children. *Journal of Political Economy* 81, 2, part 2 (March/April): S128-64.
―――. 1975. Education and fertility. Pp. 339-64 in *Education, income and human behavior*, ed. F. Thomas Juster. New York: McGraw-Hill for Carnegie Foundation and NBER.
―――, and Becker, Gary S. 1973. On the new theory of consumer behavior. *Swedish Journal of Economics* 75 (4): 378-96.
Mincer, Jacob. 1958. Investment in human capital and personal income distribution. *Journal of Political Economy* 66, 4 (July/August): 281-302.
―――. 1962. On-the-job training: costs, returns and some implications. *Journal of Political Economy* 70, 5, part 2 (October): 350-79.
―――. 1963. Market prices, opportunity costs, and income effects. In *Measurement in economics: studies in mathematical economics and econometrics in memory of Yehuda Grunfeld*, ed. Carl Christ et al. Stanford: Stanford University Press.
―――. 1970. Comments. Pp. 147-51 in *Education, income and human capital*, ed. W. Lee Hansen. New York: Columbia University Press for NBER.

Mitchell, Wesley, C. 1937. The backward art of spending money. In *The backward art of spending money and other essays*. New York: McGraw-Hill.
Parsons, Donald O. 1975. Intergenerational wealth transfer and educational decisions of male youth. *Quarterly Journal of Economics* 89 (November): 603-17.
Rosen, Sherwin. 1977. Human capital: a survey of empirical research. In *Research in labor economics* I, ed. Ronald G. Ehrenberg. Greenwich, Conn.: JAI Press.
Schultz, Theodore W. 1961. Investment in human capital. *American Economic Review* 51 (March).
———. 1963. *The economic value of education*. New York: Columbia University Press.
———. 1964. *Transforming traditional agriculture*. New Haven: Yale University Press.
———. 1967. The rate of return in allocating investment resources to education. *Journal of Human Resources* 7, 3 (Summer): 293-309.
Schwartz, Aba. 1971. On efficiency of migration. *Journal of Human Resources* 6, 2 (Spring): 193-205.
———. 1976. Migration, age and education. *Journal of Political Economy* 84, 4, part 1 (August): 701-20.
Sewell, William H., and Hauser, Robert M. 1975. *Education, occupation and earnings*. New York: Academic Press.
Sindelar, Jody. 1979. Why women use more medical care than men. Ph.D. thesis, Stanford University.
Smith, James P. 1977. Family labor supply over the life cycle. *Explorations in Economic Research* 4, 2 (Spring): 205-76.
Solmon, Lewis C. 1975. The relation between schooling and savings behavior: an example of the indirect effects of education. Pp. 253-94 in *Education, income and human behavior*, ed. F. Thomas Juster. New York: McGraw-Hill for Carnegie Foundation and NBER.
Stapleton, David C. 1978. Analyzing political participation data with a MIMIC model. Pp. 52-74 in *Sociological methodology*, ed. Karl F. Schleussler. San Francisco: Jossey-Bass.
Stigler, George J. 1961. The economics of information. *Journal of Political Economy* 69, 3 (June): 213-25.
Taubman, Paul. 1975. *Sources of inequality in earnings*. Amsterdam: North Holland.
Welch, Finis. 1974. Comment. Pp. 390-93 in *Economics of the family: marriage, children and human capital*, ed. Theodore W. Schultz. Chicago: University of Chicago Press for NBER.
Withey, Stephen B. 1971. *A degree and what else*. New York: McGraw-Hill for Carnegie Commission on Higher Education.

CHAPTER 7

The Monetary Returns to Education as Partial Social Efficiency Criteria

WALTER W. McMAHON AND ALAN P. WAGNER

Do the monetary rates of return to higher education, which tend to be lower than those for primary and secondary education, continue to make higher education, and particular types of higher education, efficient investments for individuals and for society?

To put the question this way is to put it very conservatively, for the total returns to education include the non-monetary private returns discussed in the preceding chapter. These include the contributions to efficiency in consumption, to asset management, to health, and to the education and health of one's children. There are, in addition, external benefits to the society, and significant contributions of education to intergenerational equity. The weight of the evidence in the preceding chapter is that the non-monetary private returns are positive, if the external benefits are assumed to be either positive or at least zero; therefore, if the monetary rates of return alone are higher than can be obtained on alternative investments, education definitely is a socially efficient investment.

But there are all kinds of education, and some kinds have higher rates of return than others, just as do some kinds of physical and financial assets. And all these rates vary somewhat over time. To address the question of whether or not education is worth the cost, it is *relative* rates of return that matter, as well as the longer-run lifetime rates that do not merely reflect transitory fluctuations. This chapter will focus on three issues. First, most attention will be given to rates of return to higher education, including whether the longer-term relative monetary rates of return to higher education are or are not falling over time. This issue has been raised by Freeman (1975, 1980) and challenged by Smith and Welch (1978) and Witmer (1980). Second, are rates of return at higher-cost types of public and private institutions as high as or higher than those available through attendance at lower-cost institutions? Finally, in which major fields or occupations are the rates of return highest in relation to alternative choices of fields?

Our system of higher education is based fairly heavily on the choices made by students and their families with respect to whether they should invest in education through choosing to attend college in relation to the alternatives, whether to choose a public or private institution of any given type, and what major occupational field to select. The expected private monetary rates of return offer efficiency criteria for assessing which of these private decisions are most worth the investment cost. The monetary rates studied in this paper do not include the non-monetary private benefits mentioned above, however, and hence are likely to understate total returns. Furthermore, some social benefit externalities are relevant to educational policy that is implemented as budget decisions are made within institutions and by state and federal educational policymakers. To partially accommodate the latter, some social rates of return (which reflect the full social costs and some of the social benefits) will also be discussed.

Part of the data for addressing these issues is from the College Placement Council (for starting salaries) and from *Current Population Reports*, but most is from a nationwide survey containing 2,765 usable responses from students and their families collected by the authors with the help of the National Institute of Education and the American College Testing Program. This latter survey, when weighted to be representative of the national student population, has the strong advantage of microeconomic data in that the costs for each student are extremely specific (including, for example, not just the formal tuition costs, but tuition net of scholarship aid to the specific student). This--as well as specific expected earnings and other earnings data--facilitates a calculation of a pure internal rate of return that is specific to each student. The resulting microeconomic rates of return permit controls for ability, and also facilitate comparisons of private and social rates of return among types of institutions as well as among occupational fields chosen.

The usual cross-section, and the more unusual expected rates of return reported in this chapter, are useful in analyzing the influences of expected returns and costs on the investment behavior of families. But to go beyond this and use them as criteria for analyzing the potential profitability of new decisions in the future requires the additional assumption, which we have explored (McMahon and Wagner 1981) that the real earnings expected by students in the future are reasonably accurate guides as to what those earnings will actually be. The cohort studied finished bachelor's degrees in 1976 and could have finished Ph.D.'s in 1980. Without some capacity to predict, there is no way of telling what their earnings will be, say, twenty-five years hence without waiting twenty-five years to see. Richard Freeman (1976) has predicted a permanent decline, beginning in the 1970's, in the returns to college graduates. Questions are raised about this below based on 1) the more recent evidence showing an absolute and a relative recovery in the job markets for college graduates in 1976-79, and 2) the mounting evidence that returns at the overtaking age 7-8 years after graduation should be used, allowing each new cohort to be better assimilated into the labor force. If these points are accepted, the result is an overcrowded new entrant rather than the "Overeducated American", mostly because of the passing demographic wave and the relatively transitory 1974-75 and 1980-82 inflationary spurts and recessions. The implication of this result is that rates of return based on the long-run age-earnings profiles are much more relevant to college investment decisions than are Freeman's rates of return that heavily reflect transitory dips in real starting salaries. The results of our study of expected starting salaries by occupation of white males (McMahon and Wagner 1981) and of females (Ferber and McMahon 1979) find these expectations to be reasonably accurate both in terms of job market trends and in terms of the relative peaking of age-earnings profiles.

Monetary Rates of Return over Time

Let us start with a brief summary of the method of calculating private and social rates of return to investment in higher education. This will be useful when interpreting the rates of return over time being found by others such as Smith-Welch (1978) and Joseph Liberman (1979) below, as well as for interpreting the monetary rates of return calculated for each family in our microeconomic data.

Rate of Return Concepts and Method

The monetary rate of return is merely a type of cost/benefit comparison. It can be visualized in Figure 1 as that internal rate of return that discounts the stream of net monetary benefits attributable to higher education (Area A) back to its present value and sets it equal to the stream of compounded investment costs (Area T + D). This would be a *private* rate of return, with the costs limited to the private tuition and foregone earnings costs net of term-time earnings borne by the student and his family and the benefits limited to those private returns received after taxes.[1] The *social* rate of return can also be visualized in Figure 1 by letting area A represent pre-tax earnings, including the value of output contributed to the society through taxes paid, and by letting costs include the full costs to society. Full costs would include the tuition subsidies received from tax funds, endowment funds, and other financial aids (Area S), as well as private costs. This should not imply that the incremental taxes paid by college graduates are a fully adequate measure of the external benefits of education, or of education's overall contribution to equity, but they are the best available measures of society's estimate of the value of these social contributions.

Returns to education
and costs

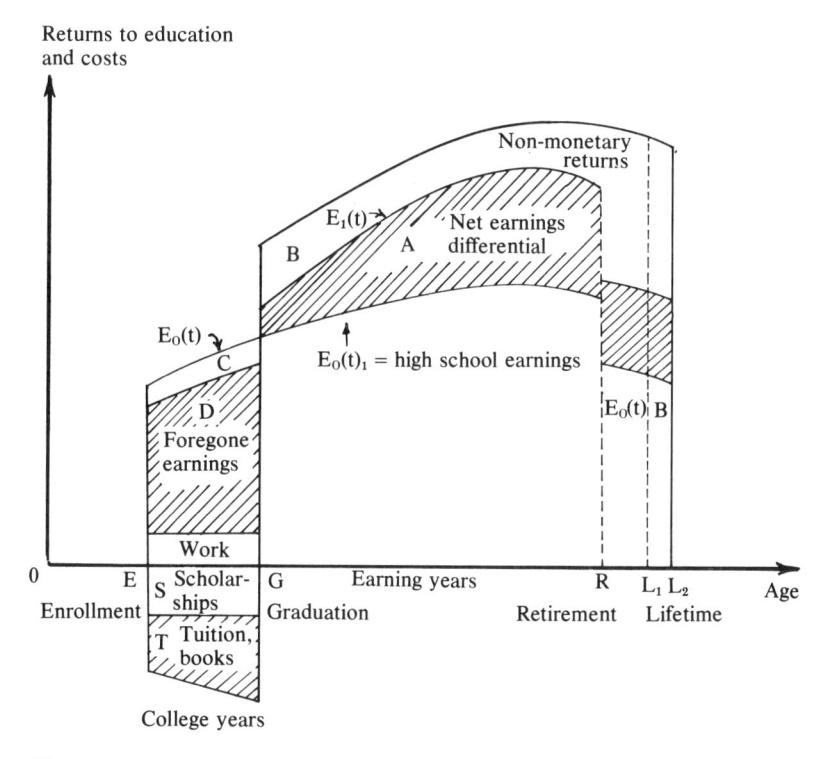

Figure 1. Investment in Higher Education and Private Returns over the Life Cycle

The non-monetary private returns discussed by Robert Michael are also illustrated in Figure 1, consisting of 1) those accruing to the student and his family following the investment made during the college years (Area B) and 2) the current consumption benefits he mentions that are enjoyed while attending college (Area C). Area B includes non-monetary job satisfactions, greater consumption efficiency during leisure hours, satisfactions during retirement, and the benefits of a longer life ($L_2 > L_1$), since more education of the individual and spouse are both known to contribute to better health and longer life.

Specifically, the monetary rate of return is calculated as the internal rate of return (r^*), that equates investment costs (on the left) to the present value of the benefits in the form of the net earnings differentials (on the right):

$$(1) \quad \sum_{t=1}^{G-E} I_t(1 + r^*)^t = \sum_{t=1}^{R-G} Y_t/(1 + r^*)^t$$

where Y_t = the annual net earnings differential attributable to higher higher education, $E_1(t) - E_0(t)$ in Figure 1,

I_t = annual investment costs consisting of tuition and fees, books, and foregone earnings, and

r^* = the private rate of return when Y_t is reduced by a 20% marginal rate for taxes on incremental earnings and I_t is net of earnings from part-time work (which does not represent study time invested) and net of scholarships and other financial aids.

r^* = the social rate when earnings, Y_t, are measured *before* taxes and investment costs, I_t, are net of part time earnings but do include total tax, endowment fund, and other eleemosynary institution subsidies.

These rates of return (r^*) are computed primarily in two ways in the new results reported below. Joseph Liberman's computation of rates of return over time uses estimates of earnings functions by regression methods for population subgroups based on Consumer Population Reports census data. The McMahon/Wagner computations are a pure internal rate of return solving Eq. (1) iteratively for each of the 2,765 student respondents in the sample, using a computer algorithm explained in more detail in Appendix A. These latter rates are computed to apply as of the date of graduation, with investment costs compounded forward at rate r^* to point G in Figure 1, so that students at different stages in their degree program can be grouped by degree objective and compared. These rates are also calculated to apply to the entire post-secondary degree program (e.g., bachelor's degree = four years, master's degree = five years, etc.), rather than to the marginal year or degree, on the assumption that most students contemplate the entire occupation-oriented degree program at one time.

Are Rates of Return Declining?

A definitive answer as to whether the decline in the economic rewards to a college education since the early 1970's is temporary or permanent must await the end of the 1979-82 recession and also the end of the wave entering the labor force due to the large population cohort born in the period surrounding 1957. But in the meantime considerable evidence has accumulated, and a tentative answer is available.

The issue raised primarily by Richard Freeman (1975, 1976, 1979), in the *Overeducated American*, is that the decline in the relative earnings of those finishing a college education since the mid-1970's is likely to persist for many years to come. He estimates that average social rates of return for all persons completing a bachelor's degree has fallen from the 11-14 percent range characteristic of 1950, 1960, and 1970 to 7.5-9.5 percent in the 1970's, presumably to persist into the 1980's.

Are Freeman's short-run rates of return, based on adjusting all points on the age-earnings profile by the percent change in starting salaries, relevant to this type of an investment decision? Or are the longer-run rates of return after each cohort is assimilated into the labor force the more relevant? We take the latter position. Evidence is presented below to this effect, followed by evidence indicating that these longer-run rates of return have not fallen. The longer-run rates of return relative to the rates of return obtainable on alternative investments are the test of whether the monetary returns to college education alone continue to be worth the investment cost.

Starting Salaries

Starting salaries are important in the three-equation recursive model that Richard Freeman (1976, Appendix B) uses to predict the continuing oversupply of college-trained manpower. Current starting salaries of college graduates relative to those of high school graduates (CSAL-ASAL) are the behavioral component in his first equation relating to the enrollment decision of potential freshmen. Smith and Welch (1978: 12) raise a question about the statistical role of the CSAL-ASAL variable, suggesting that, if it were deleted, the size of the 18-19-year-old population alone would offer nearly as good a statistical explanation of freshman enrollment (R_2 = .970, as opposed to .987). Smith and Welch (1978: 15) also suggest, on logical grounds, that "This kind of model is the antithesis of the full-career view ... where high entry wages signal *low* subsequent wages."

Our studies of the expectations of students about earnings after graduation (see McMahon and Wagner 1981) suggest that students may not be as myopic in their behavior as Freeman's CSAL-ASAL variable suggests. They have expectations of earnings twenty-five years after completion of their degree program that are quite realistic, when compared to the shape of age-earnings profiles at different degree levels and for different occupational choices seen in the long-run age-earnings profiles revealed in the 1970 census data. To be sure, blacks and females especially appear to be relatively optimistic, but this optimism could be interpreted as reflecting a long-run improvement in the job markets they face. Smith and Welch (1977, 1978) have argued that this improvement is due to an improvement in the quality of education received by blacks, and Freeman (1976) suggests that the relative improvements for both blacks and women have also been due to declining discrimination and changing sex roles.

For starting salaries, Freeman uses the College Placement Council data shown in Figure 2 below, which we have extended up through 1980 using the same source. This reveals a recovery or leveling out of the market for college graduates since 1975. There have been large increases in starting salaries in all fields shown, but when salaries are adjusted for the extraordinary inflation rates in 1973-74 and in 1979-81, those in some occupational fields are not keeping up. Although the 1971-72, 1975, and 1979-82 recessions coincided with the entry into the job market of the largest and most educated population cohort in U.S. history, there was a stabilization of starting salaries following 1975 at the level characteristic of the 1960-67 period. Comparing 1975-80 to 1960-67, no permanent trend in the average real starting salaries of college graduates is evident.

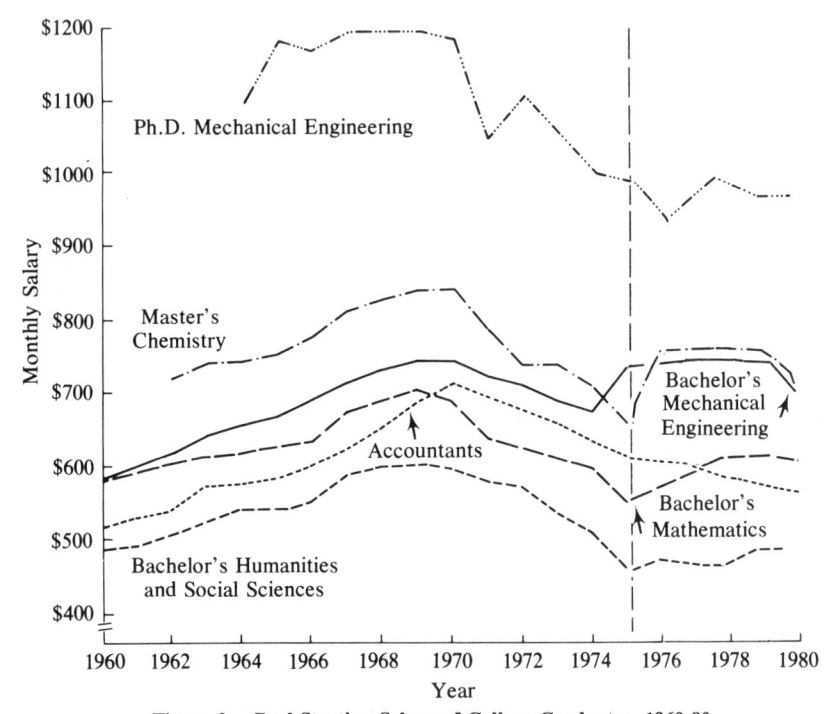

Figure 2. Real Starting Salary of College Graduates, 1960-80

Source: 1960-75: Freeman (1976: 11); 1976-80: College Placement Council July Surveys (1980). All are in 1967 dollars, deflated by the Consumer Price Index.

Ratio of Mean Income of College to High School Graduates

While the job market was absorbing this wave of new entrants during the 1970's, the relative earnings of college graduates aged 25-34 did decline from 1969 to 1974, as can be seen in Table 1. But note the stabilization and partial recovery from 1975 through 1977. This is indicative of some recession- and inflation-induced effects on new entrants. The stagflation of 1979-81 makes it harder to absorb the tail end of the large wave of

Table 1. Ratio of Mean Income of College to High School Graduates

All workers Ages	67	68	69	70	71	Year 72	73	74	75	76	77	78	79
25-34	1.33	1.32	1.33	1.33	1.27	1.22	1.19	1.15	1.19	1.26	1.21	1.24	1.22
35-44	1.53	1.47	1.58	1.54	1.55	1.55	1.52	1.55	1.56	1.55	1.48	1.47	1.52

Source: *Current Population Reports*, Series P-60.

new entrants, and is likely to have some effects similar to those shown in the inflation-recession of 1974-75.

These data show that there has not yet been a trend-type decline since 1968 in the relative market value of a college eduation for those aged 35-44, the age range that most reflects the greater peaking of the college-level age-earnings profiles. The huge wave of new entrants into the 25-34 age group during 1971-79 therefore has not yet affected the premium paid to college graduates in older age groups, and there is hope that before it does so, the wave can be assimilated.

Rates of Return to Elementary School, High School, and College, Calculated at the Overtaking Age

All of this suggests that estimates of returns to investments in education at each level should not be based exclusively on starting salaries, but should instead be based on returns at the overtaking age and/or later points in the age-earnings profile. This comes closer to a more stable long-run rate of return after a bulge of new entrants has been more adequately assimilated.

An interesting study by Joseph Liberman (1979) allows for this assimilation and for net post-schooling investment by calculating rates of return using earnings functions at the overtaking age. The concept of the "overtaking age," as originally introduced by Jacob Mincer (1974: 109), suggests that post-school investments related to job search and learning through experience on the job keep the individual's observed wage below the wage predicted from his schooling for 7-9 years. As the return from post-school learning on the job grows, the actual observed wage grows as well, finally overtaking and exceeding the schooling-predicted wage. For elementary, high school, and college graduates, this schooling-predicted wage could be read off his or her earnings profile the eighth year after his or her formal education ends.

To estimate marginal rates of return at the overtaking age, Liberman fits Jacob Mincer's "expanded schooling model" with cross-section *Current Population Reports* data for males. Mincer's expanded schooling model contains not only schooling (S) and years of work experience (t and t_2) terms, but also a squared schooling term (S^2) and an interactive schooling-times-work-experience term, as shown in the footnote to Table 2. Joseph Liberman's cross-section regression results using this model for each year from 1958 through 1976 fit the data quite well, with all R^2 greater than .96 and all regression coefficients significantly different from zero. The method of estimating the marginal rates of return for elementary school, high school, and college is to first obtain the derivative of the regression equation (one for each year) with respect to S as shown at the top of Table 2, and substituting the 8, 12, and 16 year levels of interest while holding t constant at the overtaking age of 8 years.

The portion of Joseph Liberman's more extensive results which are most relevant to the questions raised in this chapter are shown in Table 2, which he has very kindly given us permission to reproduce. The results are probably most comparable to a social rate of return, since pre-tax income is used in the regressions, although some inaccuracy is introduced by the inclusion of property income and the lack of specific investment-cost data. They show the social rate of return to education in 1976 at the overtaking age (i.e., for all who left school in 1968) to be 9.7 percent for elementary school leavers, 12.4 percent for high school graduates, and 15.2 percent for college graduates. This is not a clear test of Freeman's hypothesis because the rates of return refer to those who left school in 1968 and hence had been in the labor force for eight years in 1976. But it is notable that these longer-run rates of return, which are more significant because they do not depend so exclusively on the more transitory movements in starting salaries, *have not declined for either high school or college graduates* since 1958. Tight monetary policies and high interest rates used to fight inflation in 1981-82 continue to hold unemployment high, *especially* for those with less education. But the sources of these transitory business-cycle effects on job markets do not lie within the educational system, or dictate that longer-run rates of return are falling. They also mean that on efficiency grounds there is no case that real investment in education per high school or college-age young adult should be cut back.

Microeconomic Internal Rates of Return

The results reported above can be compared to the microeconomic internal rates of return computed for each student in our national sample. Those rates reflect very specific individual cost data, as mentioned above, for each student graduating in 1976. The sample was weighted to be representative of the entire population of U.S. students, as shown in Appendix B. For comparison to the results obtained by Joseph Liberman, we have computed the "realized" social rate of return for students in our

Table 2. Estimates of the Marginal Rates of Return to Elementary School, High School, and College

(Derived from the derivative of the Expanded Model* regression results at eight years of experience: $r_m = \frac{d \ln Y_t}{dS} = \hat{b}_1 + 2\hat{b}_2 S + 8\hat{b}_3$)

Year	Elementary school (8 years) (1)	High school (12 years) (2)	College (16 years) (3)
1958	.1104	.1264	.1424
1961	.1102	.1262	.1422
1963	.1069	.1205	.1341
1964	.1075	.1203	.1331
1966	.0981	.1165	.1349
1967	.0994	.1186	.1378
1968	.0892	.1156	.142
1969	.0988	.1206	.1414
1970	.0973	.1205	.1437
1971	.1006	.1254	.1502
1972	.0939	.1195	.1451
1973	.1029	.1205	.1381
1974	.1070	.1230	.1390
1975	.1023	.1255	.1487
1976	.0976	.1248	.1520

Year of schooling	Mean	Standard deviation	Coefficient of variation
Elementary school	.1015	.0061	.0601
High school	.1216	.0035	.0288
College	.1416	.0057	.0403

* $\ln Y_t = \hat{a} + \hat{b}_1 S + \hat{b}_2 S^2 + \hat{b}_3 St + \hat{b}_4 t + \hat{b}_5 t^2 + \hat{u}$

160 *Monetary Returns to Education*

national sample using 1970 census data on earnings at each age adjusted by a 2 percent per year growth factor for persons of the same sex, race, and occupational choice. The 13.3 percent for white males shown in Table 3 compares to the 15.2 percent obtained by Joseph Liberman (in Table 2) for 1976. The earlier cohorts of blacks in the census data did less well. This 13.3 percent long-run rate of return for white males that we obtain is also considerably above the 7.5 percent-9.5 percent (short-term) rate of return obtained by Richard Freeman, as indicated above.

Table 3. Long-Run Expected and Realized Social Rates of Return to Bachelor's Degree

	Expected rate of return, 1976	Realized rate of return, 1976
All males	17.0%	13.0%
White	17.0%	13.3%
Black	17.1%	8.3%

The expected rate of return in Column 1 of Table 3 reflects the real earnings students expect to receive twenty-five years later. The latter was used as a benchmark to estimate their entire expected age-earnings profile by the method described in Appendix A. These expected rates of return also should be interpreted as applying to 1976 bachelor's degree graduates. The 17.1 percent that we obtain for blacks includes optimistic expectations by blacks, based on trends in the college-educated labor market that raise their expected rates above those found in the cross-section census data. The 17.0 percent for white males compares to the 15.2 percent obtained by Joseph Liberman for 1976 in Table 2, perhaps reflecting some optimism about growth in earnings, but also reflecting what we have found to be relatively realistic expectations about starting salaries (See McMahon and Wagner 1981: 280-81).

Over Time, Are the Returns Worth the Cost?

We conclude that the returns *are* worth the cost. Realized rates of return have remained in the 13.3-15.2 percent range throughout the 1970's, when estimated either at the overtaking age or using the entire cross-sectional age-earnings profile. Expected rates of return in 1976 were as high or higher. All of these are relatively high when compared to the average rate of return on financial assets as measured by the New York Stock Exchange Composite Index, as can be seen in Figure 3. These longer-run rates of return to a college education have also been stable

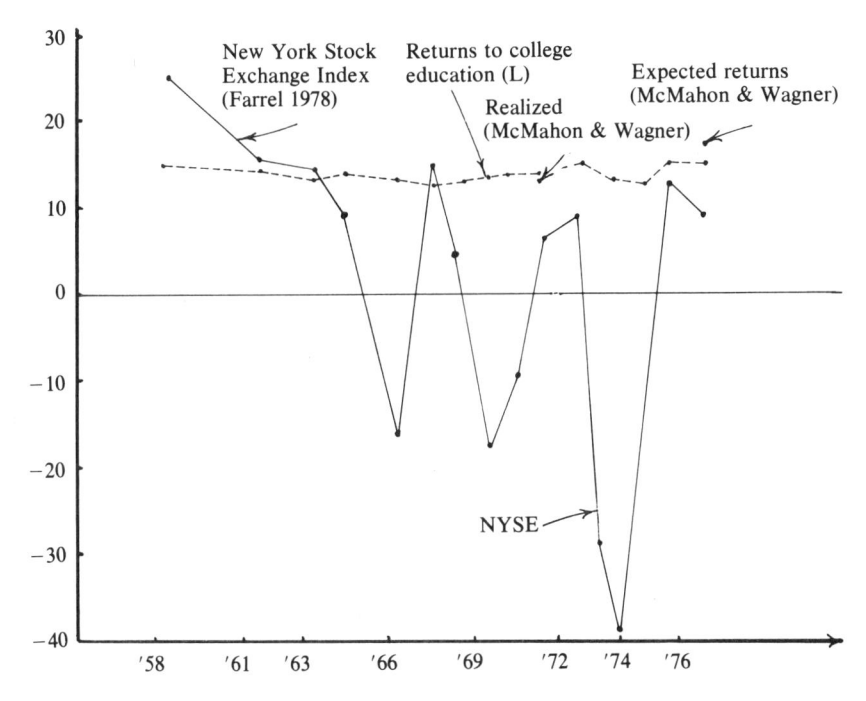

Figure 2. Long-Run Rates of Return to College and
Rates of Return to Financial Assets

and, as Joe Liberman (1979: 22) says, "The risk is minimal." A final answer will not be available from the data until several years after the entry of the large 1979 college population cohort into the labor market, but the evidence currently available is very suggestive.

Finally, the consideration of monetary returns understates total returns to the extent that there are significant non-monetary returns such as those considered in the preceding chapter.

Monetary Rates of Return by Type of Institution

Higher education in the U.S. involves a diverse set of institutions, each providing a unique set of education programs at widely different costs. An examination of rates of return across the broad types of institutions which takes into account their individual cost differences net of scholarships (for the private rates of return), as well as the differences in their expected earnings (which do predict earning differences and earning trends reasonably well), provides interesting insights as to where further investment may be most socially efficient.

Table 4. Annual Private and Social Investment Costs and Expected Earnings of White Males by Four-Year Institution Type and Control, in 1979 Dollars
(standard errors, computed as $s/\sqrt{n}$, are shown in parentheses below each mean)

Cost, return component	Research universities Public	Research universities Private	Comprehensive four-year colleges Public	Comprehensive four-year colleges Private	Liberal arts colleges Private
		Mean private investment costs			
Total private costs	$4,115 (180)	$3,506*	$4,117 (152)	$4,271 (189)	$4,642
Tuition and fees	801 (15)	1,001*	926 (61)	1,061 (91)	1,565 (131)
Books and supplies	287 (23)	234*	244 (12)	178 (6)	222 (20)
Foregone earnings net after taxes	3,773	3,773	3,773	3,773	3,773
Net of term-time earnings[b]	3,214 (113)	3,773*	3,140 (135)	3,147 (157)	3,140 (145)
Grants and scholarships (-)	188 (76)	1,502*	198 (46)	115 (75)	284 (122)

Institution type and control[a]

			Mean social investment costs	
Total social costs	$7,444 (175)	$8,027*	$6,676 (156)	$5,999 (303)	$6,498 (140)
Instructional costs per FTE	3,000 (120)	3,077*	2,333 (71)	1,730 (97)	2,210 (90)
Books and supplies	287 (23)	234*	244 (12)	178 (6)	222 (20)
Foregone earnings before taxes	4,716	4,716	4,716	4,716	4,716
Net of term-time earnings[b]	4,157	4,716*	4,083	4,090	4,083
			Mean expected salary	
Expected monetary returns					
Starting	$17,716 (777)	$20,025*	$17,119 (907)	$16,543 (486)	$15,556 (329)
In 25 years	36,518 (1,958)	33,375*	29,209 (1,657)	32,905 (1,440)	22,688 (938)

*Fewer than 6 respondents in cell
[a]Institutional Groups by Carnegie Commission classification
[b]"Net of term time earnings" calculated as gross earnings, over 40 weeks, *less* earnings from part-time job during school year.
Source: ACT College Investment Decision study sample of 2,765 students, contacted in early 1972, who could have completed bachelor's degrees in 1976.

Expected rates of return calculated for each respondent in our nationwide sample of 1976 college graduates reflect very specific individual tuition costs net of scholarships; they also reflect their expected earnings. To ensure the accuracy of the financial data, respondents provided their estimates of financial aid funds received from eight possible sources and of gross tuition. Those who returned the original questionnaire with incomplete financial data received a one-page supplement requesting the information. The student expense and financial aid responses of these students appear to be quite reasonable in relation to the information available from published college catalogues, other student surveys, and financial aid program data (see McMahon and Wagner 1973; Wagner and Tenison 1976).

Since it appears that students estimate their returns among occupations fairly accurately (McMahon and Wagner 1981), and since breakdowns of earnings by type of institution which are not available in census data also reflect differences in choice of occupational field objectives, it is reasonable to assume that students' expected earnings will reflect many differences in actual earnings of graduates attributable to the type of institution attended.

The results reported here in Tables 4 and 5 on costs, expected earnings, and rates of return all control for race and sex differences by focusing on white males (although the rates for blacks and females also were computed). In reporting rates of return by type of institution, we also attempt to control for the self-selection by higher-ability advanced-degree-seekers at research universities and liberal arts colleges by controlling for differences in ability by reporting results by ability quartiles, using composite test scores on the ACT assessment,[2] as shown later in Table 5. This is an important control, although it does not control for all variaton in this factor. It serves to partially eliminate entering ability as a factor, and to control for the selectivity (i.e., non-price rationing) of the more prestigious institutions, which would otherwise distort the results. The analysis thereby concentrates more closely on the differences in the costs and quality of the education added.

Cost Differences

The variation in costs, and returns, averaged within the Carnegie Commission's four-year institution type and control classes is evident in Table 4.[3] All cost and return data have been re-expressed in 1979 dollars. "Private costs," referring to the costs actually incurred by the student and his family during the school year, are shown in the first row. Composed of tuition and fees, books and supplies, and net after-tax earnings foregone (i.e., part-time earnings have been subtracted) *less* any grant and scholarship aid, the average annual costs faced by white males at private liberal arts colleges were the highest, at $4,642. Families with white male students at public research universities invested a smaller average of $4,115 for the academic year. Surprisingly, white males attending private research universities invested the least ($3,506), due to larger scholarships and tuition waivers, but the sample in this cell is small. The private costs at private liberal arts colleges are the highest. White males attending comprehensive colleges, whether public *or* private, and those attending public research universities incurred very similar middle-range investment costs of $4,115 to $4,271, however.

Social costs, which include the full costs of instruction, reveal a different picture. Looking across the middle row of Table 4, they are highest at private research universities ($8,027, although the sample in this cell is small) and next-highest at the public research universities ($7,444). These figures reveal a pattern similar to Bowen's (1980) educational expenditure per student unit where he also finds that instructional costs are highest at research universities and lowest at comprehensive colleges.[4] The research institutions have larger instructional cost per average student FTE than do other institutions, as might be expected, but the full instructional costs at private and public research institutions are remarkably similar at about $3,000 per student. Social costs at liberal arts colleges and at four-year comprehensive colleges are lowest ($6-6,700) and remarkably similar.

The higher private costs at the liberal arts colleges and the higher social costs at the private and public research universities can be justified, however, if there are also differences in the returns that follow this pattern.

Expected Earnings

As the last two rows in Table 4 reveal, those attending the larger private research institutions expect to earn several thousand dollars more upon completion of a bachelor's degree, and those attending the public research institutions expect to earn $1-2,000 more than those attending private liberal arts colleges or private comprehensive four-year institutions. The low expected earnings for those in liberal arts colleges may be misleading, however, since those with a terminal bachelor's degree objective shown in this table may not be typical. It will be interesting to see, in a rate-of-return calculation that also shows those planning advanced degrees and includes a control for ability, whether or not the larger expected returns are worth the larger costs.

Earnings expected in twenty-five years by white males attending research universities, *both public and private*, on the average are also significantly larger. This may reflect the effect of faculties who are actively contributing to new knowledge, better libraries, computers, and lab facilities, as well as screening and credentialing. The social costs are lower in the four-year comprehensive public and private colleges, but the returns are also lower. A rate of return calculation can best reveal whether investment at the lower- or at the higher-cost institutions is more advantageous.

Private Rates of Return

Table 5 combines investment-cost differences, earnings differences, and differences in the growth of earnings over the life cycle in one summary statistic, a long-run internal rate of return. We have sought to control for the student ability mix among institutions, and hence to some extent for equity considerations consistent with the first and lowest-level humane growth criterion suggested in Chapter 1, by reading across the rows of the table. The overall result is not a simple statement that rates of return are high at some types of institutions and low at others, but that where the highest rates of return are found depends upon the student's ability and degree-level or occupational field objective.

Private rates of return for white males, irrespective of ability level or degree objective, are almost always several percentage points higher at public institutions and at private research universities (although the latter cells are small) than at private four-year institutions and liberal arts colleges. Considering only the top ability quartile and students with advanced degree objectives, however, the liberal arts colleges do very well, with expected rates of return in the 9-11 percent range—very similar to the rates for comparable students at public four-year and public research universities. The higher private rates of return at private research universities undoubtedly reflect the large tuition waivers received by the few students in these cells, all of whom were in the top two ability quartiles. The large expansion of economic opportunity grants since the Education Amendments of 1972 and 1980 will serve to further increase private rates of return by reducing private investment costs, especially at private four-year institutions and liberal arts colleges, which would operate to offset the modest comparative advantage shown by the private rates in the public sector.[5]

A second finding emerges from Table 5. At the bachelor's level, private rates of return tend to be highest at comprehensive colleges, while at the doctor's/professional degree level the highest rates are exhibited at research universities. Consider, for example, white males planning to complete only a bachelor's degree who largely come from the third ability quartile. Within this lower ability group, the private rates of return are relatively high (25 percent), but only at comprehensive four-year colleges. Students expecting advanced degrees, and who are in the top ability quartile, anticipate private rates of return in the 10.2-11.9 percent range if they are completing their undergraduate program of study at research institutions or public four-year institutions, but not at private comprehensive colleges that may have more of a trade-school orientation.

Finally, students attending liberal arts colleges expect to fare somewhat less well than their peers, as shown in most degree and ability groups in the last column of Table 5. This may reflect the heavier mix of scientific, social scientific, and humanities fields chosen, as compared to the more vocationally oriented fields offered especially at the bachelor's level at the four-year comprehensives.[6]

Social Rates of Return

The expected social rates of return are shown in the bottom half of Table 5. These rates reflect the measurable part of the payoff to society

Table 5. Expected Rates of Return on Investment of White Males by Ability, Degree Level, and Four-Year Institution Type and Control (standard errors, computed as $s/\sqrt{n}$, are shown below each mean)

Ability quartile[a] and degree level	Institution type and control[b]				
	Research universities		Comprehensive four-year colleges		Liberal arts colleges
	Public	Private	Public	Private	Private
Mean private rate of return						
All ability quartiles					
Bachelor's	19.0	26.0*	21.0	18.5	8.7
	(1.2)	(1.8)	(2.0)	(2.4)	
Master's	9.6	17.3*	6.2	-.7	7.7
	(1.4)	(2.4)	(1.6)	(2.4)	(.6)
Doctor's/professional	19.3	11.6	9.0	-1.8	10.3
	(4.1)	(.2)	(1.0)	(4.1)	(1.7)
Top ability quartile					
Bachelor's	16.4	26.0*	19.9		-8.9
	(3.5)	(1.3)			(5.4)
Master's	8.7	23.0*	9.7		11.0*
	(2.9)	(3.0)			(1.8)
Doctor's/professional	10.2	11.9	11.4	-11.9	9.3
	(1.6)	(.1)	(1.4)	(5.2)	(2.0)
Second ability quartile					
Bachelor's	19.0		15.0	5.2	
	(1.9)		(2.0)	(4.0)	
Master's	8.6	14.5*	3.9	6.1	8.1
	(2.4)	(2.1)	(2.6)	(1.6)	(1.2)
Doctor's/professional	10.6	8.0*	6.8		
	(4.0)	(1.8)	(2.5)		
Third ability quartile					
Bachelor's	20.6		27.2	25.0	16.1
	(1.7)		(3.8)	(2.3)	(1.1)
Master's	12.4		7.4	4.3	7.5
	(.6)		(.7)	(3.6)	(.4)
Doctor's/professional	38.4		1.3		
	(11.1)		(.3)		

Table 5. (Continued)

Mean social rate of return

All ability quartiles					
Bachelor's	15.5	18.0*	17.7	15.9	7.1
	(1.6)		(1.6)	(1.7)	(2.3)
Master's	8.0	15.0*	4.8	-1.4	6.9
	(1.4)	(2.4)	(1.5)	(2.3)	(.4)
Doctor's/professional	17.9	10.5	9.3	-5.0	10.1
	(4.1)	(.2)	(.8)	(4.4)	(1.9)
Top ability quartile					
Bachelor's	12.1	18.0*	16.1		-11.4
	(2.8)		(1.7)		(4.1)
Master's	6.9	21.0*	7.7	-9.0	9.1*
	(2.7)		(3.0)		(1.4)
Doctor's/professional	8.9	10.81	8.7	-15.6	9.2
	(1.5)	(.1)	(.8)	(5.2)	(1.8)

*Fewer than 6 respondents in cell
[a]Ability quartiles established from the distribution of ACT composite test scores within the sample.
[b]Institutional groups by Carnegie Commission classification.
Source: ACT College Investment Decision study sample of 2,765 students, contacted in early 1972, who could have completed bachelor's degrees in 1976.

from the investment, and thus require measures of full social costs, including the costs of public and private tuition subsidies at each institution, as well as the full returns before taxes.

Perhaps the most significant finding is that the social rates of return tend to be highest for students seeking master's, doctoral, and professional degrees who also choose public or private research universities or liberal arts colleges for their undergraduate work. This is a pattern that emerged among the private rates, and therefore suggests that the public subsidies that affect the private rates do not distort private investment decisions.

For those seeking terminal bachelor's degrees, the social rates of return are highest at the comprehensive four-year colleges (and at the private research universities, but there the sample is small). This pattern also is similar to that found for the private rates.

Therefore, the lower costs at the comprehensive four-year colleges do show up in higher social rates of return *at the bachelor's level*, whereas the higher costs at the research universities and liberal arts colleges seem to be warranted by the returns expected by those whose objective is an advanced degree.

Overall this evidence suggests that the private institutions are not at so great a competitive disadvantage with public institutions as the differences in tuition would imply. This is especially true at private research universities when private costs are lowered through tuition waivers and grants. But even without sizable grant aid, the comprehensive four-year colleges have a competitive advantage at the bachelor's level (although the private comprehensives are quite inefficient in serving students who have advanced-degree objectives). The private liberal arts colleges are both privately and socially competitive in serving students who anticipate graduate study. The higher costs at the research institutions are covered by higher expected earnings, perhaps because of the effects of institutional quality, credentialing, and specialized fields of study.

Monetary Rates of Return by Intended Occupation

Each year, college students also choose fields of study leading toward particular occupational goals. To consider expected earnings, as we have done recently (see McMahon and Wagner 1981), is not enough. Expected earnings are higher in some fields, as well as at higher degree levels. But costs there are often also higher. An examination of *rates of return* by degree level and by intended occupation that *takes into account* not only the differences in earnings but also the cost differences can provide much better insight into which degree levels in which fields are likely to be the best candidates if expansion there is to be socially efficient.

Private Rates of Return

Separate occupation-specific rates are most justifiable for those occupations that require a significant and specialized human capital investment acquired through formal education and to some extent through experience (e.g., doctors, lawyers, engineers, architects). In these occupations, once a significant portion of the investment is made, it is costly to switch later--a locking-in process that has been called a "putty-clay" effect in capital theory. For some other occupations, inter-occupational mobility may be easier and a means of raising the returns realized on earlier investment (e.g., liberal arts graduates may be selected as managers on the job). In the case of these occupations, the calculated rate of return *to education per se* is likely to be distorted. But with the two qualifications in mind—that for some occupations specialized education is less important, and that nonmonetary returns to education and social benefit externalities must still be added—this rate-of-return test of which kinds of education at least equal the rate of return to financial assets, and hence are socially profitable, can be applied.

The expected private rates of return calculated for each white male respondent are averaged within occupational groups in Table 6. Those fields revealing the highest rates of return appear toward the top of the table; those with lower rates appear toward the bottom.

Table 6. Expected Private Rates of Return of White Male Students by Intended Occupation and Degree Objective
(standard errors, computed as $s/\sqrt{n}$, are shown below each mean)

Occupation	Associate	Bachelor's	Master's	Doctor's/ professional
Health				
Doctor, dentist				14.0
				(1.2)
Health technician		11.6		
		(3.2)		
Pharmacist		23.3		4.4
		(1.9)		(4.8)
Lawyer				16.4
				(2.0)
Engineering-technical	41.5	28.2	10.3	8.2
	(7.5)	(2.2)	(.8)	(.8)
Architect		26.6	12.7	
		(2.4)	(1.7)	
Engineer		25.5	12.0	8.6
		(2.9)	(1.1)	(.5)
Electrical technician	48.2	45.9		
	(4.1)	(9.8)		
Business	26.7	22.4	11.9	
	(1.7)	(1.7)	(.9)	
Accountant	27.2	22.8	12.7	
	(1.8)	(1.7)	(1.5)	
Manufacturing manager		28.0	11.9	
		(7.4)	(1.1)	
Sales, retailing		17.9		
		(1.6)		
Other professional		10.3	8.8	3.1
		(1.7)	(1.0)	(1.5)
Clergyman				-1.6
				(3.0)
Natural scientist			8.9	4.5
			(3.0)	(2.8)
Social scientist				-.1
				(4.0)
Education		12.3	1.6	3.9
		(1.7)	(1.6)	(1.9)
Elementary & secondary teacher		12.3	.8	1.8
		(1.7)	(1.6)	(2.7)
College professor				5.4
				(1.3)

Source: same as Table 5.

First, there are wide differences in the implicitly expected rates of return to college investment by occupational fields for white males. The rates are highest in medicine, law, and engineering-technical fields, in spite of the higher costs, and lowest in the clergy, natural science, social science, and education fields, where there have been somewhat larger supplies in relation to the effective demands. Aspiring doctors, pharmacists, and engineering-technicians exhibit expected private rates of return in the 14-28 percent range, while the rate for clergymen is low, illustrating the fact that monetary rates of return do not include social benefit externalities. For future doctors and lawyers, the private rates fall in the 14.0 to 16.4 percent range, the highest among advanced-degree-seekers. In contrast, the expected private rates of return to fields other than medicine, law, and engineering at the doctoral level ranges from -1.6 to 5.4 percent. Many of the latter students will confront a market in which there are few opportunities other than academic employment, while at the same time federal support for research is being cut.

Second, the usual pattern of lower rates of return at the more advanced levels can be observed within every field. However, slightly higher rates for professionally oriented degrees can be seen at the doctoral level for elementary and secondary school teachers (where pay scales and administrative appointments reflect advanced degrees), in addition to medicine and law. In the other cases, the rates fall with more advanced schooling, due primarily to rising foregone earnings costs.

Third, the private rates of return are generally highest where expected earnings are highest. For example, the quite high (28.2 percent) average expected private rate of return among white males in engineering-technical fields at the bachelor's degree level reflects their relatively high estimated starting and twenty-five-year-later salaries ($19,914 and $34,355, in 1980 dollars). Business students represent an exception, where expected earnings somewhat lower than this, combined with lower private investment costs (reduced further through part-time earnings, grants, and scholarship aid), produced a relatively high expected private rate of return of 22.4 percent.

Social Rates of Return

Although the private rates in Table 6 are better for the analysis of behavior, the social rates of return in Table 7, which reflect the full tax costs and full before-tax earnings, are better for use as an input in the formation of social policy.

The most significant result is that the average expected social rates of return in medicine, law, engineering, and business fields of 12.7, 15.5, 19.0, and 15.9 percent respectively are all above the 10 percent rate of return on financial assets in 1976 (as measured by the New York Stock

Table 7. Expected and Realized Social Rates of Return of White Male Students by Intended Occupation and Degree Objective
(standard errors, computed as $s/\sqrt{n}$, are shown below each mean)

Occupation	Degree objective				Average, all degree levels[a]	
	Associate	Bachelor's	Master's	Doctor's professional	Expected	Realized[b]
Health and medicine						
Doctor, dentist		16.1 (1.5)		11.1 (1.0)	12.7	7.2
Health technician				12.2 (.8)	12.2	11.7
Pharmacist		9.1 (2.5)			9.4	
		20.1 (1.1)		3.9 (4.8)	15.2	12.4
Lawyer				15.5 (2.1)	15.5	14.1
Engineering-technical						
Architect	36.4 (8.0)	24.4 (2.2)	8.5 (.7)	7.2 (.8)	19.0	12.6
Engineer		23.6 (2.3)	10.5 (1.6)		17.2	8.5
Electrical technician		18.9 (2.0)	10.0 (.6)	7.4 (.4)	14.2	11.0
	41.3 (4.1)	43.8 (1.0)			40.8	24.6

Business	22.1	17.1	10.4	15.9	11.3
	(1.4)	(.9)	(.7)		
Accountant	23.0	17.8	10.7	17.3	9.0
	(1.1)	(1.5)	(1.2)		
Manufacturing manager		16.0	10.8	13.2	15.2
		(.8)	(.9)		
Sales, retailing		16.6		15.5	12.4
		(1.1)			
Other professional		7.6	7.8	6.5	3.7
		(1.6)	(1.0)		
Clergyman				1.4	
				(1.6)	
				-2.1	-2.8	-17.5
				(3.6)	
Natural scientist			7.4	3.2	9.4	7.7
			(3.0)	(3.1)		
Social scientist				-4.8	-4.1	8.0
				(4.5)		
Education		10.3	0.0	3.1	3.8	-2.8
		(1.6)	(1.6)	(2.0)		
Elementary & secondary teacher		10.3	-.8	2.0	3.3	-3.8
		(1.6)	(1.6)	(3.0)		
College professor				5.2	7.8	5.5
				(1.2)		

[a] Averages include observations in cells that contain less than six respondents and are left blank.
[b] For method of computation, see Appendix A and also the first part of this chapter.

Source: ACT College Investment Decision study sample of 2,765 students, contacted in early 1972, who could have completed bachelor's degrees in 1976.

Exchange Composite Index), and hence, if these rates persist, are clearly socially efficient investments. Expected monetary returns alone do not make an equally strong case for music, advanced education, social science and natural science fields. However, it should be kept in mind that this test is a conservative one that leaves out non-monetary private job satisfaction discussed by Lucas (1977) and other non-monetary benefits discussed by Michael in the preceding chapter, as well as most of the social benefits associated with these fields. From the point of view of the contribution of investment in higher education to measured economic growth, the rate-of-return criterion for investment would suggest that educational investment should be expanded where the social rate exceeds some estimate of the average social discount rate, such as the 10 percent average return available on financial assets. This criterion would call for expanding investment in medicine, pharmacy, law, engineering, and business fields, for example. Alternatively, raising admission standards in education, social science, and humanities fields, all with some eye to externalities and to independent forecasts of future trends, would increase the social efficiency of the system.

Second, subsidies to students and institutions are not what seriously distort student choices with respect to occupations, since the private and the social rates of return are both highest in the same medicine, law, engineering, technical, and business fields.

Third, at the advanced graduate levels, expected social rates of return to education for white males in medicine and law tend to remain among the highest (12-15 percent), similar to those found by Eckhaus et al. (1974) for 1960. For medicine, this takes the higher costs of medical education into account through the higher foregone earnings and through most of the full institutional costs over the longer period of years required for a degree. The high rate of return is a more meaningful economic criterion for the existence of a static shortage of physicians than are head counts of doctors relative to the population. The latter do not reflect the economist.s concept of scarcity. The current tendency to emphasize the number in the pipeline, and to quickly move to shut the pipeline down, is likely to guarantee that this static shortage of physicians will persist, and that limits will remain tighter in these health fields than in those fields at the bottom of Table 7. Should there be further increases in the demand for medical care with an aging population and with increases in the income, the returns to society from continued expansion in medical education may be underestimated. On the other hand, white males choosing Ph.D. programs primarily oriented to college teaching (e.g., college professors, natural scientists, and social scientists) anticipate significantly lower social rates of return, as can be seen in Table 7. Short of a major national effort in research and science aimed at faster productivity growth, the decline in college enrollments due to the decline in fertility rates means that the rates of return in those Ph.D. programs oriented to research and to academic job markets could fall even further.

Finally, it is important to make more detailed comparisons between these new microeconomic occupation rates and those computed by Eckhaus et al. (1974) for 1960. The social rates in Table 7 are appropriate to longer-range decisions in that they apply to the entire degree program (not just the marginal years), and, in contrast to Eckhaus, they use the expected earnings of individual respondents (rather than cross-section means). They also employ a standardized opportunity cost (average earnings for those with the same education and of the same race and sex), rather than a different opportunity cost for each field. Nevertheless, his rates are about the same at the bachelor's level in most fields as the social rates in Table 7.[7] This suggests what could be an important tendency toward persistence for many of the differences in rates among occupations. For example, from 1960 to 1976, the implicit 17.8 percent social rate of return at the bachelor's level for accountants remained close to the 16.5 percent estimated by Eckhaus. Among engineers, his approximate 12 percent rate of return for 1960 is somewhat lower than our expected 18.9 percent 1976 rate. The rate of return for pharmacists stayed in the 20 percent range over this period as well.

Differences in rates of return among fields at the more advanced levels also persist. The rates of return we find in 1978 for doctors and pharmacists, in Table 7 of 12.2 to 15.2 percent, which are relatively high for the advanced levels, are very similar to those found by Eckhaus for 1960. Eckhaus reports actual rates of return for college professors for 1960 of 0-10 percent (depending on the choice of field for computation of opportunity cost), very similar to the 5.2 percent social rate for 1978 reported in Table 7.

Since differences in rates of return among occupations appear to persist over time in spite of some response in the choices made by students and their families, the differences at each degree level take on greater significance as one basis for educational planning. At the advanced levels, rates tend to be the highest in the fields where there are outlets other than into teaching, and in fields where there are enrollment quotas and other non-market barriers to entry. At the bachelor's level, expected social rates are highest in technical fields (24.4 percent), accounting (17.8 percent), and health areas (16.1 percent). The low rates for persons who enter college expecting to become teachers or social and natural scientists suggest fields where there is oversupply (in the case of elementary, secondary, and college teachers) as well as lower national priorities in the support of social and natural science and research that now prevail.

Conclusions

Overall, it can be tentatively concluded that long-run rates of return to investment in higher education, estimated at the overtaking age eight years after graduation or by use of later points on the age-earnings profile, have remained relatively steady at 13-14 percent, at least up through 1977. The rates of return implicitly expected by students based on their own costs and expected earnings as of 1976 averaged 17 percent. These rates also remained relatively high in relation to the 10-12 percent rate of return available from investment in financial assets. Long-run corporate bond rates rose to the 12-14 percent range in 1980-82. But these do not seem as high when converted to real terms, which are more relevant for investment decisions, or when regarded as a relatively transitory phenomenon.

Differences in private rates of return among fields both at the bachelor's and at advanced levels reveal patterns similar to differences in the social rates of return, suggesting that the structure of financial aids does not distort private choices. Comparing our results to those obtained by Eckhaus et al. for 1960, there is a clear suggestion that wide differences in rates of return tend to persist, perhaps in part because of internal budget allocations and related enrollment limits. From a measured economic growth perspective, the persistence of these shortages and surpluses is one evidence of social inefficiency.

There is also a pattern of differences in the rates of return to investment at different types of institutions. These rates are of particular interest because there are significant differences in costs among institutions, and private and social decisions depend upon whether or not these cost differences are justified by differences in returns. The earnings expected by the students over their life cycle, which were found to be reasonably realistic in reflecting differences among occupational fields, degree levels, and age, also reflect these sources of differences in earnings among graduates of different institutions, quite apart from differences in institutional quality. The results suggest that although per-student total costs are highest at the private and public research universities, the expected returns also tend to be higher there, as do social rates of return, especially for students seeking advanced degrees. For students at private liberal arts colleges, the higher private costs result in low private rates of return for those planning to terminate with a bachelor's degree, especially in relation to the higher private rates of return available at private or public four-year comprehensives, which may reflect the less vocationally oriented bachelor's level fields at the liberal arts colleges. But for those students planning to seek advanced degrees, much of the private cost disadvantage disappears, and attendance at a liberal arts college is more advantageous than attending a public or private four-year comprehensive institution. Finally, the place where the comprehensive four-year colleges have their best competitive advantage is among those students seeking a terminal bachelor's degree. At this level both the private and the social rates of return are among the highest available.

These results do not suggest that certain institutions will not face increasing financial distress. As the large wave of college-age young adults produced by the fertility rates that peaked in 1957 pass on out of the educational institutions, the problems brought on by declining enrollments will be felt at the more recently established and less well endowed institutions. Unusually high inflation rates will also continue to adversely affect all institutions. High fixed costs are likely to create new problems, especially at the less well established public institutions, as well as cuts in federal student loan funds that affect more heavily the private institutions, deterring expansion and new building. But institutional distress does not mean that for each student enrolled on the average, investment in higher education will not continue to be an advantageous investment both from a private and from a social point of view.

These conclusions are predicated on the emphasis on a longer-run rate of return, which brings later points in the life cycle into view, rather than a shorter-run more exclusive focus on starting salaries which does not emphasize the assimilation of new entrants into the labor force. However, real starting salaries of college graduates stabilized in the 1975-79 period following their decline in the early 70's, and at about their 1964 levels. Following the inflation and recession of 1979-82, there is no reason to think that job markets will not recover so that real salaries will stabilize again, especially as the large population wave that is passing out of the colleges also ends. As technological advances continue to stimulate the job markets for college graduates, and as the large population-recession shock is assimilated, it is interesting to note that the *relative* advantage of college graduates over high school graduates in the older (35-44) age bracket has not fallen below the level of the 1960's. No clear trend is apparent for that group, at least as yet.

Finally, the conclusions offered here are not sweeping, but are instead specific. Higher education has continued to be well worth the investment cost over time, but on a short-term basis this can vary. Social efficiency could be increased by some expansion in the dollars budgeted for, and hence the numbers admitted to, the high-return fields and (at specific degree levels) the higher-return institutions, with some contraction of real budgets and numbers in the surplus fields and other less cost effective institutions. This applies the first social-efficiency-oriented humane growth criterion from Chapter 1 and does control for ability. But budgeting steps of this nature also need to weigh the non-monetary returns and equity considerations in qualitative judgments before taking final action, considering both social efficiency and maintaining equity as the most practical means of enhancing the contribution of education to humane growth.[10]

APPENDIX A

Computation of the Internal Rate of Return

To compute the pure internal rate of return, Equation (1) below (which is repeated for convenience from the text) was solved for r* by iteration for each rate for each student. r* is defined as the *expected* rate of return when Y_t in Equation (1) is the expected real net earnings differential given by Equation (2). r* is the *realized* rate of return when Y_t in Equation (1) is the realized real net earnings differential as defined by Equation (4):

(1) $\sum_{t=1}^{G-E} I_t(1 + r^*)^t = \sum_{t=1}^{R-G} Y_t/(1 + r^*)^t$

For students planning graduate programs, the investment cost to the student and his family was increased during the graduate school years by replacing high school earnings with the earnings of a college graduate as the measure of foregone earnings costs. To measure monetary returns, the retirement age (R) was used rather than the length of life (L_2), since earnings before retirement include earnings saved and major contributions to pension plans.

Y_t^e, the expected real net earnings differential, was estimated using the following algorithm:

(2) $Y_t^e = \alpha(E_1^e - E_1^{HS})(1 + g)^t$, in order to get Y_t^e at any year t,

where g, the implicit rate of growth of real earnings was computed from:

(3) $E_{25}^e - E_{25}^{HS}(1 + .02)^{25} = (E_1^e - E_1^{HS})(1 + g)^{25}$.

Here: E_i^e = earnings expected by the student at graduation (i=1) and twenty-five years later (i=25) expressed in real terms, and

E_1^{HS} = earnings realized by high school graduates of the same race and sex at age 21 (i=1) and twenty-five years later (i=25).

High school earnings are increased by a 2 percent annual growth factor to allow for economy-wide growth in productivity in which high school graduates share. College students were assumed to include this productivity growth when asked to estimate the earnings they expect to receive "before taxes, and assuming no inflation, 25 years from now."

Y_t, the realized net earnings differential, was estimated in the same manner:

(3) $Y_t = \alpha(E_1 - E_1^{HS})(1 + g)$,

computing g from:

(4) $(E_{25} - E_{25}^{HS})(1 + .02)^{25} = (E_1 - E_1^{HS})(1 + g)^{25}$,

where E_i = earnings of college graduates at graduation (i=1) and 25 years hence (i=25) who are of the same race and sex and in the same occupational field being chosen by the student.

The only difference between this and the expected rates in Equation (2) and (3) is that E_{25} as well as E_{25}^{HS} must be adjusted for expected productivity growth. Note that g in both cases is independent of α and of the tax rate, say T, since both sides in Equations (2) and (4) would be multiplied by both α and (1 - T).

α, the percent of the net earnings differential attributable to college, is assumed to be .66. This represents a conservative estimate of the contribution of education to earnings, since some have estimated it at closer to 1.0, and hence leads to a more rigorous test of whether the returns to college are worth the costs. Denison (1964: 78-79) originally concluded, after examining the evidence, that about 66 percent of the gross earnings differentials between college and high school graduates can be attributed to education alone after controlling for IQ scores, rank in high school class, and father's occupation—a result that has been confirmed by Becker (1975: 158-66) and by Weisbrod and Karpoff (1968). It is also close to the 55 percent of variation in earnings explained on the average by schooling and schooling-related factors by Mincer (1964: 92, Equation 2). Layard and Psacharopoulos (1974) suggest that α = .90 is more plausible. It can be seen in Appendix B which follows that the α's obtained by many others tend to average about .88 or .90, so that if our .66 errs, it is on the conservative side.

APPENDIX B

Proportion of Earnings Differentials due to Education Relative to Ability and Other Factors (U.S.)

Level of schooling	"Other" (Adjustment reference)	Education α	Source
Higher education	Ability + other	.66	Denison (1964)
Primary	Ability + other	.88	Denison (1974)[a]
Secondary	Ability + other	.88	
B.A.	Ability + other	.88	
One year graduate study	Ability + other	.48	
Higher	Ability	.80[b]	Becker (1975)
Higher	Ability + other	.65[c]	
Higher	Ability + other	.74[d]	
Higher	Ability + other	.81[e]	
Secondary	Ability + other	.52[d]	
Secondary	Ability + other	.73[e]	
Secondary	Ability + other	.40	Morgan and David[f]
B.A.	Ability + other	.88	
Graduate study	Ability + other	1.00	
Two years post-secondary technical	Ability + other	.73	Carroll and Ihnen
Graduate study	Ability	.90	Ashenfelter and Mooney
Higher	Ability + other	.75	Weisbrod and Karpoff (1968)

Years of schooling	Ability	.49	Hansen, Weisbrod and Scanlon
Secondary	Ability + other	.86	Rogers
Higher	Ability + other	.73	
Years of schooling	Ability	.96	Griliches
Years of schooling after military service	Ability + other	.88	Griliches and Mason
Higher education	Ability	.94	Hause
Primary	Ability	1.00	Hause
Higher	Ability	.97g	
B.A.	Ability	.87h	
Graduate study	Ability	.89g	
Years of schooling	Mostly ability only	.85i	Gintis
Higher	Ability + other	.65	Taubman and Wales
Years of schooling	Ability	.81	Hauser et al.

[a] Based on Table 3.1.
[b] Using the Bell data or the Wolfe and Smith data and class rank as a proxy for ability.
[c] Using the Wolfe and Smith data.
[d] Using the Morgan and David results; averages for ages 18-34 and 35-74.
[e] Based on Gorseline; not corrected for underreporting of earnings.
[f] Refers to the ages 35-44.
[g] Using the NBER-TH sample.
[h] Using the Rogers sample.
[i] Overall average of the alphas implied in Gintis.

Sources: G. Psacharopoulos (1975, p. 56). Full citations for items in the last column above not datekeyed to our reference list may be found in Psacharopoulos, pp. 59-61.

APPENDIX C

Distribution of Respondents in Each Wave and in the Census of All Students

	1977 Graduates before weights	Census of all students[a]	1977 Graduates weighted[b]
Public institutions	73.8	75.5	75.5
Universities	28.0	21.8	21.8
Male	11.9	10.0	10.0
Female	16.1	11.8	11.8
Four year	29.0	30.7	30.7
Male	12.5	20.3	20.3
Female	16.5	10.4	10.4
Two year	16.9	23.0	23.0
Male	7.3	13.0	13.0
Female	9.6	10.0	10.0
Private institutions	26.1	24.6	24.3
Universities	5.0	5.5	5.5
Male	2.2	2.8	2.8
Female	2.8	2.7	2.7
Four year	17.6	17.1	17.1
Male	7.8	8.8	8.8
Female	9.8	8.3	8.3
Two year	3.5	1.7	1.7
Male	1.8	.7	.7
Female	1.7	1.0	1.0
All institutions[c]	99.9	100.1	99.8

[a] Source: U.S. Office of Education
[b] Weights simultaneously correct for type of institution, sex, and percent receiving financial aid, although the latter dimension is not shown separately.
[c] Totals vary from 100% only because of rounding.

	1976 Graduates before weights	Census of all students[a]	1976 Graduates sample weighted[b]
Public institutions	80.0%	75.5	75.5
Universities	37.0	21.8	21.7
Male	15.0	10.0	9.8
Female	22.0	11.8	11.9
Four year	29.1	30.7	29.9
Male	9.9	20.3	19.8
Female	19.2	10.4	10.1
Two year	14.0	23.0	23.9
Male	5.6	13.0	12.7
Female	8.4	10.0	11.2
Private institutions	20.0	24.6	24.6
Universities	2.3	5.5	5.3
Male	.6	2.8	2.7
Female	1.7	2.7	2.6
Four year	16.3	17.1	17.6
Male	5.5	8.8	9.5
Female	10.8	8.3	8.1
Two year	1.3	1.7	1.7
Male	.5	.7	.7
Female	.8	1.0	1.0
All institutions[c]	100.0	100.1	101.0

NOTES

1. Returns also include increments to earnings attributable to learning on the job by college graduates, part of which is made possible by the prior schooling. But it is assumed for the purposes of this paper that formal schooling ends upon graduation, and that the investment costs of learning on the job are captured by the lower beginning and steeper slope of the after-college age-earnings profile.

2. The ACT test, taken by entering freshmen, gives a composite score covering reasoning ability in each of four areas: English, math, social science, and natural science.

3. The Carnegie Commission's classification attempts to distinguish among institutions of higher education according to the size of graduate and research programs, faculty quality (i.e., percentage of Ph.D.'s on the staff), student quality, institution size, and the range of academic fields of study available to undergraduates. Among four-year institutions, for example, research universities rank high on all measures, while liberal arts colleges score low on several.

4. Small differences may be attributable to Bowen's "student unit" (weighting for graduate, upper division, and lower division enrollment) in place of our FTE weighting, and Bowen's median versus our mean measure of "average."

5. Available grant aid has increased by a factor of ten over the 1970's (see Wagner 1978), and information from a wide variety of sources indicates that the most important influences on the amount of grant aid a student receives are in negative relation to family income, and in positive relation to costs of attendance (tuition, books, room and board) (Wagner and Rice 1977). In 1977-78, the grant at a private four-year institution was more than double the gift aid received by a peer at a four-year public institution (Augenblick and Hyde 1979).

6. In 1973-74, about one-third of the baccalaureate degrees conferred by private liberal arts colleges were from humanities, social sciences, and other "liberal arts" fields, compared to a one-fifth share of baccalaureates granted by all four-year institutions together. Alternatively, over one-fourth of the bachelor's degrees in 1973-74 were in professional-technical fields (engineering, architecture, business, etc.). Less than 10 percent of liberal arts college graduates received degrees in these fields.

7. Eckhaus et al. (1974) calculates internal rates of return under the assumption that direct costs are cancelled out by part-time earnings. If this conventional assumption holds (as well it might for 1960, when direct costs of tuition and books were low and financial aid funds were limited), then his "unadjusted" rates come closest to our social rates of return.

8. The authors are indebted to Nguyen Hoang and to Len Nichols, who helped with the computations, to Robert Michael for helpful suggestions, to Thomas James and the Spencer Foundation for early support, and to N.I.E. for assistance in collecting the data.

REFERENCES

Augenblick, John, and Hyde, W. 1979. *Patterns of funding, net price and financial need for postsecondary students.* Report No. F79-1. Denver: Education Commission of the States. March.

Becker, Gary S. 1975. *Human capital.* 2nd ed. New York: Columbia University Press.

Bowen, Howard R. 1980. *The costs of higher education.* San Francisco: Jossey-Bass Inc.

Carnoy, Martin, and Marenbach, D. 1975. The return to schooling in the United States, 1939-1969. *Journal of Human Resources* 10 (Summer): 312-31.

Cohn, Elchanan. 1978. *The economics of education.* Rev. ed. Cambridge: Ballinger.

College Placement Council. 1980. C.P.C. salary surveys. Bethlehem, Penna. (July, 1980, and earlier issues.)

Denison, E. F. 1964. Proportion of income differentials among education groups due to additional education. In *The residual factor and economic growth,* ed. J. Vaizey. Paris: Organization for Economic Cooperation and Development.

———. 1974. *Accounting for United States economic growth, 1929-69.* Washington, D.C.: Brookings Institution.

Eckhaus, Richard S.; El Safty, A.; and Norman, V. 1974. An appraisal of the calculation of rates of return to higher education. Pp. 333-71 in *Higher education and the labor market,* ed. Margaret S. Gordon.

Farrel, Maurice L., ed. 1978. *The Dow Jones investor's handbook.* Princeton: Dow Jones Books.

Ferber, M. and McMahon, W. W. 1979. Womens' expected earnings and their investment in higher education. *Journal of Human Resources* 14 (Summer): 405-20.

Freeman, Richard. 1975. Overinvestment in college training? *Journal of Human Resources* 10 (Summer): 287-311.

———. 1976. *The overeducated American.* New York: Academic Press.

———. 1980. The facts about the declining economic value of college. *Journal of Human Resources* 15, (Winter): 124-42.

Layard, Richard, and Psacharopoulos, G. 1974. The screening hypothesis and returns to education. *Journal of Political Economy* 82, 5 (September/October): 985-98.

Liberman, Joseph. 1979. The rate of return to schooling: 1958-1976. Faculty Working Paper, Department of Finance, University of Illinois, Chicago Circle.

Lillard, Lee. 1979. Rates of return to higher education. *American Economic Review* (September).

Lucas, Robert E. B. 1977. Hedonic wage equations and psychic wages in the returns to schooling. *American Economic Review* 67, 4 (September): 549-58.

McMahon, Walter W., and Wagner, Alan P. 1973. A study of the college investment decision. *ACT Research Reports* 59. Iowa City: American College Testing Program.

―――. 1981. Expected returns to investment in higher education. *Journal of Human Resources*.
Mincer, Jacob. 1974. *Schooling, experience, and earnings*. New York: National Bureau of Economic Research.
Psacharopoulos, George. 1973. *Returns to education*. San Francisco: Jossey-Bass.
―――. 1975. *Earnings and education in OECD countries*. Paris: OECD.
Ribich, Thomas I., and Murphy, J. 1975. The economic returns to increased educational spending. *Journal of Human Resources* 10 (Winter): 56-77.
Smith, James P., and Welch, Finis. 1978. *The overeducated American? A review article*. Rand Paper P-6253. Santa Monica, Calif.: Rand Corporation. November.
―――. 1977. Black-white wage ratios: 1960-1970. *American Economic Review* (June).
Wagner, Alan P. 1978. Determinants of parental contributions toward post-secondary education expenses: the effects of student aid subsidies. Manuscript, Purdue University.
―――, and Rice, Lois D. 1977. *Student financial aid: institutional packaging and family expenditure patterns*. Final Report. Washington: National Center for Education Statistics, Department of Health, Education and Welfare. August.
Wagner, Alan P., and Tenison, Laurence J. 1976. Data check summary report for the study of student financial aid. Working Paper No. 1. Washington: College Entrance Examination Board. February.
Weisbrod, B. A., and Karpoff, P. 1968. Monetary returns to college education, student ability, and college quality. *Review of Economic Statistics* (November).
Witmer, David R. 1980. Has the golden age of American higher education come to an abrupt end? *Journal of Human Resources* 15, 1 (Winter).

PART II

Equity

Concerns for equity are based on widely held and deeply ingrained philosophical values relating to perceptions of our society's and our citizens' sense of fairness and justice. These concerns are expressed in many formal statements of public policy, and are emphasized in the literature of educational finance. Whereas social efficiency criteria in Part I have been basically concerned with the growth in the total returns from education, equity criteria in Part II are concerned with the distribution of these benefits. Total returns consist of both the important monetary and non-monetary benefits that significantly affect the quality of life, so the distribution of these benefits among students has important effects on the distribution of earnings and on the distribution of the quality of life later in their life cycle. The chapters in Part II are concerned primarily with the notion of distributive justice within each generation, another aspect of humane growth in the society.

A rapidly growing body of economic research focuses on the determinants of the distribution of personal income and wealth. Sahota (1978) has comprehensively surveyed the theories and related research that have appeared in an attempt to explain inequality in the distribution of personal incomes. This research explores the relationship between human capital formation and lifetime income distribution, and also develops further the theory of equity and distributive justice. As Atkinson (1975) has observed, however, many factors affect income distribution, so it is extremely difficult to make sweeping judgments about justice and injustice based only on differences in earnings. Smith (1975) similarly explores many other important dimensions of the personal distribution of income and wealth.

The overriding concern in Part II is limited, however, to the relationship between current inequalities in educational opportunities and later inequalities in the distribution of monetary earnings, as well as non-monetary satisfactions over the life cycle. On the horizon is the newest income distribution front, which is just beginning to connect the inequality in the distribution of educational benefits among children as human capital is formed during the primary and secondary school years (which in turn is correlated with the investment made during the college years) to inequality in the distribution of earnings and of non-monetary satisfactions in later life.

Different concepts of equity all require interpersonal comparisons of utility which take the subject beyond the range of pure economics and require philosophical and ethical judgments. Considerations of horizontal and vertical equity in educational finance are generally applicable both to the tax side and to student equity on the expenditure side. Horizontal equity considerations in educational finance tend to focus on the disparities in per-pupil expenditures in school districts, within school districts, among school districts, and across states, and sometimes on the disparity among outcomes. There has also been a continuing concern with intergenerational equity in the sense of reducing the intergenerational transmission of inequality. Thus, one important public policy concern in school finance has been to attempt to diminish the disparities in expenditure per pupil (an important first step toward horizontal equity among comparable groups of pupils) by seeking to equalize the fiscal capacities among parents or school districts (an important aspect of intergenerational or vertical equity among those with unequal ability to pay). Recent research and literature in school finance now generally treats three distinct types of inequalities involving selection of a vertical equity principle: the lack of fiscal neutrality (i.e., the fact that differences in property and income wealth lead to differences in expenditure per child), differences in student educational needs, and differences in educational costs and prices.

Chapter 8, by Kern Alexander, puts recent school finance reforms in perspective and provides considerable conceptual direction for reforms in the 1980.s. He points out that, during the early 1970.s, considerable judicial activity resulted in the widespread adoption of the standard of fiscal neutrality to evaluate the equity implications of school finance programs. He argues that the notion of fiscal neutrality which implies a mathematical measuring of equality, although not achieved in practice, does not go far enough toward achieving vertical equity among children. Drawing upon both philosophical equity and legal equity, he develops the equity hierarchy in depth. He then uses this framework to analyze the equity implications of district power equalizing formulas and of other attempts at equalization. G. Alan Hickrod, in reviewing this paper, suggested that a time dimension could also be incorporated into the achievement of given levels in the equity hierarchy, because there is at least some evidence to suggest that progress toward equity appears to involve an ebb and flow process.

While Chapter 8 is basically concerned with equity issues in financing the elementary and secondary schools, Chapter 9, by Susan C. Nelson, focuses on equity concerns in higher education. Nelson discusses alternative approaches for considering equity in higher education, including equity in terms of redistribution of current income and in terms of lifetime redistribution of income. She opts for a perspective on equity which views the benefits and the tax costs of subsidies for higher education separately, arguing that this approach is more workable from both methodological and policy perspectives. She then considers tuition charges at community colleges and suggests that higher tuition, combined with federal BEOG grants and state student aid, is not inconsistent with achieving equity among college-age young people and relatively equal educational opportunity.

Chapter 10, by Stephen J. Carroll, explores the effects of key state-level finance reform movements on student equity, tax equity, and school district expenditure levels. Principles emerging from this study suggest that underlying forces (that also may be present in most school finance reform efforts) tend to propel reform efforts away from the achievement of much improvement in student equity and toward tax reform and increased tax revenue. Gilbert Ghez and another anonymous referee of this paper feel that the student access and equity accomplishments of school finance reforms in recent years may be somewhat understated in Carroll's study because it does not take into full account the large increase in expenditures for special education programs. When these programs are included in the calculation of expenditure per pupil, however, the discrepancy between the amount spent per pupil (including grants in aid) in rich vs. poor districts, and in rich vs. poorer states, still remains large (McMahon 1970, 1978).

In the anchor position in Part II, John F. Due places the tax revolt and budget limitation movements within the context of the trends that have been occurring in tax systems for some time, and discusses the implications for efficiency and equity in educational finance. In developing the causes of the tax revolt, Due cites the growing share of revenue from the property tax in California in relation to the trend toward greater use of state income tax sources nationwide, the higher overall level of taxation there, and the massive budget surplus prior to the passage of Proposition 13. Tax-expenditure limitation movements of this scope have not been successful in most other states. The dramatic point emerges that one initial effect of the tax revolt is to achieve substantial equalization in expenditure per child among districts by reducing reliance on local property taxes. As Bruce Gensemer has pointed out in reviewing this paper, one side effect of the tax revolt in California (and to a lesser extent of the property tax-expenditure limitation movement elsewhere) is to achieve what school finance reform has often failed to achieve: greater equality in expenditure per student, even if at a somewhat lower overall level of total support.

Inflation and other forces apart from tax revolts have been operating simultaneously, however, to increase the inequity among children.

REFERENCES

Atkinson, A. B. 1975. *The economics of inequality.* Oxford: University Press.
McMahon, W. 1970. An economic analysis of determinants of expenditures on public education. *Review of Economics and Statistics* 52 (August): 242-52.
McMahon, W. 1978. A broader measure of wealth and effort for educational equality and tax equity. *Journal of Education Finance* 4 (Summer): 65-88.
Sahota, Gian. 1978. Theories of personal income distribution: a survey. *Journal of Economic Literature* (March): 1-55.
Smith, James D., ed. 1975. *The personal distribution of income and wealth.* New York: Columbia University Press for NBER.

CHAPTER 8

Concepts of Equity

KERN ALEXANDER

Advanced nations today recognize the value of education not only as an important civilizing agent, but also as the means by which a country can maintain both political and economic stability. Mankind is enhanced and progresses as individuals gain more knowledge about themselves and others. The educated are more humane and tolerant in their intercourse, whether acting individually or collectively, than are the ignorant.

Regardless of the many faults of our society, there is a consuming demand for education and a desire for greater human rights and dignity. The dark and middle ages of the past, on the other hand, as well as many less developed nations, have been notable for their indifference to human rights and have exhibited a persistent "acquiescence in poverty, inequality, and oppression" (Schlesinger 1978: 503). The humanitarian ethic which Tocqueville attributed to the age of equality has gained momentum, and even with some notable backward steps has by in large had a forward progression. Certainly the Declaration of Independence and the great expansion of the equal protection clause of the Fourteenth Amendment are significant manifestations of a rationality and humanity of social purpose which are somewhat extraordinary in history.

Ironically, though, the public education system which best conveys these broad and noble purposes from generation to generation in our own country itself manifests inequitable traits which have not yet been successfully remedied. Moreover, in spite of the great public interest, one finds continuing disagreement as to what the people and state should do to improve the justice and fairness of the system of public education.

Many things have been accomplished of course, particularly during the past two decades. The vestiges of serious past racial discrimination have largely been erased. Due process of law has given the child an unrefuted constitutional interest in education. The free exercise of religious beliefs has been guaranteed, and freedom of expression has been assured.

193

When one realizes that this great enunciation of freedoms and rights has transpired largely since the 1954 *Brown* v. *Board of Education* decision, only then can the true magnitude of the trends in human rights be adequately evaluated.

Even with these strides, however, there is continuing concern for existing conditions of inequity which are still of major significance in our educational system. Most notable are the economic disparities which exist among individuals, educational programs, school districts, and even states. A litany of such differences in fiscal capabilities has been reiterated over the years and continues to be one of the most controversial issues facing legislatures and courts today. Some school districts have as much as three to five times the fiscal resources of others. Beyond the district fiscal disparities, wide variations in social, economic, and physical conditions of individuals within and among states exacerbate the problems in attempting to treat all children equitably.

Underlying this dilemma is a basic question: What do equity and justice require of the state in providing for a system of education? Is it implicit in the idea of mass public education that the products of the educational system be equal? That is, does equity require an economic redistribution of the resources of society so as to level or create greater uniformity in the fiscal conditions of all individuals? Does equity require that the fiscal capacity of units of government be equalized in order that all students may have equal access to educational fiscal resources? Does equity require that the state fiscally supplement the educational program of each individual in such a way as to compensate for mental, physical, cultural, social, and economic conditions which may place an individual student at an educational disadvantage in the educational process? To answer these questions requires a philosophical definition of equity, a legal definition of equity, a review of the status of school finance equity, and finally an application of the concepts of equity to practice.

Philosophical Equity

Equity in its broadest sense encompasses justice, equality, humanity, morality, and right. To deal with the term requires substantial delimitation, for what is equitable depends to a great extent on the orientation of both the dispensers and receivers of equity. Equitable treatment may find its basis in the natural law of Thomas Aquinas, but yet be tempered by the utility of Jeremy Bentham, as well as by modern Rawlsian concepts of freedom and justice. Within these boundaries falls the necessity of government to deal with human wants and needs and to serve the common good.

In the context of today's government it is quite difficult to reduce the grand design of natural law to an operational definition. Provision for the common weal may create conditions which are favorable to many but harmful to a few. In accommodating the individual, the state should certainly not be imperiled; however, that which is perceived to imperil the state is not always clear. The necessity of assertive governmental determination is always open to question regarding actual or perceived needs of individuals.

Justice, Equity, and Equality

Most would contend that the issue of equity is simply one of justice: facts are determined, evidence is weighed, and alternatives are delineated. Justice in the abstract is easy enough to expound, but without more specific standards it is rendered useless by vagueness and overbreadth. In its relationship to equity, what does justice require? Niebuhr observes (in Robertson 1957: 14) that "equality is the pinnacle of the ideal of justice." Of the attributes of natural law, Western man has given most of his attention to justice and equality. Undeniably, the goal of equality is a basic standard against which equity must be judged, whether it involves de facto social inequalities or various disparities created by power and politics. The essentiality of equal treatment to the concept of equity is presumed by most philosophers. Even Hobbes notes, "If man is to be trusted to judge between man and man, it is a precept of Law of Nature, that he deal equally between them" (in Moris, 1971: 117). Equity, then, as a basic element of the law of nature requires equal distribution of goods and benefits.

But equity is more than equality. Like justice, it is abstract and less susceptible to definition. Equality, on the other hand, as a general standard conveys an element of prescription and measurability. While justice may be commonly defined as giving everyone his due, the term "equality" more specifically refers to division, partition, and redistribution.

Kant (in Moris 1971: 243) relates equity to right, saying that equity is founded not on any principle of beneficence, benevolence, or charity, but upon "right." His "right" was both natural and positive, the former being based on pure rationality while the latter emanated from the will of the legislator. To him an innate right is vested in every person at birth, a birthright, while acquired rights are founded upon juridical acts. For Kant, this innate right is the obligation which equity must address.

Depending on one's orientation, equity and justice may be viewed as attributes of each other and as virtually interchangeable. In the eyes of the jurist, equity is an essential element of the broader concept of justice, while the economist will almost certainly view equity as an a priori condition of which justice is a basic part. Regardless of this semantic relativity, though, justice and equity entail the virtue of attributing to everyone his right. Dabin (in Moris 1971: 490), recognizing the inherent problems in quantifying justice, said it must be defined by *aequalitas* rather than by the *aequum*. He says, "The virtue that renders to everyone his right or his dignity deserves to be defined, in a strict sense, not merely by the loose idea of equity (acquum et bonum) but by the mathematical idea of equality (aequalitas)." Regardless, however, of problems of measurement, most agree that equity and justice have broader qualities than those which are measurable in terms of equality.

Commutative and Distributive Equity

Equity may be classified in several categories, two of which are commutative and distributive. Commutative equity entitles a person to something simply because it is his, leaves the distribution produced by the market place unaltered, and is libertarian in its orientation. Here someone owns something by virtue of a private and individual relationship (Hayek 1976: 31). This particular element of equity includes what is commonly known in other countries as private law, the inviolability of property, freedom to contract, and duty to compensate another for damages. It maintains that the order in which certain operations are performed, and hence presumably initial endowments, do not matter.

Distributive equity, on the other hand, consists of conditions created by various kinds of redistributions of social benefits which every society is called upon to make. It is here that the issues of equality and public school finance most commonly arise (Hayek, 1976: 86). The redistribution of the resources of society to the individual is one side of the equation, while the debt of the individual (what is owed to society) is the other. These interact to circumscribe the degree of equity which can be maintained in the educational system.

In a free society the rewards of the system may not be distributed in accordance with any recognizable principle of equity. Some theoreticians observe that we are in error when we conclude that the pattern of rewards in a free society is either just or unjust. Hayek, the Nobel laureate, has observed, "In a free society in which the position of the different individuals and groups is not the *result of anybody's design*--or could within such a society not be altered in accordance with a principle of general applicability--the difference in rewards cannot meaningfully be described as just or unjust." (Hayek 1976: 83; emphasis added). The operative words, "result of anybody's design," are, of course, extremely important to the validity of the statement when applied to public education. Where by design of special interests or by conscious distribution of governmental influence or resources some persons are placed in a more advantageous position than others, the injustice is not merely the result of natural processes. This is what has transpired in the organization of school districts into enclaves of relative wealth and poverty.

Hayek believes that equity is served if government does not grant benefits in unequal proportions to certain persons, to the detriment of others. The best result which government can effectuate is that all players in the game will have equal chances to succeed, or that legislation will not be responsible for determining who will win or lose. If government does intercede in the natural processes, creating imbalances and disparities in the opportunity to develop one's abilities, then remedial action through legislation may be necessary to effectuate equity. Since in all organized societies most governmental actions are designed to achieve particular goals, and as side effects impair opportunities for some individuals or whole classes of people, remedial governmental action is justified. Hayek maintains that affirmative action is not required to achieve justice unless the condition was itself created by government.

Rawls's Positivism

Rawls, on the other hand, advances the philosophy that an unequal distribution of goods by government is justified if these goods operate to the advantage of the "least favored." In other words, he believes that positive and affirmative relief is justified regardless of whether the condition was created by previous government action. "All social primary goods, liberty and opportunity, income and wealth, and the bases of self-respect--are to be distributed equally unless an unequal distribution of any or all of these goods is to the advantage of the least favored" (Rawls 1977: 303). That is, any initial disadvantage, regardless of reason-- innate physical or mental condition, cultural incapacity, social or economic deprivation--may be justifiably mitigated by the state through its redistributive processes. A legal positivism to the effect that an unequal distribution is made by the state is just conduct if it is visited upon the disadvantaged or least favored (Hayek 1976: 45). (This relates to the genre of legal positivism, not necessarily to philosophical positivism, which falls into another realm.) Such affirmative response is probably not only justifiable but actually required if equity is to be achieved.

Thus, in their philosophical context, equity and justice are presumed to have similar attributes of right and humanity of purpose. In the very broad and unrestricted context, equity may be coextensive with the wide moral expanse of natural law and Western man's ideals of charity, but in a more restricted sense the terms may be presumed to espouse simple justifiable fairness. In this regard, then, social and economic philosophy may be interpreted as having four types of equity. Each depends to some extent on the conditions which are extant in society generally, and in government in particular. Equity in education therefore will be viewed in light of the concepts of (1) commutative equity, (2) equal distribution of the fiscal resource base, (3) restitution, and (4) positivism.

With commutation, government is not required to redistribute resources. Instead, it is assumed either that there is no action, or that the state action manifested produces no disparate or unjust results on any segment of the population. In such a state of affairs no further government action is necessary and desirable and individualism, libertarianism, and the results of the market prevail. Commutative equity provides for no corrective or remedial state action to redress disparate conditions created in the private sector.

Equal distribution entails a limited equity concept which requires only mathematical equality of fiscal resources.

Restitution as a concept of equity recognizes that unjust distribution of advantage in society may be exacerbated by undesirable state action, and it seeks to compensate for its impact. With full knowledge that providing justice to one party may create injustice for another, the government proceeds with redistributive (non-Pareto type) tax and expenditure policies as discussed in Chapter 1 to correct for inadvertent or inappropriate antecedent governmental actions.

Positivism as a concept of equity requires that government act affirmatively to correct inherent or innate disadvantages and disparities among individuals. Such may not issue from a basic right, but from a moral and humanitarian necessity to alleviate a condition which has befallen a segment of the population through no fault of the state government itself. Under this theory anyone who is disadvantaged, even by nature or misadventure, has a right to have the condition ameliorated by state action. Positivism suggests that there is a moral obligation to assist those who are disadvantaged, even though their inferior position is not the result of governmental action. Kant supports this in his argument for a duty of beneficence, and Rawls justifies it with his principle of benefit to the "least advantaged."[1]

Each of these concepts of equity may be applied to educational finance in establishing a framework through which educational opportunity may be viewed.

Legal Equity in Educational Finance

While equity generally evolves from precepts of philosophy and natural law, legal equity as we know it in school finance cases emanates more directly from precedents founded in the context of constitutional law. Indeed, in the various court decisions which bear on school finance, there is no assumption that considerations of equity emanate from sources other than constitutional law.

The law of equity itself evolves from a period in history when the English common law became so bound in writs and their attendant precedents that in many instances fundamental fairness could not be served. Equity law developed as a gloss around common law, allowing a party, in the absence of precedent, to argue that fundamental fairness and right had not been served. Although equity was never developed into a unified theory of law, it did have certain percepts which could be loosely described as evolving from "conscience" and "natural law" (Plucknett, 1956: 675). This concept was formalized as early as 1275 in statutes of Westminister which asserted that "the King, who is sovereign lord, shall *do right* unto all such as will complain" (emphasis added). Equitable considerations--to do right, provide justice, and generally act in fairness and good conscience--are ancient legal principles which have bearing today.

The concepts of equity in education in the United States today spring from common weal and good conscience interpretations of the courts in reference to constitutions and statutes of the various states and the federal government. Even though any student of jurisprudence will quickly assert that equity and law are quite different and probably should not even be considered remotely related, it is nevertheless interesting to note that recent legal precedents indicate that equitable considerations do exist. For example, in viewing the unequal educational opportunity brought about by language deficiencies of non-English-speaking children, the Supreme Court enunciated a kind of equitable relief by maintaining that the Civil Rights Act of 1964 assumed a fundamental fairness which required that all children have the opportunity to acquire basic English skills, and that to provide less would be a mockery of public education. The court cited Senator Hubert Humphrey's statement that "Simple justice requires that public funds, to which all taxpayers of all races contribute, not be spent in any fashion which encourages, entrenches, subsidizes, or results in racial discrimination" (*Lau* v. *Nichols* 1974). The reference by the Supreme Court in this case to "simple justice" should not go unnoticed, since it represents a kind of equitable standard by which the court recognizes that equality of educational opportunity is not fulfilled "merely by providing students with the same facilities, textbooks, teachers, and curriculum; for students who do not understand English are effectively foreclosed from any meaningful education."

In effect, the Supreme Court says that educational deficiencies should be corrected in order to give all students a reasonable chance to succeed in life. That the educational needs of each student are a necessary consideration of the law is reinforced by this position. On the other hand, a more limited but definitive standard is advanced by the court in *Hobson* v. *Hansen* (1967), wherein equal opportunity is measured by a quantitative determination of equal educational resources distributed among schools (Dorfman 1978: 24).

The view of educational opportunity as having an intrinsic requirement of fairness and equitability beyond mathematical quantification is not foreign to the thinking of many concerning educational opportunity. Much has been written about equality of education, and in much of the literature a standard of equity emerges which exceeds mere mathematical nicety. Tumin (1965) explains that equal education does not mean the same education, but it does mean equal concern "that each child shall become the most and the best that he can become."

Tyler has observed that the measure of equality should be that every child is learning and that the conditions for learning are equal among all the children. Accordingly, every child must be able to perceive the opportunity and advance according to his ability (Tyler 1972: 428). In the same vein, other investigators argue that the school should be held responsible for providing differential educational experiences designed for the special abilities that the child brings to the educational setting (Johns, Alexander, and Rossmiller 1969).

That the state should provide for an adequate level of education and compensate for background variations for each student suggests not only equal treatment but also a supplementary standard based on individual needs. This accommodation of educational needs departing from a strict adherence to mathematical equality is the nature and essence of educational equity. In legal philosophy, sometimes the grossest discrimination can lie in treating things that are different exactly alike (*Jenness* v. *Fortson* 1976). At this point strict adherence to mathematical equality is insufficient, since equity and justice cannot be obtained through equal treatment of unequals.

This is precisely the issue which has perplexed educators and lawyers alike since the late 1960's, when educational finance litigation began in earnest. Throughout the litigation three major issues have prevailed. First, how and to what extent can school district fiscal capacity be equalized? Second, how can educational needs be measured, and should such measures be used to allocate funds to local school districts? Third, should the tax effort among school districts be mandated at a uniform level? These issues circumscribe reasonably well three concepts of school finance equity which carry into the latest litigation. Litigation, to date, can be tracked along the lines of these three issues: fiscal equalization, educational needs, and uniformity of effort.

Fiscal Equalization, Educational Needs, and Uniformity of Effort

At the outset of significant litigation in the arera plaintiffs in *McInnis* v. *Ogilvie* (1969) and *Burruss* v. *Wilkerson* (1969) relied on the arguments of fiscal equalization and educational need. The courts in both instances shied away from rendering decisions for the plaintiffs because of judicial uncertainty; "discoverable and manageable standards" to determine constitutionality were not apparent. Such vaguenessess of measurable relief could in retrospect be attributed to a lack of definitiveness in the measurement of fiscal capacity among local school districts, and to an inability to determine the educational standards needed to compensate certain children who have educational disadvantages. The *McInnis* (1969) decision summarized the situation thus: "the courts have neither the knowledge, nor the means, nor the power to tailor the public moneys to fit the varying needs of these students throughout the state." At that time problems in the measurement of educational needs were obvious to everyone, including the courts, but the complexities of accurate quantification of local school district fiscal ability were unforeseen (Coons et al. 1970: 206). Concerning the measurement of educational need, one school of thought was to assess children's deficiencies and apply cost differentials (Johns, Alexander, and Rossmiller 1969) while another felt that compensation in school finance formulas for variations in educational needs and deficiencies created intractable problems and should be largely ignored in state aid formulas. Coons et al. clearly enunciate this latter attitude: "By the no-wealth principle we disengage ourselves from the bootless argument for a Fourteenth Amendment obligation to treat disadvantaged children differently, that is, according to some occult perception of the personal characteristics of each. . . . It may be that constitutional arguments for preference according to personal need will eventually succeed, but we neither expect such a result nor support it" (Coons et al. 1970: 309). This difference of position in the role of state finance formulas constitutes a formal departure from the educational philosophy of the foundation program. On a philosophical theoretical basis, it is the neutrality theory of Hayek versus the "least favored" philosophy of Rawls.

Herein lies the essential difference between the educational finance definition of mere equality and a more pervasive standard of equity. A system of educational finance which merely fiscally equalizes, or neutralizes, or provides equal distribution to local school districts with low fiscal capacity is admittedly inferior, on this scale of social justice, to a system which attempts to fully fiscally equalize and, in addition, to provide resources to the "least-favored" children in the Rawlsian tradition.

Problems surrounding fiscal effort create an additional complicating factor which holds philosophical implications for considerations of equity. At one end of the continuum there are those who maintain the desirability of total or local determination of fiscal effort. To advocate this position Coons et al. coined the term "subsidiarity" (Coons et al. 1970: 14-15). It is maintained that subsidiarity and equality are compatible values, but that local choice should be permitted even if it creates unequal educational opportunity. A contrary position is that a child's education should not be a function of low aspiration or local disregard for the value of education: "A child's education may be seriously impaired if local aspiration levels prevent local school authorities from utilizing resources which are present in the tax base of the community" (Alexander and Jordan 1976: 347-49).

These three issues--fiscal equality, educational needs, and uniformity of effort--have been viewed in different ways by the courts. As pointed out above, plaintiffs in both *McInnis* and *Burruss* maintained that the state must assure the child that neither fiscal inability nor educational need disparities should work to create an inferior education. Even though the plaintiffs in these cases were unsuccessful, they nevertheless presented the rationale which has apparently become most popular in the major state court decisions of the present. Their concept of equity is that the state must 1) erase the fiscal disparities among school districts, 2) correct with cost differential programs for variations in educational needs, and 3) require a uniform local effort at a level high enough to assure adequate resources in every school district. These cases propound a much more comprehensive concept of equity than the mere fiscal equality standard which was first advanced in *Serrano* (1971) and in *San Antonio Independent School District v. Rodriguez* (1973).

The Supreme Court of California delineated the difference between *McInnis* and *Serrano*: "contentions of Plaintiffs here are significantly different from those in *McInnis*. The instant complaint employs a familiar standard . . . discrimination on the basis of wealth. . . . By contrast, the *McInnis* Plaintiffs repeatedly emphasized 'educational needs'" (*Serrano v. Priest* 1971).

To contrast the two positions is to more clearly identify the basic difference of simple equality and a more pervasive concept of equity. The mathematical equality of *Serrano* is deficient in accommodating a full range of equitable considerations. *McInnis*, more complex constitutionally and not as susceptible to "judicially manageable" measurability, nevertheless conveyed the attributes of a more full-blown concept of equity.

The limited standard of *Serrano* has been reflected in some other state cases, best exemplified by *Horton v. Meskill* (1977), wherein the Supreme Court of Connecticut found the state's system of school financing to be constitutionally deficient because it failed to correct for the "great disparity of local communities to finance local education." Of primary concern to the court was the issue of fiscal equality. This was certainly appropriate, in this instance, in view of Connecticut's woefully primitive method of financing, but the court did not expand on the educational ramification which disparities in educational needs and variation in fiscal effort would create in imbalancing educational opportunity. Although the court did not foreclose inclusion of correction factors of need and effort, it seemed more concerned that the local community have a high degree of choice. Absolute equality, the court maintained, is not required, nor are precisely equal educational advantages. Such departure apparently permits the legislature to address the more pervasive issues of equity but does not by any mean require it. Here, as in *Serrano*, the court is apparently content to tolerate very wide effort differentials among the school districts with no provision by the state for correction of educational need variations.

Most recent court decisions, contrarily, follow the rationale advanced by the plaintiffs, in *McInnis*, that educational needs and wide effort variation must be accounted for in the state school aid program. Thus, in Colorado a lower court held a system of financing unconstitutional, stating that even though the "educational needs of school children vary to some degree among school districts because of geographical, ecological, social, and economic factors" (*Lujan* v. *Colorado State Board of Education* 1979) neither the legislature nor the state education agency had taken steps to formulate an educational finance system which had the ingredients required of a "thorough and uniform" educational program which was required by the Colorado Constitution. The court observed that the state had not undertaken any analysis of the extent of variations in "educational needs throughout the state." The court, therefore, took a broad view of the legal concept of equity, apparently requiring that the system reflect more than mere fiscal equality.

This more comprehensive view of educational equity was followed in a Levittown, New York, case in which the court reasoned that the state finance program must account for non-educational demands on the local property tax (municipal overburden), costs of educational services, and the educational needs of particular children or groups of children which vary greatly from district to district (*Board of Education, Levittown Union Free School District of Nassau Country* v. *Nyquist* 1978).

A lower court in Ohio, in holding the Ohio system of school finance unconstitutional, found that the state constitution's "thorough and efficient" provision required that the "state has a commitment not merely to provide minimal educational opportunity but to maintain the finest public school system possible in a free government" (*Board of Education of the City School District of Cincinnati* v. *Walter* 1978). This court ruled that vast disparities in expenditures denied equality of educational opportunity and that overall substantial educational services were not delivered to the majority of the children in Ohio. The court pointed out that the state financing formula did provide for fiscal equalization of local property disparities, but that it was inadequate in amount of funds available. It did not properly account for educational need differences among students, and the local tax effort provision had collapsed of its own weight. The Ohio court established criteria for a valid system--an equitable system. It must provide 1) realistic appraisal of educational needs, 2) equal opportunity, and 3) high-quality general education, with arrangements for meeting the special educational needs of certain students. 4) It must compensate urban districts for special costs. 5) Quality of child's education can be dependent only on educational needs, not on irrelevant factors. 6) The state's role must be primary. 7) Variations in local effort can only result in differences in educational offerings *above* a level of high-quality general education. 8) The system must be financed at adequate level.

This view of educational equity is consistent with an earlier decision in which the Supreme Court of New Jersey said that a "thorough and efficient system of public schooling must be understood to embrace that educational opportunity which is needed in the contemporary setting to equip a child for his role as a citizen and as a competitor in the labor market" (*Robinson* v. *Cahill* 1973). As in the Colorado and Ohio cases, the court of New Jersey was not satisfied to allow the state to delegate away its educational responsibility to the local school districts. It was held to be the state's responsibility to "define in some discernible way the educational obligation and *compel* the local school districts to raise the money necessary to provide that opportunity."

From these legal definitions of equality, thoroughness, uniformity, and efficiency of education, it becomes quite clear that fiscal equalization of the taxpaying capacity of the local school district is only one element in the judicial definition of a concept of equity. As a concept governing the distribution of educational funds, equity must necessarily include all those elements which contribute to the provision of equal access to a basic educational program. Factors which tend to limit any child's equal access may theoretically be found detrimental to attainment of equity. Certainly, as the courts have indicated, among the many essential considerations must be finance-formula redress for local school district incapacity created by economic, social, geographical, and personal conditions which may impair the child's full enjoyment of his or her public educational entitlement.

It appears, from reviewing the court decisions, that equal protection provisions of the state constitutions are more likely to be narrowly interpreted to refer only to equalization of taxpaying ability of local school districts, while education provisions of state constitutions requiring the state to provide "thorough," "efficient", "uniform," etc., systems of education are more comprehensive, mandating a higher level of educational equity. Fiscal equalization, therefore, is an essential element in an overall concept of equity of state school finance, but it alone does not meet the legal standard of equity prescribed by *Levittown* (New York), *Robinson* (New Jersey), and *Walter* (Ohio). On the other hand, the minimal requirements of *Serrano* (California) and *Horton* (Connecticut) may be met by equalizing taxpaying ability of local school districts.

A School Finance Equity Model

Combining the more rigorous requirements of the New York, New Jersey, and Ohio cases into a taxonomy describing the components of a model of educational finance equity, the following emerge. Equity requires:

1) Adequate funding of basic *developmental educational programs* in such a way as to establish thorough, efficient, and uniform educational opportunity throughout the state.

2) A basic formula adjustment which will fully *fiscally equalize* among all school districts in the state. This is probably the most important single element in the determination of equity, but it cannot stand alone if true equity is to be achieved. The term "fiscal neutrality" will suffice as a reasonably definitive standard.

3) A level of *fiscal effort uniformity* at such a high level as to prevent a child's education from being a function of low educational aspiration of the community, or to prevent external local political influences, unresponsive to or unconcerned with education, from denying appropriate educational opportunity. Local tax leeway, unlimited local choice, or subsidiarity are all earmarks of an inequitable system.

4) Financing for *corrective educational programs* designed to meet particular and individual needs of children which are due to congenital deficiencies adversely affecting educational achievement. Such programs must not establish unreasonable or legally irrational classifications of children.

5) Financing for *remedial educational programs* designed to provide measures to offset educational disadvantage caused by social or economic distortions. Such financing may be justified as offsetting individual deficiencies of the least advantaged.

6) Financing for *diseconomies of scale* created by geographic and demographic conditions.

7) Financing for *governmental overburdens* which tend to drain local tax resources on which the local school district must rely.

8) Financing which is designed to correct for differences in the *cost of delivering comparable educational services* throughout a state. Such a factor goes beyond a simple adjustment for cost of living as determined by an economic marketbasket; instead, its purpose is to correct for disparities in school district power to purchase educational services.

Prevailing legal precedents, therefore, suggest that true educational equity is obtainable only through a complexity of financial considerations, no one of which can accommodate the desired standard. Fiscal equalization among school districts is probably the most important single component in an equitable system, but it is insufficient in and of itself.

School Finance Equity Today[2]

The development of state school finance systems designed to provide equity for students and taxpayers has long been a major concern of writers in the field of public school finance. The concept of equality of educational opportunity has been central to discussions of state school finance equity. Many years ago, Cubberley concluded that the magnitude of local fiscal capacity disparities was such that "any attempt at the equalization of opportunities for education, much less any attempt at equalizing burdens, is clearly impossible under a system of exclusively local taxation" (Cubberley 1906: 54). Recognizing the limitations inherent in school finance models based entirely or predominantly on local taxation, Cubberley recommended that general state aid be used to facilitate movement toward greater educational equity.

Reviewing the concepts of "equalization of educational opportunity" and "equalization of tax support," Strayer and Haig early observed that strict interpretation of these concepts would imply that "the state should ensure equal educational facilities to every child within its borders at a uniform effort throughout the state in terms of the burden of taxation; the tax burden of education should throughout the state be uniform in relation to tax-paying ability, and the provision of schools should be uniform in relation to the educable population desiring education" (Strayer and Haig 1923: 173). Noting that most individuals would insist on the provision of at least a minimally educational program in all school districts, but would not preclude individual districts from going beyond that minimum at their own expense, Strayer and Haig recommended that the concepts of educational equity and equalization of school support be operationalized by furnishing all children within the state with equal educational opportunities up to a prescribed minimum, and raising the funds necessary for this purpose through state and local taxation adjusted so as to bear upon taxpayers in all districts at the same rate in relation to local fiscal capacity.

Discussion of educational equity for students has concentrated primarily on the provision of resource inputs necessary for the attainment of equality of educational opportunity (see Mort and Reusser 1974: 99-100). Beginning in the early 1960's, numerous writers focused on the shortcomings of the traditional foundation method of equalizing educational opportunities. Reflecting a general movement in the United States toward the elimination of inequality of opportunity based on social and economic factors, the generally accepted definition of educational equity was broadened to include substantial equality in the provision of educational services beyond the minimum level and equality of educational outputs as well as inputs.

Johns and Morphet (1960: 5) observed that most Americans apparently believed that "everyone should have equality of opportunity for the kind and quality of educational program which will best meet his needs and those of the society in which he lives." They noted that this standard had not been attained in many communities due to such factors as inefficient school districts organization, inadequate state school finance programs, ineffective local policies, and inept educational leadership. However, they reasoned that more complete attainment of equality of educational opportunity would be forthcoming because of growing acceptance of the concept as a public policy objective.

The foundation program concept has been roundly criticized because of the wide disparities it permits between rich and poor school districts. It does not suffice to say that the more affluent, with their greater ability to obtain greater funding from local sources, merely use this money to add on a few unnecessary educational frills. On the contrary, these additional funds tend to give these districts a higher degree of quality which comes about from being able to attract better teachers by paying higher salaries and to generally provide those services which enrich the educational programs (Benson 1965: 86). As an alternative definition to the foundation concept, Benson (1965: 62) suggested that equality of educational opportunity "implies that any two children of the same abilities shall receive equivalent forms of assistance in developing those abilities, wherever they live in a given state and whatever their parental circumstances are."

Fiscal Neutrality

Through the writings of Wise (1967) and Coons et al. (1970), the fiscal neutrality principle was developed as a legal definition of fiscal equality. During the 1970's, fiscal neutrality emerged as a major standard for evaluating state school finance programs. Fiscal neutrality has received varying interpretations in the school finance literature, being viewed as a fiscal equity standard for both students and taxpayers. Wise advanced the argument that the failure of a state to provide for substantial equality of educational opportunity may consitute a denial of equal protection of the laws in violation of the Fourteenth Amendment.

Following Wise, Coons et al. (1970) developed a detailed rationale for school finance litigation which formulated a negative definition of equal educational opportunity based on a fiscal neutrality standard, challenging the constitutionality of state school finance systems on equal protection grounds. The standard of school finance equality developed by Wise (1967: 146) provided that the quality of a child's education may not be a function of either local wealth or geographic location, while the standard developed by Coons was only concerned with wealth.

Fiscal neutrality is a limited concept. It only applied to measurement of the degree of equalization of taxpaying capacity among local school districts; it does not attempt to measure the more pervasive standard of equality of educational opportunity or educational equity. In spite of its limitations it is an attractive concept, from an economist's point of view, primarily because it suggests a quantifiable definition of fiscal equalization. Benson made the following observation concerning the definition of fiscal neutrality: "The heuristic use of the concept of fiscal neutrality in *Serrano* and related cases has no thorough development in the literature of public finance. I suggest that we are free, those of us who are interested in social policy, to define the term in any sensible way we wish" (1973: 55). Benson then defined fiscal neutrality broadly as existing "when we see no warping or distortion of choice in consumption of tax-financed goods and services on irrational or socially undesirable grounds."

Barro categorized alternative interpretations of fiscal neutrality as follows: "The *ex post* interpretation is that the actual level of educational support must not correlate with wealth. On that basis, a system that resulted in both higher spending and higher tax effort in wealthy districts would not be acceptable. The *ex ante* formulation is that the *ability* of a district to support schools should not depend on wealth. This means only that a unit of effort must produce the same support everywhere. In that case a correlation between expenditure and wealth might be acceptable" (Barro: 34).

The *ex post* fiscal neutrality standard requires that variations in revenue per educational need unit not be systematically related to variations in local fiscal capacity. Measurement of *ex post* fiscal neutrality involves quantitative analysis of the relationship between local fiscal capacity and revenue per pupil unit. The *ex ante* fiscal neutrality standard requires that equal tax effort result in equal revenue per unit, irrespective of variations in local fiscal capacity. Measurement of *ex ante* fiscal neutrality involves quantitative analysis of the relationship between local tax effort and revenue per pupil unit.

Measures of Equity

The development of quantitative measures of school finance equity was stimulated by Congress in 1974 through the enactment of an amendment to Public Law 81-874 (P.L. 93-380, Sec. 5 d 2). This amendment provided that states with public school finance systems "designed to equalize expenditures" would be permitted to include P.L. 874 funds as a local resource in the calculation of state equalization aid to local school districts. The U.S. Commissioner of Education was required to issue regulations establishing operational tests for determining whether a state's public school finance system was designed to equalize expenditures.

As a result, two statistical measures were developed: an expenditure disparity test, and a wealth neutrality test (Magers, 1977: 124-128). The expenditure disparity test reflects a resource equality standard of school finance equity. Essentially, this test requires that the 95th to 5th percentile range in expenditure (or revenue) per educational need unit not exceed 25 percent of the 5th percentile level after adjusting for cost differentials recognized by the state (*Federal Register* 1977: 15540-50). The wealth neutrality test is based on the equal yield for equal effort principle, reflecting the *ex ante* fiscal neutrality standard. It requires that 85 percent of total state and local revenues be wealth neutral (*Federal Register* 1977: 65524-27). Procedures used for determining which revenues are wealth neutral and which are not were summarized by Johns and Magers (1978: 381-82), who proposed a national school finance equity assessment model. The model focused on two classes of individuals directly affected by state school finance systems: pupils and taxpayers. Resource disparity and resource sufficiency were incorporated as conditions of pupil equity, while wealth disparity was incorporated as a taxpayer equity condition. Quantitative measures of wealth disparity, resource disparity, and resource sufficiency were included, respectively, "to produce coefficients reflecting (1) the extent to which the access to resources vary, (2) the extent to which resources vary, and (3) the extent to which the level of resources is sufficient to provide an adequate educational program" (Johns and Magers 1978: 381-82). Statistics proposed for the measurement of wealth disparity, resource disparity, and resource sufficiency were the P.L. 81-874 wealth neutrality test, the relative mean deviation in expenditure per pupil, and the percentage by which state mean expenditure per pupil falls below national mean expenditure per pupil, respectively. It was suggested that the model could be used "as a national standard for judging the relative equity of state school finance models" (Johns and Magers 1978: 373).

Efforts to quantify equity as it relates to school finance have, thus, evolved primarily around methodologies to more accurately measure the relationships between school district fiscal capacity and educational resource inputs. Employed to do this have been the standard statistical tools of economists, Gini coefficients, and various other measures of relative variation and deviation. Few attempts have been made to fully define what equality of opportunity is, or what a concept of equity implies for school financing mechanisms. Part of the problem has been that there is no overall theoretical base from which to work--a problem common to the nebulous concept of equity, whether its application is to educational finance or any other field of endeavor.

It is certain, though, that more is required than simple fiscal neutrality or full fiscal equalization. The complexity of the educational enterprise creates financing problems which transcend mere mathematical equalization of local taxpaying capacity.

Equity Hierarchy

Although philosophical equity, legal equity, and the practice of school finance are not easily reconciled, commonalities can be found. As shown in Figure 1, a hierarchy of equity can be fashioned, progressing from the lowest philosophical level of commutative equity upward to the highest level of positivism. The steps in the hierarchy, when related to school finance legal theory, produce a pattern of supplementary attributes which, if combined, produce an equitable school finance system. Any one taken alone would be equitably defective.

Commutative Equity

Beginning at the lowest level, commutative equity would simply be an exchange of resources which are indifferent to considerations of equality, educational need, initial endowments, etc. Shifting taxation to the local level produces almost this result, wherein the state and federal systems allow the individual district to retain its own resources regardless of ability. Assets are maintained, and no redistribution takes place. In this sense local tax prerogative and choice maintain economic homogeneity, but only within local boundaries.

Commutative equity may also suggest a system of laissez-faire self-interest which is not unlike the result of a governmental allocation system, the proceeds of which flow to the private sector, benefiting those who in large measure already have financial resources. It brings to mind the dual systems of public education in Europe, where state financial support has in many instances served to strengthen private schools, maintaining the elitism and advantage of the wealthy few. Today, in this country, proposals for tax credits and other devices to aid private schools must be classified as examples of this lowest scale of equity. These are commutative in the sense that they would tend, without extraordinary restrictions, to per-

Philosophical Equity

```
                                                    POSITIVISM
                                                    Fiscal neutrality
                                                    Uniformity of effort
                                                    Cost of delivering education
                              RESTITUTION           Economies of scale
                              Fiscal neutrality     Governmental overburden
                              Uniformity of effort  Corrective programs
                              Cost of delivering    Remedial programs
              EQUAL           education
              DISTRIBUTION
                              Economies of scale
              Fiscal neutrality
                              Governmental overburden
              Subsidiarity
              (Local choice)
COMMUTATIVE   Unlimited local effort
Local leeway
Subsidiarity
  (Local choice)
Unlimited local effort
                         Legal Equity
                                         Rawls
                   Hayek     ─────────────────────►
            ◄──────────────
             (Conservative)                  (Liberal)
            ◄──────────────────────────────────────►
```

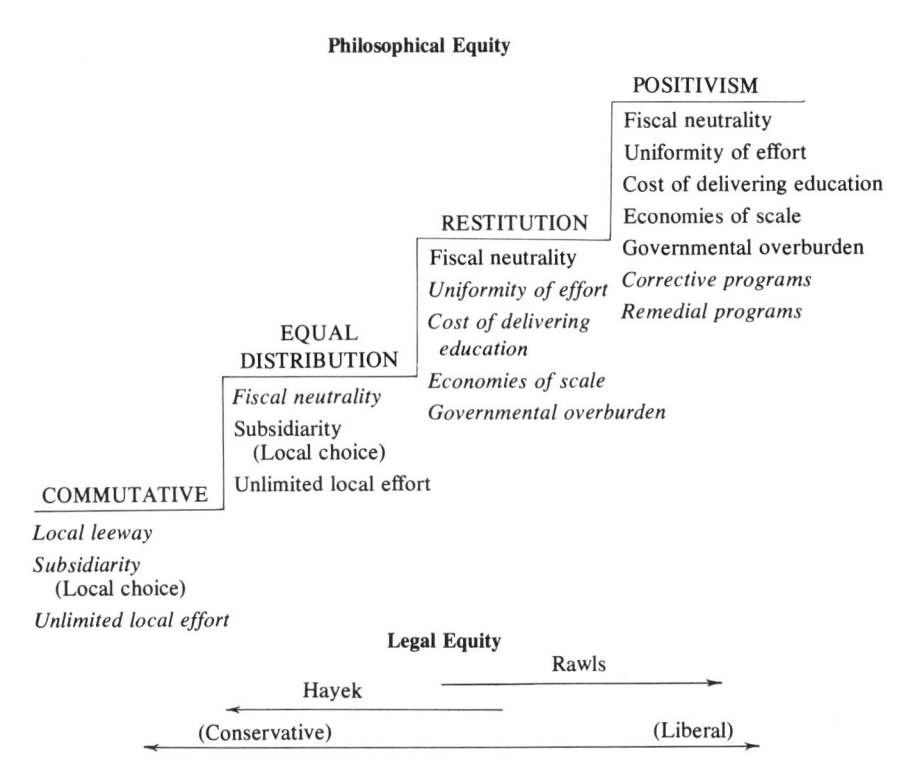

Figure 1. Equity Hierarchy

petuate and even crystalize the differences between caste and class in America. The derivative effect would be to siphon from the public educational system the resources which would otherwise go for a public purpose.

Equal Distribution

At the next-highest step of philosophical equity, seeking a more equal distribution, we find a presumption that the educational system is an obligation of the state and that in implementation the state treats all local school districts in a fiscally neutral manner; all have access to the same amount of money per pupil. The state here is not primarily concerned with uniformity of services, efficiency of operation, or thoroughness of the educational program. An equal fiscal base is provided for all the schools regardless of where they are located, and it is a local prerogative to decide entirely on what level of educational program is desired. This is, of course, the fiscal neutrality concept which became the rationale on which *Serrano* was decided. At this level, educational equity is defined as full fiscal equalization, the only prescribed standard.

The school finance formula most closely associated with this level of equity would be district power equalization. In its most primitive form, as recommended by Coons et al. (1970) originally, district power equalization would fully fiscally equalize, but subsidiarity gaps in educational opportunity would be permitted and would continue to exist.

Restitution

The third level of philosophical equity is classified as restitutionary because it requires that the state recompense local school districts for problems created by either economic or social conditions. Here the state responds to local conditions which cause educational opportunity to vary from some established norm. Implicit in this level of equity is an established desirable level of educational opportunity. Restitution, though, is only provided for those structural weaknesses of the system, whether social or economic, and is not related to the child's personal educational needs.

Restitution requires the state to mitigate fiscal inequities created by diseconomies of scale of schools or school districts, cost variations in delivering comparable educational services, and adjustments for effort disparities among school districts.

Most important among these is the role the state must play in equalizing the fiscal effort among school districts. This can be accomplished by high levels of required local effort or charge-backs of the foundation program variety. Traditional, unembellished percentage-equalizing formulas did not have the capacity to correct for low effort, and standing alone were more nearly associated with Level II equity than with Level III.

Restitution or restoration constitutes a high level of equity when combined with full fiscal equalization or fiscal neutrality. Restitution conveys the philosophy that education is a state function, and as such has not only the responsibility but also the obligation to rectify and idemnify shortcomings at the local school district level.

Positivism

At the highest level of educational equity in Figure 1, positivism demands that the unique and high-cost programs which are designed to meet individual needs of children be fully financed. This is Rawlsian equity, which justifies intervention if it is designed to assist the least advantaged. These types of needs include corrective programs for those children with congenital deficiencies which can be moderated by effective education processes. Programs for handicapped children fall into this category. Herein, also, is justified a kind of fiscal affirmative action whereby those who suffer disadvantages because of societal or cultural conditions receive the benefits of specially designed and financed remedial educational programs.

Equity of educational finance constitutes a complexity of issues related to equal educational opportunity. It is instructive to note that, from both the philosophical and legal viewpoints, equity is much broader than the simple fiscal equalization. Fiscal equalization alone, while probably the most important building block to an equitable system, is less than adequate alone. Its deficiencies may be related to overall fiscal inadequacy, a lack of uniformity in fiscal effort, failure to identify and accommodate appropriate costs, and the lack of recognition of educational needs.

NOTES

1. A problem which cannot be completely resolved emerges with the definition of disadvantage. It is always difficult to distinguish between needs and wants. Of course, it may be easy to determine when someone is severely physically or mentally handicapped, but minor exceptionalities are not so easily identifiable. Health care, housing, and food should be classified as needs, along with basic education. The problem arises in trying to assess just what is minimally necessary, and in determining what action is required to obtain the essentials. Of course, one may assert that it is not the minimum that is required, but a higher level of appropriate ness on the average.

2. I express my appreciation to Thomas R. Melcher, research associate, Institute for Educational Finance, for his contribution in preparing the school finance equity statement included herein.

REFERENCES

Alexander, Kern, and Jordan, K. Forbis. 1976. *Educational need in the public economy*. Gainesville: University Presses of Florida.

Barro, Stephen M. 1974. Alternative post-Serrano systems and their expenditure implication. In *School finance in transition: the courts and educational reform*, ed. J. Pincus. Cambridge: Ballinger.

Benson, Charles S. 1965. *The cheerful prospect: a statement on the future of public education*. Boston: Houghton Mifflin.

―――. 1973. Accomplishing fiscal neutrality. In *School finance in transition: proceedings of the 16th national conference on school finance*. Gainesville: National Educational Finance Project.

Board of Education, Levittown Union Free School District of Nassau County v. Nyquist, 409 N.Y.S. 2d 606 (1978).

Board of Education of City School District of Cincinnati v. Walter, No. A7602725, Court of Common Pleas, Hamilton County, Ohio, 1978.

Brown v. Board of Education, 347 U.S. 483 (1954).

Burruss v. Wilkerson, 310 F. Supp. 572 (1969), aff'd mem. sub. nom., 397 U.S. 44 (1970).

Coons, John E.; Clune III, William H.; and Sugarman, Stephen D. 1970. *Private wealth and public education*. Cambridge: Harvard University Press.

Cubberley, Ellwood P. 1906. *School funds and their apportionment*. New York: Columbia University, Teachers College.

Dorfman, William B. 1978. *Educational opportunities: the concept, its measurement, and application.* Washington: National Center for Education Statistics, U.S. Department of Health, Education and Welfare. P. 24.
Federal Register 42, March 22, 1977, pp. 15540-50; December 30, 1977, pp. 65524-27.
Hayek, Freidrich A. 1976. *Law, legislation and liberty*, II. Chicago: University of Chicago Press.
Hobson v. Hansen, 269 F. Supp. 401 (1967).
Horton v. Meskill, 1972 Conn. 615, 376 A. 2d 359 (1977).
Jenness v. Fortson, 403 U.S. 431, 91 S.Ct. 1970 (1976).
Johns, Roe L.; Alexander, K.; and Rossmiller, R. 1969. *Dimensions of educational need.* Gainesville: National Educational Finance Project.
Johns, Roe L., and Morphet, Edgar L. 1960. *Financing the public schools.* Englewood Cliffs, N.J.: Prentice-Hall.
Johns, Thomas L., and Magers, Dexter A. 1978. Measuring the equity of state school finance programs. *Journal of Education Finance* 3: 373-85.
Lau v. Nichols, 414 U.S. 563, 94 S.Ct. 786 (1974).
Lujan v. Colorado State Board of Education, Civil Action No. C-73688, Dist. Court City and County of Denver (1979).
Magers, Dexter A. 1977. Two tests of equity under impact aid Public Law 81-874. *Journal of Education Finance* 3: 124-28.
McInnis v. Ogilvie, 394 U.S. 322 (1969).
Moris, Clarence, ed. 1971. *The great legal philosophers.* Philadelphia: University of Pennsylvania Press.
Mort, Paul R., and Reusser, Walter C. 1941. *Public school finance.* New York: McGraw-Hill.
Plucknett, Theodore F. T. 1956. *A concise history of common law.* Boston: Little, Brown.
Rawls, John. 1977. *A theory of justice.* Cambridge: Harvard University Press.
Robinson v. Cahill, 62 N.J. 473, 303 A.2d 273 (1973).
Robertson, D. B. 1957. *Love and justice: selections from the shorter writings of Reinhold Niebuhr.* New York: Meridan Books.
San Antonio Independent School District v. Rodriguez, 411 U.S. I, 93 S.Ct. 1278 (1973).
Schlesinger, Arthur, Jr. 1978. Human rights and the American tradition. *Foreign Affairs* 57 (3): 503.
Serrano v. Priest, 5 Cal. 3d 584, 96 Cal. Rptr. 601, 487 P.2d. 1241 (1971).
Strayer, George D., and Haig, Robert M. 1923. *The financing of education in the state of New York.* New York: Macmillan.
Tumin, Melvin. 1965. The meaning of equality in education. Paper presented at the Third Annual Conference of the National Committee for Support of Public Schools, Washington, D.C.
Tyler, Ralph. 1972. Personal correspondence, October 9, 1967, cited in *On equality of educational opportunity*, ed. Frederick Mosteller and Daniel P. Moynihan. New York: Random House.
Wise, Arthur E. 1967. *Rich schools, poor schools: the promise of equal educational opportunity.* Chicago: University of Chicago Press.

CHAPTER 9

Equity and Higher Education Finance: The Case of Community Colleges

SUSAN C. NELSON

From the perspective of public policy, the world of higher education is fundamentally different from the one a person leaves behind at high school graduation. While the high school graduate undergoes no magical transformation during the following summer, society has decided that its responsibility for his education shifts from guaranteeing a right to providing opportunities.

The change is reflected in the different criteria used to judge the equity of public subsidies at the two levels of education. While earlier chapters of this volume emphasize equity in the context of elementary-secondary finance, this chapter focuses on its extension into higher education. In the first section I shall examine and evaluate the ways in which equity has been analyzed in the literature on higher education finance. In the second section I apply the lessons from the literature to community colleges, the sector of higher education with the closest kinship to elementary-secondary schooling. In particular, I discuss the question of imposing tuition in California's community college system.

Equity: Some Theoretical Perspectives

The notion of equity in higher education finance is a normative one: people disagree on what strikes them as equitable, but it is hard to say that one view is right and another wrong. However, if equity is to be considered in policy decisions, it becomes necessary to choose among versions of equity which have conflicting implications. The fundamental choice in the literature is between 1) treating higher education subsidies like any other government programs that transfer income among people, and 2) viewing them as special and recognizing their inter-generational implications. Specifically, should equity for higher education subsidies be defined simply as a pro-poor redistribution of current income? Or should equity be defined more broadly?

Most of the empirical work adopts the former narrow view, extending from other areas of public policy the concern with the distribution of current economic well-being among the general population. "What impact do the benefits and burdens of government have on the current distribution of income? Some variant of this question has frequently been asked of government policies (Reynolds and Smolensky 1977). The studies discussed below apply this question to subsidies for higher education. Although this "net benefit" approach is popular, serious conceptual and practical problems limit its usefulness for examining the equity of higher education subsidies.

A second view of equity would judge the subsidies more in accordance with the nature of higher education. Since higher education represents an investment in future income, one version might test subsidies according to their impact on the long-run, or lifetime, distribution of income. While this approach has fewer conceptual problems than evaluating equity in terms of current redistribution, it is impractical. An alternative version would judge the costs of the subsidies separately from the benefits. The first aspect would involve focusing on the distributional consequences of raising revenues through the tax system, while the second would concentrate on the distribution of both educational opportunities and income. This approach to equity seems the most reasonable and practical of the three and is the one I shall later apply to the particular question of imposing tuition at California's community colleges.

Before turning to the previous studies of equity, it is necessary to stress the role of efficiency--the allocation of resources so that they may generate the greatest value of output, whether it be airplanes or intangible benefits to society--in justifying *any* subsidies for higher education. It is generally accepted that higher education produces current and future private benefits for the student as well as public benefits for society. If higher education were viewed as having only private benefits, there would be no *efficiency* grounds for subsidizing it and for inducing people to consume more higher education than they otherwise would. Inherently, the external benefits of the higher level of education are consumed collectively and accrue equally to everyone (except possibly for spatial variations). Since people may place different values on these benefits, the political process is charged with finding a level of subsidy that is acceptable to a majority of voters, and with combining the concerns of equity and efficiency into a single finance system. Economic evidence can affect those judgments.

Equity as the Redistribution of Current Income

Reflecting the general concern that public policy improve (or at least not worsen) the distribution of economic well-being, a number of studies have examined higher education subsidies in terms of their effects on the current distribution of income. Although the approach is quite common and appealing, it is also problematic. Three factors in particular challenge the reliability of the conclusions on redistribution, and a fourth questions its use as a measure of equity. Because of the popularity of this approach, its problems will be discussed at some length.

Perspectives on Net Benefits. In these studies, "net benefits" (that is, subsidies minus payments) hold the key to equity: subsidies are generally pronounced equitable if low-income households receive larger net benefits than more affluent households. But a major problem with attempting to determine the redistributional consequences of higher education subsidies is that examining net benefits in different ways, even for a single set of data, can reverse the conclusions.

A prime example of this problem involves the well-known study by Hansen and Weisbrod (1969) that is the source of the conventional wisdom that the poor subsidize the rich through public higher education. Using data for California in 1964-65, Hansen and Weisbrod distinguished between families with students in California public higher education and those without. The latter received no subsidies, so their net benefits were negative, equal to their state and local taxes. For families with children in state-supported colleges, net benefits were positive, equal to the difference between the subsidy at the type of institution attended and the state and local taxes paid. By comparing net benefits for the median families in each group, Hansen and Weisbrod found, not surprisingly, that 1) the families receiving the lowest net benefits (those without students) had the lowest median incomes, and 2) among student families, the median *community college* student had both lower net benefits and lower family income than his counterpart attending a *state college*, who in turn had lower net benefits and income than the median *university* student. From this evidence, Hansen and Weisbrod concluded "that the current method of financing public higher education leads to a sizeable redistribution of income from lower to higher income." (1969: 77).

This conclusion of an anti-poor redistribution is reversed if net benefits are calculated for each income class, rather than only for the median student or household in each group of users or non-users. Using Hansen and Weisbrod's data, Pechman (1970) and Machlis (1973) distributed benefits across income classes according to the distribution of students at each level of institution, and they distributed an equal amount of taxes according to the income of taxpayers. Looking at the net benefits for the average family in each income class (Pechman) or for the income class as a whole (Machlis), net benefits were negative for high-income groups and positive for low- and middle-income people, implying that high-income households were subsidizing the low- and middle-income ones. Even if net benefits were calculated only for students, thereby focusing on the average student in each income class, Hansen and Weisbrod's conclusion is still reversed. (See Nelson 1978a: Table 6).

There are arguments on behalf of each approach.[1] Hansen and Weisbrod's method, however, masks the wide variation in tax payments among families with different incomes; even with regressive taxes, higher-income families invariably pay higher taxes.[2] Nearly all other empirical attempts to determine the effect of higher education subsidies on the distribution of current income have adopted the Pechman-Machlis approach.[3] Clearly, the choice between examining net benefits by income class versus examining income by net benefit level is not an esoteric question. The fact that reasonable methodologies can produce opposite conclusions reflects a problem inherent in determining the current redistributional consequences using this net benefit approach.

Treatment of Non-Users. The fact that the primary redistribution in higher education subsidies involves a transfer from non-students to students creates a second problem for judging equity according to net benefits. Some studies separate users and non-users throughout the analysis, but most implicitly (if not explicitly) assign a student's benefits to the whole income class. This practice hides the fact that, in the low-income groups, a few families receive substantial benefits, while at the other end of the income scale the benefits are more widespread. The studies of Pechman (1970), Windham (1970), Machlis (1973), the State of New Jersey Commission (1976), Crean (1975), Moore (1978), and Vredeveld (1978) all suffer from this problem.

Examining users and non-users separately has its drawbacks, however, due to the life-cycle patterns of college attendance and earnings. As long as college attendance generally begins right after high school graduation, the parents of most students will be between forty and sixty years old, near the peak of their lifetime earnings cycle. Consequently, students' families will inevitably have higher average incomes than the population at large. This point was the focus of the contributions to the literature by Crean (1975), Miklius (1975), and McGuire (1976). Although simple analyses such as Hansen and Weisbrod's, comparing incomes of families with and without students in public higher education, technically reflect the redistribution that is occurring, it seems inappropriate to consider such findings inequitable. In the context of a study on life-cycle aspects of income inequality, Moss (1978) has stated: "Inequalities in income associated with differences in age and experience during the prime years of work life are largely salutary....There is obviously no sense in trying to correct such sources of inequality in income associated with age."

To isolate inequality not related to age, McGuire suggests comparing student families with families in a comparable age cohort. This comparison permits judgments on whether students come from the more or less affluent part of the relevant population, but it says nothing about income redistribution. Even if the tax side is included—as Crean attempts, by comparing the distribution of benefits with the distribution of taxes paid by each age group—the implications for redistribution remain unclear, since all age groups are contributing to the subsidies. Because of the difficulty in evaluating the equity of these intergenerational transfers, the net-benefit approach produces a perplexing situation: evidence of income redistribution cannot be judged for its equity, and evidence of equity does not provide information on income redistribution.

The Importance of Data. As with most questions involving empirical tests, problems with data and definitions plague the researcher investigating the redistributional consequences of higher education subsidies. The danger in settling for only an approximation of desired data (as is commonly done) is particularly acute.

Two studies have reached inaccurate conclusions to their own questions because they used inappropriate data. Specifically, Windham (1970) and to a lesser extent the State of New Jersey Commission (1976), when calculating net benefits by income class, used tax payment information that predated the student income distribution data by several years. Due to inflation and the general growth in incomes, the tax distributions were unrepresentative of the populations from which the students came. For example, in his study of Florida, Windham distributed benefits according to student family incomes in 1967, but he allocated the costs according to 1960 and 1961 tax burdens. His conclusion that the poor were paying for the children of the rich to attend public higher education in Florida resulted primarily from the fact that the *whole population* had lower incomes in 1960 and 1961 than in 1967.

At least two alternative approaches could be used in order to avoid this inconsistency. First, the 1960 and 1961 tax distributions could be updated to reflect the 1967 distribution of income by assuming that each 1 percent of the population in a given income class essentially pays the same fraction of total taxes in 1960 or 1961 and in 1967. For example, since a smaller fraction of the population's income falls below $3,000 by 1967, this income class also carries a smaller fraction of the tax burden in that year. When the tax burdens that Windham used are revised to reflect the 1967 distribution of income (but not to reflect any changes in the tax system), it appears that the highest income groups have negative net benefits, while the less affluent classes generally receive positive net benefits. This reverses Windham's conclusion.[4]

A second way to avoid the problems that plague Windham's study would be to use contemporaneous tax and benefit information. When the 1966 Brookings MERGE file, which combines estimates of the 1966 burden of federal, state, and local taxes with 1967 demographic data,[5] is substituted for the 1960 and 1961 tax studies, Windham's conclusion is reversed again, and even more strongly, under both progressive and regressive incidence assumptions.[6] Again, findings on the redistributive impact of public subsidies for higher education, using the net benefit approach, are quite sensitive to the data on which they are based.

Judgments on the redistributional consequences of higher education subsidies are susceptible to other data problems that may not be as easy to rectify. The definitions of income in the cost data are apt to differ from those on the benefit side of the equation. In addition, the reliability of the student income information is questionable, since students are called upon to estimate their parents' incomes. Apart from the conceptual problems with the redistributional approach to equity, caution is required in accepting any of the empirical results because they could be severely distorted by these data problems.

Redistribution: Inconsistent with Other Views of Equity. A final problem inherent in the redistribution of current income net benefit approach to equity is that its conclusions are not necessarily consistent with the other interpretations of equity. Consequently, it becomes necessary to choose among the alternative approaches. Conlisk (1977), in a theoretical model of the effects of subsidies on the distribution of lifetime incomes (to be discussed further below), finds that the implications of the net benefits approach frequently conflicts with conclusions based on the redistribution of lifetime incomes. In addition, it is possible that in a good situation on educational opportunity grounds, with progressive taxes and a "pro-poor" distribution of benefits, the poor could appear to be subsidizing the more affluent due to life cycle considerations and to features in the tax laws that are outside of the control of educational policy decisions. (See Example A.) This anomaly results from the life cycle of earnings: if students come from families whose incomes are higher simply because they are older, then the transfer from non-students to students could appear to redistribute income from poor to rich, even if the lowest-income students receive the largest benefits. Alternatively, a situation with a regressive tax system and an "anti-poor" benefit distribution, which would fail any equity test in terms of equalizing educational opportunities, could also redistribute some income from the rich to the poor. (See Example B.) This second anomaly is due to the fact that, even with regressive tax systems, higher-income people almost inevitably pay higher taxes.

Only if equity is *defined* in terms of current income redistribution should that approach be used, since it cannot serve as a reliable proxy

EXAMPLE A. *Anti-Poor Distribution of Net Benefits: Pro-Poor Tax and Subsidy Distributions*

In State A, taxpayers fall into either of two distinct groups: the young and the old, distributed across income classes (as in Rows 1 and 2 below). All of the old group and none of the young receive benefits from the subsidies (i.e., have family members attending college) this year, while next year all of the young group is assured of receiving benefits. Subsidies for higher education are distributed progressively among students (Row 3), with students from low-income families receiving larger subsidies than their more affluent counterparts. The subsidies for higher education are raised through progressive taxation of all households (Row 5).

According to the net benefit approach, benefits are attributed to the average taxpayer (not the average recipient)in each income class (Row 7). Consequently, the net benefit calculations indicate a redistribution of income from poor to rich (Row 8), although the largest redistribution occurs between young and old taxpayers.

Hypothetical Benefits and Tax Distributions in State A

	\$10,000	\$15,000	\$20,000	\$25,000
1. Number of young families	50	30	15	5
2. Number of old families	5	15	30	50
3. Benefits per old family	\$520	\$460	\$420	\$390
4. Benefits per young family	0	0	0	0
5. Tax rate	1.0%	1.1%	1.2%	1.3%
6. Average tax payment	\$100	\$165	\$240	\$325
7. Average benefit	\$47	\$153	\$280	\$355
8. Average net benefits	\$-53	\$-12	\$40	\$30

Mean annual family income

Explanation:
Rows 1 - 5: assumed.
Row 6: tax rate × income.
Row 7: Benefits per old family × number of old families
Number of old families + number of young families.
Row 8: Average benefit-average tax payment.

for the other interpretations of equity. The current redistributional consequences of subsidies for higher education do not necessarily reflect either their long-run redistributional impacts, or their effects on educational opportunities. Furthermore, in view of the three problems discussed earlier--the sensitivity of the conclusions to the perspective on net benefits chosen; the dilemma of non-users and the intergenerational nature of the transfers; and the sensitivity to choice of data--even defining equity as income redistribution does not guarantee that an accurate net benefit assessment can be made. Consequently, it seems unwise to rely on findings about the effects of net benefits on current income redistribution to determine the equity of higher education subsidies.

EXAMPLE B. *Pro-Poor Distribution of Net Benefits; Anti-Poor Tax and Benefit Distribution*

State B confers greater higher education subsidies (benefits) on students from high- than from low-income families (Row 1), even though there is no difference in overall attendance rates across income classes. Financial support for higher education is raised through regressive taxes (Row 2). Because high-income families have larger tax bills even with regressive taxes (Row 3), net benefit calculations indicate a redistribution of income from rich to poor (Row 4).

Hypothetical Benefits and Tax Distributions in State B

	Mean annual family income			
	$10,000	$15,000	$20,000	$25,000
1. Benefits per family	$130	$160	$170	$180
2. Tax rate on income	1.1%	1.0%	0.9%	0.8%
3. Average tax payment	$110	$150	$180	$200
4. Average net benefits	$20	$10	$-10	$-20

Explanation: Rows 1 & 2: assumed.
Row 3: tax rate X income.
Row 4: benefit per family-average tax payment.

Equity as Lifetime Redistribution

Higher education can be distinguished from most other publicly supported social programs in two important ways. First, expenditures on higher education are rightly considered investments in human capital with substantial payoffs, some private and some public, in the future. Second, unlike other programs where redistribution of current income is a prime concern--such as housing subsidies, food stamps, public works programs, and health care, as well as straightforward income-transfer programs--higher education subsidies do not contribute substantially to the current economic well-being of the recipients. These differences suggest that subsidies for higher education should be judged in terms of their long-run influence on economic welfare and its distribution. As Pechman has stated, "The real question is whether public higher education makes the distribution of *lifetime* incomes of the recipients of its benefits and of society in general more or less equal" (1970: 368).

A few contributions to the literature have adopted this long-run intergenerational income distribution view, which is discussed in connection with Figure 3 in Chapter 1 and which is also the one that Pechman recommends. In the most elaborate attempt, Conlisk (1977) developed a sophisticated simultaneous equation model of intergenerational changes in income distribution. A child's lifetime income is affected by (among other factors) his parents' after-tax income, which is in turn related to the amount of higher education subsidies society provides. Unfortunately, the impact of tuition subsidies or other policy alternatives on lifetime incomes remains indeterminate in Conlisk's model.

Robert Hartman (1972) suggested a simpler but less complete approach. His method would focus on a cohort of high school seniors with various family incomes and would predict, under alternative tuition and subsidy policies, what their incomes would be at age fifty. He suspects that family income is a much stronger determinant of educational attainment (and of future earnings) than the cost of college, implying that tuition subsidies would not substantially alter the distribution of future income. Although Hartman's method is more tractable than Conlisk's, it is an incomplete projection of the cohort's future income since it does not consider the alternative uses to which the tax money could be put, in either the public or the private sector.

Even if a workable model could be developed, it is unclear how equity should be evaluated across generations, since with higher education the generation that pays for the subsidies is usually not the one receiving the benefits. Some taxpayers may have benefited in a similar manner in the past, and some may benefit through their children, but it is unclear how to judge the overall equity of taking from one generation (with the resultant effects on its income distribution) and giving to another (with another set of distributional consequences).

Equity of Costs and Benefits

In addition to a concern with the distribution of economic well-being that is achieved, either currently or prospectively, public higher education has long been advocated for its role in equalizing opportunities. As Arthur Okun wrote, "Equality of opportunity is a value in itself." He explains this value as reflecting "a conviction that economic inequalities that stem from inequality of opportunity are more intolerable (and, at the same time, more remediable) than those that emerge even when opportunities are equal. But the concept of equality of opportunity is far more elusive than that of equality of income.... Basically it is rooted in the notion of a fair race, where people are even at the starting line.... Presumably, it would be desirable to have fairer races" (Okun 1975: 75, 84).

Higher education is one of the prime ways in which society assists individuals in moving up to the starting line. It therefore seems incomplete to consider the impact of the subsidies only on the distribution of income, particularly only for current income, while ignoring their contribution to equalizing educational opportunities—to promoting Okun's fair race.

An approach that has been suggested, most notably by Pechman (1970), for examining the contribution of higher education subsidies both to the redistribution of income and to the provision of educational opportunities is a separate analysis of the costs and benefits of the subsidies. This approach implicitly recognizes that society views one dollar paid in taxes as different from a dollar received in education; it assigns the task of redistributing current income to the tax system, and that of equalizing educational opportunities to the benefit side. The standards for judging the equity of the taxes are straightforward, reflecting the consensus that, on equity grounds, progressive taxes are preferable to regressive ones. A minor complication arises, however, in deciding whether or not it is the average tax dollars that really are the ones paying for the higher education subsidies. Ideally, one should examine the marginal tax dollars—on the grounds that these are the taxes that would be increased or decreased if the subsidy level changed. Lacking information on the true marginal tax revenues, the average tax dollar is a logical substitute.

The benefit side is more complex. Defining equality of educational opportunities is only slightly easier than defining equity. Presumably equality refers to a situation in which an individual's investment in higher education is not constrained by his family income. There are many possible indicators, some of which conflict. Again, the literature suggests several ways to examine educational opportunity. For example, Hansen and Weisbrod (1969) compared the income distribution of families with students attending each of the three levels of public higher education with those of all families without students in public higher education, and then related this attendance pattern to eligibility for and aspirations to attendance at the four-year institutions on the part of high school graduates in 1966. Because of the attendance patterns among students, larger subsidies went to the more affluent. Overall, the comparisons suggested that students from low-income families were less likely to receive the same amounts of higher education as their more affluent counterparts.

McGuire (1976) recognized that the life cycle of earnings predetermines that families of the traditional college age student will have higher incomes than the population as a whole. He revised Hansen and Weisbrod's comparison between students and non-students, substituting families headed by people thirty-five to sixty years old as the comparison group. This substitution suggested that students are approximately representative of the relevant population. Machlis (1973) made similar comparisons for New York City and the United States as a whole, comparing students to the population with eighteen to twenty-four-year-old dependents. Rather than simply looking at the income distributions for the two groups, he created an "educational opportunity index" comparable to the Lorenz curve and Gini coefficient which are used to measure income inequality. He found that the indices for New York City were substantially better than those for the nation as a whole. Although Hansen and Weisbrod's comparison would be relevant in the context of income redistribution, McGuire's and Machlis's revisions are more appropriate in a consideration of educational opportunities.

While only a few studies chose to examine the equity of higher education subsidies by separating the costs from the benefits, this approach has much to recommend it, conceptually, practically, and for policy purposes. Given a decision that higher education merits any subsidy, the concern that the revenue to provide the subsidies be raised in an equitable manner is separated from the concern that those subsidies be distributed appropriately. This approach is also consistent with the investment nature of higher education, since it examines the subsidies for their effect on the inputs to the process of investing in human capital, not just on the outcomes of that investment. The life-cycle pattern of consumption of and payment for higher education also poses no problem.

In practical terms, this approach is more workable than the other two that focus on the redistributional consequences of the subsidies. Although inaccurate data could affect the conclusions on equity, the distortions would not be as severe as with a net benefit approach, where consistent as well as accurate information is required on both the tax and the benefit sides. Since the empirical tests are current rather than prospective, this approach does not involve the same uncertainties of forecasting as does focusing on lifetime redistributional effects.

Furthermore, for policy purposes, the source of any inequity is readily apparent--whether that source is a regressive tax structure, low attendance or persistence rates on the part of low-income students, or barriers imposed by eligibility standards. Perhaps the only drawback is that this approach does not satisfy the common desire for information on the overall net effect on the distribution of income. In view of the many problems with the net benefit approach, it seems much wiser and more useful for policy purposes to examine the equity of the costs and benefits of the subsidies separately.

Equity: An Application to Community Colleges

The concern with equity in higher education is perhaps most acute at the community college level. More than their senior counterparts, these two-year public institutions are charged with opening the doors to higher education for educationally and economically disadvantaged groups. Community colleges are the vehicles through which a phenomenal number of people gained access to higher education in the 1960's and 1970's. In 1960 10 percent of all college students attended community colleges; in 1976 that figure had reached 34 percent. While the 1960's were the years of the meteoric increase in community college enrollments, witnessing a tenfold rise, in the 1970's community colleges outpaced the rest of higher education in enrollment growth in absolute as well as percentage terms. From 1970 to 1976 two-thirds of the increase in higher education enrollment came at the community college level, and much of this growth has come from populations traditionally underrepresented in higher education. Compared to their four-year counterparts, community college students in 1976 were more likely to be black or hispanic (20 percent vs. 12 percent), to be attending part-time (43 percent vs. 15 percent), to be first-generation college-goers (59 percent vs. 48 percent), to have low family incomes (25 percent with less than $10,000 in family income vs. 16 percent), and to be older (more than 29 percent over 25 years old vs. 13 percent).[7]

This evidence reflects the impressive role that community colleges have played in providing educational opportunities to non-traditional clienteles. However, a full evaluation of their contribution to equity in higher education not only must examine their finance mechanisms, along the lines suggested in the previous section, but must also answer two questions: What would have happened in the absence of community colleges' proliferation?[8] And what are these new students gaining access to—is it really "higher" education, or mainly "high schools with ashtrays"? In other words, is the open door really a revolving door?

Pending answers to these last two fundamental and complex questions, the rest of this chapter describes how the theoretical analysis of the preceding section might be applied to community colleges and in particular to the equity effects of a very real policy decision in the nation's most prominent community college system. The issue of imposing tuition in California's community colleges became particularly acute in 1978, in the wake of Proposition 13's mandated reduction in property tax support, and similar types of pressures to raise tuition face other community colleges in the United States. In 1979 the major program of federal student assistance, Basic Educational Opportunity Grants (BEOG), renamed Pell Grants in the Higher Education Amendments of 1980, was substantially expanded to encompass more middle-income students, presenting an unusual opportunity to have the federal government, in effect, pay the new tuition for many low- and middle-income students. In 1978-79, tuition of $400 per ADA (average daily attendance) would have generated approximately the $260 million in bailout funds which the state provided the community college system for that year; tuition of $200, comparable to the charges at the California State College and University system, would have raised about half that amount.

How would the equity of community college finance have been affected if much of the lost property tax revenue had been replaced by tuition revenues instead of by the state bailout? In preparing to address this question, it is necessary first to consider whether the particular characteristics of community colleges require any modification in the approach to equity recommended in the preceding section. The most obvious difference is that community colleges are only one part of the total system of higher education. Consequently, in analyzing changes in community college finance, the impact on the four-year sector should not be ignored. For example, students who responded to community college tuition by choosing a university should be distinguished from others who were discouraged from attending anywhere. In addition, this difference reinforces the conclusion that we should avoid viewing equity in terms of the overall income redistribution resulting from the subsidies for this one component of higher education.

Community colleges also tend to serve a different clientele than their four-year counterparts. Because community college students are older, there is less intergenerational transfer involved and the concern with evaluating intergenerational equity is reduced. Age also affects efficiency issues, such as the rate of return on the investment in the education of older people, who have fewer years in which to capture the return and who have higher foregone earnings. Community colleges draw from the less affluent segments of society too. But none of these differences affects the approach to equity.

Finally, while interdistrict equity is an issue for community colleges and not for the four-year sector, it is less critical here than in elementary-secondary education, primarily because community college education is not mandatory, and there is greater mobility.[9] Nevertheless, since greater interdistrict equity is still presumably preferable to less, it merits inclusion among other equity issues.

Although community colleges are a unique component of public higher education, the preceding discussion indicates that the equity issues in subsidizing them can be approached in essentially the same way as can equity issues for higher education in general. Specifically, the consequences of imposing tuition should be examined by analyzing the tax side separately from the enrollment response, with attention also given to interdistrict equity and the impact on the four-year sector where relevant. As already discussed, progressivity is the logical standard for judging tax equity. While there is less consensus on the quantitative indicators of equity on the expenditure side, as discussed in the preceding chapter by Alexander, two reasonable goals for equality of opportunity will be used here: 1) the probability of attending college should be independent of family income within ability levels, and 2) among students, higher education subsidies should be inversely related to family income.

In terms of tax equity, the tax burden was distributed slightly more progressively with the state bailout than it was in the pre-proposition 13 days. This conclusion rests on the reasonable assumption that the funds for the bailout came from the state budget surplus, which was produced largely by increases in the state personal income tax (45 percent), by corporate taxes (25 percent), and by sales tax increases (26 percent).[10] According to the consensus on the incidence of these three types of taxes, the bailout therefore reflected a more progressive mixture of taxes than does the state budget as a whole (of which these three main taxes contribute 36, 15, and 37 percent, respectively). It was also more progressive than the other $865 million in subsidies for community colleges, which came 60 percent from state apportionment and 40 percent from local revenues.[11]

On the benefit side, the bulk of the equity impact of tuition would have occurred through an enrollment response. Tuition would have discouraged some students from attending and thereby would have altered the distribution of subsidies. The size of the enrollment response is uncertain, however. Estimates of the responsiveness of general enrollment to tuition changes vary widely. One thorough synthesis of the literature by McPherson (1978) suggests that an across-the-board $100 increase in tuition would lower the fraction of young people attending any college by about 1 percentage point, reflecting a price elasticity of about -0.3.[12]

For several reasons, the responsiveness to tuition at California's community colleges may differ from McPherson's estimates. First, those estimates were based on average tuitions of the institutions studied. For instance, McPherson's estimates apply to an average tuition of $1,000. Presumably, moving from zero to $100 tuition would have a larger effect on enrollment than going from $1,000 to $1,100. Low-income students who had avoided applying for financial aid to offset only living expenses because of the hassle and paperwork involved might have to face the choice between not enrolling and entering the student aid maze. While Chicago and New York City also imposed tuition for the first time within the last decade, their experiences were complicated by non-tuition factors (such as an end to open enrollment at the senior institutions of the City University of New York) and provide little generalizable guidance on enrollment response. Perhaps the most comparable case was Wisconsin's "tuition experiment" in 1973, when the University of Wisconsin reduced tuition at two of its two-year colleges from about $500 to $165 and then raised it again in 1975. The results suggested a $100 increase produced a 4.5 percent drop in enrollment (American Association of State Colleges and Universities 1977; Stampen 1974).

Second, the studies that have looked at non-traditional clienteles such as those in California community colleges consistently find that lower-income, lower-ability, and adult students are more sensitive to tuition than are traditional students.[13] While direct evidence is scarce, presumably part-time and non-degree credit enrollments would also be particularly responsive to tuition.

The impact of tuition depends also on the tuition response of senior public institutions. If only community colleges raise tuition, their enrollment loss will be larger than if the four-year institutions follow suit. With no change in state college or university tuitions, some students would find them relatively more attractive than the community colleges—but how many students will be drawn away is unclear. Estimates of the responsiveness between public and private sectors suggest that, if the public sector lowered its tuition relative to private institutions, about half the increase in public enrollments would come at the expense of private attendance (McPherson 1978: 183-86). This probably overstates the enrollment substitution between two- and four-year public colleges in California, for two reasons. First, only about half of the recent high school graduates attending the community colleges would have been eligible for a senior institution (University of California–Systemwide Administration 1978). Second, for many students two- and four-year public colleges are not equal alternatives; location and program have strong influences on their choice. Indeed, Bishop and Van Dyk's study (1975) finds that the presence of a four-year public institution has little effect on adults' decisions to attend college at all. This suggests that the bulk of any enrollment response for community colleges will be in the form of dropouts, independent of tuition levels in the four-year sector.

A final problem with the existing estimates of tuition sensitivity is that they are all based on student responses before the federal Basic Educational Opportunity Grant program became massively available and well known. Many studies at least recognize that *net* tuition (tuition minus financial aid), not just the institution's *stated* tuition, affects enrollment. Nevertheless, low-income students are probably less sensitive to tuition than those earlier results would imply, now that the assurance of aid is greater and independent of the institution chosen.

This discussion reflects the uncertainty inherent in any prediction of the enrollment response to the imposition of tuition at California's community colleges. In terms of equity, however, several points are clear.

1) In the absence of student aid to offset some of the tuition for low-income students, the very population that community colleges most want to attract into higher education would be most deterred by the policy shift. Clearly, tuition alone would be a step backward from the first equity goal of making the probability of college attendance independent of family income, at given ability levels. Nor would any progress be made toward the second goal of improving the distribution of subsidies among students: everyone would receive a subsidy reduced by the amount of tuition imposed.

2) The actual equity impact of tuition would not be nearly this severe, however, because of the existence of the federal basic grant program (BEOG). In fact, both measures of equity might be improved by the imposition of tuition. As Table 1 shows, if there had been tuition of $200 in 1979-80, the federal government would effectively have paid at least half of it for students who lived in a family of four with less than approximately $25,000 in income.[14] Indeed moderate income students

Table 1. Basic Grant Awards, 1978-79 and 1979-80, at Alternative Tuition Levels

Family Income	Basic grant, 1978-1979[1]	Basic grant, 1979-80 with tuition of: $0	$200	Additional cost of attendance, 1979-80, compared to 1978-79 with tuition of $200[2]
	(1)	(2)	(3)	(4)
		(in dollars)		
4,000	750	750	850	100
8,000	750	750	850	100
12,000	616	750	850	-34
16,000	0	750	850	-650
20,000	0	685	685	-485
24,000	0	375	375	-175

[1] For dependent student living off campus in hypothetical family of four with one wage earner, no outside income, no special expenses, no assets, one child in college.
[2] Additional cost to a student (after basic grant) of attending college in 1979-80 with tuition of $200, compared to the after-BEOG cost in 1978 with no tuition. Column (4) = tuition minus (3) - (1).
Source: Author's calculations.

with income between approximately $12,000 and $25,000 would not have felt the tuition charge because with the higher BEOG, they would have paid less for college out of their own resources in 1979-80 than they did in 1978-79 when community colleges were "free". Consequently unless low-income students are twice as tuition sensitive as their higher-income counterparts,[15] the drop in enrollment might have been less severe among low-income than among high-income students. Enrollment of moderate income students should have increased in spite of the tuition charge. If so, imposing tuition would not have worsened the disparity between college-going rates of low- and high-income students of given abilities (the first equity goal) and could even have improved the distribution of public subsidies among students (the second measure of equity). This assumes that the basic grant program effectively operates as an entitlement program. In the current climate of constant or declining budgets for basic grants, an increase in the volume of aid to California students would reduce the funds available in other states. Although imposition of tuition would still represent progress in California toward the two equity goals, it might have some adverse effects in other states by lowering the basic grants to their students.

3) While economists focus on tuition and net tuition as determinants of enrollment, non-price barriers can be just as effective in deterring low-income students from enrolling, as mentioned earlier. The actual enrollment and equity impact of tuition would depend in large measure on efforts to minimize these non-price impediments. Such efforts could include publicity of the student aid that is available, well-staffed financial aid offices, simplified aid application processes, and sensitivity to the particular handicaps of hispanic students[16] whose parents might have particular language problems filling out the forms. While tuition does not erect these hurdles to receiving aid, it does make their existence more of a threat to the provision of equal educational opportunities.

4) Whatever the effect of non-tuition barriers and whatever the relative tuition sensitivity of high- and low-income groups, presumably there is some level of student aid that would reduce the difference among the college-attendance rates of various income groups. Tuition coupled with increased student aid would represent a clear step toward the equalization of educational opportunities.[17] While the problems with the empirical evidence on tuition sensitivity discussed above indicate that an optimal level of tuition cannot be determined a priori, the massive increase in basic grants that came in the fall of 1979 with the implementation of the Middle Income Student Assistance Act (MISAA) presented a unique opportunity to impose tuition and offset it dollar for dollar for low-income students at a low cost to the state. According to column 4 in Table 1, tuition would not have resulted in higher net costs of attendance in

1979-80 than in 1978-79 for students with family income between about $12,000 and $25,000; the cost would actually have dropped for these students. And with only about $5 million in state student aid, California could have offset the remaining cost increase for those with family incomes below $12,000.[18] This is a small price to pay for the more than $100 million in net revenue that the higher tuition would have generated, at the same time as it made the college attendance rates more equal across income classes and increased the concentration of community college subsidies on lower-income students.

Summary

An examination of the literature on the equity of public subsidies for higher education suggests important reasons why it is better to evaluate the costs separately from the benefits of educational finance systems with separate attention given to tax incidence and the contribution to equality of educational opportunities. When this approach is applied to the decision to raise tuition, as in the case of California's community colleges, the lower tuition policy is not necessarily superior on equity grounds if need-based student aid is also increased.

On the tax side, financing with the state bailout was slightly preferable in terms of equity to the pre-Proposition 13 days, because the revenues in the budget surplus were raised more progressively than were general revenues. The budget surplus in California appears to have ended, so the choice is not relevant for the future. While the magnitude of the enrollment drop that would result from the imposition of tuition is uncertain, the BEOG (i.e. Pell Grant) program is a significant force contributing to equity on the benefit side. Because basic grants offset half of any moderate tuition increase for the lowest-income students, the enrollment loss is not as large and does not come disproportionately from the low end of the income scale. And because the basic grant program became much more generous in 1979-80, the imposition of a modest tuition in that year would probably have produced an equity gain relative to 1978-79. At a relatively low cost to the state, all low and moderate-income students would have found attending a community college to be no more expensive in 1979 than it had been in 1978. The stated tuition and the problems involved in applying for aid would still have deterred some low-income students however.

Although the opportunity is past for states to raise tuition and have the federal government offset most of the effect on low and moderate income students, equity still should not be used as an excuse for spending scarce state resources in order to avoid higher tuition. Particularly in the present climate of budget stringency at both the state and federal levels, higher tuition accompanied by substantial increases in assistance for public sector students could improve a state's budget picture and the equity of educational opportunities.[19]

NOTES

1. For a concise comparison of the two approaches, see Hartman (1970).

2. Indeed, tax payments varied more among income classes than subsidies did among types of institutions. The average subsidy at the University of California in 1964 exceeded the average for community colleges by less than $1,000, while the wealthiest families paid almost $4,000 more in taxes than the poorest.

3. These include Windham (1970), Zimmerman (1973), Crean (1975), State of New Jersey Commission on Financing Post-Secondary Education (1976), Vredeveld (1978), and Moore (1978).

4. The following table compares Windham's original estimates of net benefits from higher education subsidies accruing to each income class in Florida with revised calculations based on tax burdens that are contemporaneous with the benefit distributions:

Net Benefits (in thousands of dollars)

Family Income:	Less than $3,000	$3,000-4,999	$5,000-9,999	$10,000+
Windham's original estimates:				
Based on 1960 tax incidence	-7,123	-12,900	-6,037	26,120
Based on 1961 tax incidence	-3,840	-8,683	-12,123	24,675
Revisions, adjusting tax burdens for income growth:				
Based on 1960 tax incidence	-945	600	7,307	-6,954
Based on 1961 tax incidence	735	2,337	-1,121	-1,865
Revisions, using Brookings 1966 MERGE file inflated to 1967:				
Progressive assumptions	1,593	8,811	23,933	-34,335
Regressive assumptions	-1,282	6,448	14,574	-19,844

5. See Pechman and Okner (1974) for a description of this data base.

6. See note 4.

7. These figures generally refer to 18-34-year-old undergraduates, except the distribution by family income applies to 18-24-year-old primary family members who are not married. Also, the age statistic applies to all two-year colleges, not just to public ones; U.S. Bureau of the Census (1978). The figures for race refer to all full-time students and come from the National Center for Education Statistics (1978).

8. Several recent studies find that the presence of a community college per se does not increase the college attendance rate of able youngsters from low- or middle-income families, except perhaps for black men and white women. Community colleges *do* seem to induce more people over twenty-five to enroll. See Anderson, Bowman and Tinto (1972), Sandell (1976), and Bishop and Van Dyk (1975).

9. For more elaboration on this perspective, see Nelson (1978b) and Garms (1979). For empirical evidence and a contrasting perspective, see Augenblick (1978).

10. Actual revenues in 1977-78 compared with what they would have been if each revenue source (including "other revenues") had grown at the same rate as expenditures between 1975-76 and 1977-78. Office of the Legislative Analyst (1978: Table 3).

11. Since both alternatives involve the same level of local support, interdistrict tax equity does not emerge as an issue here.

12. That is, a 10 percent increase in tuition would cause the enrollment rate to fall by 3 percent (or 1 percentage point, since about one-third of 18-24-year-olds are enrolled).

13. For evidence on adult enrollments, see Bishop and Van Dyk (1975). Bishop also controlled for ability and income in a separate study (1975).

14. These figures apply to full-time students. Since students who attend at least half-time are eligible for basic grants, they would receive some protection from tuition, but up to a lower income level. Students taking one course would receive no assistance.

15. The evidence on this is unclear. See McPherson (1978) for a brief discussion.

16. According to Gilbert (1979: 11), 10.3 percent of the enrollment at California's community colleges is hispanic, 9.6 percent black.

17. Most student aid programs do not help less-than-half-time students. The Higher Education Amendments of 1980 allow up to 10 percent of the federal Supplementary Educational Opportunity Grants to go to less-than-half-time students. Selective tuition waivers are an alternative strategy for helping low-income populations to take one course at a time, if they so desire.

18. This approximation was derived as follows: In 1978-79, about 72,000 California community college students received basic grants. If even two-thirds of these recipients needed state assistance of $100 each to hold them harmless against the tuition charge, this would cost the state only about $5 million.

19. This paper was written while the author was a research associate at the Brookings Institution as part of a study with David Breneman entitled *Financing Community Colleges: An Economic Perspective* (The Brookings Institution: 1981) with support from the Ford Foundation and the Carnegie Corporation. The opinions and any errors are the author's responsibility and should not be attributed to the officers, staff, or trustees of the Brookings Institution.

REFERENCES

American Association of State Colleges and Universities. 1977. Wisconsin low tuition experiment ends: tuitions up, enrollments down. *AASCU Special Report*. Washington. August.

Anderson, C. Arnold; Bowman, Mary Jean; and Tinto, Vincent. 1972. *Where colleges are and who attends*. Berkeley: Carnegie Commission on Higher Education.

Augenblick, John. 1978. Issues in financing community colleges. *Papers in Education Finance* No. F78-4. Denver: Education Commission of the States. October.
Bishop, John. 1975. Income, ability, and the demand for higher education. Discussion paper No. 323-75. Madison: Institute for Research on Poverty, University of Wisconsin. August.
———, and Van Dyk, Jan. 1975. Can adults be hooked on college? Some determinants of adult college attendance. Discussion paper No. 319-75. Madison: Institute for Research on Poverty, University of Wisconsin. December.
Conlisk, John. 1977. A further look at the Hansen-Weisbrod-Pechman debate. *Journal of Human Resources* 12(2): 147-63.
Crean, John F. 1975. The income redistributive effects of public spending on higher education. *Journal of Human Resources* 10(1): 116-22.
Garms, Walter I. 1979. On measuring the equity of community college finance. Rochester: University of Rochester. June.
Gilbert, Fontelle. 1979. Minorities and community colleges. Washington: American Association of Community and Junior Colleges.
Hansen, W. Lee, and Weisbrod, Burton A. 1969. *Benefits, costs, and finance of public higher education*. Chicago: Markham.
Hartman, Robert W. 1970. A comment on the Pechman-Hansen-Weisbrod controversy. *Journal of Human Resources* 5(4): 519-23.
———. 1972. Equity implications of state tuition policy and student loans. *Journal of Political Economy* Supplement 80(3): S142-S171.
Machlis, Peter D. 1973. The distribution effects of public higher education in New York City. *Public Finance Quarterly* 1(1): 35-58.
McGuire, J. W. 1976. The distribution of subsidy to students in California public higher education. *Journal of Human Resources* 11(3): 343-53.
McPherson, Michael S. 1978. The demand for higher education. In *Public policy and private higher education*, ed. David W. Breneman and Chester E. Finn, Jr. Washington: Brookings Institution.
Miklius, Walter. 1975. The distributional effects of public higher education: a comment. *Higher Education* 4(3): 351-55.
Moore, Gary A. 1978. Equity effects of higher education finance and tuition grants in New York State. *Journal of Human Resources* 13(4): 482-501.
Moss, Milton. 1978. Income distribution issues viewed in a lifetime income perspective. *Review of Income and Wealth* 24(2): 119-36.
National Center for Education Statistics. 1978. *The condition of education – 1978 Education*. Washington: U.S. Government Printing Office.
Nelson, Susan C. 1978a. The equity of public subsidies for higher education: some thoughts on the literature. *Papers in Education Finance* No. 5. Denver: Education Commission of the States.
———. 1978b. Interdistrict equity and community college finance. Working paper. Washington: Brookings Institution. March.
Office of the Legislative Analyst. 1978. Statement to the Senate Finance Committee. Sacramento. November.
Okun, Arthur M. 1975. *Equality and efficiency: the big tradeoff*. Washington: Brookings Institution.
Pechman, Joseph A. 1970. The distributional effects of public higher education in California. *Journal of Human Resources* 5(3): 361-70.

Pechman, Joseph A., and Okner, Benjamin A. 1974. *Who bears the tax burden?* Washington: Brookings Institution.
Reynolds, Morgan, and Smolensky, Eugene. 1977. *Public expenditures, taxes and the distribution of income.* New York: Academic Press.
Sandell, Steven H. 1976. The demand for college: the effect of local colleges on attendance. Columbus: Center for Human Resource Research, Ohio State University. June.
Stampen, Jacob. 1974. The University of Wisconsin center system experiment in low fees, 1973-74. Madison: University of Wisconsin System. April.
State of New Jersey Commission on Financing Post-Secondary Education. 1976. An analysis of the monetary benefits and costs of higher education in New Jersey in 1975-76. June.
U.S. Bureau of the Census. 1978. School enrollment − social and economic characteristics of students: October 1976. *Current Population Reports*, ser. P-20, no. 319. Washington: U.S. Government Printing Office.
University of California − Systemwide Administration. 1978. *Beyond high school graduation: who goes to college?* Berkeley: Office of Outreach Services. May.
Vredeveld, George M. 1978. Distributional impacts of alternative methods of financing higher education. *Journal of Higher Education* 49(1): 47-69.
Windham, Douglas M. 1970. *Education, equality and income redistribution.* Lexington, Mass.: D. C. Heath.
Zimmerman, Dennis. 1973. Expenditure-tax incidence studies, public higher education, and equity. *National Tax Journal* 26(1): 65-70.

CHAPTER 10

The Search for Equity in School Finance

STEPHEN J. CARROLL

During the last seven years, at least twenty-two states have modified their educational financing systems. To date no standard model of reform has dominated the field.[1] States have employed different approaches in different degrees and in different combinations. It is frequently asserted (and it seems reasonable to believe) that these differences are justifiable because the reforms undertaken should be appropriate to the prevailing circumstances in the states. At present, however, there is no consistent body of information either on what these reforms have accomplished or on the relative effects of various approaches to reform.

This report summarizes the results of the reforms enacted in five states--California, Florida, Kansas, Michigan, and New Mexico--whose new financing laws represent the major approaches to reform in the post-*Serrano* era. The first section summarizes the principal findings of the analysis of the effects of reform in each state, the tables for which are presented in the appendix. A detailed discussion of that analysis is presented in Carroll (1979). The second section summarizes the results of the econometric analysis of Michigan school districts' budgetary behavior. Park and Carroll (1979) presents the details of that part of the larger study. The third section offers observations on why the observed outcomes occurred.

The Effects of Reform on Revenues, Instructional Expenditures, and Tax Rates

This section summarizes the effects of each state's reform on: 1) the level and distribution of current revenues,[2] instructional expenditures, and tax rates; 2) the relationships between instructional expenditures and districts' fiscal capacities; and 3) expenditures by various kinds of districts. Because California's pre- and post-reform school finance systems specify different formulas for elementary, high school, and unified districts, the results are presented separately for the districts of each type. Similarly, Kansas's post-reform plan differentiates among small, medium, and large districts; we performed separate analyses for each type.

Background

Reform advocates generally agree on the need for more equitable school finance systems, but they agree far less on what kinds of systems are best for the purpose. Several types of systems have been championed in the reform debate. Some represent alternative means to accomplish the same objectives, but others reflect quite different notions of what would constitute an equitable school finance system.

Most, but not all, reform proposals embrace one or the other of two basic themes, or some compromise between them. The first is *equalization of fiscal outcomes* among the school districts within a state. The state's school finance system, in this view, should not allow any student (or taxpayer) to obtain a more expensive public education (or lower tax burden) than is available to others in the state. The pre-reform systems were inequitable because they allowed students and taxpayers in wealthy districts (high per-pupil tax base) to obtain a more expensive education while enjoying a lower tax burden.

The second theme is *equalization of fiscal opportunities* among the state's school districts. From this point of view, the pre-reform plans were inequitable because low-wealth districts had to levy much higher tax rates to achieve the same level of spending as high-wealth districts. The numerical disparity in school spending was less troublesome than the fact that low-wealth districts did not have the same ability to raise school revenues. This theme leads to fiscal neutrality as the objective of reform: a finance system in which any district can obtain the same level of funding as any other district, provided only that it put forth the same effort.

The tension between equalization and fiscal neutrality is reflected in the reforms studied here. Before reform, California, Florida, Kansas, and Michigan distributed state aid to the schools through foundation plans. New Mexico distributed flat grants to its school districts. The typical foundation system guarantees each district a minimum amount of funding per pupil (the foundation level) at a stipulated property tax rate. A district's state aid is the difference (if greater than zero) between the foundation level and the amount per pupil that the district could raise locally at the specified rate.[3]

After reform, *California* combined a high-level foundation plan with differential expenditure growth limits. The foundation program very substantially increased state aid to low-wealth districts, while the expenditure growth limits allowed greater expenditure increases by lower-spending districts. *Florida* also retained the foundation program approach in its reform plan. An extensive system of adjustments for the distribution of a district's pupils among twenty-six different categories, and an adjustment for the cost of living in a county served by a district, enter the computation of each district's guarantee. Local districts are limited to a narrow range of tax rates. *Kansas* adopted a Guaranteed Tax Base (GTB) plan constrained by strict limits on expenditure growth.[4] The growth limits allow low-spending districts to increase their budgets more rapidly than can high-spending districts. The state's districts are divided into three enrollment categories; a separate guarantee is specified for each category. *Michigan* introduced an unrestricted GTB plan with an upper limit on the tax rate for which state aid is paid. Districts may levy higher rates. *New Mexico* has assumed full responsibility for school finance, while retaining the local district as the operating unit. The New Mexico plan allows no local discretion on districts' revenues or tax rates. A pupil-weighting system with adjustments for teacher cost differentials is used to determine each district's budget, and the schools are financed out of state funds plus a state-mandated local levy.

The main reform themes directed our interest toward the effects of each state's reform on the distributions of fiscal outcomes among its school districts and on the relationships between its districts' fiscal outcomes and their fiscal capacities or efforts. Even casual observation confirms that many interested parties evaluate reforms in terms of their impacts on certain kinds of communities or people (e.g., central cities, low-income people); accordingly, we examined how various types of districts fared under each state's reform.

Data

We obtained data from state sources on districts' revenues, expenditures, tax rates, wealth, and numbers of pupils. Data on the characteristics of the community served by the school district were obtained from the 1970 census, fifth count, compiled to 1974 school district boundaries. We used the census definitions of household income, urbanity, race, and poverty level. We obtained data for the following years:

State	Year Reform Introduced	Years for which data were available
California[5]	1973-74	1970-71 through 1976-77
Florida	1973-74	1972-73, 1975-76
Kansas	1973-74	1972-73 through 1974-75
Michigan	1973-74	1971-72 through 1975-76
New Mexico	1974-75	1972-73 through 1975-76

In computing any measure employed in the descriptive analysis, we include all the districts in a state for which data were available. The distributions of revenues, instructional expenditures, and the tax rates--and the relationships between them and size, wealth, or tax rates--are generally computed over all the districts in the state. The measures relating the distributions of those variables to income, urbanity, race, and poverty are computed over all districts that could be matched to the census data.

To facilitate interstate comparisons, we adjusted all districts' assessed values to market values and computed the effective property tax rate on market value. In making these adjustments we used ratios of property sales prices to assessed values for the given year at the lowest level of aggregation (district, county, or state) for which the data were available in each state.

What Did Reform Cost?

Table 1 presents the pre- and post-reform revenues per pupil, instructional expenditures per pupil, and adjusted tax rates for each state in each year.

In all five states, the post-reform years saw impressive revenue growth. (Not all of which is solely attributable to reform--the states probably would have increased school revenues even if they had not modified their finance systems.) The post-reform growth in revenues is even more impressive when contrasted with the pattern of school tax rates, which generally dropped sharply in the first year of reform. Tax rates were higher after reform only in Michigan and in Kansas's small and medium districts.

The results for Michigan are particularly interesting. Michigan imposed no limits on school districts' revenues or taxes, but neither one increased dramatically. Nor did the shift from the foundation plan lead districts to cut their spending or even fail to keep pace with the rates of growth in revenues in other states.

Neglecting the California data, instructional expenditures per pupil have grown in every state in every year, but their rate of growth is in every case lower than the rate of growth of revenues. The same is true for all three types of California districts in the pre-reform years and over the 1974-75 to 1976-77 period. It seems to be generally true that school districts do not translate increases in their per-pupil revenues into proportional increases in their instructional expenditures per pupil. This is similar to the pattern that Bowen (1980) finds in the data for higher education institutions.

These results are consistent with previous studies of school districts' expenditure behavior (Alexander 1974; Barro and Carroll 1975; Carroll 1976) which found that as districts' per-pupil budgets increase, they allocate decreasing proportions of their budgets to expenditures for

Table 1. Revenues per Pupil, Instructional Expenditures per Pupil, and Adjusted Tax Rates

	Pre-reform			Post-reform			
State and variable	1970 -71	1971 -72	1972 -73	1973 -74	1974 -75	1975 -76	1976 -77
Revenues							
California							
Elementary	745	780	860	999	1,076	1,196	1,327
High school	1,007	1,058	1,148	1,230	1,274	1,388	1,519
Unified	825	882	992	1,078	1,162	1,277	1,412
Florida			815			1,149	
Kansas							
ADM below 400			1,200	1,274	1,488		
ADM 400 to 1,299			881	996	1,119		
ADM 1,300 and above			772	907	1,035		
Michigan		845	901	1,014	1,123	1,242	
New Mexico			650	659	874	983	
Instructional expenditures							
California							
Elementary	553	591	634	717	684	746	821
High school	723	769	809	869	781	830	899
Unified	628	665	712	792	715	757	833
Florida			625			853	
Kansas							
ADM below 400			746	761	843		
ADM 400 to 1,299			595	621	688		
ADM 1,300, and above			563	575	643		
New Mexico			512	551	614	709	
Adjusted tax rates							
California							
Elementary	7.2	7.4	7.6	6.7	6.7	7.0	6.9
High school	5.6	5.7	6.0	5.3	5.2	5.5	5.4
Unified	11.3	11.8	12.1	11.1	11.6	11.8	11.7
Florida			8.1			6.5	
Kansas							
ADM below 400			5.0	5.7	5.9		
ADM 400 to 1,299			5.8	5.4	6.0		
ADM 1,300 and above			8.1	7.4	7.7		
Michigan		12.3	12.1	12.7	13.2	13.6	
New Mexico			3.9	3.7	3.7	3.0	

Instructional expenditures were unavailable for Michigan. California eliminated its instructional expenditures compilation in 1975-76. We aggregated the accounts that had been included in instructional expenditures prior to then; the 1975-76 drop in per-pupil instructional expenditures in all three types of California districts probably reflects some difference between our calculation and the procedure California had used to calculate instructional expenditures. All results are based on student-weighted observations. Parallel results, obtained using the district as the unit of analysis, are available in Carroll (1979).

teachers. Taken together, these observations suggest the following hypothesis. School districts broadly agree on what constitutes an acceptable instructional program, and they exert every effort to provide one. In doing so, low-revenue districts concentrate on necessities and make do with disproportionately few non-instructional resources. Districts with higher revenue per pupil provide a somewhat costlier instructional program, but they devote much larger shares of their budget to non-instructional purposes. When a district's budget is increased, it improves its instructional program somewhat, but it devotes a much larger share of its additional revenues to non-instructional resources.

Did Reform Contribute to Equalization?

We computed indexes of the distributions of revenues per pupil,[5] instructional expenditures per pupil, and adjusted tax rates in each state each year. The results suggest three conclusions: 1) Reform efforts in these five states have brought about somewhat more equal distributions of per-pupil revenues. 2) Reform reduced disparities in per-pupil instructional expenditures very little, if at all. 3) Reform has generally led to more equal distributions of adjusted tax rates.

Regardless of what these states sought to accomplish, their reform plans wrought little change in the distributions of per-pupil revenues,[6] and (as we shall see below) the same kinds of districts are found in the upper and lower portions of the distribution. In each of these states the districts that have relatively high per-pupil revenues before reform also have high revenues after reform.

It may be that a distribution of revenues is "inequitable" when it stems from one finance system and "equitable," or at least less inequitable, when it is generated by another. But most of the arguments put forward by reform proponents suggest that the distribution itself is at issue. From that perspective, only New Mexico and California (in its unified districts) have substantially reduced the inequality of per-pupil revenues. California (in its elementary and secondary districts), Florida, Kansas, and Michigan have changed the rules whereby districts raise local revenues and receive state general aid, but they have not much changed the consequences.

In general, instructional expenditures per pupil are no more equally distributed after reform than they were before, in spite of the impressive growth in revenues.

In all five states, districts that enjoy high revenues allocate a large share of them to non-instructional purposes. Furthermore, in those cases where disparities in per-pupil revenues declined, there were smaller declines in disparities in instructional expenditures. This reinforces our earlier conjecture that when reform results in substantial increases in a previously low-spending district's revenues, it tends to put those funds to non-instructional uses. It is also consistent with the behavior of higher educational institutions found by Bowen (1980).

What all this implies depends on one's view of the relationship between non-instructional expenditures and the objectives of reform. At one extreme, if all school resources are equally important, it is a matter of little consequence how districts use the additional revenues they derive from reform. At the other extreme, if educational quality is determined by instructional expenditures, and if the object of reform is to equalize the quality of the education afforded students who live in different places, then the states have dissipated much of the additional resources they have put into their reform efforts.

In every state except Florida, disparities in the distribution of adjusted tax rates fell by more than 25 percent between pre-reform and post-reform years. New Mexico entirely eliminated variation in local educational property tax rates. Even in Michigan, where reform was accompanied by an increase in the average adjusted tax rate, the distribution of tax rates was dramatically equalized by reform.

Did Reform Improve Fiscal Neutrality?

A school finance system is fiscally neutral if differences among districts' per-pupil revenues are independent of their abilities to pay; that is, if they reflect only interdistrict differences in effort. The school finance community has traditionally defined a district's ability to support education in terms of its property tax base per pupil. From this perspective, progress toward fiscal neutrality is signaled by a reduction in the relationship between per-pupil revenues and property tax bases; i.e., a decline in the elasticity of per-pupil revenues with respect to property tax base per pupil.[7]

But a community's wealth includes its stocks of human capital as well as its stocks of physical capital, and the salary income derived from human capital is an important component of ability to pay. Several recent studies attempt to develop broader measures of wealth which combine both property and human capital.[8] However, that work is still in its formative stages. Accordingly, we separately explore the effects of each state's reform on the relationship between per-pupil revenues (or expenditures) and the per-pupil property tax base and household income.

Post-reform elasticities of revenues with respect to the tax base are below those for the pre-reform period in California, in Kansas's large districts, and in New Mexico. The results for Florida, Kansas's small and medium districts, and Michigan show little or no improvement in wealth neutrality.[9]

Turning to the results for instructional expenditures, a little improvement occurred in Kansas's small and medium districts. Otherwise, the post-reform elasticities in each case are not much different from the pre-reform period. In sum, 1) Reform has generally reduced the degree to which revenues depend on property wealth. 2) Instructional expenditures per pupil are generally as closely related to property tax bases after reform as they were before.

Reform improved the income neutrality of per-pupil revenues in California and Michigan, and worsened it in Kansas. Florida's reform introduced substantial income bias into what had been an income-neutral distribution of revenue. In New Mexico, district revenues were independent of income both before and after reform.

Reform has reduced the income bias of the distributions of instructional expenditures in California's high school and unified districts. More income-biased distributions of instructional expenditures have resulted from reform in Florida, and in Kansas's small districts. Although income neutrality improved in some cases, the distributions of revenues and instructional expenditures per pupil are, in other cases, *more* income-biased after reform than they were before. Some school finance reforms have worsened the relationship that originally gave rise to the reform movement.

Who Were Reform's Winners and Losers?

We find that the division of per-pupil revenues between pupils in small and large districts was mostly unaffected by reform in eight of the nine cases. Similarly, reform has not much affected the division of revenues between less and more urban districts in six of nine cases, between less and more white districts in seven of nine cases, and between districts where the incidence of poverty is low and those where it is high in seven of nine cases. (See Appendix, Table A-4.) There are even fewer exceptions in the case of instructional expenditures. See Carroll (1979) for detailed results.

More substantial reform effects pertain to the distribution of adjusted tax rates between districts with high and low incidence of poverty. Before reform, adjusted tax rates were often substantially higher in the higher-income districts. In every case reform was accompanied by relative reductions in these tax burdens, and often the reductions were large. (See Appendix, Table A-5.)

Otherwise, there are few departures from the general pattern of little change in the distributions of tax rates between different types of districts.

Conclusions

Its original proponents viewed school finance reform as an issue of educational equity. They assumed that more spending is associated with better schooling, so that disparities in school spending imply disparities in educational quality. They also assumed that poor people live in property-poor districts, at least more so than in property-rich districts. Finally, they observed that state finance systems were only mildly equalizing at best, and they argued that existing systems discriminated against poor chidren by affording them an inferior education.

In a few cases, reform has improved either (property) wealth neutrality or income neutrality or both, but *reform has not generally brought about distributions of revenues or instructional expenditures that correspond more to fiscal efforts or correspond less to wealth.*

All in all, reforms in these five states have not dramatically altered the relationships that originally gave rise to reform efforts. Reform has worked some improvements in educational equity, but *each state's post-reform inequality of per-pupil revenues and instructional expenditures is remarkably similar to what it was before.*

These reforms have made considerable progress toward other objectives, however, such as tax equity. In every case except Florida, disparities in adjusted tax rates have narrowed dramatically. And reform promoted greater equality in the distributions of adjusted tax rates between large and small districts, between more and less urban districts, between districts serving many and few whites, and between districts with high and low incidence of poverty. *Reform seems to have been a generally effective device for equalizing the tax burdens of supporting education.*

It also appears that *reform has generally furthered the objective of increasing statewide total spending for education.* In principle, equalization could have taken the form of redistributing revenues from high-spending to low-spending districts. Presumably, however, such an approach is politically unworkable. Reform states have instead chosen to increase state educational aid, attempting thereby to raise lower-spending districts' revenues without significantly reducing those of higher-spending districts. The result is to increase the share of state revenues going to public education above what it would otherwise have been. To be sure, the states might have increased their support for education even if they had not modified their finance systems. But legislators' reluctance to tax the residents of high-spending districts to support education in lower-spending districts has so far required that equalization, if it is to be obtained at all, be obtained by leveling up the distribution of revenues. This approach, in turn, requires increased state contributions to education.

School Districts' Budgetary Behavior

This section summarizes an analysis of the budgetary behavior of Michigan school districts over the 1971-72 through 1975-76 school years.[10] We estimated econometric models that relate expenditures per pupil to different types of grants (federal or state, categorical, unrestricted block, or matching), to the "prices" (or matching rates) of revenues per pupil, and to characteristics of districts' populations. Our data were for 451 districts in each of the five years.

Background

The class of finance plans variously termed "guaranteed tax base," "district power equalizing," or "variable matching systems" figures prominently in the school finance debate.[11] These plans provide more equal fiscal opportunities to school districts if they wish to take advantage of them; the choices are left up to the local citizenry. Any district can obtain the same revenues per pupil as any other district if it levies the same local property tax rate, regardless of any differences in their property tax bases or other characteristics.[12] It is also free to choose a higher or lower tax rate. Local governments are able to select whatever level of service they (their constituents) desire and are willing to support.

But GTB plans give rise to important distributional issues. Low-income communities may not be able to afford tax rates they would have to levy to keep pace with higher-income communities. What if disproportionately minority communities systematically levy lower tax rates than do heavily white communities? Other things being equal, they would get less state aid, and in any event they would spend less than other districts. The question of how school districts will respond to the incentives inherent in a GTB plan is central to the debate over what constitutes an appropriate school finance system.

In 1973, Michigan introduced a GTB plan according to which the state guaranteed each district $38 per pupil for each mill of property tax effort up to 22 mills. Districts levying less than 22 mills received per-pupil matching grants equal to their tax rate times the difference (if positive) between $38,000 and their per-pupil tax base. Districts that levied 22 mills or more received unrestricted block grants per pupil equal to .022 times the difference (if positive) between $38,000 and their per-pupil tax base. By matching locally raised tax dollars with state aid, the plan effectively lowered the "price" of expenditures to school districts and, presumably, provided an incentive to increase their expenditures.

In theory, we would expect a district faced with a lower price to "buy" more educational revenues. But how much more? And how do other factors affect its budgetary behavior, such as the amounts of state and federal categorical aid available to a district, or the "tastes" of its population for public education as opposed to private education and other goods and services?

Results

Table 2 lists the variables used in the analysis and presents our results. The "price" faced by a district is one for all districts in 1971-72 and 1972-73. In the last three years, for districts whose assessed value per pupil (AV) is below the guarantee and whose tax is below the matching limit, it

Table 2. Elasticities of Expenditures per Pupil

Variable	1974-75 Cross-section	Pooled
Cost to district of $1 per pupil increase in expenditures (price)	-.12 (4.23)	-.02 (2.90)
Unrestricted state block grant/pupil	.03 (7.65)	.005 (5.08)
State categorical aid/pupil	.07 (6.45)	.02 (6.50)
Federal categorical aid/pupil	.02 (3.60)	.02 (7.99)
Dummy variable for fifth year		-.06 (13.24)
Pupils this year/pupils last year	-.57 (4.84)	-.32 (11.26)
Product of pupils/household, residential share of tax base, and median/mean value of owner-occupied home	-.02 (1.04)	.003 (1.28)
Assessed value/pupil	.20 (7.63)	.10 (10.20)
Median household income	.08 (2.74)	.04 (1.52)
Ratio of owner-occupied to total dwelling units	-.20 (3.79)	-.20 (4.06)
K-12 private school pupils per capita	-.05 (.22)	-.08 (.38)
Fraction of families in poverty status	-.03 (2.10)	-.04 (2.42)
Fraction of employed persons 16 or older working as professional, technical, or kindred	.02 (1.20)	.04 (2.39)
Nonwhite fraction of population	.36 (4.44)	.50 (6.30)

Table 2. (Continued)

Urban fraction of population	.10 (3.78)	.13 (5.52)
Fraction of population 55 or older	-.02 (.94)	.01 (.51)
Fraction of population 55 or older still in same house as 5 years ago	.05 (1.24)	.03 (.96)
Population	-.01 (1.79)	-.005 (.85)
Year (1 in 1971-72, ..., 5 in 1975-76)		.04 (8.38)
Year squared		.02 (11.99)
Constant	5.14 (20.41)	5.80 (25.91)
R^2	.69	.80[a] (.96)[b]

The dependent variable is the natural log of per-pupil expenditures; all independent variables except the dummy for fifth year, year, and year squared are also in natural logs. The pooled equation assumed an autoregressive error structure and was estimated by an iterative GLS procedure. T-statistics given in parentheses.

[a]Corresponds to R^2 conventionally reported for OLS regressions; obtained from sum of squared errors using reported coefficients to compute fitted values of the dependent variable.

[b]R^2 based on sum of squared errors from the regression using the GLS transformed variables.

is the ratio of assessed value to the guarantee. For all other districts, it is one.

Michigan's state aid program was not fully funded in 1975-76. We introduced a *dummy variable for the fifth year* to control for the effects of the shortfall.

If we take the representative household to be the one in a median-valued, owner-occupied house, the cost of a $1 per pupil increase in total revenues is the cost to the district (AV/GTB) times the product of three terms: 1) the number of *pupils per household*, 2) the *residential share of the property tax base*, and 3) the *ratio of median to mean value of owner-occupied housing*. That is,

$$\frac{V}{GTB} = \frac{AV}{GTB} \frac{N}{H} \frac{R}{AV \cdot N} \frac{V}{R/H}$$

where V = the assessed value of the median-valued house, GTB = the state guarantee, AV = assessed value per pupil, N = number of students, H = number of households, and R = total assessed value of residential property.

We estimated several alternative cross-sectional models for the individual years. The results were similar across models in a given year and across years. The second column in Table 2 provides a representative equation from 1974. We also estimated several alternative models that pooled cross-sectional and time-series data.[13] The last column in Table 2 presents the results for a representative model. Of all the equations, it was the most plausible. In any case, the results differ little from those obtained with other models.

We find that the coefficient of the "price" of education to the district is very small, and only marginally significant at best. As a practical matter, it does not matter much whether it is significant or not, since an elasticity of -.02 (in the pooled equation) is hardly useful as a policy tool. For example, changing the matching rate from 0 to 1--a 50 percent reduction in the price of education to the district--would increase spending only 1 percent. We also find that state block grants exert a very small influence on expenditures. The elasticity of .005 (in the pooled equation) implies that a 1 percent increase in unrestricted state aid, about $1.00 per pupil for the average district, would cause a .005 percent increase in spending-- only 6 cents per pupil.

The coefficients for the other forms of aid are much larger. They imply that expenditures increase about 32 percent of the amount of state categorical aid, and about 38 percent of the amount of federal aid.

The price of education to a household (as distinct from the price of education to a district) is also significant. It appears that districts are responsive to their constituents' perceptions of the cost of education.

We find significantly higher expenditures in school districts serving populations that are wealthier, higher-income, employed in higher-level positions, more minority, and more urban. Expenditures are significantly lower in school districts serving populations that more frequently live in owner-occupied housing and that are more frequently in poverty.

Did the GTB Plan Encourage Greater Expenditures?

The Michigan data provide no evidence that state matching or block grants stimulate school district expenditures. For whatever reasons, school districts in Michigan have not (as yet) responded appreciably to changes in the implicit price of school expenditures.

It may be that Michigan school district decisionmakers or voters, or both, simply do not value educational expenditures very highly. Even if they are concerned about school quality, they may base allocative decisions on some measure of quality that has little to do (at least in their minds) with educational expenditures. Nor are they necessarily wrong. An immense volume of research has yet to establish a relationship between school spending and students' achievement.[14] In any event, Michigan's school districts may not have tried, or succeeded when they did try, to convince the voters to the contrary. The "price" inherent in the GTB plan would then be irrelevant to their decisions.

Alternatively, school districts or voters may equate the "cost" of education with the local property tax *rate*. As Feldstein notes, the education community in general and the school finance community in particular have confused the school tax rate with the "price" of education. The GTB plan provides every district (below the matching ceiling) with identical marginal trade-offs between local tax rates and expenditures. Those may not be the relevant trade-offs, but they may be what actually motivate budgetary decisions in most districts. There would then be no "price" response because there would be no perceived "price" differences among districts.

Finally, it should be noted that our data pertain only to the first three years of Michigan's GTB plan. Michigan districts may become more responsive to price in the future.

Why Reform Did Not Achieve More

School finance reforms are ostensibly designed to bring about more equal or fiscally neutral distributions of revenues. By those criteria, reform has not accomplished a great deal. In general, the kinds of districts that had greater per-pupil revenues before reform turned out to have greater ones afterward, and the inequalities between them and lower-spending districts are much the same as they were before reform. One is led to wonder why the complete restructuring of state school finance systems has fallen short of its ostensible goals. Below, we offer some possible explanations.

Diverse Objectives

Each of the reforms appears to have been designed to serve several different purposes simultaneously. We do not mean to imply that the plans' developers, or the legislators who enacted them, or the governors who signed them into law, necessarily had any particular set of objectives in mind. But regardless of what they wanted to accomplish, or thought that the plans would accomplish, the structures of the plans are compromises among diverse and sometimes conflicting goals.

We have noted the tension between equalization and fiscal neutrality. Although much of the school finance literature describes these concerns as alternative paths converging on the same goal of equity, they are in fact two separate paths leading to two separate goals based on differing concepts of equity. It is unlikely that all the districts in a state would choose to levy the same tax rate under any school finance system, even if they would all thereby obtain the same revenues per pupil. The only way to achieve a high degree of equalization, consequently, is to narrowly constrain school districts' freedom of decision regarding budgets and tax rates, which means a loss of local control. But local control is central to the concept of fiscal neutrality.

A school finance plan can be oriented toward fiscal neutrality, as is Michigan's, or toward equalization, as is New Mexico's. Or it can compromise. California, Florida, and Kansas enacted compromise plans in the sense that (unlike New Mexico) they permit districts to determine their own tax rates and hence revenues, but (unlike Michigan) they limit districts' choices. The limits hinder progress toward fiscal neutrality, while the permitted discretion impairs equalization.

We are not suggesting that such compromises are in any sense wrong or improper. Rather, we are suggesting that local control over budgets and tax rates is the "price" of equalization, and that revenue and tax rate disparities are the "price" of fiscal neutrality. More generally, equalization comes at the expense of local discretion over spending and tax levels; and one reason why these plans have not provided greater equality is that they have attempted to preserve some degree of local discretion.

These plans also reflect the three-way conflict among "holding harmless" high-spending districts, tax relief, and state support for education. None of the reform plans we studied cut the revenues of previously high-spending districts. In fact, none even capped spending. Their various revenue and tax-rate limits only constrained the growth of revenues in high-spending districts. Consequently, low-spending districts had to chase a moving target in trying to "catch up" to their higher-spending counterparts. The states increased their aid to low-spending districts, but the limits that held down revenue growth in the high-spending districts also applied, though not always as tightly, to low-spending districts, which had to translate some of their increased state aid into tax relief.

Political realities may impose a "leveling up" equalization strategy. But that approach is expensive, and the amount of equalization accomplished at a given cost to the state diminishes as state funds are translated into tax relief.

It is not within our province to judge whether equalization is more important than tax relief, or whether the revenues of high-spending districts should be cut to improve equalization, or whether states should contribute more to the support of education. We merely point out that the cost of "leveling up" is greater state support for education or higher local property taxes, or both. States can obtain greater equality at a given level of support only by redirecting revenues from high-spending to low-spending districts or allowing lower-spending districts to increase their tax rates. They can provide more tax relief or greater equality of tax burdens only by redirecting revenues from high-spending to low-spending districts or by increasing state aid to education. The five states' reforms generally eased local property tax rates and very substantially equalized tax efforts across districts. The "price" of these results was less progress toward revenue equalization, given the states' ability or willingness to support education and their inability or unwillingness to cut the revenues of high-spending districts.

Add-ons and Adjustments

Each of the reform plans can be viewed as a combination of a basic plan and various add-ons and adjustments that modify the distribution of state aid among districts.[15] California adds a flat grant program ($125 per pupil) to its foundation program and permits districts to override their revenue limits with approval of the voters. Florida adjusts the distribution of state aid for the distribution of pupils among twenty-six categories in each district for the cost of living in the district. Kansas rebates a share of the state personal income tax receipts collected in each county to the county's school districts. Michigan's municipal overburden provision provides additional state aid to cities where nonschool tax burdens are particularly high. And New Mexico adjusts state aid according to the distribution of districts' pupils among grades and to an index of teacher costs.

These provisions have been justified on several different grounds: California's flat grant program is constitutionally mandated; its override provision presumably allows districts that are willing to exert greater tax effort for the schools an opportunity to do so. Florida's, Michigan's, and New Mexico's provisions ostensibly direct additional state aid to districts judged to have needs that are not well accommodated by the basic plan. And the income tax rebate in Kansas is supposedly a means for shifting part of the school support burden to the income tax.

Some subtle parliamentary maneuvering apparently has gone on behind the scene as well, however. Persons familiar with state school finance systems have told us, off the record, of instances where states have included add-ons or adjustments to "hold harmless" high-spending districts. States that are under political or judicial pressure to reform but that are unable either to cut the revenues of high-spending districts or to provide enough additional state aid to "level up" low-spending districts have allegedly found an ingenious way out. They searched for a characteristic that was common to high-spending districts and rare in low-spending districts, and they then provided an aid adjustment to "offset the unusual costs" incurred by districts with that characteristic. The result was an ostensibly equitable school finance plan that preserved the revenues of high-spending districts but did not require additional state support to the others.

In any event, whatever the purposes of add-ons or adjustments might have been, and however appropriate they might be to the circumstances of a particular state, their effects on equalization and fiscal neutrality are of interest.

California's flat grants are counted against a district's foundation aid, and thus add nothing to the revenues of districts receiving foundation support. Nearly half the districts in the state, however, are not entitled to foundation support because their tax bases are so large. But these districts receive the flat grants which thereby partially offset the equalizing effects of the foundation program.

The ability to override the revenue limit (formally, to levy a tax rate in excess of the rate which yields the revenue limit) reduced the equalization effect of the revenue limits. More important, high-wealth and high-spending districts most frequently obtained overrides. Thus both equalization and fiscal neutrality were impaired by the override provision.

Florida's pupil-weighting system has no impact whatsoever on the distribution of revenues. The correlation between weighted pupils and unweighted pupils across Florida's districts is extremely high (greater than .999). A foundation plan that guaranteed about 1.26 times as much support per unweighted pupil would have led to exactly the same distribution of revenues. The cost-of-living adjustment, however, has a decided effect on the distribution of revenues; it introduces substantial revenue disparities. Moreover, the cost of living tends to be high where wealth, and particularly income, are high. The adjustment therefore directs additional revenue to high-wealth and high-income districts, adversely affecting wealth neutrality and introducing very substantial income bias into the distribution of revenues.

Kansas's income tax rebate essentially provides support in proportion to the taxable income of a county's residents. School districts in high-income counties therefore levy lower property tax rates to stay within their budget limit. The net effect is a reduction in the property taxes paid by residents of higher-income counties.

Michigan's municipal overburden provision distributes a small amount of funds, most of which go to Detroit. Because Detroit has above average per-pupil revenues and wealth, the provision is disequalizing and reduces fiscal neutrality. However, the amount of funds involved is so small relative to state equalization aid that the adverse effects on equalization and fiscal neutrality are negligible.

The teachers' cost-adjustment provision in New Mexico's reform plan allows greater revenues to districts whose teachers are relatively highly educated and experienced. We suspect that this provision accounts for the rather surprising New Mexico results. The state shifted from the least equalizing pre-reform finance system--flat grants--to a plan tantamount to full state assumption. Yet this shift accounted for a reduction of only about 20 percent in revenue disparities. The puzzling question is why a shift from a flat grant system to a system that ostensibly guaranteed equal revenues to every district failed to bring about greater equality. The reason, we suspect, is that some of New Mexico's districts had taken advantage of their opportunities prior to reform and raised greater per-pupil revenues than did other districts. They then used these funds to employ more educated and experienced teachers than lower-wealth districts could afford. Their teachers' experience and education index accordingly would be relatively high in the post-reform years, raising their revenue entitlements according to the formula.

We could not explicitly test this hypothesis, because the data we obtained did not provide information on teachers' experience and education adjustment factors. However, it is consistent with the available data. Note also that this feature of New Mexico's plan has a tendency to "lock in" revenue disparities whether or not they are associated with wealth. A district that entered the reform era with a highly educated and experienced staff had a high adjustment factor, generating high revenues that allowed it to retain a highly qualified staff. In contrast, a district with a much less qualified staff at the outset of reform had a low adjustment factor, generating lower revenues, and therefore could not as readily hire highly qualified new teachers. This feature of the plan consequently appears to run counter to the ultimate objective of reform: reducing inter-district disparities in the quality of education offered to children.

The fiscal limits or constraints imposed by California, Florida, Kansas, and New Mexico have also figured importantly in their reforms. Depending on one's point of view, revenue or tax rate limits may be interpreted as devices for bringing about gradual equalization, for delaying equalization, for limiting disparities in a system that permits local discretion, for controlling the cost of state aid, or for forcing local districts to translate a part of their state aid into local property tax relief.

Reform as a Preventive to Further Disparity

Our study compared pre-reform and post-reform distributions and relationships in five states. Most states annually reset their school finance systems' parameters, and year-to-year increases in state aid to education are common. It is beyond the scope of this study to speculate on what changes the five states would have made if they had not restructured their finance systems, and how those changes would have affected the distributions and relationships of interest. But it is possible, perhaps even likely, that disparities in these states would have widened in the absence of reform. If so, these reforms have been more successful than suggested by the data examined here.

Summary

We examined the reforms enacted between 1972 and 1974 in California, Florida, Kansas, Michigan, and New Mexico. Using data generally covering 1972 through 1976, we recount what happened to school taxing and spending in each state's districts, describe what happened to districts' spending opportunities, estimate how reforms and other factors affected the budgetary behavior of Michigan school districts in response to the state's Guaranteed Tax Base plan, and speculate on why reforms in the five states had unexpected outcomes in light of equalization aims.

The following are our principal findings: 1) Reform brought impressive growth in district revenues in all five states, and declines in local property tax rates for education in all but Michigan. It appears that reform has contributed to the objective of increasing statewide total spending for education and reducing local educational property tax rates. 2) The five states have made some progress toward a more equal distribution of revenues per pupil, but these improvements have generally been small. However, local property tax rates are now significantly more equal among school districts. To the extent that reform aimed at more equal spending, its accomplishments were very minor. To the extent that tax equalization was an aim, the results of reform have been substantial. 3) Reform has done little to equalize the distribution of per-pupil instructional expenditures. (This result is consistent with other studies which have found, for example, that as districts' per-pupil budgets increase, they allocate decreasing proportions of their budgets to expenditures for teachers.) If educational quality is closely linked to instructional expenditures, and if the object of reform is to equalize the quality of education afforded students who live in different places, the states have dissipated much of the additional resources they have put into their reform efforts. 4) Before reform, school revenues were ordinarily tied closely to the size of the local property tax base. Reform has substantially loosened that tie. Much of the fiscal advantage previously enjoyed by high-wealth districts has been eliminated by reform. 5) Poor children--or, more accurately, districts serving disproportionate numbers of poor children--have not fared well in the wake of reform, in comparison with their higher-income counterparts. Before reform, poor children generally had about the same school revenues and lower school tax rates compared with those of higher-income children.

Reform has not much affected the distribution of revenues between poor children and rich children, while the tax rates levied by disproportionately poor districts increased relative to those levied by districts serving higher-income populations. 6) Judging by the Michigan data, state matching grants have no effect on school district spending, and state block grants have very little effect: spending increases by an average of only six cents for every dollar of state unrestricted grants. Federal and state categorical aid has a much stronger effect: A dollar of categorical aid increases district spending by 32 to 38 cents.

Two factors probably explain why reform accomplished relatively little in attempting to equalize spending outcomes and opportunities.

First, reform commonly tried to pursue objectives that were at once diverse and conflicting, such as equalizing revenues, preserving some local control over spending, trying to avoid the political hazards of cutting back on high-spending districts, providing tax relief, and avoiding excessive growth in state spending for schools. Because all these goals could not be achieved together, it was difficult to achieve much progress on any one front.

Second, each state tended to make add-ons and adjustments to its basic school finance plan usually with disequalizing effects. For example, Kansas's income tax rebates are disequalizing, as is Florida's cost-of-living adjustment. However appropriate such provisions may be for the needs of a particular state, they make it harder to reduce inequality.[16]

APPENDIX

Table A.1. Coefficients of Variation for Revenues, Instructional Expenditures, and Adjusted Tax Rates

State and variable	Pre-reform 1970-71	1971-72	1972-73	Post-reform 1973-74	1974-75	1975-76	1976-77
Revenues							
California							
Elementary	.22	.23	.22	.21	.20	.18	.18
High school	.17	.18	.18	.19	.17	.17	.16
Unified	.18	.19	.18	.16	.14	.14	.13
Florida			.12			.13	
Kansas							
ADM below 400			.23	.21	.22		
ADM 400 to 1299			.21	.18	.20		
ADM 1300 and above			.12	.11	.10		
Michigan		.15	.17	.15	.14	.16	
New Mexico			.17	.18	.12	.10	
Instructional expenditures							
California							
Elementary	.17	.17	.17	.16	.18	.16	.15
High school	.14	.15	.15	.14	.16	.15	.14
Unified	.17	.17	.18	.17	.18	.15	.13
Florida			.12			.14	
Kansas							
ADM below 400			.21	.21	.20		
ADM 400 to 1299			.19	.17	.19		
ADM 1300 and above			.11	.09	.09		
New Mexico			.11	.11	.10	.09	
Adjusted tax rates							
California							
Elementary	.22	.23	.23	.22	.17	.17	.17
High school	.17	.17	.17	.15	.13	.14	.14
Unified	.17	.16	.17	.15	.14	.13	.12
Florida			.11			.10	
Kansas							
ADM below 400			.28	.20	.19		
ADM 400 to 1299			.28	.23	.18		
ADM 1300 and above			.22	.23	.15		
Michigan		.20	.24	.18	.15	.14	
New Mexico			.29	.31	.10	.00	

Table A.2. Elasticities of Revenues per Pupil and Instructional Expenditures per Pupil with Respect to Adjusted Wealth per Pupil

State and variable	Pre-reform 1970-71	1971-72	1972-73	Post-reform 1973-74	1974-75	1975-76	1976-77
Revenues							
California							
Elementary	.195	.214	.241	.202	.180	.150	.148
High school	.380	.399	.396	.388	.329	.331	.307
Unified	.289	.320	.332	.250	.236	.203	.205
Florida			.199			.214	
Kansas							
ADM below 400			.471	.349	.444		
ADM 400 to 1299			.420	.326	.352		
ADM 1300 and above			.219	.111	.141		
Michigan		.253	.235	.236	.233	.238	
New Mexico			.147	.179	.102	.046	
Instructional expenditures							
California							
Elementary	.096	.105	.108	.090	.117	.101	.104
High school	.266	.267	.286	.261	.266	.268	.247
Unified	.224	.235	.256	.249	.248	.217	.179
Florida			.183			.213	
Kansas							
ADM below 400			.381	.371	.328		
ADM 400 to 1299			.352	.326	.285		
ADM 1300 and above			.127	.145	.145		
New Mexico			.058	.046	.047	.045	

Table A.3. Elasticities of Revenues per Pupil and Instructional Expenditures per Pupil with Respect to Household Income per Pupil

State and variable	Pre-reform 1970-71	1971-72	1972-73	Post-reform 1973-74	1974-75	1975-76	1976-77
Revenues							
California							
Elementary	.197	.199	.198	.197	.185	.160	.149
High school	.268	.274	.255	.262	.219	.184	.134
Unified	.210	.185	.099	.151	.101	.106	.093
Florida			.087			.306	
Kansas							
ADM below 400			.176	.204	.240		
ADM 400 to 1299			.227	.275	.375		
ADM 1300 and above			.201	.240	.231		
Michigan		.274	.252	.251	.233	.150	
New Mexico			.044	.017	.001	.000	
Instructional expenditures							
California							
Elementary	.145	.146	.152	.135	.136	.126	.124
High school	.153	.150	.153	.116	.099	.072	.077
Unified	.183	.204	.182	.131	.135	.118	.110
Florida			.099			.348	
Kansas							
ADM below 400			.159	.232	.226		
ADM 400 to 1299			.273	.331	.326		
ADM 1300 and above			.291	.264	.233		
New Mexico			.180	.177	.198	.209	

Table A.4. Ratios of Average Per-Pupil Revenues in Districts below the Median on a District Characteristic to Average Per-Pupil Revenues in Districts above the Median on the Characteristic

State and characteristic	Pre-reform 1970 -71	1971 -72	1972 -73	Post-reform 1973 -74	1974 -75	1975 -76	1976 -77
Size							
California							
Elementary	1.04	1.05	1.06	1.04	1.08	1.07	1.05
High school	1.05	1.05	1.10	1.11	1.02	1.07	1.07
Unified	1.00	0.98	0.92	1.00	0.98	0.98	1.00
Florida			0.97			0.89	
Kansas							
ADM below 400			1.32	1.23	1.30		
ADM 400 to 1299			1.16	1.13	1.12		
ADM 1300 and above			0.96	0.91	0.93		
Michigan		0.90	0.93	0.90	0.91	0.91	
New Mexico			1.09	1.12	1.06	1.05	
% Urban							
California							
Elementary	0.93	0.93	0.93	0.94	0.96	0.95	0.96
High school	0.96	0.97	0.99	1.00	0.98	1.02	1.02
Unified	0.95	0.93	0.89	0.96	0.95	0.95	0.97
Florida			0.96			0.88	
Kansas							
ADM below 400			1.10	1.09	0.99		
ADM 400 to 1299			1.11	1.04	1.11		
ADM 1300 and above			0.95	0.90	0.94		
Michigan		0.90	0.93	0.88	0.88	0.88	
New Mexico			1.09	1.10	1.04	1.01	
% White							
California							
Elementary	1.01	1.01	1.02	1.02	1.00	1.01	1.02
High school	1.07	1.06	1.05	1.07	1.05	1.05	1.06
Unified	1.05	1.06	1.14	1.04	1.06	1.05	1.04
Florida			1.06			1.05	
Kansas							
ADM below 400			0.84	0.91	0.99		
ADM 400 to 1299			0.90	0.93	0.94		
ADM 1300 and above			0.98	1.03	0.99		
Michigan		1.04	1.00	1.04	1.03	1.03	
New Mexico			1.08	1.06	0.99	0.98	

Table A.4. (Continued)

% Poverty

California							
Elementary	1.15	1.16	1.15	1.10	1.10	1.08	1.08
High school	1.10	1.09	1.09	1.07	1.07	1.03	1.02
Unified	0.99	0.97	0.93	1.00	0.97	0.98	0.98
Florida			1.06			1.18	
Kansas							
ADM below 400			0.97	1.08	1.20		
ADM 400 to 1299			1.00	0.99	1.01		
ADM 1300 and above			1.06	1.08	1.07		
Michigan		1.06	1.10	1.05	1.06	1.06	
New Mexico			0.98	0.99	1.00	1.01	

Table A.5. Ratios of Average Adjusted Tax Rates in Districts below the Median on a District Characteristic to Average Adjusted Tax Rates in Districts above the Median on the Characteristic

State and characteristic	Pre-reform 1970-71	1971-72	1972-73	Post-reform 1973-74	1974-75	1975-76	1976-77
Size							
California							
Elementary	0.86	0.85	0.84	0.89	0.93	0.91	0.90
High school	0.91	0.90	0.88	0.99	0.95	0.98	0.97
Unified	1.00	0.98	1.00	0.97	0.93	0.96	0.96
Florida			0.93			0.96	
Kansas							
ADM below 400			0.95	1.17	0.99		
ADM 400 to 1299			0.93	0.93	0.97		
ADM 1300 and above			0.78	0.73	0.80		
Michigan		0.88	0.92	0.87	0.88	0.88	
New Mexico			1.07	1.16	0.97	1.00	
% Urban							
California							
Elementary	0.88	0.89	0.90	0.90	0.93	0.95	0.95
High school	0.98	0.97	1.00	0.99	1.00	1.06	1.01
Unified	1.04	1.02	1.05	1.00	0.93	0.98	0.97
Florida			0.95			0.99	
Kansas							
ADM below 400			1.00	1.04	0.95		
ADM 400 to 1299			0.89	0.96	0.94		
ADM 1300 and above			0.75	0.72	0.80		
Michigan		0.89	0.93	0.86	0.86	0.87	
New Mexico			1.03	1.08	0.97	1.00	
% White							
California							
Elementary	1.01	1.02	1.02	1.02	1.02	1.04	1.06
High school	0.94	0.92	0.91	0.95	0.96	0.98	1.01
Unified	0.99	0.99	0.98	1.02	1.07	1.02	1.04
Florida			1.05			1.05	
Kansas							
ADM below 400			1.12	0.96	1.03		
ADM 400 to 1299			1.11	1.03	1.07		
ADM 1300 and above			1.16	1.18	1.11		
Michigan		0.99	0.93	1.01	1.02	1.01	
New Mexico			1.17	1.18	1.04	1.00	

Table A.5. (Continued)

% Poverty

California							
Elementary	1.17	1.17	1.16	1.17	1.10	1.07	1.05
High school	1.09	1.06	1.06	1.09	1.06	1.00	0.98
Unified	1.07	1.07	1.09	1.04	0.97	1.01	0.99
Florida			0.97			0.99	
Kansas							
ADM below 400			0.90	1.05	1.08		
ADM 400 to 1299			1.05	1.07	1.02		
ADM 1300 and above			1.24	1.20	1.12		
Michigan		1.18	1.26	1.14	1.11	1.11	
New Mexico			0.99	0.98	1.05	1.00	

NOTES

1. The word "reform" has normative connotations; it suggests that something is wrong and that change will improve or correct the situation. While we do not wish to imply that all recent changes in state school financing systems were necessarily for the better, we follow contemporary usage in the school finance community and refer to these changes as "reforms."

2. Revenues equal the sum of local revenues, state non-categorical aid, and federal impact aid. This measure, in our view, best reflects the concepts expressed in the reform debate. Readers who take differing views, or who are interested in the effects of categorical programs, will find parallel analyses for alternative revenue measures that exclude impact aid and/or include state and/or federal categorical aid, in Carroll (1979).

3. See Carroll (1979) for detailed descriptions of each state's pre- and post-reform school financing system.

4. The typical GTB plan guarantees each district a given minimum revenue per pupil at each property tax rate. A district's state aid equals the difference, if positive, between the revenues it would raise at its rate if it had the state-guaranteed tax base per pupil and the revenues it actually raises at that rate.

5. Table A.1 (in the Appendix) presents the results for one commonly used distributional index, the coefficient of variation, which is the standard deviation divided by the mean. A value of, say, .22 means that approximately two-thirds of the students in a state attend districts where revenues (instructional expenditures, tax rates) are within 22 percent of the mean; about one-sixth are more than 22 percent above the mean, and about one-sixth are more than 22 percent below the mean. Thus, a reduction in the coefficient from one year to the next implies that districts are, on average, relatively closer to the mean in the second year; the distribution has become more equal.

6. Inequality declined substantially in New Mexico, but approximately half that decline is attributable to the treatment of impact-aid revenues in the state's reform plan. New Mexico's virtually complete assumption of school finance responsibilities accounted for the other half of the decline.

7. The elasticity of one variable with respect to another is the percentage change in the first variable that is, on average, associated with a 1 percent change in the second. An elasticity of revenues with respect to wealth of .195 means that the average district's revenues increase by .195 percent with each 1 percent increase in its wealth. The elasticities reported here were obtained from quadratic regressions of revenues per pupil (or instructional expenditures per pupil) on wealth (or on household income per pupil or on tax rates).

8. See, e.g., McMahon (1978).

9. Table A.2 presents the elasticities of revenues per pupil and of instructional expenditures per pupil with respect to property wealth per pupil. Table A.3 provides parallel results for income per pupil.

10. Rolla E. Park designed the econometric approach and performed most of the work reported here. See Park and Carroll (1979) for further details.

11. The terms "guaranteed tax base" and "variable matching" generally refer to a formula that ensures each district a minimum revenue per pupil for each unit of tax effort. "District power equalizing" (DPE) generally refers to a plan that also allows each district no more than the guaranteed amount of revenue per unit of tax effort. That is, a DPE plan is a GTB plan with full recapture of "excess" local revenues.

12. Fiscal opportunities are equalized up to a point, if, as in Michigan, there is an upper bound on tax rates beyond which the guarantee no longer applies. Districts whose tax bases exceed the guarantee continue to have a fiscal advantage in the absence of a "recapture" provision.

13. These included models assuming an auto-regressive error structure, variance components models, and fixed-effects models. The results were surprisingly robust. No coefficient changed more than 5 percent across models.

14. See, e.g., Averch et al. (1974).

15. The add-ons and adjustments discussed here are those in operation in each state in the years covered by our data. Some of the states have recently added, deleted, or modified such provisions, but we lack the data to assess the consequences.

16. I am indebted to Arthur Alexander, Richard Cooper, Dennis Doyle, Richard Fernandez, James Fox, Paul Hill, James Kelly, David Lyon, David Mandel, and Daniel Weiler for useful advice and comments on various aspects of the study. I am particularly indebted to my colleague, Rolla Edward Park, who performed most of the work reported in the second section. The research was supported by the National Institute of Education. The opinions expressed herein are mine and are not necessarily shared by the Rand Corporation or its research sponsors.

REFERENCES

Alexander, Arthur. 1974. *Teachers, salaries, and school district expenditures*. Santa Monica, Calif.: Rand Corporation. R-1588-FF.

Averch, Harvey, et al. 1974. *How effective is schooling?* Englewood Cliffs, N.J.: Educational Technology Publications.

Barro, Stephen. 1974. Alternative post-*Serrano* systems and their implications. Pp. 25-80 in *School finance in transition*, ed. J. Pincus. Cambridge: Ballinger.

———, and Carroll, Stephen J. 1975. *Budget allocation by school districts: an analysis of spending for teachers and other resources*. Santa Monica, Calif.: Rand Corporation. R-1797-NIE.

Berne, Robert. 1978. *A methodological assessment of education equity and wealth neutrality measures*. New York: New York University, Public Policy Research Institute.

Bowen, Howard. 1980. *The costs of higher education*. San Francisco: Jossey-Bass.

Brown, Lawrence, et al. 1977. *School finance reform in the seventies: achievements and failures*. Washington: Technical Analysis Paper, Office of the Assistant Secretary for Planning and Evaluation, Department of Health, Education and Welfare and Killalea Associates, Inc.

Carroll, Stephen J. 1976. School district expenditure behavior. *Journal of Human Resources* 11 (Summer): 317-27.

———, 1979. *The search for equity in school finance: results from five states.* Santa Monica, Calif.: Rand Corporation. R-2348-NIE.

Coons, John; Clune, William III; and Sugarman, Stephen. 1970. *Private wealth and public education.* Cambridge: Harvard University Press.

Feldstein, Martin. 1975. Wealth neutrality and local choice in public education. *American Economic Review* 65 (March): 75-89.

McMahon, Walter W. 1978. A broader measure of wealth and effort for educational equity and tax equity. *Journal of Education Finance* 4 (Summer): 55-88.

Johns, Roe L.; Alexander, Kern; and Stollar, Dewey H., eds. 1971. *Status and impact of educational finance programs.* Gainesville: National Educational Finance Project.

Park, Rolla E., and Carroll, Stephen J. 1979. *The search for equity in school finance: Michigan school district response to a guaranteed tax base.* Santa Monica, Calif.: Rand Corporation. R-2393-NIE/ASE.

United States Office of Education. 1972. *Public school finance programs, 1971-72.* Washington: Department of Health, Education and Welfare. Publication No. (OE) 73-00001.

Wise, Arthur. 1968. *Rich schools, poor schools.* Chicago: University of Chicago Press.

CHAPTER 11

Shifting Sources of Financing Education and the Taxpayer Revolt

JOHN F. DUE

The financing of education, perhaps more than any other single governmental activity, is confronted with a major hazard in the form of what we have come to call the "taxpayer's revolt." A question of major importance is: What has caused this "revolt"? What implications does it have for education? As a preliminary step, it is necessary to review the shifts that have occurred over the years in the financing of education and to examine the major sources of state tax revenue--the growing source of education finance.

Changing Patterns of State and Local Finance

Changing Sources of School Finance

A very substantial shift has occurred over the last four decades from local to state financing. As shown by Tax Foundation (1979a) data in the 1930 fiscal year, only 17 percent of the cost of financing education came from state sources, and 83 percent came from local sources. By 1941-42 the local share had fallen to 67 percent, by 1961-62, 57 percent, in recent years to 48 percent, the state share rising to 44 percent (the remaining 8 percent being federal). The shift has been slow and steady, propelled by opposition to higher property taxes and the desire for equalization of educational opportunities by region.

But the trend has been by no means uniform among the states, as illustrated in Advisory Commission on Intergovernmental Relations publications. In Hawaii the support is almost entirely from the state; in Alaska only 17 percent of the total is raised locally (1978-79), and in New Mexico and North Carolina less than 20 percent. In general the southern states show the least reliance on local sources and thus on the property tax. By contrast, in New Hampshire 86 percent of the school support is

267

local; the state in this respect has not moved out of the nineteenth century. But South Dakota and Nebraska show local support percentages in excess of 70 percent, and Oregon, Connecticut, Massachusetts, Vermont, Wyoming, and Wisconsin, 60 percent.

Changing State Tax Sources

The shift from local to state financing has of course greatly reduced the relative reliance on the property tax for the financing of education. Local governments themselves have been making increased use of nonproperty tax sources, but this trend has had little effect on the school districts, which (with minor exceptions) lack access to these non-property tax sources.

U.S. Bureau of the Census publications (1980) provide a summary of shifting relative state reliance on various tax sources, as noted in Table 1. There have been no revolutionary changes in state tax legislation in recent decades, with new state taxes or rate changes. But rising incomes and inflation have produced two very significant trends.

First, the yields of the state income tax, particularly the personal income tax, have been rising rapidly. In the early 1970's the combined yield of the personal and corporate tax exceeded the yield of the sales

Table 1. State Tax Revenues by Major Source for Selected Years, 1927-78

Tax	1979	1975	1970	1960	1950	1940	1927
Sales tax	31	31	30	24	21	15	0
Individual income tax	26	24	19	12	9	6	4
Corporate income tax	10	8	8	7	7	5	6
Motor fuel and vehicle license	12	15	19	27	29	37	35
Tobacco	3	4	5	5	5	3	-
Liquor	2	3	3	4	5	6	-
Property	2	2	2	3	4	8	23
Death duties	2	2	2	2	2	3	7
Other	11	11	12	16	18	17	25

Source: Advisory Commission on Intergovernmental Relations (1977:29); U.S. Bureau of the Census (1980:5).

taxes for the first time since the latter were introduced in the 1930's. The use of fixed-dollar exemptions and, in the majority of the states, progressive (though not very progressive) rates cause the yield of the income tax to rise faster than the price level and total incomes, while the sales tax simply keeps pace with total consumer expenditures.

Second, the deterioration of fuel taxes and motor vehicle license fees as a revenue source has been great, in real terms. These have declined from 37 percent in 1940 to 27 percent in 1960, 15 percent in 1975, and 12 percent in 1978. (Little wonder that the roads are full of potholes!) The liquor and tobacco taxes have also fallen sharply; the relative yields of both have dropped by roughly half since 1960. The reason is simple: these levies, with minor exceptions, have specific rates. Legislators and voters rarely raise them, so they continuously decline in yield relative to total revenues to personal income taxes.

There is, of course, a wide range of patterns among the states. There are groups at each extreme: the states currently relying primarily on sales and related taxes, and those relying primarily on income taxes, as shown in Table 2.

These are Bureau of the Census calculations and include in the sales tax data some related levies that other states do not have, such as gross receipts taxes. Thirteen states receive 40 percent or more of their tax revenues from the sales tax; fourteen do so from the income tax. Several states in each group receive over half from the tax involved. Oregon's 70

Table 2. States Relying Primarily on Sales and Income Taxes, 1979

Sales Tax States		Income Tax States	
State	Sales and related taxes as % of state tax collections	State	Income tax as % of state collections
Washington	57	Oregon	70
South Dakota	53	Massachusetts	59
Tennessee	51	New York	54
Mississippi	50	Delaware	54
West Virginia	49	Wisconsin	52
Hawaii	49	Minnesota	52
Indiana	49	Michigan	49
Arizona	47	Alaska	46
Florida	45	Virginia	45
New Mexico	44	Montana	44
Connecticut	43	Iowa	44
Utah	42	California	44
Wyoming	41	Maryland	44
		North Carolina	43

percent reliance on the income tax is the highest dependency of any state on a particular levy. Several, but by no means all, in each group do not use the other levy, or at least with general coverage.

The result is widespread difference in the distribution of burden by income class, as shown in Advisory Commission on Intergovernmental Relations publications (1977). For the states as a whole the distribution is somewhat regressive by income class, but not to a high degree. This pattern is also found with states making substantial use of both sales and income taxes, with property taxes at the local level. But the high-income-tax states, such as Oregon, show a progressive pattern throughout or over a wide range, whereas the non-income-tax states, such as Washington, show a strikingly regressive burden.

While there is an ongoing dispute over the incidence of the property tax by income group because of varying assumptions about shifting of portions of the tax, the studies typically show some regressivity by income groups. This is particularly evident in the lowest income group, made up in part of retired persons owning their homes, and of others whose current incomes are far below their lifetime incomes. Table 3 shows the results of a typical study. Thus a shift to financing education with income taxes instead of with property taxes clearly produces a more progressive distribution of burden, so far as individual property-owners are concerned. Even the shift to a sales tax lessens regressivity, if it is assumed that the proportion of the property tax on business property is shifted to the consumer. If it is assumed that the property tax is primarily a tax on capital, however, then the distribution of burden is progressive and a shift to a sales tax increases regressivity, as shown by Aaron (1975). This is not the popularly held view, however.

The studies thus far available of distribution of the property tax burden were made before most of the circuit-breaker and other provisions to lessen the burden on the elderly poor were introduced. The present property taxes, as explained below, are undoubtedly less regressive than the tax was a decade ago.

Changes in Major Taxes

Recent decades have not seen drastic changes in the structure of the three major tax sources, although some have occurred, as summarized by Welch (1976). The concepts of regressive, proportional, and progressive rates as they relate to the concepts of equity on the tax side were discussed in Chapter 1. The desirability of separating tax equity from the appraisal of equity on the benefit side has also been discussed in Chapter 9.

Property Taxes. The major change in property taxes has been the introduction of "circuit-breaker" features, designed to lessen the impact of the tax on those persons most severely burdened--the elderly owning

Table 3. Real Estate Taxes as a Percentage of Family Income, Owner-Occupied Single-Family Homes, by Income Class and by Region, 1970

Family income[1]	U.S. total	Northeast	North Central	South	West	Homeowners No. (000)	% dist.[2]
Less than $2,000	16.6	30.8	18.0	8.2	22.9	1,718.8	5.5
$2,000-2,999	9.7	15.7	9.8	5.2	12.5	1,288.7	9.7
3,000-3,999	7.7	13.1	7.7	4.3	8.7	1,397.8	14.1
4,000-4,999	6.4	9.8	6.7	3.4	8.0	1,342.8	18.5
5,000-5,999	5.5	9.3	5.7	2.9	6.5	1,365.1	22.8
6,000-6,999	4.7	7.1	4.9	2.5	5.9	1,530.1	27.8
7,000-9,999	4.2	6.2	4.2	2.2	5.0	5,377.4	45.0
10,000-14,999	3.7	5.3	3.6	2.0	4.0	8,910.3	73.6
15,000-24,999	3.3	4.6	3.1	2.0	3.4	6,365.6	94.0
25,000 or more	2.9	3.9	2.7	1.7	2.9	1,876.9	100.0
All incomes						31,144.7	
Arithmetic mean	4.9	6.9	5.1	2.9	5.4		
Median	3.4	5.0	3.5	2.0	3.9		

[1] Census definition of income (from all sources). Income reported received in 1970.
[2] Cumulated from lowest income class.

Source: U.S. Bureau of the Census, *Residential Finance Survey, 1970* (conducted in 1971), special tabulations prepared for the Advisory Commission on Intergovernmental Relations. Real estate tax data were compiled for properties acquired prior to 1970 and represent taxes paid during 1970. Medians were computed by ACIR staff. Reproduced from Advisory Commission on Intergovernmental Relations (1977): 143.

their own homes but having little current income. The primary feature is that a credit is given to low-income taxpayers, either as a deduction from taxable income or as a cash refund. With one group of states, if the property tax exceeds a certain percentage of the taxpayer's income, the taxpayer receives a credit for all or part of the excess; in the other, all taxpayers in a specified lower-income group receive a percentage reduction in property taxes, the percentage falling with increases in income, and reducing the regressive aspect of property taxation. Five states provide the credit regardless of age; in the others only the elderly receive the credit. Several states allow credit for tenants, under the assumption that a certain percentage of rent paid (usually 20%) reflects the landlords' property tax shifted to the tenant. By 1977, twenty-nine states had some form of property tax relief for the low-income elderly.

One other change has been the move to check rising property taxes on farmland by requiring assessment on the basis of farm use rather than on the land's value for other purposes, and to shift to a farm productivity basis instead of sales value. This measure was designed in part to meet the problem created by increases in farmland values out of proportion to increasing yields from the properties.

Income Taxes. State income taxes, personal and corporate combined, have become the number one source of state tax revenue for the states as a whole. The last major shift to this tax occurred between 1967 and 1971, when ten states, including the major industrial states of Michigan, Illinois, Ohio, and Pennsylvania, imposed the tax. Thereafter only one individual income tax was added (New Jersey in 1976). Only five states lack individual income taxes, although three have taxes with limited scope. Forty-five had imposed corporate income taxes by 1975; of the larger states, only Texas and Washington have not done so. The one exception to the general trend was Michigan's repeal of its corporation income tax in 1975, in favor of a value-added type of levy. This new tax, called the single business tax, was intended mainly to stabilize state revenue, as explained by the Advisory Commission on Intergovernmental Relations (1978).

The rates of many state income taxes have remained unchanged for decades. There has been little or no upward trend. Some states readjust their rates from year to year for budget-balancing purposes, and Nebraska does so under an automatic formula. In 1978 five states actually reduced their income tax rates, and in 1979 ten states lowered income taxes in various ways. There has been a definite but difficult to measure or summarize trend toward liberalizing exemptions and granting additional deductions, thus in effect reducing the overall burden. A trend to index the brackets is now beginning. Colorado and Arizona made the change in 1978; by 1980, seven states were indexing.

Sales Taxes. Changes in sales taxes have not been dramatic; no new state has added the sales tax since 1969, as noted by Due and Mikesell (1980).

1) *Rates.* As shown in Table 4, there has been a steady but very slow upward trend in sales tax rates. In 1962, the great majority of the states used 3 percent; in 1971, 3 percent was still the most popular (20), but there were twenty-two states above and only three below. By 1979, there were almost as many 4s as 3s, with only one state below 3 percent and twenty-seven above. The maximum rate was 4 percent in 1962, 6 percent in 1971, 7 percent in 1979. But there are still only three states in excess of 5 percent. In the 1971-78 period, fourteen of the rates were increased (one by only .125 percent), but only two by as much as 2 percentage points. Two were decreased, but one by only .25% to make way for a similar increase in the local sales tax rate, the other (North Dakota) by 1 percent. Thus the rate changes have been slow and not drastic. The Nebraska rate is adjusted automatically from year to year on the basis of revenue needs, but in a very narrow range.

2) *Coverage.* In the last decade, there has been little basic trend toward change in structure; such trend as there has been is toward slight broadening of exemptions, rather than broader coverage of the tax, as was occurring to some degree in the 1960's.

a) *Food.* In most sales-tax states, proposals for exemption of food come up in every legislative session or before the voters. Since 1971 this exemption has been granted in six additional states: Kentucky, Louisiana, Michigan, Indiana, North Dakota (which had exempted a few food items previously) and Washington. This exemption causes a substantial revenue loss (20-25%), adds to complications in operation and enforcement, and frees substantial expenditures of the middle- and upper-income groups, but it nevertheless has great political appeal. As of October 1, 1980, twenty-one of the sales-tax states exempt food (but not restaurant meals), and two tax it at reduced rates.

Table 4. State Sales Tax Rates, Selected Years

Rate (%)	1938	1962	1971	1979
2	16	11	3	1
3	6	20	20	17
4	0	5	15	16
5	0	0	6	8
6	0	0	1	2
7	0	0	0	1

Fractional rates are grouped on the major fraction rule.

A decade ago there was considerable spread of a superior alternative to food exemption: a credit against income tax (with cash rebate if the credit exceeded income tax liability) representing tax paid on minimum necessary purchases. But the spread has been relatively slow; while the procedure has great advantages over food exemption in terms of equity, protection of revenue, and operation of the tax, it has less political appeal. Four states abandoned the plan: Colorado, Iowa, Michigan, and Indiana, the last two shifting to food exemption instead. Hawaii, Kansas, Nebraska, and New Mexico use the system in lieu of food exemption. Two states, Massachusetts and Vermont, provide both the credit and food exemption, thus adding to complications unnecessarily. Idaho provides a credit but no cash refund for low-income groups; Wyoming uses the system only for the elderly.

b) *Drugs and Medicines.* This exemption, which has particular justification because of uneven incidence of medical expenditures, is now provided for prescription drugs in all except six states, compared to all except nineteen in 1971, and in several for all drugs.

c) *Others.* Five states have made the mistake of exempting clothing, making the tax more regressive, as shown by Schafer (1969). Several states, most recently Maine and Minnesota, have exempted gas and electricity for home use. But adding exemptions has not been a common pattern.

d) *Services.* A decade ago there was a move in a number of states to broaden the base by adding specified services. But the trend slackened. There were serious objections to *general* inclusion of services (still found only in Hawaii and New Mexico) and inclusion of a *limited* number adds little to revenue and does not make the tax more progressive, as demonstrated by Davies (1969) and Nelson (1971).

e) *Industrial Machinery and Equipment.* The sales taxes were presumably designed to reach final consumption expenditures, but as a result of the definition of retail sales used, certain purchases by business firms were brought within the scope of the taxes. Because many commodities may have either production or consumption use, exclusion of all non-consumption purchases is almost impossible under the retail sales tax. Typically the states that introduced the sales tax in early years tax these industrial machinery items, while many of those that introduced the tax later do not. There is also an important regional concentration; in general, the industrial states, from Wisconsin and Indiana east, exclude the industrial items. There has been a slight tendency to add the exemption of machinery and no tendency to eliminate the exemption, except temporarily in New Jersey.

The general overall trend, therefore, has been some lessening of regressivity by exempting food, or by a sales tax credit against income tax (and both, in two states), and by almost complete exemption of drugs and medicines. There is substantial evidence that a sales tax with food taxable is regressive; with food exempt, more or less proportional.

The Revolt

One of the first bits of evidence of increasing taxpayer dissatisfaction was provided by voter action on bond issues, the aspect of governmental finance most subject to popular vote. Between 1950 and 1959, 79 percent of all state and local bond issues (by amount) were approved; from 1960 through 1967, 73 percent; from 1968 through 1975, only 50 percent; and in 1975, the all-time low, 29 percent, as shown by the Advisory Commission on Intergovernmental Relations (1977).

But until 1978, most proposals to restrict state or state-local spending were defeated. In June, 1978, however, California voters approved Proposition 13, drastically reducing property taxes and making state and local tax increases much more difficult. In brief, the provisions were as follows: 1) Property tax rates are limited to 1 percent of "full cash value." 2) "Full cash value" is the 1976-77 assessed value figure; the assessments cannot be increased until property is sold or new property is constructed, except to the extent of increase in the consumer price index to a maximum of 2 percent a year. 3) Any future increases in state taxes require a two-thirds vote of all members of each house of the legislature. 4) Local governments, by a two-thirds vote of the electors, may impose special taxes, but not on real property.

The action of the California voters led to the placing of tax and expenditure limitation measures on the November ballot in a number of states. (In many states no such measures are possible; in others, such as Illinois, the vote is not binding.) Arizona, Hawaii, Michigan, and Texas voters approved measures limiting the growth in state expenditures to the rate of growth in income or related measures (Tennessee had previously done so), but Nebraska voters defeated a similar proposal. Idaho and Nevada voters approved measures to roll back the property tax rates drastically. (There is doubt about the constitutionality of the Idaho measure, and in Nevada the voters disapproved the proposal on a second note.) But Oregon voters turned down a similar measure, as did Michigan voters (who approved a milder proposal). South Dakota voters approved a two-thirds vote requirement for tax increases. As a consequence of this voter action, gove ors in a number of states proposed substantial cuts in expenditures in the 1979-80 budgets. In 1980, despite conservative trends, the major tax limitation proposals were defeated, except in Massachusetts.

Causes of the Revolt

How can this relatively sudden change in voter attitudes be explained? There have been a number of analyses of this question, in a symposium volume of the *National Tax Journal* (1979), in Laffer and Seymour (1979), and in Mushkin (1979).

Tax Increases? One obviously possible explanation was that taxes had been rising sharply. Popular literature is fond of referring to soaring and skyrocketing state and local tax burdens. What is the evidence? As shown by the Tax Foundation (1979a), state and local expenditure (from own source) as a percentage of GNP is virtually the same as it was a decade ago (10.6) and less than in the mid-1970's; the high was 11.5 percent in 1979. Expressed as a percentage of personal income (Advisory Commission on Intergovernmental Relations 1979) the figures show some rise, from 10.5 percent in 1965 to 12.3 percent in 1975 in 1977, as personal income has risen less rapidly than GNP. But the increase over a decade relative to incomes has been relatively small, as has been the increase in federal taxes and expenditures.

Data on property taxes as a percentage of GNP and of personal income show an increase up to 1971-72 and a decline since, as shown in Table 5. The most hated of the major state and local taxes has not been increasing at all relative to personal income.

Table 5. Property Taxes as a Percentage of GNP, Selected Years 1902-77

Year	Property Tax Collections	Property Taxes as % of GNP
1976-77	$62,535	3.5
1971-72	41,500	4.0
1969-70	34,083	3.7
1964-65	22,583	3.6
1962	19,054	3.4
1960	16,405	3.3
1954	9,967	2.7
1950	7,349	2.6
1946	4,986	2.4
1944	4,604	2.2
1942	4,537	2.9
1940	4,430	4.4
1936	4,093	5.0
1932	4,487	7.7
1927	4,730	4.9
1922	3,321	4.5
1913	1,332	3.3
1902	706	2.9

Sources: Advisory Commission on Intergovernmental Relations, *Financing Schools and Property Tax Relief – A State Responsibility* (Washington, 1973), p. 16, and Bureau of the Census publications.

As shown in Figure 1, farm property taxes as a percentage of farm values has remained almost constant for a long period.

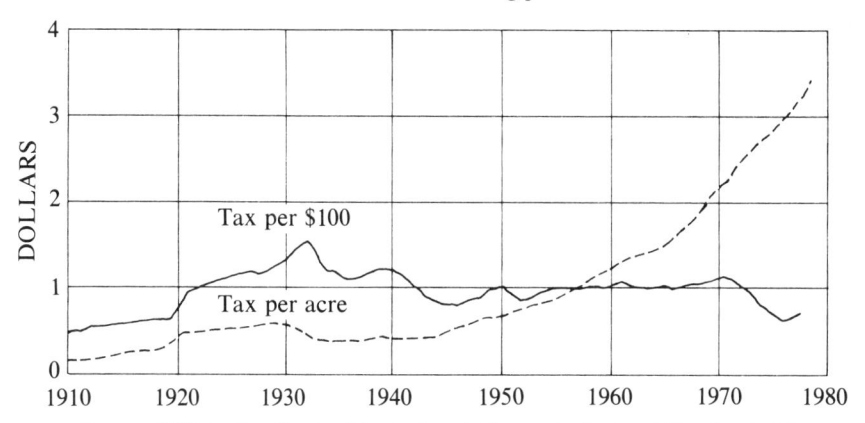

[Figure: graph with DOLLARS on y-axis (0 to 4) and years 1910-1980 on x-axis, showing "Tax per $100" and "Tax per acre" curves]

Source: USDA, *Handbook of Agricultural Charts*, Agricultural Handbook 551, November 1978. Tax based on market value.

Figure 1. Farm Real Estate Taxes

Furthermore, there was no overall shift toward the taxes regarded as least fair. There was a slight shift away from the property tax (the levy consistently regarded as the worst) and some shift from the motor fuel tax (regarded as the most acceptable) to the other levies, but on the whole the changes were not significant. Table 6 indicates that there was no sharp increase in dislike of the property tax (and a decrease since 1978). The property tax has been far more unpopular in the West than elsewhere-- despite the high property taxes in much of New England.

There were, however, certain changes in taxes that were adversely affecting various people. At the federal level, and to a lesser extent at the state level, inflation was pushing persons into higher tax brackets and increasing their tax liabilities when their real incomes were not rising. At the same time, social security payroll taxes have been rising--they are the only type of levy in the United States that has risen significantly in recent years. These are not state-local levies; nevertheless, they produce reactions against taxes generally. Adjustments in the tax structure in general offset much of these increases for the lower-income groups, but there was no equivalent offset for the large numbers of middle-income voters.

In addition, in some states (particularly California) some homeowners experienced very rapid increases in property taxes, as house values rose much more rapidly than the general price level and assessments kept pace with increased values.

Table 6. Which Do You Think Is the Worst Tax – That Is, the Least Fair?

	% of U.S. Public							
	May 1980	May 1979	May 1978	May 1977	May 1975	April 1974	May 1973	March 1972
Federal income tax	36	37	30	28	28	30	30	19
State income tax	10	8	11	11	11	10	10	13
State sales tax	19	15	18	17	23	20	20	13
Local property tax	25	27	32	33	29	28	31	45
Don't know	10	13	10	11	10	14	11	11

Reproduced from Advisory Commission on Intergovernmental Relations, *Changing Public Attitudes on Governments and Taxes* (1980), p. 1.

All in all, however, changes in taxes can hardly explain the massive change in attitude that appears to have occurred toward state-local taxes. Other forces must be explored.

Inflation? It is clear that the great majority of the population regards inflation as the number one problem facing the economy. A portion of the population--perhaps a quarter--has been actually injured by inflation because their incomes have lagged behind increases in the cost of living. Retired persons are the most obvious victims, but other fixed-income receivers are also injured. Most of the population clearly is not adversely affected; incomes have kept up with the cost of living, and values of typical assets have risen even more rapidly. The evidence for this is that per capita real incomes have risen, though slowly (there was a decline in 1975). But many persons see only one side of the picture; they intensely dislike the increasing cost of living *without* recognizing that their incomes have kept pace, or more than kept pace.

Accompanying this hatred of inflation is the very widespread conviction that inflation results from government deficits. The states as a whole have run surpluses in recent years. But, unable to hit the deficit spender directly, the voters hit at anything in reach--and this means states and local governments, when they have the opportunity.

Dissatisfaction with Government Efficiency and Government Services? Another element of dissatisfaction arises from the widespread belief that all levels of government are inefficient, corrupt, and do not provide high-quality service. Many families are critical of the educations their children receive, and they complain about too many "frills." Others are disturbed at the inability of the police to stop large-scale crime, especially in metropolitan areas, and they believe that criminals are coddled. Watergate, G.S.A., and comparable patterns on the part of some state and local officials further the view that corruption is widespread. The belief that government services could be provided at half the present cost is nonsensical--but is widely accepted.

In addition, voters in many cities are unhappy with the effects of unionization of municipal employees and teachers. Strikes of school teachers, policemen, and firemen are repugnant, as a matter of principle, to many, and the inconvenience resulting from closed schools magnifies this attitude. There is little doubt that unions in some cities have pushed wages of certain types of municipal employees above those of the private sector for comparable work--quite the reverse of a few decades ago. And the uncompromising attitudes of some union leaders in these fields have aggravated the attitudes. A portion of the vote for Proposition 13 sought to teach the public employees a lesson: the taxpayers have the final say, after all. In Canada, the imposition of wage and price controls was designed more to keep the pay of government employees in line than to control wages in the private sector.

There is well-known and long-standing concern with the welfare programs, due to the belief that there is extensive chiseling and that the programs given recipients incentives not to work. And a minority of the population still believes that the appropriate solution for the low-income groups is to send them over the hill to the poorhouse.

The problems with Amtrak and Conrail and BART (Bay Area Rapid Transit) furthered the belief that governments never do anything well, while the public forgets about the gross mismanagement of Penn Central and the financial problems of Chrysler, Sambo's, Braniff, and A&P.

Irritating Regulatory Policies? Another element of dissatisfaction is related to the introduction in the last decade of a number of regulatory measures which, while having justification and support, irritate many persons. The combined effects of these measures are not negligible. Only a few examples--some perhaps petty--need be noted. The 55-mile-an-hour speed limit is one. However significant the gains may be in lessening accidents and saving fuel, many drivers feel that it is an unreasonable restriction on their freedom. Mandatory helmet laws for motorcycle riders create similar resentments. Pollution controls have been a source of tribulation to many firms and have resulted, in some instances, in loss of employment. No matter how strongly people favor pollution control in principle, they are resentful if the measures result in loss of jobs. Anyone who has had the experience of being stranded in a remote community with a car taking only unleaded gas when the gas stations have no such gas is hardly sympathetic to this regulation. Similarly, anyone who has struggled in the middle of the night with an aspirin bottle cap that will not come off does not look with favor upon the government action that requires childproof caps. Many people quite legitimately feel that many such rules are issued without regard to the costs as compared to the benefits--that bureaucrats become obsessed with the particular change and do not consider the cost side at all. (The auto interlock mechanism was perhaps the prime example.)

There has also been widespread belief that long-standing regulatory policies of the Interstate Commerce Commission and the Civil Aeronautics Board were primarily concerned with protection of the industries and not of the public, and that they led to wasteful empty-truck movements and excessively high air fares and at the same time have not prevented deterioration of the railroads.

Minority Rights? A basic rule for the satisfactory functioning of a democratic society is that while the majority must rule, the rights of minorities must be protected. For a long period this second rule was violated, at least as far as certain minorities were concerned. The last two decades have seen great progress in the improvement of their position. The great majority of the population finds this as a desirable change, regarding improvement of the position of minorities as a public good. But in the process obviously many individuals have felt harmed by the procedures and programs. There is always a basic issue of just how far the majority is willing to go in improving the position of minorities. In the end the will of the majority must prevail, and if it is temporarily prevented from doing so by institutional factors, the result is a backlash against government generally, including against taxes. The absolute rights position taken by some minority groups increases the danger of this type of backlash.

Several examples will illustrate the argument. Attempts to ensure equal treatment of women, blacks, and other minorities have resulted in a substantial amount of paper work for business firms and universities. Some of this work appears to be highly unproductive in the attainment of the actual objectives. The line between increased minority participation and establishing outright quotas is a very fine one, as witnessed by the *Bakke* case, and many people object to the principle of quotas. Universities, schools, and government agencies alike feel that at times they are caught in a cross fire of conflicting priorities--veterans versus minorities, for example. Busing for school integration has been highly unpopular with many families who fear deterioration of schooling for their children and dislike the long bus rides that may result. Not all of this opposition to busing reflects dislike of integrated schools per se, as it did initially in the South.

In the field of women's rights, changes in terminology to avoid obviously sexist implications are generally accepted, but other changes have proven annoying to many and to result in awkward grammar. Many people find the word "chairperson" is very irritating. And the federal government has virtually come to blows with the commercial fishing industry over its insistance that fishermen be called "fishers."

Obviously not everyone is affected by all of these irritations, but the total number of individuals affected by various ones is obviously substantial--and without a question a source of taxpayer revolt, a reaction against financing activities that produce the irritations.

In a sense, the voters as a whole have come to conclude that the benefits from public goods, from adjusting for externalities, and from redistribution of income are not as great as they anticipated they would be. Alternatively, it may be argued that the voters have come to conclude that legislative bodies have gotten out of hand; by logrolling and pork-barreling they have pushed programs beyond the limits the majority of society will accept. But both of these statements are simplistic; much of the anti-tax sentiment has little to do with taxes per se. The votes are votes against inflation and irritating regulations and government actions, not just against taxes.

The Dangers of the Taxpayer Revolt

One of the greatest dangers of the revolt is irrational behavior. If voter reaction against government becomes strong, especially when fed by skillful proponents of lower taxes, it produces results that are not rational in terms of the voters' considered preferences. Their reactions are much like yanking the telephone off the wall in response to reaching a wrong number, or smashing a door open when the lock is sticking.

Proposition 13 provides a good example of irrationality. First, one of the chief beneficiaries was the U.S. Treasury, since state taxes are deductible for federal income taxes. The result is a transfer of perhaps a billion dollars of real income from Californians to the rest of the country annually. Second, a very large portion of the tax savings went to business firms, and much of this to large firms. The *Wall Street Journal* (Feb. 13, 1979) reports that of the $6.4 billion tax cut, only $2.3 billion went to homeowners (and much of this was lost through higher income tax payments), $1.2 billion to landlords, and $2.9 billion to business. For example, the *Journal* reports tax savings of $47 million to Standard Oil of California, $12 million to Getty Oil, $20 million to the Southern Pacific Railroad, $10 million to Atlantic Richfield, and at least this much to two other oil companies that will not release their data. Furthermore, the *Journal* reports that many firms have not been passing the tax savings on to consumers. The public utilities did--but much of the gain went to large industrial customers. While tax savings to business firms obviously offer some advantages, it is hard to believe that the California voters really would rationally seek to aid Standard Oil to the extent of nearly $50 million dollars a year.

Proposition 13 contains another provision that has potential for serious nuisance and economic distortion: the rule that assessments of property cannot be raised until the property is transferred. Such a rule is irrational by any standards. It will encourage freezing of property in the hands of the present owners, as well as creating numerous interpretative questions.

A significant example of irresponsible behavior on the part of state legislatures reacting to the taxpayer revolt is their endorsement of the calling of a constitutional convention to provide for the requirement of an annually balanced federal budget. It is believed that such a convention can consider other matters as well; it could easily end up in a battle over abortion and the ERA, for example, rather than over the federal budget. Such a straitjacket amendment would render effective fiscal policy impossible. It is also irrational from the standpoint of the states, because they would almost certainly be the first losers--revenue-sharing would be the first budget item to be eliminated permanently. The proposal is based upon the assumption that the federal deficit is the source of inflation, a widely held view that is almost certainly incorrect. The deficit is far too small, as a percentage of total spending in the economy, to have any significant effect. (It is equal to about 1.5 percent of GNP.)

Quite apart from irrationality, there are some serious objections to the meat-axe tax reductions that Proposition 13 and similar measures produce. One is the drastic cutting of "unprotected" services. The initial impact in California appears to have been on libraries and parks. One tendency is to freeze state and local employee wages and welfare payments. The former causes loss in personnel and in morale; the latter, inequity by usual standards. The more moderate proposals in other states do not have this "meat axe" effect.

Second, the movement is leading to constitutional requirements for two-thirds or similar legislative requirements to raise taxes. Such a rule substitutes minority rule for majority rule. While there may be some merit, at times, for requirements in excess of a majority, it is hard to believe that tax increases constitute one of them. Sixty-six percent of the population of a state may strongly favor increased expenditures for various purposes and may be willing to vote higher taxes to pay for them--but the 34 percent minority opposing can block the change. One voter in opposition equals two votes in favor--a violation of the one man, one vote rule if there ever was one.

Further undesirable effects can arise when the attack is centered too exclusively upon the property tax, leading to drastic reductions in this levy. A property tax *with adequate circuit-breaker provisions* to protect the poor and improved administration has significant advantages. It is the only tax from which school districts can effectively raise large sums of money and thus maintain some financial autonomy. It is the only means by which local governments can obtain substantial tax revenue from outside-owned business firms gaining large benefits from the local community. Properly designed, it is not seriously regressive. It avoids the potential adverse effects of the marginal income tax rates affecting additional income earned. Any sharp reduction in property taxes will almost certainly raise property values, concentrating the gain in the hands of those persons owning property at the time of the reduction and making it more difficult for young couples to purchase homes and for young farmers to acquire farms. The alternatives--higher sales and state income taxes--are not without their own disadvantages.

An anomaly of the California tax action is that it greatly reduces the financial autonomy of the local units, shifting power to the states and likely leading to long-run increasing demands on Washington. Yet, because the local units are the ones in which voters have greatest direct control, this shift is completely contrary to the principles of the conservatives who support tax revolts. Analyses of the consequences of Proposition 13 are provided by a Report to Congress by the Comptroller General (1979) and by Bell (1979).

The Implications for Education

A survey in California by the Education Finance Center of the Education Commission of the States (1979) suggests that education was not a major target of the affirmative votes for Proposition 13. Interviews of 1,049 respondents showed that the public schools were second only to police and fire departments as categories that people did not wish cut back. Welfare was by far the category most favored for cutback, followed by children's day care, recreation, and parks. Nevertheless, the general anti-tax sentiment which Proposition 13 reflects has serious potential consequences for schools. The attack is aimed more directly at the property tax than at any other levy, and of course, despite the relative increase in state funding. this levy remains the chief source of school financing. Further increases in state funding can be obtained only by raising state taxes or taking funds from other state activities. The taxpayer revolt will make the former increasingly difficult, and the other activities have their strong supporters. The lag in motor fuel levies, for example, by resulting in deteriorating highways, increases the pressure to quit using highway funds for auxiliary activities such as state police and to use general revenue funds for road use. Thus education is almost certain to suffer. The California survey noted above shows summer schools and interscholastic sports to be most favored for cuts, followed by music, art and drama, adult education, physical education, and administrative expense.

The greater sympathy for education than for many other functions, however, and the recognition that improved education aids economic development of a state and thus the flow of tax revenue, may result in special measures to protect against the overall cuts. But this can occur

284 *Shifting Sources of Financing Education*

only by increased state financing. Along with the increased state financing is certain to go increased state control over the schools.

The Future

The California revolt was obviously facilitiated by several special circumstances. The most important was the very large state surplus of about $5 billion. Second, property values had been rising rapidly and assessments were keeping up with them, with little change in tax rates. In 1978, the average increase in assessed values of homes was 120 percent. Third, the percent of personal income paid in state and local taxes is relatively high in California. Finally, it can be argued that California voters are politically particularly volatile.

In most other states the situation is different. Several states did have surpluses--Washington, Wisconsin, and Texas, for example. But today few states have any significant surpluses. Unlike in California, the cutbacks at the local level cannot be averted for a year or so by distribution of state surpluses. Property tax bills in many states have *not* been rising substantially, and usually they have not been rising at all in real terms. But the bandwagon effect is significant; the *Wall Street Journal* (February 16, 1979) reported that governors proposed an overall tax revenue cutback of more than $5 billion in 1979-80 budgets. A number of states have been considering amendments to their constitutions and other measures to restrict state and local spending. In addition, many states were considering reductions in various taxes, particularly in the property tax. Many of the proposals were relatively innocuous, some merely designed to distribute surpluses built up from rapidly rising income tax yields. Some have positive merits, such as exemption of medicines and industrial machinery from state sales taxes. But others go much farther. Some freeze property taxes at existing levels--a measure that has very little justification because of changing relative property values. In many states, of course, there are no direct initiative and referendum measures, and voters can restrict legislative powers only through constitutional amendments, a much slower process. But governors and legislature can act quickly if they wish. A summary of several referenda is provided by the Education Finance Center (1980).

Conclusion

The hazards of the tax revolt expenditure limitation movement for education as well as for other basic state and local government functions are obvious. How serious they will prove to be remains to be seen. The bandwagon was rolling at full tilt in 1981, with politicians leaping on at each opportunity. But the bandwagon appears to be slowing down--as the consequences of drastic tax reduction and federal budget cuts become apparent. Services that people want must be reduced, and competent personnel must be let go. California voters in 1980 rejected a proposal to cut state income taxes in half, and most of the proposals in 1980 and 1981 were defeated at the polls.

In a paper given at the annual conference of the Canadian Tax Foundation, Richard Musgrave offered several suggestions to diminish the dangers of the tax revolt. The following to some extent parallel his, but by no means fully:

1) Avoid sharp increases in property tax assessments. However meritorious may be the principle that assessments should keep pace with property values, it can be disastrous politically.
2) Take measures to offset automatic increases in tax yields that run well in excess of inflationary trends. The simplest solution is to index the state income tax.
3) Replace specific rate levies by ad valorem levies. It is very doubtful that the voters as a whole have preferred that the tobacco, and liquor and motor fuel taxes (the ones most widely accepted) decline for a decade in real terms--even though this has occurred.
4) Avoid state surpluses of any substantial magnitude.
5) Do not facilitate initiative and referendum measures at the state level, even though these appear to be "democratic." They lend themselves to demagoguery; they prevent coalitions that compromise and balance the interests of various groups; they lead to irrationality; they encourage single-issue voting.
6) All levels of government should seek to minimize petty annoyances, to balance benefits and costs of various regulatory measures, and to ensure that the protection of the rights of minorities does not go so far as to produce a serious backlash. In the end, the majority will must prevail--and there are no absolute rights in this world.
7) Given the obvious sympathy of voters for education over most other state and local functions, seek to protect it against the meat axe by specially allocated funding at the state level.[1]

NOTE

1. I am greatly indebted to the Advisory Commission on Intergovernmental Relations and the Tax Foundation for the use of material compiled by them.

REFERENCES

Aaron, Henry. 1975. *Who pays the property tax? A new view*. Washington: Brookings Institution.

Advisory Commission on Intergovernmental Relations, 1977. *Significant features of fiscal federalism, 1976-77.* Washington: U.S. Government Printing Office.

―――. 1978. *The Michigan single business tax.* Washington: U.S. Government Printing Office.

Bell, Douglas D. 1979. What Proposition 13 did to the California Board of Equalization and the county assessors. Paper presented to Western States Association of Tax Administrators.

Davies, David. 1969. The significance of taxation of services for the pattern of distribution of tax burden by income class. Pp. 138-46 in *Proceedings of the National Tax Association for 1969.*

Due, J. F., and Mikesell, J. L. 1980. State and local sales taxation. Working paper in public finance and economics. Bloomington: Indiana University School of Public and Environmental Affairs.

Education Finance Center. 1979. *Public opinions and Proposition 13.* Denver: Education Commission of the States.

―――. 1980. *Tax and expenditure limitation referenda.* Denver: Education Commission of the States.

Laffer, Arthur B., and Seymour, Jan P. 1979. *The economics of the tax revolt.* New York: Harcourt Brace Jovanovich.

Mushkin, Selma J., ed. 1979. *Proposition 13 and its consequences for public management.* Cambridge: Abt.

Nelson, E. O. 1971. Progressivity of the Ontario retail sales tax. *Canadian Tax Journal* 18 (September-October): 411-15.

Proceedings of a conference on tax and expenditure limitations. 1979. *National Tax Journal* 32 (June).

Report to Congress by the Comptroller General. 1979. *Proposition 13-- how California governments coped with a $6 billion revenue loss.* Washington: U.S. General Accounting Office.

Schaefer, J. M. 1969. Clothing exemptions and sales tax regressivity. *American Economic Review* 59 (September): 596-99.

Tax Foundation. 1979a. *Facts and figures on government finance.* Washington: Tax Foundation.

―――. 1979b. *Monthly Tax Features* 23 (January).

U.S. Bureau of the Census. 1980. *State government tax collections in 1980* Washington: U.S. Government Printing Office.

Welch, Ronald. 1976. Property tax developments: modernization, classification, site value taxation. *National Tax Journal* 29 (September): 323-27.

PART III

Policy and Emerging Prospects: Combining Efficiency and Equity

Equity and efficiency within education—and productivity in the economy at large—can be advanced through educational planning, finance, and budgeting policies, as has been developed in earlier parts of this volume. But this would require that current educational financing systems and policies do more to encourage increased efficiency and to achieve greater student and taxpayer equity. A socially optimum policy must incorporate both efficiency and equity considerations.

In Part III, questions are raised with regard to why efficiency and equity do not appear to be the cornerstone of our current educational financing systems, against the background of what in fact has occurred over the years. Part III also offers insights into emerging prospects for the future. With respect to efficiency considerations, for example, why is there a preoccupation with inputs rather than with educational outcomes and their more ultimate "full" earnings and social benefits? Why are most educational administrators not trained in cost effectiveness techniques? Why does the use of wasteful cost-plus reimbursement schemes for many categorical services persist? Why are resources wasted on programs that are high in cost but low in quality and effectiveness? Part of the problem may be that efficiency concepts are too vague when the weights to be given to different benefits are not sufficiently defined or comprehensive. Part may be due to the lack of adequate incentives, and part to a lack of adequate knowledge of what works. If so, this volume has attempted to add to the body of knowledge which contributes to the continuing development of output-related efficiency incentives, comprehensive benefit concepts, and efficiency criteria.

With respect to equity, why does the vast inequality in expenditure per pupil--to use a rough but easily available index of student equity-- persist within and among states? Is it because school finance reform movements have tended to be diverted toward tax reform and/or toward sources for increasing school revenues? (There is some evidence of this.) Or is it because there is only gradual movement in preferences, as expressed through the courts and through the political mechanism, toward higher-level equity criteria? There is also some evidence of this, as suggested by the huge expansion of community colleges, the rapid expansion of special education programs, and the large increase in federal funding of Basic Educational Opportunity Grants for students from low-income families. There are also movements in the other direction with inflation and federal budget cuts. Most would probably agree that progress toward greater equity has been slow, erratic, and that there is still a long way to go.

Chapter 12, by Elchanan Cohn, brings together the cost and the more immediate outputs of education within the context of an optimization model. His state-support model accommodates the many and often diversified goals that school districts typically pursue, including student equity goals in the objective function. It assumes that various trade-offs will be involved in that attainment of any one goal conflicts with the attainment of other goals because of limited resources. Cohn illustrates how the prototypical model would be applied to school districts and even individual schools in an effort to optimize resource allocation within state school systems. This model is unique in that it focuses on educational outputs rather than on educational inputs, and that it pursues simultaneously both efficiency and equity objectives. This type of research should ultimately lead toward introducing considerations of the quality of school outputs, and toward integration of the possible long-term effects of the tremendous disparities in per-pupil expenditures on the quality of life that students ultimately enjoy.

In Chapter 13 Allan Odden suggests that the courts are now beginning to look at the output side--and that this has efficiency implications. Many practical budget decisions deal implicitly with efficiency in the production of human capital, more than might be surmised from purusal of the literature or of formal state and federal education finance policies. In recent key court decisions dealing with equity, Odden feels that there has been a trend toward stronger student equity criteria (one of the more recent decisions in Ohio to the contrary). Outside the courts, Odden cites the accelerating trend toward competency testing that is creating pressures for efficiency in learning processes and in school organizations. There are fears that equity could be sacrificed, but if raising low scores becomes a practical method of raising average test scores, student equity could actually be advanced.

The concluding chapter, by Terry Geske, summarizes and integrates what might be regarded as the more significant findings in relation to our theme of efficiency, equity, and humane growth as drawn from the preceding chapters. These findings relate primarily to the means of increasing efficiency in education in the entire human capital-formation process, as well as to ways of improving student equity with implications for the distribution of lifetime benefits within each generation. The findings are especially pertinent in the current era of financial stress, when criteria for finding wasteful and ineffective uses of funds can be an important source for the maintenance of educationally sound and equitable programs. In addition, if joint improvements in efficiency and equity can be found and emphasized -- that is, if educational financing, planning, and budgeting changes can lead to improved efficiency and/or equity without losses in either -- the political opposition to such changes is likely to be reduced. The final chapter is directed toward these possibilities, their implications, and the emerging policy prospects.

CHAPTER 12

Combining Efficiency and Equity: Optimization of Resource Allocation in State School Systems

ELCHANAN COHN

The financing of public elementary and secondary education in the United States has undergone tremendous change during the past 50 years. During 1929-30, only 16.9 percent of total public school revenues came from the states, whereas 82.7 percent were derived from local sources. By 1969-70 the proportion of state aid increased to 40 percent, and the local share declined to 52.1 percent (Grant and Lind 1976: Table 65). With school finance laws having been declared unconstitutional in New Jersey, Connecticut, California, and elsewhere, the state share is likely to increase even further. Without doubt, much of the change is due to the intensive campaign for improvements in the equity aspects of state educational systems. Educational reformers argue that poorer districts should receive disproportionate aid in an effort to equalize their chances for providing "quality" education to all children.

An assessment of the successes or failures of the reform movement is outside the scope of this article.[1] What is apparent, however, is that the reformers concentrate on *equalization*, and their concept of "equality" or "equality of educational opportunity" was ultimately cast largely in terms of disparities in *expenditures per pupil*--in other words, in terms of educational *inputs* (Cohn 1974: 25-31). Efficiency considerations have been largely left out.

My objective here is to change the focus of state aid from a process of input equalization to an optimization procedure combining educational production efficiency, equity, and "need." The new state aid model is built around the concepts of the educational production function, goal programming, and state-local partnership in educational finance. Before the model is presented, however, it is necessary to provide a brief review of current state aid plans, models of resource allocation, and earlier proposals for efficiency incentives in state aid formulas.

The Current Status of State Aid to Education

Public school finance currently is based mainly on the Strayer-Haig-Mort "Foundation" Program. The foundation program is based on the notion that each school must provide a minimum-quality education by spending a certain foundation sum (F) per pupil. The state selects a minimum "mandated" property tax rate (r_m) and state aid is equal to the difference between F and the property tax revenue which a tax rate of r_m would generate:

$$SA_d = E_d [F - r_m (V_d/E_d)] \qquad (1)$$

where SA_d is state aid to district d, E_d is a measure of student enrollment or attendance, and V_d is taxable property valuation in the district.

The measure of student enrollments used is usually weighted average daily attendance or membership, with differential weights attached to different levels of schooling or special programs. The weighting procedure has become quite complex in many state aid formulas, in an attempt to provide special consideration for special needs of particular children or school districts.

It should be pointed out that alternative models of school finance are in use, including the percentage equalizing, resource equalizer (or guaranteed valuation), and power equalizing schemes. As shown elsewhere (Cohn 1974: 32-36; Cohn 1979: 270-80), all of these are either special cases of the foundation program or close kins thereof. Also, "flat grants" are frequently disbursed as part of the formula, and a significant portion of the state share of local school costs might be provided as special-purpose (categorical) grants which lie outside the scope of the basic aid formula. Likewise, transportation and capital costs may be financed through a different procedure.

Reform in recent years served to increase the proportion of educational revenues derived from state sources, as indicated in the preceding chapter by Due. A key objective not always achieved (as shown in the chapter by Carroll) has been to reduce interdistrict disparities in per-pupil expenditures. In many cases school finance reform was spurred by a court ruling or by the threat of court action.[2] Reform has also been directed toward inclusion of modifiers in the state school finance system for such things as sparsity of population, inflation, and declining enrollments.[3]

Although the discussion here must gloss over many aspects of recent changes in educational finance, it is clear that the main activity has been directed toward improving equity aspects of school finance systems.[4] Efficiency criteria have by and large been completely left out. In fact, it may be argued (as has Schultz in Chapter 2) that some of the new modifiers have served to *reduce* efficiency. For example, school finance statutes in some states include a provision under which more per-pupil state aid is given to smaller districts, *on the basis of the argument* that costs per pupil increase as the size of the school district decreases.[5] But such increased state aid reduces the economic pressure on high cost per pupil, inefficient school districts to consolidate (where possible) or to reduce costs by other means, thus providing a counter-efficiency incentive. Similarly, some state aid formulas aid the very large urban districts where there may be inefficiencies due to excessive size and diseconomies of scale. And although many states have statutes requiring some degree of accountability, including competency testing, there are no direct links between the state aid formula and these measures of internal efficiency of schools. My purpose here is to reverse the encouragement of inefficiency and to promote efficiency, while not omitting equity considerations.

Models of Resource Allocation in Schools

Efficiency of any enterprise is measured by the ratio of output to input. It is generally agreed that, other things being equal, an enterprise reaping higher profits is a more efficient economic unit, because with a given input it can generate a greater output. The same principle holds for public enterprises such as schools. Those school districts which are able to generate greater "output" from a given set of inputs will be regarded as the more efficient districts.

There are significant differences, however, between most private enterprises and school districts. First, the school district produces "outputs" which are not sold (at least not directly) in the marketplace. As Rossmiller and Geske (1976: 499) point out, educational outputs may be classified into "a number of different but not mutually exclusive ways, such as short-range and long-range, cognitive and non-cognitive, or monetary and non-monetary." In the long run, the outputs of the educational system should be reflected in human capital formation, which has been measured by such proxies as discounted lifetime earnings differentials attributed to education, internal rates of return to education, or the contribution of education to economic growth.[6] In addition, education should have an impact on tastes, leisure, and a host of other non-monetary benefits.[7] Although the long-run effects are perhaps the most relevant educational outputs, they are generally useful only in studying the ultimate value of education, as opposed to the productivity of a specific educational enterprise over a very short time period. Therefore, if it is desired to evaluate the performance of a school district over, say, a one-year period, it is necessary to examine the short-range outputs.

The short-range (or intermediate) outputs consist of "cognitive, affective, and psychomotor achievement--possession of basic knowledge, exhibits of intellectual and manual skills, demonstrations of analytical capabilities, displays of values, attitudes, and aspirations, and the like" (Rossmiller and Geske 1976: 500). To measure such outputs, a multidimensional output vector must be specified. Without market prices it is almost impossible, given the state of the art and without substantial additional research, to measure the aggregate value of a school's output, and hence its output/input ratio. Also, the inputs include not only those purchased by the schools (teachers, plant and equipment, etc.) but also those associated with students, which exacerbates the problem of measuring the output/input ratio. Finally, we know all too little about the learning *process*, so it would be very difficult to explain *why* the output/input ratios vary among schools--even if we could to overcome the above-listed difficulties.

Nevertheless, no progress in improving educational efficiency is possible unless we attempt to analyze the educational production process, to model the relationship between inputs and outputs, and to find means by which output per unit of input could be increased. The educational production function must, therefore, be developed.

The Educational Production Function

Suppose we identify n outputs, denoted by $Q_1, Q_2, \ldots, Q_n$, m instrumental inputs (over which the school administration has some control), denoted by $X_1, X_2, \ldots, X_m$, and k nonschool inputs (over which the administration has no control), denoted by $Y_1, Y_2, \ldots, Y_k$. Let us assume, furthermore, that an educational *process* can be identified, showing the manner by which inputs are transformed into outputs. Denote this process by the letter $\underline{f}$. Then we have the following educational production function:

$$\underline{f}(Q_1, Q_2, \ldots, Q_n; X_1, X_2, \ldots, X_m; Y_1, Y_2, \ldots, Y_k) = 0 \qquad (2)$$

That is, in an educational production function of the type discussed in the chapter by Rossmiller, the levels of the outputs are determined by the levels of the instrumental inputs, given the levels of the nonschool inputs, according to the process $\underline{f}$.

It was noted earlier that a learning theory from which the nature of the process ($\underline{f}$) would be discerned is lacking. One could, instead, surmise what $\underline{f}$ might look like by employing a curve-fitting technique. Empirical research generally has not followed this route, showing preference for the simplest form, i.e., a linear relationship.[8] For example, an equation for Q_1, the first output, would have the following linear form:

$$Q_1 = \alpha_1 + \sum_{i=2}^{n} \beta_{1i} Q_i + \sum_{j=1}^{m} \gamma_{1j} X_j + \sum_{h=1}^{k} \delta_{1h} Y_h + e_1 \qquad (3)$$

where α_1 is the intercept, β_{1i} is the coefficient of the ith output, γ_{1j} is the coefficient of the jth instrument variable, δ_{1h} is the coefficient of the

294 Combining Efficiency and Equity

hth nonschool variable, and e_1 is a stochastic error term. The coefficients ($\alpha, \beta, \gamma, \delta$) may be estimated using multiple regression analysis.

Since educational outputs are not likely to be mutually independent, estimating a separate equation for each output could result in biased coefficients. A simultaneous-equation system may be developed instead, and coefficients estimated using techniques such as two-stage least squares (Johnston 1972: chs. 12, 13). After some manipulation, one can derive the reduced-form equations which express each output in terms of the inputs alone.

$$Q_1 = a_1 + \sum_{j=1}^{m} b_{1j} X_j + \sum_{h=1}^{k} c_{1h} Y_h$$

$$Q_2 = a_2 + \sum_{j=1}^{m} b_{2j} X_j + \sum_{h=1}^{k} c_{2h} Y_h \qquad (4)$$

.

.

.

$$Q_n = a_n + \sum_{j=1}^{m} b_{nj} X_j + \sum_{h=1}^{k} c_{nh} Y_h$$

where the a's, b's, and c's are constants. From equation systems of this kind it is possible to appraise the impact of any one input on any of the educational outputs, other things being equal.[9]

Mathematical Programming Approaches

To improve the efficiency of resource allocation in schools, one may employ the technique of mathematical programming. All mathematical programs contain an objective function and constraints. For example, the objective function could be the minimization of resource costs, the maximization of output, or minimization of deviations from target output levels. Constraints include limitations on school resources, technical aspects of the educational process, and the requirement that a solution must only involve "relevant" activities. As examples of confinement of the solution to relevant activities, negative values of inputs are excluded, and the number of teachers in the system must not fall below some reasonable minimum.

An example of the objective function might be to maximize some measure of intermediate outputs, such as the sum of verbal and mathematical achievement of students in the fourth grade. Constraints would include requirements 1) that the costs of inputs do not exceed a certain maximum; 2) that certain inputs fall within a pre-specified range; and 3) that all inputs and outputs assume non-zero values. The system may also include the production functions for other ouputs as constraints. The solution of the problem would yield the input levels which would maximize achievement within the restricted domain of the problem.

Another possibility is to minimize the costs of schooling subject to the production function constraints plus the latter two constraints from the preceding paragraph. An empirical counterpart of these two cases is given in Boardman (1978).

The problem with the first example is that it singles out cognitive achievement to the exclusion of other important educational outputs. Use of linear programming methods for more than one output is impossible, however, because we do not have a pricing (or other) mechanism for weighting the multiple outputs. The cost minimization case overcomes this problem, but it is questionable whether schools should strive either to minimize costs for a given output or to obtain maximum output subject to input and production constraints.

A third case has therefore been developed, utilizing the technique of goal programming. Here the objective function is to minimize deviations from target levels of the educational goals (or outputs). The target levels may be set sufficiently high so that, in practice, we approach the objective of output maximization. Constraints include the educational production process, input limitations, and other relevant constraints. Since the main thrust of this paper hinges on the development of a goal programming framework, I shall discuss it in more detail in the next section.

Goal-Programming Model

The model assumes that we have multiple educational goals or outputs (outcomes), and that the attainment of any one goal conflicts with the attainment of other goals (principally because attainment of each goal competes for resources that are needed for the attainment of other goals). The objective is to minimize deviations from target goal levels, subject to an array of constraints. An example of educational goals is presented in Table 1, based upon the Pennsylvania goals of education.

The objective function includes two main elements: preemptive priority factors, and coefficients of regret. The preemptive priority factors (P_j) indicate which of the goals should be attained first (P_1), second (P_2), and so on, as in the middle column in Table 1. Note that it is possible, however, for two or more goals to occupy the same priority level. In that case, the coefficients of regret (σ_i^+ and σ_i^-) in the last two columns indicate which output will be attained first. Also, since both positive and negative deviations may be subject to minimization, the coefficients of regret determine whether priority should be given to minimizing underachievement or overachievement.

Table 1. Pennsylvania Goals of Quality Education, Estimated Preemptive Priority Factors and Estimated Coefficients of Regret

Output number	Short name	Estimated preemptive priority factors	Coefficients of regret σ_i^+	σ_i^-
1	Self-concept	P_3	1.302	4.308
2	Understanding others	P_3	1.513	2.950
3	Verbal basic skills	P_1	1.056	18.660
4	Math basic skills	P_2	1.076	14.000
5	Learning attitudes	P_1	1.400	3.500
6	Citizenship	P_4	1.250	5.920
7	Health habits	P_7	1.474	3.110
8	Creativity potential	P_5	1.750	2.330
9	Creativity output	P_8	1.865	2.155
10	Vocational development	P_8	1.272	4.666
11	Knowledge of past accomplishments	P_9	1.866	2.155
12	Readiness for change	P_6	2.545	1.647

Source: Cohn and Morgan (1978: Tables 2, 3, and Equation [1] on p. 97).
Note: For additional information about the outputs, consult Cohn and Millman (1975; Table A-1). A discussion of the preemptive priority factors of the coefficients of regret is contained in Cohn and Morgan (1978) and in Morgan (1977).

The set of constraints include technical relationships constraining the achievement of outputs, resource availability, and non-negativity requirements.

The major difficulty with this approach is the estimation of the pre-emptive priority factors and the coefficients of regret. On what basis can one determine whether verbal achievement should receive priority over mathematical achievement, which in turn should receive priority over non-cognitive goals? And how is one to determine whether overachievement of any one goal should be preferred to underachievement?

In seeking to answer such questions, Morgan (1977) has developed a survey instrument which elicited information from school principals in Pennsylvania about their perceptions regarding priorities for educational goals.[10] They were asked to rank the twelve outputs in Table 1, and to indicate which of the outputs they desire to attain exactly, on which they are willing to overachieve, and on which they are willing to underachieve. From this information Morgan constructed an aggregate voting table, and an aggregate priority schedule was obtained. Although no principal was allowed to rank any two goals equally, some goals did occupy the same priority level in the aggregate ranking. In such cases the coefficients of regret determined which of the goals had priority.

Drawing on Cohn with Millman (1975), Morgan then developed a prototypical goal-programming model for Pennsylvania secondary schools. The target output levels were set at the Pennsylvania mean plus three standard deviations, which represent the output attained by the upper 5 percent of the schools in the sample. The results of the exercise indicated that all except two goals could be attained exactly or overachieved.

A goal-programming model only slightly different from that developed by Morgan is presented here. The outputs $(Q_1, Q_2, \ldots, Q_n)$ may be represented by the list in Table 1. Inputs are divided into manipulable inputs $(X_1, X_2, \ldots, X_m)$ and non-manipulable inputs $(Y_1, Y_2, \ldots, Y_k)$. Manipulable inputs are those over which school administrators exert some control. The contribution of nonmanipulable inputs and the intercept (a_i) to the ith output is given by $S_i = a_i + \sum_{j=1}^{k} c_{ji} Y_j$, where c_{ji} is the reduced-form coefficient describing the effect of input Y_j on output Q_i. A list of manipulable inputs (used in the Pennsylvania input/output model) is given in Table 2. The goal-programming model is described in Table 3.

Equation (1) in Table 3 describes the objective function. We seek to minimize deviations from target output levels $(T_1, T_2, \ldots, T_n)$, where

Table 2. Manipulable Input Variables

Label	Description
TEDUC	Teacher's education
GUIDANCE	Counselor/pupil
TLOD	Teacher load
CSIZ	Class size
AEE	Average extracurricular expenditure/pupil
TSALARY	Teacher's salary
PSUP	Paraprofessional support
CUG	Curriculum units/grade
PRCO	Preparation coefficient (teacher specialization)
SFRAT	Student/academic faculty ratio
BOOKSP	Library books/pupil
TEXPER	Teacher's teaching experience
LIBRARY	Accessibility of library
CLPRACT	Teacher classroom practices
INNOVATE	School usage of innovations
BRAT	Ratio of actual enrollment to building capacity
AMAN	Administrative man hours/pupil
AXMAN	Auxiliary man hours/pupil

Source: Cohn with Millman (1975: 59).
Note: For additional information about both manipulable and nonmanipulable inputs, consult Cohn with Millman (1975: Tables A-2 – A-4).

positive deviations are denoted by d^+ and negative deviations by d^-. P_1, $P_2, \ldots, P_n$ are the preemptive priority factors, with P_1 the highest priority, P_2 the next, and so on. The coefficients of regret are given by $\sigma_1 \pm, \sigma_2 \pm, \ldots, \sigma_n \pm$, and become part of the functions $g_i, \ldots, g_U$ as shown in the definitions below Table 3.

Equation system (2) is a production-function constraint. It is required that the production of the n outputs, in accordance with the underlying production process exhibited in the equation system, will differ from the target values by the values of the deviational variables, d^+ or d^-. Equation system (3) simply states that the level of inputs (X_j) must not fall below legal or institutional requirements (L_j) and cannot exceed input availability (H_j). Finally, the constraints in system (4) invoke non-negativity restrictions to confine the solution to relevant activities.

Elchanan Cohn

Table 3. Goal-Programming Model

Minimize the objective function:

$$Z = P_1 [g_1(\bar{d}^-, \bar{d}^+)], \ldots, P_U [g_U(\bar{d}^-, \bar{d}^+)] \tag{1}$$

Subject to the following constraints:

a. Production possibilities

$$b_{11} X_1 + b_{12} X_2 + \ldots + b_{1m} X_m - d_1^+ + d_1^- = T_1 - S_1 \tag{2}$$
$$b_{21} X_1 + b_{22} X_2 + \ldots + b_{2m} X_m - d_2^+ + d_2^- = T_2 - S_2$$

$$\cdot$$
$$\cdot$$
$$\cdot$$

$$b_{n1} X_1 + b_{n2} X_2 + \ldots + b_{nm} X_m - d_n^+ + d_n^- = T_n - S_n$$

b. Legal and institutional boundaries

$$L_1 \leq X_1 \leq H_1 \tag{3}$$
$$L_2 \leq X_2 \leq H_2$$

$$\cdot \ \cdot \ \cdot$$
$$\cdot \ \cdot \ \cdot$$
$$\cdot \ \cdot \ \cdot$$

$$L_m \leq X_m \leq H_m$$

c. Non-negativity conditions

$$(T_i - S_i), d_i^+, d_i^- \geq 0, \quad i = 1, 2, \ldots, n \tag{4}$$

where

- Z = The objective function of the model with the priority factors, determined by the administrator's preference function, associated with each goal.
- b_{ij} = the reduced form input coefficients estimated by a simultaneous-equation estimation technique from the data for a relevant set of schools or school districts.
- X_j = the inputs over which the administrator has control. These inputs may be altered by the decisionmaker when he attempts to optimize his objective function.
- d_i^+ = deviational variable representing the overachievement of goal i with its value determined ex post in solution.
- d_i^- = deviational variable representing the underachievement of goal i (also determined ex post).
- P_u = the preemptive priority factor for the uth objective. $1 \leq u \leq U$

$$g_u(\bar{d}^-, \bar{d}^+) = \sum_{i=1}^{n} (\sigma_{ui}^- d_i^- + \sigma_{ui}^+ d_i^+) = \text{the uth priority objective, using the coefficients of regret.}$$

Table 3. (Continued)

T_i = the predetermined target level for each goal.

S_i = the contribution to the ith goal attributable to the nonmanipulable variables over which the educational administrator has no control. The expression for S_i is additive and linear.

H_j = the level of resource availability.

L_j = legal and institutional minimum levels of input utilization.

$\sigma_{ui}\pm$ = an ex-ante determined coefficient of regret (weighting factor) associated with goals which occupy the same priority level in the objective function. The coefficient of regret gives the relative importance of goal i to goal j when each occupies priority level u. Also, it is required that $\sigma_{ui}\pm \geqslant 0$.

n = the number of goals.

m = the number of inputs over which the administrator has control.

U = the number of priority levels.

A prototypical goal-programming model of this kind could be developed for each state and then applied to any school, district, or division thereof. The model solution provides an optimal input vector which, if adopted, would achieve the desired deviations from these target output levels. If attainment of such an optimum is too costly, some of the target output levels may be lowered until input cost meets the available amount of resources. Alternatively, a cost constraint may be added to the model, yielding a solution which guarantees operation within a given budgetary constraint.

Earlier Proposals for Efficiency Incentives in State Aid to Schools

It was mentioned earlier that an important omission of state aid plans is any serious connection to efficiency. Yet we have noted the availability of techniques that could improve efficiency through the utilization of the production function concept and/or mathematical programming.

I have made proposals for inclusion of efficiency aspects in the state aid formulas in my earlier writings. One proposal dealt with the incorporation of a penalty factor or an incentive fund corresponding to either school size or output attainment, or both (Cohn 1974: Chs. 6, 7; Cohn 1975). A second proposal is to require employment of a goal-programming model in each school district as a prerequisite for state aid (Cohn forthcoming).

Penalty Factor or Incentive Funds for Scale Economies

Studies have shown that school size is related to costs per pupil, other things being equal. The fact that most schools are either too large or too small suggests that society might reap considerable savings if schools can be coaxed to organize themselves more efficiently. An explicit inclusion of a penalty factor (the "stick") or an incentive fund (the "carrot") might be helpful. My suggestion was to study scale economies for each state, and to measure the difference between per-pupil costs in each school (properly adjusted) and the per-pupil costs that would prevail had the school been organized to tap all possible scale economies. That difference is denoted by $C_i - C_m$ (i.e., district i costs less minimum costs).

Penalty Factors. After C_i is measured for each district, the legislature decides on a proportion (p) such that a penalty factor equal to $p(C_i-C_m)$ per pupil is imposed on each district and subtracted from its state aid allotment.

Incentive Payment. Alternatively, the change in $C_i - C_m$ over time (say, over the past two years), denoted by ΔC_i, could be calculated for each district, representing the resource saving to society due to organizational changes. Total savings to the state amount to the sum of such savings to individual districts, given by $\Sigma \Delta C_i$. Then the proportion of total savings accomplished by the ith district is given by $g_i = \Delta C_i / \Sigma \Delta C_i$. Suppose the state appropriates an incentive fund of a fixed amount, say $IF. Then each school district receives a share of IF in accordance with its *relative* contribution to total savings, or $g_i IF$.

Other Features. The penalty and incentive payment features could be combined. For example, total penalties may be set equal to IF, so that the system will be self-financing. Schools in which substantial economies can be reaped through reorganization will be penalized, whereas those showing improvement over time will be rewarded. Although some schools may be penalized and rewarded simultaneously, the financial rewards to increasing efficiency should, in general, lead to political pressure on schools to organize more efficiently. It is also possible to limit implementation of the plan to those schools where significant savings could be reaped through reorganization, eliminating "necessarily existent small schools" from the plan. Finally, an adjustment for interdistrict "equity" may be made in the formulas, so that the state bears more of the burden in the poor districts.

Output Incentives

A similar plan was suggested for output incentives (Cohn 1974: Ch. 7). The main feature of the plan is the construction of an "output index," based on the technique of canonical correlations. Once such an index is established, penalty factors and incentive payments may be constructed analogous to our construction of the scale economies plan. The main problem, however, is the construction of the output index, and it is not clear whether the canonical correlation technique provides a viable solution.

Goal-Programming Requirement

Finally, it was suggested that each state develop the capacity to perform goal-programming routines for each school or school district (Cohn forthcoming). State aid to schools would be conditional upon the district's willingness to examine its resource allocation in light of the goal-programming solution. Although the proposal does not require the schools to adhere to the results of the goal-programming solution, it is assumed that the very act of carrying out such an exercise would make state aid systems more efficiency-conscious and would provide guidance on optimal input combinations that would lead to more efficient and equitable resource allocation in education.[11]

A New School Finance Model

The efficiency-related proposals in the preceding section are designed to improve resource allocation in education *within* each school district (and thereby within the state as a whole), and to provide some link between state aid to education and efficiency objectives. This section takes a much more radical view, proposing a new school finance model in which internal efficiency is, in a sense, *optimized*.[12] Moreover, it is proposed that the implementation of "equity" objectives be cast in terms of educational *outputs* rather than *inputs*. The new statewide finance model is unique, in the sense that it satisfies both equity[13] and efficiency goals *simultaneously*. While caveats in the proposal are recognized, it appears to hold tremendous promise for the future.

The conceptual development of the new finance plan is detailed in the following paragraphs.

Goal-Programming Models

Each state will develop several prototypical statewide goal-programming models. The state's elementary and secondary education sector might be classified by level of education and type of community (for example, elementary-urban, elementary-rural, secondary-urban, and secondary-rural). Some of the goal-programming elements should be determined on a statewide basis, while others would depend on local conditions.

Objective Function. Educational goals, preemptive priority rankings, and coefficients of regret could be determined on a statewide basis via surveys of school administrators, parents, teachers, and taxpayers. Alternatively, each school district might be allowed some flexibility in choosing and ranking goals. It would be administratively simpler, however, if a single set of goals and priority weights were to be imposed from the state level.

Target Output Levels

Target output levels must be determined on a statewide basis for each prototype. "Best practice" or other desired target levels may be set initially.

Production Function. The construction of input-output models to derive reduced-form coefficients of the educational production functions must be based on aggregate data. An input-output system should, therefore, be specified for each prototype based on the best available data.

Application to Individual Schools. Once the objective function, target output levels, and production-function coefficients are specified, only resource availability constraints must be determined. Because such constraints are likely to vary from school to school, they must be respecified for each school or district. Adding the non-negativity constraints, the state analysts are now in a position to run the goal-programming model to find input needs for an individual school or school district.

Goal-Programming Solution. Once the goal-programming model is solved for a specific school district, a solution vector of manipulable inputs, $X_1^*, X_2^*, \ldots, X_m^*$, is determined, indicating the levels of input utilization required to minimize deviations from target output levels.

Educational Costs

The minimum cost required to achieve the objective function for each school district is given by the formula:

$$C_d = \sum_{j=1}^{m} p_j X_j^* \qquad (5)$$

where C_d are costs in district d, and p_j is the market price of input X_j. Market prices of inputs may vary from district to district (e.g., teacher salaries) due to supply-demand factors.

Local Share of Educational Costs

It is assumed that districts rely primarily on property tax revenues. The state will impose a minimum mandated tax rate, r_m. Local revenues (LR_d) will be, then:

$$LR_d = r_m V_d + \text{other revenues (other than state aid)} \qquad (6)$$

where V_d is assessed valuation of taxable property in district d.

State Share of Educational Costs

The state share (SA_d) is given by the difference between educational costs (C_d) and local revenues (LR_d):

$$SA_d = C_d - LR_d \qquad (7)$$

If C_d exceeds LR_d, local revenues generated by a property tax at the rate r_m are insufficient to cover the costs of inputs suggested by the goal-programming solution. Ideally, state aid should be given to the district to make up the difference. If state aid is provided on the basis of Equation (7), target output levels will be attained as closely as possible by all school districts. Equity, measured in terms of equality of *output*, will be attained to the best possible extent. Equity in the conventional sense (e.g., equalization of expenditures per pupil) will *not* be achieved, since schools endowed with a larger percentage of "disadvantaged" pupils or more expensive inputs would require greater expenditures, *ceteris paribus*, to achieve the output target levels.

Suppose that $LR_d > C_d$. In that case the district raises more revenues than required to cover the costs of the inputs suggested by the goal-programming solution. If the local tax rate r_m is required for the school district to receive state aid, surplus funds will be accumulated by the district. At least two possibilities may be considered. First, let the district use the extra funds as it sees fit. This could lead to attainment of output beyond the target output levels, and thus create some degree of inequity in the distribution of educational outputs. Alternatively, require the district to send extra funds to the state, as suggested by the District Power Equalizing plan (a recapture clause).[14] This latter plan is superior on equity grounds (since under the former plan schools for which $LR_d > C_d$ could attain output levels higher than target output levels), but the former plan is politically more attractive, since wealthier districts will be less reluctant to vote for it. Although the political considerations must not be overlooked, it appears that an attempt should be made to incorporate a recapture clause into the educational finance plan.

Total state aid to school districts is the sum of its share for all districts:

$$\text{Total state aid} = \sum_{d=1}^{D} SA_d \qquad (8)$$

where D is the number of districts in the state.

Total state aid required to attain the initial target output levels might exceed the amount which the state legislature is willing to appropriate. A common resolution of a discrepancy between desired and appropriated funding levels has been to reduce all districts' funding by an equal percentage, satisfying an aggregate state budget constraint. Such a procedure may not be desirable in the present analysis, because of our focus on *output attainment* as opposed to input equalization. An alternative process is, therefore, suggested.

Aggregate State Budget Constraint

Suppose the maximum state appropriations to public school districts are denoted by A_0. If required total state aid (from Equation 8) exceeds

A_0, it is necessary to change some of the parameters in the school finance plan to satisfy the budgetary restriction.

Upon examination of steps 1-4 of the new plan, it appears that total state aid to schools is a function of the mandated tax rate, target output levels, input prices, and input availability. (The state share is also a function of other parameters in the goal-programming model, but it does not appear that the state can exert any control over these parameters, at least in the short run.) In symbols,

$$SA_d = f(r_m, T_i, p_i, L_j, H_j) \qquad (9)$$

It is obvious that a higher r_m will produce more local revenues and hence will require less state aid. Lower input prices and lower target values for the goals would require less state aid.[15] Finally, varying legal and institutional constraints over the inputs would also alter the state share, but the direction of change is not clear a priori.

The analysis might begin with target output levels chosen to represent "best practice." Best practice could be measured by the top performance in the state, top performance anywhere in the United States, or average performance in the highest-ranking state. Then goal-programming models will be run for each district and total state aid evaluated. If total state aid exceeds what the legislature is willing to appropriate, alternative strategies may be examined. For example, it is possible to raise the mandated tax rate, which would increase local revenues and hence reduce the total state share. Or target output levels might be reduced from the "best practice" level to a more moderate level. The state could also attempt to reduce the prices of educational inputs by imposing ceilings on teacher salaries and other inputs which are not purchased in a national market. Finally, all three possibilities may be used simultaneously until total state aid computed from Equation (8) is equal to state appropriations.[16]

Caveats

There exists *no* plan for social action which does not suffer from at least some shortcomings. The new finance model is no exception. First, it depends critically on the valid construction of the objective function and the educational production function. It is not possible to claim total success in the formulation of either of these relevant functions, although many aspects of each have been discussed in varying chapters in this book. Recent work by Summers and Wolfe (1979) also suggests that reliable educational production functions can be constructed.[17]

Educational finance, moreover, continues to depend on the property tax for generating local revenues. The programming plan also does this, and is deficient to the extent that the property tax is undesirable. It should be noted, however, that implementation of the new finance plan is *not* contingent on the existence of any type of local taxation. It could easily be amended to be financed exclusively through statewide, less objectionable taxes, such as proportional or progessive income or wealth taxes.

Perhaps the most important bone of contention is the selection and measurement of educational outputs. A plan focusing on educational outputs must rest on reasonably firm grounds regarding agreement about which educational outcomes should matter and how one may go about measuring them. This aspect of the plan will require considerable study by each state, although advances made through the Pennsylvania Plan (among others) should make the job a lot easier.

Finally, our model is static, as opposed to dynamic, and does not address the question of the "interaction in educational outputs over time" (Ritzen and Winkler 1979: 33). Although it is possible to redesign the model to include dynamic features, the complexity of the model would increase substantially and use of the conventional input/output framework --and hence of goal programming--would be ruled out. Considerable work must, therefore, be done before a dynamic model of the Ritzen-Winkler (1979) variety could be incorporated into the school financing mechanism.

Conclusions

The principal purpose of this chapter is to develop the outline of an alternative school finance plan which combines equity and efficiency. The equity concept is redefined in terms of equalization of *outputs* rather than of *inputs* (as the current notion of fiscal or wealth neutrality implies). The new school finance model, furthermore, automatically takes into account interdistrict differences in "need," because districts in which costs of inputs are higher or the number of disadvantaged or "hard to educate" pupils are greater will receive such amounts of extra state aid as are necessary to minimize deviations from target output levels. The model is also relatively simple, requiring only moderate levels of additional expertise at the state level and no additional personnel at the district level.

To implement the model, it is first necessary to collect the data for school districts, to obtain the relevant parameters (input-output coefficients, preemptive priority factors, etc.) and to study the results of the model's application in detail. As a first approximation, it might be desirable to implement the model alongside an existing finance plan, until sufficient data and experience are accumulated for it to supplant present plans. It is necessary to stress, however, that unless the new plan ultimately is directly incorporated into the budgeting process, it is likely to have negligible real consequences--as was the fate of the Planning-Programming-Budgeting System (**PPBS**) instituted in the federal government by President Johnson in 1965.[18]

Considerable space has been devoted to problems with the input-output system and other elements of the goal-programming model that should not be overlooked. The fact is, however, that present funding plans implicitly assume certain production-function relationships, such as the effect on educational outcomes of class size, teacher experience, and educational preparation of teachers. The new model attempts to study such effects *explicitly*, in order that state aid dollars might go as far as possible in achieving educational goals. The educational outcomes (or outputs), moreover, become explicit and measurable in the new plan, eliminating the possibility of school administrators hiding behind a cloak of the elusive "educational quality" syndrome in justifying expenditures and requests for state assistance.

Much more work remains to be done in order for the plan to be implemented. It is necessary to study the production function relationships over time and space in each state. Development of output indices, surveys designed to provide output ranking, and conferences with school administrators to impress them of the need to employ resources more efficiently are all necessary for the implementation of the new funding plan. With cooperation of school and state officials, federal agencies, and school finance experts in academia, the plan presented here in its bare bones might (to paraphrase Ezekiel 37: 5-6) form flesh, sinew, and skin--and, finally, have breath put into it.[19]

NOTES

1. For a brief description, see Benson (1978: 368-73).

2. See, e.g., Lawyers' Committee for Civil Rights Under Law (1977).

3. See, e.g., Johns (1975), Goettel and Firestine (1975), Hickrod et al. (1976), and Abramowitz and Rosenfeld (1978).

4. For additional information concerning school finance consult Benson (1978), Cohn (1974, 1979), and Garms, Guthrie, and Pierce (1978).

5. Cohn (1968); See also Riew (1966), and Sabulao and Hickrod (1971). See, however, the contribution by Theodore W. Schultz in this volume.

6. See Cohn (1979: Chs. 3, 6 and 7), and the contribution by McMahon and Wagner in this volume.

7. See Cohn (1979: 51-54), and the contribution by Michael in this volume.

8. A linear educational production function allows infinite substitution among the inputs and rules out input interactions. This could be ameliorated by using nonlinear models, such as the Cobb Douglas or CES (constant elasticity of substitution) production functions. Use of such production functions would, however, so complicate the present analysis that it would render it practically useless. The Cobb Douglas (log-linear) educational production function has also been criticized on theoretical

grounds by Bowles (1970). The main objection to the linear model by Brandl (1970) is not relevant in the present context, because our use of goal programming (see below) constrains each variable to within reasonable bounds.

9. One example of this approach is Cohn with Millman (1975). See also Boardman, Davis, and Sanday (1977).

10. See also Morgan and Cohn (1977) and Cohn and Morgan (1978).

11. Mention should also be made of the study by Starler and Thomas (1973) which used linear programming techniques for linking state aid to efficiency. See also Bruno (1969) for a linear programming model of school finance.

12. That is, use of educational inputs is based on their allocation necessary to minimize deviations from target output goals.

13. Equity is satisfied in the sense that all schools receive the funds necessary to minimize deviations from target output goals, regardless of local wealth.

14. The district power equalization plan was originally suggested by Coons, Clune and Sugarman (1970). For a brief discussion see Cohn (1974: 35-36, 56-59), and Cohn (1979: 274-280).

15. Mathematically, this means that $\partial SA_d/\partial r_m < 0$, while $\partial SA_d/\partial T_i$ and $\partial SA_d/\partial p_i > 0$.

16. Ideally, a simulation process should be developed to examine the effect of the new proposal on input costs, educational attainment, state aid needed to achieve a given target level, and the sensitivity of such parameters to changes in the mandated tax rate, input prices, other constraints, and target output levels. See Cohn, Sweigart, and Reeves (1980).

17. A strong attack on the educational production function was launched by Levin (1976). See, however, Hanushek's (1976) and Watts's (1976) replies, as well as my analysis of the debate (Cohn 1979: 191-92). Also, as Brown and Saks (1975) point out, if schools seek not only to optimize *total* achievement but also to reduce the variance of achievement among students, then the production function must be respecified. In addition, goal programming is only one member of the larger family of multiple-objective decision-making methods--and in fact it may not be the preferred method. See Reeves, Sweigart, and Cohn (1980).

18. See Schick (1977). An alternative view is given by Haveman (1977). See also Kramer (1979), esp. Ch. 2. The use of PPBS in the Department of Defense is generally credited with great success, but in that department PPBS was highly influential in budgeting decisions under the leadership of Robert S. McNamara.

19. I thank my colleagues Andy Barnett, Philip Jacobs, B. F. Kiker, and Blaine Roberts for valuable comments on an earlier version of this chapter. Valuable insights were also provided by Ernst W. Stromsdorfer. I am indebted to Walter W. McMahon and Terry G. Geske for their meticulous review and constructive comments which were extremely helpful in developing the final draft. Finally, my association with J. Michael Morgan, Gordon C. McMeekin, James R. Sweigart, and Gary R. Reeves has significantly increased my understanding of mathematical programming and multiple-objective decision-making.

REFERENCES

Abramowitz, S., and Rosenfeld, S., eds. 1978. *Declining enrollment: the challenge of the coming decade.* Washington: National Institute of Education.
Benson, C. S. 1978. *The economics of public education.* 3rd ed. Boston: Houghton Mifflin.
Boardman, A. E. 1978. Policy models for the management of student achievement and other educational outputs. *TIMS Studies in the Management Sciences* 9.
―――; Davis, O. A.; and Sanday, P. R. 1977. A simultaneous equations model of the educational process. *Journal of Public Economics* 7 (February): 23-49.
Bowles, S. 1970. Towards an educational production function. Pp. 11-61 in *Education, income, and human capital*, ed. W. Lee Hansen. New York: Columbia University Press.
Brandl, J. E. 1970. Comment on 'Towards an educational production function.' Pp. 61-65 in *Education, income, and human capital*, ed. W. Lee Hansen. New York: Columbia University Press.
Brown, B. W., and Saks, D. H. 1975. The production and distribution of cognitive skills within schools. *Journal of Political Economy* 83 (June): 571-93.
Bruno, J. E. 1969. A mathematical programming approach to school finance. *Socio-Economic Planning Sciences* 3: 1-12.
Cohn, E. 1968. Economies of scale in Iowa high school operations. *Journal of Human Resources* 3 (Fall): 422-34.
―――. 1974. *Economics of state aid to education.* Lexington, Mass.: Heath.
―――. 1975. A proposal for school size incentives in state aid to education. *Journal of Education Finance* 1 (Fall): 216-25.
―――. 1979. *The economics of education.* Rev. ed. Cambridge: Ballinger.
―――. Forthcoming. Macro versus micro approaches to educational planning. In *Planning and vocational education*, ed. George Copa and Jerome Moss, Jr. New York: McGraw-Hill.
―――. with Millman, S. D. 1975. *Input-output analysis in public education.* Cambridge: Ballinger.
Cohn, E., and Morgan, J. M. 1978. Improving resource allocation within school districts: a goal-programming approach. *Journal of Education Finance* 4 (Summer): 89-104.
Cohn, E.; Sweigart, J. R.; and Reeves, G. R. 1980. A new approach to financing public schools. *Journal of Education Finance* 6 (Summer): 1-17.
Coleman, J. S., et al. 1966. *Equality of educational opportunity.* Washington, D.C.: U.S. Government Printing Office.
Coons, J. E.; Clune, W. H., III; and Sugarman, S. D. 1970. *Private wealth and public education.* Cambridge: Harvard University Press.
Froomkin, J.; Jamison, D. T.; and Radner, R., eds. 1976. *Education as an industry.* Cambridge: Ballinger.
Garms, W. I.; Guthrie, J. W.; and Pierce, L. G. 1978. *School finance: the economics and politics of public education.* Englewood Cliffs, N.J.: Prentice-Hall.

Goettel, R. J., and Firestine, R. E. 1975. Declining enrollments and state aid: another equity and efficiency problem. *Journal of Education Finance* 1 (Fall): 205-15.
Grant, W. V., and Lind, C. G. 1976. *Digest of educational statistics, 1975 edition.* Washington: U. S. Government Printing Office.
Hanushek, E. A. 1976. Comment. Pp. 191-96 in Froomkin, Jamison, and Radner (1976).
Haveman, R. H. 1977. Policy analysis and the Congress: an economist's view. Pp. 577-91 in Haveman and Margolis (1977).
———, and Margolis, J., eds. 1977. *Public expenditure and policy analysis.* 2nd ed. Chicago: Rand-McNally.
Hickrod, G. A., et al. 1976. *Enrollment change and educational personnel change in the K-12 schools of Illinois.* Research Report 3-HYCH--76. Normal: Center for the Study of Educational Finance, Illinois State University.
Johns, R. L. 1975. An index of extra costs of education due to sparsity of population. *Journal of Education Finance* 1 (Fall): 159-204.
Johnston, J. 1972. *Econometric methods.* Rev. ed. New York: McGraw-Hill.
Kramer, F. A. 1979. *Contemporary approaches to public budgeting.* Cambridge: Winthrop.
Lawyer's Committee for Civil Rights Under Law. 1977. *Summary for state-wide school finance cases since 1973.* Washington: The Committee.
Levin, H. M. 1976. Concepts of economic efficiency and educational production. Pp. 149-91 in Froomkin, Jamison, and Radner (1976).
Morgan, J. M. 1977. Goal programming and resource allocation within the Pennsylvania secondary school system. Ph.D. dissertation, University of South Carolina.
———, and Cohn, E. 1977. Resource allocation within secondary schools: a goal programming approach. Pp. 646-52 in *1977 Proceedings of the Social Statistics Section, American Statistical Association.*
Reeves, G. R.; Sweigart, J. R.; and Cohn, E. 1980. Educational output goals and implementation strategies in public school finance. *Proceedings of the 12th Annual Meeting of the American Institute of Decision Sciences.*
Riew, J. 1966. Economies of scale in high school operations. *Review of Economics and Statistics* 48 (August): 280-87.
Ritzen, J. M., and Winkler, D. R. 1979. On the optimal allocation of resources in the production of human capital. *Journal of the Operational Research Society* 30: 33-41.
Rossmiller, R. A., and Geske, T. G. 1976. Toward more effective use of school resources. *Journal of Education Finance* 1 (Spring): 484-502.
Sabulao, C. M., and Hickrod, G. A. 1971. Optimum size of school district relative to selected costs. *Journal of Educational Administration* 9 (October): 178-91.
Schick, A. 1977. A death in the bureaucracy: the demise of federal PPB. Pp. 556-76 in Haveman and Margolis (1977).
Starler, N. H., and Thomas, R. W. 1973. Intergovernmental education grants and the efficiency of resource allocation in school districts. *Applied Economics* 5: 181-92.

Summers, A. A., and Wolfe, B. L. 1979. Improving the use of empirical research as a policy tool: an application to education. Paper presented at the Amerian Economic Association annual meeting, Atlanta.
Watts, H. W. 1976. Comment. Pp. 197-98 in Froomkin, Jamison, and Radner (1976).

CHAPTER 13

State and Federal Pressures for Equity and Efficiency in Education Financing

ALLAN ODDEN

Equity concerns related to both students and taxpayers have been the driving forces behind the school finance reforms of the 1970's, at the state and federal levels. Efficiency concerns, as Cohn has indicated in the preceding chapter, have been in the background, for the most part, although the question of whether spending more will result in better student achievement is often posed in school finance policy debates. Since the mid-1970's a variation of this latter theme has been interest in basic education programs and minimum competency tests. At the federal level, efficiency has become a growing concern, manifesting itself in the push for competency testing, consolidation of the numerous federal categorical programs, and budget cuts in Title I and other federal programs. Equity issues probably will continue to dominate in the 1980's, but efficiency issues will be given increased attention as a result, at least in part, of continued inflation and these revenue squeezes.

Here I shall attempt to trace the changing nature of these concerns and to suggest likely trends for education financing in the late 1980's. The first section of this article discusses equity issues related to state school finance reforms and summarizes the available information on how effective the reforms have been in meeting the various equity goals. This section concludes with a review of the efficiency issues that might come to center stage in school finance policy debates in the 1980's. The second section covers the federal interest in education financing, both in its current focus on equity and with respect to future efficiency issues.

Equity Issues in State School Finance Reforms

Equity issues have been the targets of most recent school finance reforms passed by the states. Both public school children and taxpayers have been the objects and beneficiaries of these reforms. This section discusses the relationship between state school finance reforms and numerous equity issues related to both children and taxpayers.[1]

Equity for Children

Three general equity principles for children have guided the education finance reform programs of the 1970's: equal treatment of equals, unequal treatment of unequals (horizontal and vertical equity, respectively, as developed in Chapter 1), and equal opportunity.

Equal treatment of equals. A prominent source of inequity in most school finance structures has been large per-pupil expenditure differences among school districts within a state. Differences of two or three to one are common, and in many states differences between the high- and low-spending districts reach a ten-to-one ratio. Even after adjusting the expenditure figures for factors that should cause differences--such as pupil need differences, price variations, transportation costs, and capital outlay expenditures--wide per-pupil expenditure variations still exist.

These differences have been a major target of school finance reform efforts. One goal of most new school finance systems has been to reduce spending gaps. Arizona, California, Florida, Indiana, Iowa, Minnesota, New Mexico, North Dakota, South Carolina, and Utah enacted high-level foundation programs for the purpose of bringing up the spending levels in low-expenditure districts, in order to diminish the overall expenditure gaps across the state. Washington has taken the most dramatic step on this issue; as its new program is phased in, the state fully funds a basic education program, and local school districts are allowed to supplement state aid by only 10 percent.[2]

Unequal treatment of unequals. States have recognized, though, that students and school districts are different and that such differences should be recognized in school aid programs. Special student populations have been a particular target of these school finance reforms. New state programs for handicapped students, low-income students, low-achieving students, and students for whom English is not the primary language have expanded rapidly. Arizona, Florida, Indiana, Iowa, Massachusetts, New Jersey, New Mexico, New York, South Carolina, Tennessee, Utah, and West Virginia have enacted comprehensive pupil-weighting systems that recognize a variety of special needs. Twenty-two states provide additional funds for compensatory education programs for economically or educationally disadvantaged students. Illinois and Minnesota, in recognition that concentration of poverty produces the most difficult educational disadvantage, allocate greater dollar amounts for these students as their concentration increases. Twenty-two states also have expanded programs for bilingual students. The states allocated $3.4 billion in 1979 for services to the handicapped (see Odden and McGuire 1980). Federal budget cuts effective for the 1982 fiscal year reduce support for Title I low-income minority group students, bilingual education, and a number of other categorical programs that may reduce incentives for school districts to continue to expand these in the future.

Special district characteristics also have been recognized. Sparsity factors in a number of states and increased state participation in transportation costs have been especially helpful for rural districts. Urban factors, such as per capita wealth measures, poverty student concentration factors, cost adjustments, and municipal overburden adjustments have helped target additional aid to fiscally pressed central-city school districts. Factors based on the number of pupils per school, such as additional aid for remote, one-room rural schools and regional adjustments, also have been tried.

Equal opportunity. In addition to recognizing differences among students and districts that require appropriately unequal treatment, recent school finance reforms also have sought to reduce the role of factors that should not be related to spending differentials. In particular, new school aid programs have sought to eliminate the links between equal educational opportunity and local district wealth and income, i.e., to create "fiscally neutral" school finance systems. This was the major issue in most school finance court cases and as a result has been the major objective of most reform efforts. Many new school finance programs are designed to insure that neither local school district property wealth nor household income determine per-pupil expenditure levels. In general, recent educational finance changes have been designed to funnel increases in state aid to low-wealth school districts, in an attempt to break the link between per-pupil spending and the fiscal capacity of local school districts.

Taxpayer Equity

Children have not been the only equity targets of the education finance reforms passed during the 1970's. Taxpayers also have been of concern; indeed, taxpayer concerns may have been preeminent since, in addition to the following equity goals, property tax relief was a major element in many education finance changes, as has been developed in the chapter by Carroll.

Equal treatment of equals. In its classical public finance sense, this principle relates to taxpayers with equal incomes. The principle requires that taxpayers with equal incomes have equal tax burdens. This concern has not been a central objective of school finance reform, although the school finance objective of reducing property tax regressivity (mentioned below) in a sense subsumes this issue.

In school finance circles, the principle of equal treatment of equals has been given a different emphasis. A central problem in school finance is that taxpayers in low-property-wealth districts often spend less at a given tax rate than taxpayers in high-property-wealth districts. In many states, school districts in the same geographical area can have very different per-pupil spending levels, even with similar tax rates; indeed, many times the district with the higher tax rate spends less than a neighboring district with a lower tax rate.

These phenomena also have been a target of many education finance reforms. Many states attempted to implement what is known as the "equal yield for equal effort" goal, under which the state guarantees to taxpayers in each school district approximately the same amount of local and state revenues per pupil for equal tax rates, regardless of the level of local property wealth or income. Colorado, Connecticut, Illinois, Kansas, Michigan, New Jersey, Ohio, and Wisconsin have implemented these kinds of school aid programs.

An additional aspect of the school finance definition of this equity principle concerns the definition of local fiscal capacity. States are beginning to adopt income factors in their school aid systems, in recognition of the fact that both income and property wealth affect ability to pay, and hence "effort" and fiscal decision-making. To treat taxpayers fairly, both wealth and income need to be considered. Connecticut, Kansas, Maryland, Missouri, Pennsylvania, Rhode Island, and Virginia include income in their equalization systems, thus insuring that taxpayers in districts with the same property wealth and income will be treated more similarly.

Finally, school finance reform in a number of states has been accompanied by improvements in the administration of the property tax. These changes seek to make assessment practices uniform, not only within but also across assessing jurisdictions. The purpose of such assessment reforms has been to insure that homeowners with homes of equal value and similar tax rates have similar property tax bills.

Unequal treatment of unequals. As complements of a new school finance distribution formula, many states also have sought to reduce the regressivity of the property tax burden across taxpayers who are unequal in their incomes. Michigan, Minnesota, and Wisconsin implemented circuit-breaker programs of property tax relief simultaneously with expanded school finance equalization programs. The school finance plan improved the equity of the property tax on a district-by-district basis, while the circuit-breaker program focused on individual households and limited property tax payments to fixed percentages of income. In most cases, the percentage increased as income increased, the objective being to make the property tax a less regressive tax with respect to current income.

The Effectiveness of Recent School Finance Reforms

Enacting school finance reform is a first step in assuring equity in educational finance structures. The next step is to determine whether the change produces the expected effects. A third step is to analyze the efficiency effects, i.e., the relationship between the increments to fiscal equity, learning or other outputs and the costs of the new programs. Little, if any, empirical work on the efficiency issue has been conducted. However, in the late 1970's a number of studies were conducted on the various impacts of state school finance reform efforts.

The initial study was conducted by Brown, Killalea, Rosenthal, and Tron (1978: 195-212). They used the national Elementary and Secondary General Information Survey data set, which provides information for all states. The data are based on a stratified random sample of districts which can be used to make valid generalizations for the nation. The sampling does not allow for perfectly valid generalizations for each state; nevertheless, it was the only national data set available at that time. Analyzing data from both the 1970 and 1975 school years, the authors found, using a variety of tests of inequality, that per-pupil expenditure disparities which were large in 1970 had not been reduced by 1975, and actually had increased in some states. However, in comparing school finance reform states to non-school finance reform states, the authors reached a somewhat different conclusion. In reform states, expenditure disparities tended to remain constant or marginally to decrease, while in the non-reform states disparities remained constant or marginally increased. Nevertheless, expenditure disparities had not been reduced significantly. On the other hand, important progress was made in reducing the relationship between per-pupil expenditures and local property wealth per pupil, with the reform states making more progress on this goal.

The general findings of this early study have been duplicated by nearly all succeeding studies, which have used data from all districts in a particular state, thus providing accurate descriptions of the effects of reforms. Carroll's chapter earlier in this book reporting his five-state analysis is a good example. In his extensive study of California, Florida, Kansas, Michigan, and New Mexico, he concludes, again using a variety of inequality measures, that limited progress has occurred in diminishing disparities in per-pupil expenditures per se, but that significantly more progress was made in reducing the relationship between expenditures and local district property wealth. This latter finding was interpreted as improving taxpayer equity. But according to the classification of equity issues that include the equal opportunity principle discussed in the previous section, it also can be related to equal opportunity or child equity. Moreover, as also noted, this objective was the major target of most school finance reforms. So the Carroll study shows that the reforms in those five states were remarkably effective: they dramatically reduced the link between spending and local property wealth -- the major reform objective -- and simultaneously reduced, though to a smaller degree, spending disparities per se.

Two other multiple-state evaluations of the impacts of school finance reforms produced results similar to those of the Brown et al. and of the Carroll research. Odden, Berne, and Stiefel (1979) showed that the particular statistics used often will lead to different conclusions about the impact of the change in the system. Nevertheless, using a variety of statistics, their conclusion was that school finance reform states typically improved the equity of both the distribution of per-pupil expenditures and the relationship between spending and local wealth. Further, in comparing reform to non-reform states, they found that progress was greater for the school finance reform states. Finally, they also found that many states improved on both equity goals—a finding that had not been anticipated. Hickrod et al. (1980), in a five-year study of Indiana, Iowa, and Illinois, came to similar conclusions. Over this period their study showed a reduction in per-pupil expenditure disparities for Iowa and Illinois, the reform states, but little progress on this front for Indiana, a non-reform state. For all three states, however, there were significant reductions in the relationship between spending and wealth, with the most dramatic progress again occurring in both Iowa and Illinois, the reform states. Finally, Adams and Odden (1980) found progress on both these fronts in an analysis of the impact of the Missouri school finance reform, although improvement in expenditure disparities was very slight.

These findings on the impacts of the school finance reforms in the 1970's are encouraging. The central thrust of the litigation in this decade was to break the link between local wealth, usually defined as property wealth, and per-pupil spending. Consistent and extensive progress was made in reducing this relationship in those states that attempted to do so by enacting a new school funding law. In addition, some expenditure gaps per se were also diminished. More progress on the latter is needed, and more progress than that which occurred would have been desirable. Nevertheless, the consistent findings of the results of school finance reform stand in stark contrast to the perceived lack of progress found in many other public policy reforms of the last decade. In this sense, the moderate successes of most school finance reforms are indeed a cause for optimism.

Efficiency Issues Related to School Finance Reform

Efficiency has not been a top priority issue of school finance reform. Efficiency could entail a trade off involving calculating equity gains versus the costs in efficiency terms of the reform. Improving the contribution of education to humane growth by improving both efficiency and equity, as discussed in Chapter 1, could mean maximizing equity gains while minimizing costs. This exercise was not an explicit objective in the 1970's. Indeed, the above results just on effects would not have been available a decade ago. They *are* available now, and they make it possible to discuss effects in a coherent manner—in large part because of cooperative efforts to define alternative concepts of school finance equity—and to develop alternative measurements of it (Odden, Berne, and Stiefel 1979).

The methodological gain in the 1970's was the development of an equity framework in school finance that allows for compatible discussions of the effects of reforms across states. One can hope that the gain in the late 1980's will include the next step of discussing the outputs of education in relation to the costs, i.e., the effects on efficiency of school finance reforms.

But other efficiency issues also are likely to be raised. The first includes school productivity: the relationship between school resources and student achievement. In the later 1970's, significant advances were made in researching this issue (see Murnane 1980), and strong links between resources and performance were documented. While this research now includes only intradistrict resource allocation, it is providing information on optimum ways to spend resources to enhance student learning. The next logical step for this type of investigation is to include data from more than one school district, or for all school districts in a state (as suggested by Cohn), and to analyze both inter- and intradistrict resource allocation in its relationship to student performance, and thereby to relate fiscal fairness to its impact on students.

While this would be a large-scale effort, it is a direction in which school finance must move. Given the methodological gains already made in the 1970's, important movement in this direction should be possible. Two other recent research efforts provide a foundation for this assessment. Ginsberg and Moskowitz (1980) moved the analysis of the allocation of resources beyond the school district level to the school site level in a 1980 study of New York. The focus of their study was on the equity across schools and across types of students within schools. This is one of the first analyses of the equity of a state school finance system that moves beyond interdistrict comparisons. A complementary effort by Wendling and Cohen (1980) examined the relationship between educational resources at the school level and average achievement of the students in those schools, also using New York data. The importance of both these studies is in their moving beyond school district boundaries and making statewide assessments on resource allocation and student achievement from subdistrict data. The next step for such research will be to obtain student-level data over time, to relate performance gains to resource allocation, and to draw both effectiveness and efficiency conclusions relating costs (resource allocation) to effects (student performance).

These research directions will improve the seriousness with which efficiency issues can be analyzed within the school finance field. There are also other pressures for enhancing the efficient use of school funds. The interest in defining and funding a "basic education" and the popularity of minimum competency tests are examples of issues creating these pressures. While there are many possible explanations for the increasing salience of these issues, one such explanation is a concern for efficient use of state and federal funds. Rising inflation and continued controls on the growth of government will likely keep these pressures alive. The growth of government services in the 1970's created an environment that was conducive for making equity gains, and while it is more difficult to enhance equity (which usually requires redistributive policies) in an era of no growth, equity issues and efficiency concerns are not necessarily in conflict. Interdistrict equity of resource allocation is needed, but intradistrict equity is also needed. Moreover, the relationship between resources and achievement could prove to be as important in freeing resources for enhancing ultimate student equity as is fiscal equity itself.

Equity and Efficiency Pressures from the Federal Government

Beginning in 1965 with the Elementary and Secondary Education Act (SEA) and continuing through the 1970s, the federal role in educational finance has remained fairly consistent. The federal strategy has been to target aid for particular categories of students and, except for impact aid, to ignore general-purpose aid. The concern of the federal government for the past fifteen years has been to increase services for special pupil populations, beginning with poverty and minority students in the mid-1960's and expanding over the years to include, among others, handicapped, bilingual, migrant, and native American students. These funds are now being cut back.

These federal programs have been developed on an individual basis, each with separate funding mechanisms, accounting requirements, rules, regulations, and program guidelines. To insure compliance with each of the federal programs there have been stipulations for fiscal comparability, maintenance of local effort, anti-supplanting, and annual evaluations. This fragmentation and these detailed sets of rules and regulations have resulted in some frustration and efficiency issues that continue to be debated.

Effectiveness of Federal Programs

While some research in the late 1960's indicated that some federal programs may not have been very effective, more comprehensive work in the 1970's indicates that federal programs, especially Title I of the Elementary and Secondary Education Act, have been quite effective in accomplishing their limited objectives. The major National Institute of Education study (1977a) on Title I concluded that the funds had been allocated according to congressional intent, and had financed programs that substantially increased student math and reading achievement levels (1977b). In addition, the study found the program to have some income redistribution characteristics (1977a). In addition, both Title I and the new Education for All Handicapped Children Act (P.L. 94-142) may reduce spending disparities among school districts within states and may diminish the link between spending and local school district wealth (Vescera 1978; Education Commission of the States 1979), two of the basic school finance equity goals.

These results are firm evidence that federal education programs designed for special student populations are probably producing the effects that the legislation intended. The results also suggest that a federal goal of providing more resources for different categories of needy children is compatible with the state school finance goal of reducing the relationship between spending and local district wealth.

Efficiency Issues

Although the federal commitment is to enhance the equity of the education system for special pupil populations, recent policy debates indicate that increased attention is being given to inefficiencies inherent in the current set of federal elementary and secondary education programs, both across the federal programs themselves and between the state and federal programs designed to serve the same or similar objectives.

Three major sources of inefficiency have been addressed in recent federal policy debates and are likely to be debated again in the 1980's. Each has important implications for the interactions between state and federal education programs. The first is the proliferation and fragmentation of the current set of federal programs which have produced both service overlaps and service gaps at the local district level. Some students qualify for services under a variety of programs, while others with less severe problems may qualify for no particular program but nevertheless need additional services. This situation is exacerbated by guidelines that require concentration of dollars to make service levels meaningful. As a result, a "piling on" phenomenon can occur: some students become targets of large sums of categorical dollars, while others receive none.

Second, the individual federal program guidelines are inconsistent and uncoordinated. Some, for example, call for "pull out" programs, while others mandate mainstreaming. Often the same students are served by different programs which require conflicting program delivery configurations.

Third, until recently there has been a reluctance to allow a merging of federal dollars with state dollars available for programs targeted at the same populations and designed with similar education objectives. As a result, state and federal dollars are separated artificially and inefficient service delivery can occur.

Several changes could occur to help reduce these inefficiencies while maintaining the federal and state commitments to special populations. First, the federal government may cease to make law based on the most extreme case among the states. Rather, policies may be developed or changed to recognize accomplishments that have been made by many states and to provide incentives for other states to move in the desired direction. This will reflect a need to streamline the entire federal program structure and integrate it with state efforts. Second, numerous special programs may be merged into a simpler scheme, which would relax restrictions by merely maintaining a distinction between special groups as a whole and the general population. Third, there should be increased opportunities for using state and federal funds together, especially for those programs aimed at the same students and with similar objectives.

Finally, there might be an increase in matching requirements for the receipt of federal funds, rather than the current complex web of comparability, maintenance of local effort, and anti-supplanting provisions. This change would reflect a recognition that matching requirements are more effective than the current obsession with tracking dollars, which requires costly accounting activities.

In addition, there is a growing concern in Washington, from both an equity and efficiency perspective, about the interaction between federal categorical funds and inequitable state school finance structures. Members of Congress increasingly recognize that a dollar of federal aid in a low-wealth, low-spending school district may not be used as efficiently as a dollar in a medium- or high-spending district. In other words, the Congress is concluding that an unfair state school finance structure may blunt the overall impact of federal categorical dollars. The funds made available under Section 842 of the Education Amendments of 1974 reflected this concern. This issue was also a major driving force behind the bill debated during the 1977 session of Congress that was designed to provide federal incentives for states to close spending gaps among their school districts. There is also growing awareness that substantial disparities exist in per-pupil expenditures among the fifty states, and that only the federal government is in a position to remedy the differences.

All of these concerns with state school financing systems were behind the establishment of the congressionally mandated study of school finance that is being conducted by the U.S. Department of Education. The study undertakes to define equity in education finance under a variety of standards, to measure the degree of equity among and within states, and to develop alternative federal policies to enhance inter- and intrastate education finance equity. The initial focus of the study, however, is description of the numerous federal categorical programs, their legislative intent, and a researching of issues related to their implementation, for the purpose of making them more efficient, including simplifying or consolidating them.

Indeed, many suggest that the major issue surrounding the reauthorization of the Elementary and Secondary Education Act in 1984 will be simplification and consolidation. One set of forces pushing this issue to the forefront simply opposes the federal role in education and has a conservative preference for block grants. But another set of forces has a legitimate concern for efficiency. As discussed above, 1960 through 1980 produced literally hundreds of programs for special student groups at the federal, state, and local levels. Giant equity gains were realized in meeting the needs of special students. More programs may not be needed for now. A large portion of the agenda for the future at the federal and state levels will be to streamline and integrate their management, and to work to maximize their benefits. In this sense, the efficiency issue at the federal level may take on central importance in the decade to come.

NOTES

1. For an overview of equity in school finance, see Odden, Berne and Stiefel (1979).

2. For an overview of recent trends in school financing, see Odden and Augenblick (1980). For an overview of the characteristics of each state's finance structure, see McGuire, Augenblick, and Hammond (1980).

REFERENCES

Adams, E. Kathleen, and Odden, Allan. 1980. The relationship between property tax assessments, tax burdens and Missouri school finance, and the equity impacts of the 1977 reform. Report to the School Finance Study Committee of the State Board of Eucation.

Brown, Lawrence; Ginsburg, Alan; Killalea, J. Neil; Rosenthal, Richard; and Tron, Esther. 1978. School finance reform in the seventies: achievements and failures. *Journal of Education Finance* 1, 2 (Fall): 195-212.

Carroll, Stephen. 1979. *The search for equity in school finance: results from five states*. Santa Monica, Calif.: Rand Corporation.

Education Commission of the States. 1979. *Special education finance: the interaction between state and federal support systems*. Denver: Education Finance Center, Education Commission of the States.

Ginsberg, Alan, and Moskowitz, Jay. 1980. A school based analysis of inter- and intradistrict resource allocation. Washington: AUI Policy Research Center.

Hickrod, G. Alan; Chaudhari, Ramesh; Hubbard, Ben C.; and Lundeen, Virginia. 1980. *Equity measurements in school finance*. Normal: Center for the Study of Educational Finance, Illinois State University.

McGuire, Kent; Augenblick, John; and Hammond, Joanne. 1980. School finance at a fifth glance. Denver: Education Finance Center, Education Commission of the States.

Murnane, Richard. 1980. Interpreting the evidence on school effectiveness. Paper presented to the American Educational Research Association annual meeting, March, 1980.

National Institute of Education. 1977a. *Title I funds allocation: the current formulas*. Washington: NIE.

―――. 1977b. *The effects of services on student development*. Washington: NIE.

Odden, Allan, and Augenblick, John. 1980. *School finance reform in the states: 1980*. Denver: Education Finance Center, Education Commission of the States.

Odden, Allan; Berne, Robert; and Stiefel, Leanna. 1979. *Equity in school finance*. Denver: Education Finance Center, Education Commission of the States.

Odden, Allan, and McGuire, C. Kent. 1980. Financing educational services for special populations: the state and federal roles. Working Paper No. 28. Denver: Education Finance Center, Education Commission of the States.

Vescera, Lawrence. 1978. An examination of the flow of Title I and state compensatory education aid and their effect on equalization in four states: Florida, New Jersey, New York and Texas. Paper No. 10. Denver: Education Finance Center, Education Commission of the States.

Wendling, Wayne, and Cohen, Judith. 1980. The relationship of education resources to student achievement levels in New York State. Working Paper No. 27. Denver: Education Finance Center, Education Commission of the States.

CHAPTER 14

Educational Finance: Research Findings and Policy Implications

TERRY G. GESKE

The recent past has been a tumultuous period in educational finance. The chapters in this volume provide a useful perspective on trends in financing and in research during this period, and consider new developments in research with implications for the future. These chapters report on the rapid expansion of research on human capital formation and on the substantial progress that has been made in a number of interrelated areas, including work on the value of human time, monetary and nonmonetary returns to education, educational productivity, and efficiency and equity problems in state and federal support systems for primary, secondary, and higher education.

Citizens and policymakers alike have been concerned over equity and equality of educational opportunity in state financing systems for the public schools. A series of early court cases, beginning with the *Serrano* decision in California, helped focus considerable attention on the basic inequities in school financing systems that rely heavily on local property taxes. During the latter 1970's and early 1980's some of the emphasis shifted from equity to efficiency criteria in state support models. Many states mandated minimum competency testing programs, and there were indirect incentives to promote greater efficiency through tax and expenditure limitation provisions and federal budget cuts. Inflation, slower economic growth, declining enrollments, and continuing demands for property tax relief all continue the pressure to find more efficient means of producing education so that its quality, as well as the equity with which it is distributed among children, is maintained and improved.

What, then, have been the new developments in the broader theory of educational finance and in the scientific tests of the hypotheses suggested by the theory? And what are some of the basic conclusions that can be drawn from the research reported in this volume as far as efficiency and equity are concerned? Furthermore, how do these developments relate to recent trends in the financing of elementary, secondary, and higher education? This chapter addresses these questions in terms of the efficiency and equity criteria presented by McMahon in Chapter 1, as well as in relation to the more detailed use of these concepts, measures, and empirical estimates developed throughout the book. It begins with a consideration of overall themes drawn from the findings presented and the scientific standards sought in selecting from among the research findings, before turning to develop some of the main implications for efficiency and equity.

Basic Themes

A basic theme with regard to efficiency that cuts across several of the chapters in this volume has to do with educational outputs. Traditionally, the focus in educational finance has been on the input side, despite the fact that the concept of efficiency really requires a careful examination of the output side as well.

Considering the input side briefly first, the measurement of educational inputs has improved considerably during the last decade. The development and application of the concept of opportunity costs, both in terms of foregone earnings and foregone learning that have arisen through the new developments in human capital theory, has substantially advanced our understanding of the input side of the educational process. Educational costs are now typically viewed in terms of "what is given up" rather than "what is put in" (Thomas 1971). There has also been progress in converting expenditure to real terms, and in considering capital costs so that the costs of underutilization are not overlooked. But the most significant advance has probably been the recognition of the value of time, including student time, as part of the opportunity costs relevant to efficiency considerations.

The stronger new theme element, however, has to do with the output side, where improvements in the capacity to measure and to use measures of outcomes have been made in the last decade. Several of the chapters in this volume report on that progress. The chapters by Michael and by McMahon and Wagner, concerned with measurement of the long-run non-monetary and monetary returns, discuss the relation of education to "full earnings" and its total productivity. The chapter by Rossmiller is concerned with measurement of the relation of inputs to learning rates and other more immediate outputs, and suggests that these difficulties on the output side are not insurmountable. Cohn also includes outputs in the objective function, and he attacks the difficult problem of rank-ordering the multiple outcomes of schooling. The recent emphasis on efficiency and competency testing in education is prompting a much closer look at these kinds of possibilities for measuring educational outputs. In addition, several recent state supreme court cases have begun to consider the equity implications of state support models in terms of educational outputs.

A second basic theme that links a number of the papers in this volume has to do with child equity. In spite of increased categorical funding for special student populations such as handicapped or disadvantaged students, and major federal Basic Educational Opportunity Grants for college students, only limited progress has been made toward greater child equity when measured either in terms of disparity in expenditure per pupil or in outcomes in elementary and secondary schools in the last decade. Most policy changes have attempted to break the linkage between school district wealth and spending, and thus to reduce the vast disparities in per-pupil expenditures and to increase intergenerational equity. But while recent school finance changes appear to have weakened the link between wealth and spending, these changes have by no means eliminated the differences in per-pupil expenditures among districts. For the most part, the largest effect of school finance reform has been on the tax side.

Child or student equity involves much more than horizontal equity in the form of equal educational expenditures for similarly situated students at each level. Although the former has not yet been attained, considerable attention, for example, has to be devoted to identifying and measuring the unequal educational needs of various types of students in the coming years, and to the criteria for vertical equity among unequals. To many, child or student equity suggests a proportional matching of educational resources with educational needs, while at the same time avoiding going so far that the system becomes inequitable for the normal student.

Before exploring these efficiency and equity themes and turning to the research reported in this volume, the standards that have been applied in selecting from each author's basic findings deserve mention. Accordingly, an effort has been made to focus on specific findings that appear to be firmly based in logic and accompanied whenever possible with consistent empirical evidence. Particular care also has been taken to single out general patterns or regularities that seem to emerge from several different researchers working independently on separate problems. More widely observed patterns increase the credibility of empirical results, and theoretical underpinnings can suggest a more general theory that explains a wider range of phenomena. Finally, the primary emphasis throughout this chapter is on what has been found, rather than on what is not yet known. I attempt to draw out potential additional implications for efficiency and equity, and for humane growth in the society.

Efficiency Criteria

Social efficiency was defined in Chapter 1 as the potential for increases in schooling outcomes without increases in the physical quantities of resource inputs. This definition of efficiency was then limited further for most practical applications by including an additional minimal equity principle involving Pareto efficiency, a concept that rules out situations in which some are made worse off. Efficiency criteria were presented in a progression of efficiency concepts from simple limited accountability tests all the way to cost/full-benefit analysis, including in the latter some attempt to appraise quantitatively and qualitatively the value of the benefits, even the social benefits. As several of the writers in this volume stress, the major difficulty in applying efficiency criteria involves the measurement of all outcomes.

Several chapters consider specific dimensions of efficiency as related to education. Schultz and Benson explore the important efficiency relationships among the environment, the home, and a child's learning, while Rossmiller and Thomas, Kemmerer, and Monk concentrate on efficiency within the school itself. Together these chapters serve to emphasize that efficient use of parents' time and of the child's time in the home, as well as in the classroom, is important to the efficiency of the entire educational process. While these chapters are essentially concerned with more immediate outcomes of the schooling process, Michael and McMahon and Wagner focus on ultimate outcomes of schooling by examining non-monetary and monetary returns to education, the latter in relation to the costs of the inputs, including the value of the student's time.

Environment, Home, and Achievement

Consider the possibilities for increased efficiency in education arising in the evironment. Schultz provides a perspective regarding the relationship of the organization of the school system and of limited parental involvement to greater efficiency. One approach to improved efficiency in public education is simply to make some provision for a greater degree of parental involvement and of competition among schools. These elements of involvement and competition would encourage efficiency by motivating and enabling parents to police the system more effectively, as well as providing a wide range of choices in the schooling process. If competition could force the inefficient units to be phased out (e.g., through consolidation with adjacent districts), it would surely increase incentives to improve the social efficiency of schools. Schultz suggests that greater parental involvement and hence improved efficiency would probably also result in better education even in poor families.

Benson examines the efficiency relationships among time-allocation decisions, socioeconomic status (SES) of parents, and school achievement of children. His analysis reveals no differences between SES categories in parents' attempts to exert control over their children or to help them with homework. His findings suggest that although both high- and low-SES parents appear to be equally concerned about their children and to allocate equal amounts of time in exercising control over them and in helping them with homework, the high-SES parents may be using their time to better effect. Taking the child to the library, a park, or a movie (and perhaps limiting the amount of time spent watching television), for example, were activities more characteristic of high-SES families.

There are implications here for both efficiency and equity. Consider the problem, for example, of inefficient schools and low achievement in the urban ghettos. Apparently progress is being made in certain experimental schools in Chicago which require contracts with parents to make sure that children devote ample time to their homework. This relates directly to Benson's finding that low-SES parents are as concerned about their children as are high-SES parents, and that they are willing to spend equal amounts of time in controlling them and in homework supervision. Low-SES parents, however, may need to be given opportunities and guidance in these matters by the school.

Neighborhood effects also can have an important influence on children and on their perceptions of the value of education. The perceptions of low-SES children about the worth of an education can inhibit their learning and substantially affect the quality of their later lives. This type of persistent negative feedback through lack of positive role models is reinforced by recessions such as the one in 1981 with unemployment rates of approximately 40 percent among young black people in urban ghettos. There are, however, increases in minority enrollments in colleges and professional schools, due in part to perceptions of increased market opportunities for black and female college graduates. Over time, successful minority graduates are unlikely to locate in ghetto neighborhoods. Another policy implication might lie in the possibility of urban ghetto schools specifically budgeting funds for visits by recent graduates, in an effort to counteract Benson's neighborhood effects and to provide role models for others to emulate.

The study by Benson represents a needed contribution to our knowledge about human capital formation. While researchers have extensively used the educational production function approach over the years, consistently finding a strong relationship between SES variables and student achievement, they have rarely attempted to explain systematically how SES factors influence student learning. Benson's study delves into this relatively unexplored area, searching out the effects of out-of-school influences on student learning. In a sense, he has begun to redefine and open up the "black box" over which Rossmiller and others have expressed concern. This study represents a very useful start, and additional work will help clarify how the out-of-school lives of children, including parental guidance of their time-allocation patterns, affect school performance.

The trend toward increased female participation in the labor market has implications for issues raised by both Schultz and Benson. The basic premise is that increased parental inputs, both in the home and in the educational decision-making process, can increase efficiency in schools and in children's learning. Yet women's increasing participation in the labor market represents a substitution of market work for time previously spent with children and in volunteer work. Efforts to increase parental time inputs will have to confront the major trend of increasing female participation in the labor force.

Schooling and Achievement

Rossmiller points out that cost effectiveness studies indicate that teachers also are a significant element in pupil achievement, and that the manner in which resources are mixed does make a difference. Several studies have consistently found teacher-related variables (teaching experience, verbal ability, recency of the teacher's professional training, the extent to which teachers are involved in decision-making, and the instructional strategies they employ to be related significantly to student achievement.

In addition, cost effectiveness studies examining the schooling process have begun to delineate complex teacher-student interaction effects. One study found that low-achieving elementary students did better with relatively less experienced teachers, in smaller classes, and in schools with more high achievers (Summers and Wolfe 1975). To obtain an accurate fix on whether this increase in effectiveness would be cost effective, warranting a move toward this new mode of instruction, the net cost of less experienced teachers in smaller classes would also have to be estimated.

Another study disclosed that black teachers with less than six years of experience were more effective in teaching reading to black children than were white teachers with similar teaching experience (Murnane 1975). Where black teachers are available at the same cost as white teachers with comparable education and experience, there are implications for efficiency. A change to black teachers in comparable situations would, based on Murnane's analysis, constitute an increase in cost effectiveness. This does not necessarily encompass all the benefits, and therefore, as pointed out in Chapter 1, it is a lower-level social efficiency criterion. But if additional qualitative judgments are also applied, this research result might be able to contribute to changes that result in greater social efficiency.

Research on the technology of the instructional group involving process-related variables such as the use and cost of student and staff time, certain combinations of students and teachers, and various instructional strategies and their costs, when aided by qualitative judgments, provide insights about organizing more socially efficient mixes of school resources.

Thomas, Kemmerer, and Monk conclude that substantial differences across SES categories in the percent of "time on task" allocated by students are correlated with the use of individualized instruction. Students in low- and middle-SES classrooms usually received a larger proportion of whole-class instruction than did students in high-SES classrooms. Students in high-SES classes received substantial amounts of small-group instruction, individualized seatwork, and tutoring, whereas these instructional formats were not observed in low-SES classrooms. In addition, more individualized instruction increased the percentage of time that students were actually on task. Consistent with this, achievement scores were positively correlated with the mean proportion of time in small-group instruction and negatively correlated with the proportion of time in whole-group instruction.

The work of Thomas and his colleagues suggests that high-SES classrooms are more technically efficient in that students there spend more time on task. This more efficient use of student time involves a move like that illustrated from Z to B in Figure 2a, Chapter 1. However, if individualized instruction also requires more teacher time per pupil, it could also involve a move from B to C, requiring a larger per-pupil expenditure. This establishes a direct link between expenditure per pupil, facilitating more teacher time per pupil, and pupil achievement, with implications for educational financing. That is, there is the effect of larger expenditure per pupil on the ability to attract teachers with greater verbal skills and advanced training,[1] and also the effect of larger expenditure per pupil on the ability to provide more individualized instruction such as indicated by Thomas and his colleagues, which leads to more time on task and consequently greater achievement.

More time on task produces increased learning or achievement, which in turn relates positively to students' increased earnings and non-monetary benefits later in life.[2] Research focusing on the classroom represents an attempt to open up the "black box" by examining how SES factors influence student achievement. A better understanding of the relationship between time-allocation decisions in households, as well as in classrooms, and student learning will ultimately allow greater efficiency in the formation of human capital.

Schooling and Its Longer-Run Outcomes

The studies summarized in the previous section considered more immediate schooling outcomes, such as achievement, whereas the chapters by Michael and by McMahon and Wagner consider the more ultimate outcomes of education. While earlier research on human capital formation was preoccupied with measuring the direct monetary benefits of education to individuals and to society as a whole, recent research is now confronting the more difficult task of attempting to quantify and value the non-monetary benefits associated with education. As in Chapter 1, these two research thrusts, when added together, have been referred to as dealing with "full earnings," or total private benefits.

Michael surveys the recent economic research on the non-monetary returns to education, focusing on the efficiency effect of schooling on the productivity of non-market time. He stresses the importance of controlling for the effect of schooling on earnings, since cross-effects from earnings as they are spent on the enjoyment of consumption time are not part of the non-monetary returns from education. Limiting himself to studies that control for this income effect, he critically reviews the research investigating the relationship between schooling and health, between schooling and asset management, between schooling and consumption behavior, and between schooling and migration. A review of a very large number of these studies finds significant evidence of several different types of non-monetary benefits of schooling.

Michael concludes that additional careful work would be fruitful with regard to the notion that schooling enhances the productivity of human capital through more efficient learning, although he does not discuss Mincer's extensive work on the relationship of schooling to learning on the job (e.g., Mincer 1974). While some evidence suggests that education may produce a real productivity effect in the financial capital market, Michael is somewhat skeptical of these studies because of the nature of the technological neutrality assumptions involved.

In his own study, Michael concludes that education produces a positive effect on the efficiency of consumption, and he estimates that the effect of schooling is about 60 percent as great in non-market activities as in the labor market. This result may be compared to the one arrived at independently by McMahon (1979), who through the use of survey data estimates that the non-monetary returns *expected* by students are approximately 80 percent as important and valuable to the recipients as are the increments to earnings due to education. Other studies examining the effects of schooling on specific consumer behavior suggest that people with more years of education are likely to use new products more readily, credit cards more extensively, contraception techniques more effectively, and market-search techniques more efficiently. Similarly, Benson's study suggests that high-SES parents are able to use the time spent with their children in ways that more effectively contribute to the child's achievement in school, another important non-monetary return. At the same time, the evidence in regard to the effects of education on migration is inconclusive and mixed.

On the other hand, Michael observes that Grossman's work on the positive effects of schooling on health offers some of the best direct evidence of a non-market productivity benefit from schooling. There is also some evidence that a wife's schooling increases her husband's earnings, as well as her husband's health level. Similarly, studies have shown that parental schooling levels (after controlling for differences in earnings) are positively correlated with the health status of their children.

Another important line of research examines the impact of schooling on the family. While it is very difficult to partition labor-market and non-labor-market effects here, if schooling does indeed facilitate a more productive sorting of men and women in the marriage market, then the benefits would include more stable marriage relationships and more positive assortative mating by intelligence. The findings of studies on the direct effect of parental schooling on the earnings of their sons has been mixed, but there is ample evidence of the indirect effects of schooling on children's earnings. In addition, studies have shown that more educated parents spend relatively more time with their children than less educated parents do. Based on the studies reviewed, Michael concludes that there is evidence to suggest that schooling raises productivity in non-labor-market activities and thus provides non-monetary benefits of specific kinds.

McMahon and Wagner consider the monetary rates of return over time to higher education, and the differences in monetary returns in relation to costs by degree level, by major field (and its related occupations), and by type of institution. They begin by addressing the question of whether the rates of return per student are actually declining. Arguing that rates of return should reflect a view of the entire life cycle, and should not be allowed to be overly affected by the more transitory recessions of 1974 and 1981, they conclude that long-run private rates of return to investment in higher education remained relatively stable at approximately 13 to 14 percent, at least through 1978. Furthermore, these rates of return to higher education compared favorably in level and degree of stability with the average rates of return to financial assets, which were approximately 10 to 12 percent for this same period. Since it can reasonably be assumed that non-monetary private returns and spillover social benefits are at least greater than zero, higher education *does* pay for itself and continues to remain a good investment for individuals and for society.

That is not to say that there are not vast oversupplies in some fields and shortages in others, suggesting that the social efficiency of higher education could probably be increased. McMahon and Wagner find rates of return across occupational fields that vary widely (and that appear to persist in approximately the same ranges over time when compared with earlier studies). The expected social rates of return are highest in medicine, pharmacy, engineering, law, and business, ranging from approximately 13 to 19 percent. The expected social rates of return are lowest for advanced training in teaching, natural science, and social science, ranging from approximately -4 to 7 percent. For the most part, these differences in social rates of returns are also reflected in the differences in private rates of returns for the various occupational fields. Hence, private incentives with respect to choices among fields do not appear to be seriously distorted by scholarships. But since these differences in rates of return among fields tend to persist, it suggests that if they are accepted as having some predictive capacity for the medium-term (4-6 year) future, enrollment quotas of different types (and the underlying budget decisions) may be limiting expansion in fields where returns are high relative to costs, and hence limiting the achievement of greater social efficiency within the system.

McMahon and Wagner use specific microeconomic data on the differences in private costs, e.g., tuition net of scholarships, in their analysis of differences in expected rates of return by types of institutions. While costs are highest for students at private and public research universities, the private rates of return for students who will pursue doctoral degrees are higher there as well. In addition, social rates of return are also higher for these types of institutions, especially for students pursuing advanced degrees. Private rates of return for students planning to earn only a bachelor's degree are low at private liberal arts colleges, in relation to rates of return at the four-year comprehensive colleges. On the other hand, for students planning to seek advanced degrees, a liberal arts college is a more advantageous choice than a four-year public or private comprehensive institution. Finally, the private and social rates of return are highest at comprehensive four-year colleges for those students who plan to complete a terminal bachelor's degree, perhaps in part because of the larger number of students in job-oriented terminal bachelor's degree programs at these institutions.

As Schultz has discussed in his introductory overview of the returns to education, consistent with the findings for higher education reported by McMahon and Wagner, the rates of return to investments in human capital over longer periods of time have exceeded the average rates of return to physical capital and to financial assets. This is consistent with the fact that growth in our stock of human capital in the United States has been higher than the growth of physical capital. A prominent economics journal published a debate of the case for a decline in the average rates of return to education during the 1980-81 recession, but the longer-run decisions to invest in education need to consider the longer-run rates of return to investment in education relative to other forms of investment as indicated above, not to speak of the non-monetary returns.[3] Investment also can be shifted gradually toward those fields, levels, and institutions where payoffs are the greatest, thus promoting efficiency in the creation of human resources. Fields with strong social benefits (e.g., the preservation of knowledge in the classics and philosophy) illustrate the need to add social benefits judgmentally, justifying their preservation but also justifying the need to reduce the number of majors in these areas because of over-supplies of unemployable people in these fields of study.

In addition, as Michael's survey indicates, substantial progress has been made during the last decade in conceptualizing and measuring non-monetary benefits of education. But additional steps must be taken to relate these non-monetary private benefits to the costs of obtaining them, and to measure objectively the spillover social benefits, before the "full benefit"/cost ratios as measures of social efficiency can be obtained. The inclusion of the specific non-market contributions of schooling that are mentioned by Michael in judgmental ways in the cost/benefit calculus, however, does permit a more objective judgment of education's total efficiency contribution to humane growth.

Equity Criteria

Equity refers to the notion of distributive justice and fairness in educational systems. It has been translated into public policy largely as efforts to secure more equal educational opportunity. Equity criteria were presented in Chapter 1, which considered child equity and tax equity in terms of horizontal equity (equal treatment of equals), intergenerational equity (an in-between case), and vertical equity (unequal treatment of unequals).

A number of the authors in Part II of this volume explore the application of these equity criteria. Alexander focuses on child equity and discusses the importance of considering philosophical and legal bases. Due focuses specifically on tax equity and documents changes that have occurred in it as the results of changes in the financing of elementary and secondary schools over the last decade. The chapters by Nelson, Carroll, and Odden consider different combinations of both tax equity and student equity in recent school finance reform efforts. The following considers these applications of equity criteria, and the joint implications of their contributions for 1) child equity, 2) intergenerational equity, and 3) tax equity.

Child Equity

Alexander explores the concept of equity, its application in recent school finance reforms, and its implications for needed future reforms. He develops the relation of the hierarchy of equity criteria to its philosophical and legal roots. The result provides a useful framework for evaluating the continual development of more equitable school financing programs. The hierarchy, consisting of four levels similar to those summarized in Chapter 1 -- commutative, equal distribution, restitution, and positivism -- is combined with a plea to focus these equity concepts more clearly on the students. He concludes that the fiscal neutrality standard which seeks to divorce per-pupil expenditure from the wealth of parents does not go far enough, and hence is an inadequate standard of equity for public school finance.

While limited progress is being made in achieving more fiscally neutral financing systems, fiscal neutrality is far from being achieved. In this respect, elementary and secondary school finance is way behind higher education finance. The Education Amendments of 1980 provided significant increases in Basic Educational Opportunity Grant support and hence greater fiscal neutrality and greater equity among college students. At the same time, however, federal budget cuts in 1981 in categorical funding for the public schools, and in student loan programs in higher education, are having negative effects on student equity considerations.

At the common school level, Alexander clarifies some of the shortcomings of the popular district power equalizing (DPE) schemes, which have done very little to reduce the vast differences in spending levels among school districts. These DPE schemes assure local districts a choice of spending levels and virtually ignore the more difficult problems involving the measurement of educational need and the determination of adequate support levels.

The courts, however, appear to be broadening their definition of equity to include vertical equity elements such as the assessment of educational needs. Based on education provisions in state constitutions, recent cases in Colorado, New York, and Ohio have defined equity to include equality, thoroughness, uniformity, efficiency, and adequacy. Combining the more demanding requirements of these recent court cases, Alexander feels that a model of education finance equity should include the following components: adequate funding of basic education programs, complete fiscal equalization of each district's tax-paying ability, uniform tax effort, and supplemental standards for corrective and remedial educational programs. His proposed provisions for diseconomies of scale, governmental overburdens, and cost differences have negative implications for efficiency—another example of an equity-efficiency conflict—and hence do not meet the more limiting humane-growth criteria.

As Carroll and Odden point out, approximately half of the states attempted to adopt more equitable school financing programs during the 1970's. What, then, have been the overall effects of the school finance changes on equity and on efficiency? Some states increased the level of their foundation programs; others maintained their basic financing structures but instituted more sophisticated allocation schemes; still others adopted DPE or guaranteed-tax-base types of school financing formulas. The chapter by Carroll indicates, for example, that California combined a high-level foundation plan with differential expenditure growth limits, whereas New Mexico, in effect, assumed full responsibility for school finance while implementing a comprehensive pupil-weighting system with adjustments for teacher cost differentials.

In the five states studied, Carroll reports that the school finance reform movement promoted greater tax equity and somewhat diminished the strong relationship between school district spending and school district wealth. However, it did little or nothing to equalize the vast disparities in per-pupil expenditures. (Odden's chapter comes to a similar conclusion after reviewing other studies of the effectiveness of some recent school finance reforms.) In addition, Carroll points out that while these reforms have been accompanied by substantial revenue growth for the schools, even with declining school tax rates, they have not had equally large implications for horizontal child equity in that they have done very little to equalize the distribution of per-pupil expenditures for instructional purposes.

Perhaps even more disturbing is the persistent finding that these reforms have *not* resulted in some shifting of resources from the more advantaged to the less advantaged pupils. Carroll finds, for example, that in general the division of per-pupil revenues between pupils in small and large districts, in less and more urban districts, in less white and more white districts, and in low and high incidence-of-poverty districts has remained largely unaffected by the reforms in the five states studied. Likewise, some studies reviewed by Odden indicate that the relative position of poor and minority students has not been improved by many of the reforms. In fact, at least some evidence suggests that minority students have become *more* disadvantaged since some tax changes were implemented.[4]

Hickrod, Chaudhari, and Hubbard (1979) have pointed out the importance of monitoring school financing changes over time. They conducted a longitudinal study of the effects of the school finance reform that was adopted by Illinois in 1973. In one of the few studies concerned with the impact of financing changes over time, these researchers found that Illinois made progress toward the established equity goals of less expenditure disparity between school districts and greater wealth neutrality for a period of approximately three years, from 1973 to 1976. Much of the ground gained during this period, however, was lost from 1976 to 1978. This reversal in equity trends had resulted in the loss of all the gains that had been made with regard to expenditure disparities in the bulk of

Illinois' school districts, and some of the gains that had been made with regard to wealth neutrality. Without immediate changes in the Illinois school aid formula, these authors concluded that the state would soon be characterized by the same degree of inequities that existed when the 1973 reform was implemented.

While the preceding has been concerned with the implications for child equity of various changes in the financing of elementary and secondary schools, the chapter by Nelson focuses on equity concerns in higher education. She concludes that a perspective on equity which views the costs and the benefits of subsidies for higher education separately is superior to efforts that try to link the two, and she argues that a number of aspects of equity become clearer when this approach is used. While tuition would promote somewhat greater equity on the cost side because the tax burden would be distributed somewhat more progressively, the greatest impact would be felt on the benefit side through an enrollment response. This would have implications for intergenerational equity as well.

Based on her estimates, Nelson suggests that the federal Basic Educational Opportunity Grants (BEOG) program which was extended in the Education Amendments of 1980 (now referred to as the Pell Grant Program) would largely offset any tuition charge that would be imposed on the junior college system in California. These federal grants would have, in effect, paid approximately half of the increased tuition charges for low-income students. In this situation the use of federal grants to offset increased tuition charges will tend to maintain the access of low-income students to junior colleges, thereby further reducing the relationship between college attendance rates and family income levels. At the same time, these federal grants also improve the distribution of public subsidies among students with the more needy students receiving more assistance. In addition, with a minimal amount of effort the state could supplement these with state grants to students, thereby offsetting any remaining costs that low-income families may incur because of tuition. Nelson's work discloses that a seemingly undesirable policy in terms of equity could actually be easily turned around to *promote* equity objectives because of the different state and federal arrangements involved.

Most of the authors treating equity in this volume conclude that inequity, especially student inequity, still permeates our financing structures for public schools and institutions of higher education. Vast inequalities in per-pupil expenditures and hence in horizontal equity among similarly situated students still exist. At the same time, too little attention has been devoted to vertical equity. There has been limited redistribution of resources, say from the more wealthy districts to the less wealthy districts, in spite of special categorical aid programs for the disadvantaged and for the handicapped. In my opinion, in the quest for equal educational opportunity the allocation of equal dollars for students with varying educational needs will not provide the programs necessary to enable all to develop to the fullest their innate abilities and talents. Rather, quite the opposite effect will occur. Unequal educational opportunities are assured when state support models do not take into consideration such factors as students' socioeconomic backgrounds, physical and mental handicaps, language deficiencies, and other important student characteristics.

Intergenerational Equity

Less attention has been directed to the notion of intergenerational equity in educational finance, but the rapid developments in human capital theory applied to explaining the distribution of income are likely to be of increasing importance in the future. The vast inequalities in per-pupil expenditure, along with the lack of progress in terms of vertical equity among unequal students, virtually assures an intergenerational transmission of inequality. For example, due to particular circumstances in California, Nelson concludes that the use of federal grants would improve the access of disadvantaged students to the junior college system. Because these grants would reduce the link between college attendance rates and family income levels, and also provide the more needy students with larger amounts of assistance, they would have an important intergenerational effect, enhancing the future earnings and non-monetary returns of these students.

The rising rates of college enrollment by blacks, women, and students from low-income families could help to overcome the negative neighborhood effects developed by Benson. That is, children of these more highly educated students will, in turn, be more likely to complete higher levels of education than if their parents had never attended college; they will also be able to act as role models for others in the urban neighborhoods. Considerable evidence indicates that the educational attainment of individuals today is directly related to that of their parents. Thus this intergenerational effect creates a pattern that perpetuates increased lifetime income for the better-off segments of society and decreased relative benefits for those who already are behind, unless steps are taken such as through adequate funding for the BEOG program to improve intergenerational equity.

Tax Equity

Due documents the significant shifting of the responsibility for public school financing from the local to the state level, both over time and in recent spurts as the result of property taxpayers' revolts. While there has been tremendous variation among the states in shifting the sources for financing education, the major effect has been a reduction in the relative reliance on property taxes. Since the 1978-79 school year, the average state share (approximately 47 percent) has exceeded the average local share (approximately 43 percent) of revenues for the public schools.

As states have assumed a larger portion of school costs, they have relied more heavily on state income and sales taxes. Rising incomes and inflation have permitted states to realize substantially increased yields from these tax sources without the enactment of new taxes or the altering of tax rates. Overall, this shifting of education costs from local to state tax sources, particularly to income tax revenues, has resulted in a somewhat less regressive pattern of state-local tax burdens. Due presents ample evidence that governmental expenditure as a percentage of GNP has not increased in the last decade. Similarly, the property tax burden has not been increasing relative to personal income. He therefore suggests that increased tax burdens have not been the primary reason for increasing taxpayer dissatisfaction.

Several factors other than increased total tax burdens appear to have precipitated the taxpayers' revolt, including the effects of inflation on local real estate assessments and property tax receipts, dissatisfaction with government inefficiency, dislike of irritating regulatory policies, and a backlash over minority rights. Due suggests that one characteristic of the taxpayers' revolt may be somewhat irrational behavior -- voter reactions sometimes produce results that are contrary to the voters' true preferences. For example, among the chief beneficiaries of Proposition 13 have been the federal government (because state taxes are deductible from federal income taxes) and large business firms (because of property tax savings), rather than the individual real estate owners who mounted the tax revolt. Likewise, this meat-axe approach to tax reductions shifts fiscal responsibility for various services to the states, and probably ultimately to the federal government, which significantly diminishes local financial autonomy. Yet tax revolt crusades are usually fought under the banner of returning more power to local government.

Carroll provides additional evidence consistent with Due's basic findings. He points out that many states essentially directed their practical reform efforts at the tax side rather than the expenditure side of their financing systems, perhaps forestalling tax revolts. That is, these states carefully reexamined how tax dollars were raised to support public schools, and in an effort to promote greater tax equity many of them increased state support for education in order to alleviate growing local property tax burdens. The basic notion behind many of the adopted formulas was simply to assure districts equal educational spending for equal tax rates, thus eliminating the significant advantages that property-wealthy districts had always enjoyed in financing their schools.

Carroll finds that the disparities in the distribution of adjusted tax rates fell by more than 25 percent between pre- and post-reform years in each state he studied, with the exception of Florida. New Mexico completely equalized local educational property tax rates, and in Michigan, where reform was accompanied by an increase in the average adjusted tax rate, the distribution of tax rates was significantly equalized by reform. Carroll also concluded that reform promoted greater equality in the distributions of adjusted tax rates between different types of districts (e.g., large and small, rural and urban, wealthy and poor). In addition, reform generally resulted in greater total statewide spending for education.

The reform moves undertaken appear to have achieved a greater degree of horizontal tax equity, in that tax efforts for school spending have become more equal for those who have similar income and wealth. In addition, as Odden points out, states have begun to incorporate income factors in their school aid formulas, acknowledging the fact that both income and property wealth affect school district spending patterns. Due also indicates that this shifting of the costs of education from local to state tax sources has resulted in a somewhat less regressive pattern of state-local tax burdens. Increased vertical tax equity may be achieved as higher portions of educational costs are increasingly financed by more progressive tax structures (such as the state income tax, rather than the local property tax).

The marked increase in the average level of state support of educational costs documented by Due, Carroll, and Odden raises the controversial issue of local versus state control. Schultz contends, for example, that the political process involving increased state support, perhaps for property tax relief, has resulted in a centralization of control in education which is having detrimental effects on the quality of a child's education. Yet increased levels of state support seemed justified by the need to reduce dependence on the property tax and to correct inequity in the wide differences in expenditures per child that persist, even though this growing centralization may sometimes have a detrimental effect on local control and hence on the efficiency of the schooling process. This suggests a point at which there may be some trade-off between efficiency and equity. At the college level, the Basic Educational Opportunity Grants to students seem largely to have avoided this conflict.

The underlying assumption is that these higher levels of state support will necessarily result in greater state control over education, stifling diversity, innovation, and eventually efficiency. However, we are badly in need of information about how these state increases in support levels affect educational governance structures. Some evidence suggests that increased state funding does not necessarily lead to substantial state restrictions on local school district decision-making, nor does it diminish the initiative of local school boards to adopt new educational practices. In fact, the availability of a higher percentage of state aid and higher total per-pupil expenditures have been found to be associated with the adoption of more innovation (Levin et al. 1972). Wirt (1978) also concludes, after examining the question of whether state control follows the dollar in the fifty states, that there is no relationship between the degree of state control and the state share of local school costs. He suggests that the degree of state control may better be explained by "political culture," rather than by the amount of state aid allocated to the local schools.

Progressing toward Human Growth

The two basic themes advanced in the previous sections concerned with efficiency in creating educational outputs and child equity have some complementary elements. The first has to do with growth in educational outputs obtained through greater efficiency and the growth in the resulting returns to education; the second, regarding equity, has to do with the distribution of educational outputs and the distribution of the ultimate returns or "full earnings" from education.

In Chapter 1 efficiency and equity criteria are merged into a hierarchy of humane growth criteria. The latter are a composite set of criteria for increasing education's contribution to humane growth in a society. Using this framework, an attempt is made in this section to seek out various possible combinations of the findings reported previously, and to draw out a few implications once efficiency and equity criteria are combined. This is a difficult task, since it goes beyond mere summarization of what are often quite separate and isolated research results. The difficulty is increased by the fact that, while there are situations where both efficiency and equity can be increased (or at least neither is decreased), there is a wider potential range of situations which will involve trade-offs, unless some compensation is paid or some safeguards are set up. Thus the humane growth criteria suggest that policy options be limited to those areas where both efficiency and equity changes are joint products.

Combining Efficiency and Equity Criteria

But before discussing areas wherein opportunities may exist for achieving complementarities, let us look at two contributions that emphasize the combination of efficiency and equity. The first is the state allocation goal-programming model for experimental use, proposed by Cohn, which combines the two criteria. The second is the discussion of policy by Odden. Practical policy decisions normally require mixing both efficiency and equity considerations.

Cohn attempts to advance the state of the art by devising a state-support model which emphasizes efficiency criteria. Based upon educational production function techniques, this new model utilizes a goal-programming framework which assumes that school districts pursue multiple educational goals. The objective function of the model is to minimize deviations from specified target goal levels, subject to an array of constraints. In order to use this approach, a careful effort must be made to establish priorities or rank orderings for the agreed-upon educational goals--that is, to decide which of the goals should be attained first, second, and so on, and (given similar priority levels) which goal should take precedence.

Cohn's model attempts to address both equity and efficiency criteria simultaneously by focusing on educational outputs rather than inputs. He describes how the goal-programming models would be applied to school districts and individual schools, including the specification of the objective function, target output levels, and resource availability constraints. The state's share of costs would be determined by the difference between the district's educational costs (to achieve the objective function) and the amount of local revenues generated by a state minimum mandated tax rate. Ideally, the state would provide the aid necessary to achieve the established output level in all districts across the state, thereby assuring equity as measured in terms of equality of output for all students.

Odden suggests that the federal government has an important role to play in promoting both efficiency and equity in educational finance. As he points out, the federal government has basically relied upon categorical aids to fund particular programs in the elementary and secondary schools for special pupil populations, such as the disadvantaged, the handicapped, and the bilingual. Odden reviews recent studies that indicate that federal programs have somewhat improved student equity in state school financing systems. In addition, the recent Education of All Handicapped Children Act (P.L. 94-142) has served to reduce spending disparities among school districts and to diminish the link between spending and school district wealth. Nevertheless, vast inequalities in per-pupil expenditures persist within and among states, and there is room for substantial improvement.

Simultaneous Improvements in Efficiency and Equity

To improve both efficiency and equity, and thereby to increase the contribution of education to humane growth in the society, one key question is whether, on pure efficiency grounds, the last dollar spent in the high per-pupil expenditure school districts and colleges yields as much in student achievement as it would if spent in the low per-pupil expenditure districts or colleges. Larger per-pupil expenditure and various other indices of school equality are known to lead to higher achievement, but there is also some evidence that diminishing returns eventually begin to set in. If so, greater equity would also improve the efficiency with which each dollar is spent.

The work by Thomas and his colleagues implies that more teacher time per pupil (and hence larger expenditure per pupil), permitting more individualized instruction, is related to greater student achievement. This same kind of positive association arises in the research on earnings functions. Johnson and Stafford (1973), for example, found a 10 percent increase in school expenditures per pupil increased the annual return to schooling by about 2 percent, and Wachtel (1974) found similarly strong effects when controlling for initial student test scores. When using aggregated data on school districts, a clear separation of school quality and student ability cannot be controlled (e.g., Coleman 1966), but when using micro data for individual students, the impact of school quality supported by higher per-pupil expenditure on rates of advancement in firms and on earnings is more convincing (Solomon 1973; Wachtel 1975; Wise 1975).

Growing evidence, however, points to a persistent pattern involving expenditures for instructional purposes in elementary and secondary schools (Alexander 1974; Barro and Carroll 1975; Carroll 1976), as well as in higher education (Bowen 1980), that may be cited here as an empirical law of educational finance. This law says that as spending increases in educational organizations, there may be a tendency to allocate decreasing portions of the institution's budget to the instructional component. If the residue is allocated to improvements in the quality of instruction, well and good. But sometimes it is not so allocated.

The point is not that there are differences in quality when expenditure per pupil is larger--of course there are. Rather, the point is that, in view of the tremendous variation in per-pupil expenditure which exists within and across states, there may be diminishing returns to expenditure per pupil in obtaining additional achievement at the high end. Are educational programs in wealthy districts which cost four to five times as much as those in poor districts actually four or five times "better," by whatever set of evaluative criteria might be applied? It is difficult to accept the notion that there aren't some inefficiencies and elements of waste at the extreme end of the continuum involving inordinately high expenditures. If there is waste through expenditure on non-instructional activities, this would represent another instance, when combined with careful judgments, where greater child equity through greater equality of opportunity and greater efficiency may be complementary. That is, seeking out the inefficiencies that may be involved as the more affluent school districts allocate increasing percentages of their budgets to non-instructional components which do not contribute to more qualitative programs could produce both greater equity and more efficient use of resources for new learning.

A second source of potential contributions to humane growth via joint products of improved efficiency and equity may lie in competency testing, but only if it is judiciously applied. The adoption of competency testing programs would be consistent with our focus throughout this volume on the need to place greater emphasis on the output side. Many have been quick to condemn competency testing, pointing out the numerous problems involved with any testing program; but testing does require careful examination of short-run (and to some extent longer-run) educational outputs. Competency testing programs which focus on outputs (amount learned) may help identify one result of wide differences in per-pupil expenditures. In so doing, they could actually promote a greater focus of resources on student achievement, including the development of remedial programs in attempts to begin reversing the decline in test scores. The time has come to concentrate more on the quality of schooling outputs and on the nature of corrective and remedial programs for students who are not receiving their fair share of educational benefits.

Suggesting a third area in which to seek out contributions to humane growth, in this case through emphasizing efficiency gains, Schultz contends that the organizational and administrative structure of large school systems are responsible for substantial inefficiencies in education. The control structure for these school systems has sharply reduced the role of parents, and also diminished the role and prestige of teachers in the schooling process. Schultz proposes a decentralized system of education which would increase consumer choice and secure greater parental involvement. This type of decentralization model based on choice, if equity is not to be sacrificed, leads directly to the notion of voucher systems which are receiving increased interest today. Although to many people (including Schultz) voucher systems have limitations (e.g., they have the potential for fostering racist schools, unless they are limited in some way), they do provide a vehicle for channeling federal aid through students and their parents to improve equity and, through consumer choice, to force efficiency without the spectre of federal control that would be raised by direct grants to local schools.

While some scholars have espoused the use of voucher systems and the notion of choice as a means of simultaneously achieving improved efficiency and improved equity, others have severely criticized models of choice as involving substantial trade-offs. Alexander, for example, contends that voucher systems would detrimentally affect equity in educational finance. Nevertheless, a number of policy variants could involve the use of vouchers. One possibility would be to provide vouchers for low-SES parents that could be used at the school of the parents' choice if they were willing to sign a contract ensuring that their childrens' homework would be supervised and completed. Limited in this way, the scope for inequity may be sharply reduced, and there is also the promise of increased efficiency. But at this time there is not sufficient theoretical work and empirical experimentation to allow us to conclude whether or not this type of voucher system involves trade-offs or complementarities between efficiency and equity.

These three suggestions of possible ways of implementing humane growth criteria by reducing disparities in per-pupil expenditures and simultaneously increasing efficiency suggest areas wherein opportunities for complementarities may exist between efficiency and equity in educational finance. Research is needed over the next decade in order to develop these further and to seek out and identify possible additional situations where both can be achieved simultaneously.

Most economists specialize in efficiency, although those in the cost/benefit and public finance fields also work on the development of measures of inequality and with the application of equity criteria as a necessary part of most public-sector policy decisions. Educators concentrate on equity in school financing models; in higher education they concentrate on educational opportunity grant and loan programs, with somewhat less attention devoted to social efficiency. The chapters in this volume attempt to promote a cross-fertilization of ideas applied to common problems and research interests. Economists and educators can learn from each other as they attempt to increase both efficiency and equity. Perhaps they can join together in the effort to minimize the trade-offs, and to increase the contribution made by education to humane growth in the society.[5]

NOTES

1. See, e.g., statements by Chambers (in Windham 1979: 95-107).
2. There is substantial research to document this point. See, e.g., the recent survey by Mincer (in Windham 1979).
3. See *Journal of Human Resources* (Winter, 1981).
4. See, e.g., Knickman and Reschovsky (1980).
5. I am indebted to Walter W. McMahon for helpful suggestions and comments.

REFERENCES

Alexander, Arthur. 1974. *Teachers, salaries, and school district expenditures*. Report No. R-1588-FF. Santa Monica, Calif.: Rand Corporation. October.
Barro, Stephen, and Carroll, S. J. 1975. *Budget allocation by school district: an analysis of spending for teachers and other resources*. Report No. R-1797-NIE. Santa Monica, Calif.: Rand Corporation. December.
Bowen, Howard. 1980. *The costs of higher education*. San Francisco: Jossey-Bass.

Carroll, Stephen J. 1976. School district expenditure behavior. *Journal of Human Resources* 2 (Summer): 317-27.
Coleman, James S., et al. 1966. *Equality of educational opportunity.* Washington: U.S. Department of Health, Education and Welfare.
Ferber, M., and McMahon, W. W. 1979. Women's expected earnings and their investment in higher education. *Journal of Human Resources* 14 (Summer): 405-20.
Hickrod, G. A.; Chaudhari, R.; and Hubbard, B. C. 1979. *Equity goals in Illinois school finance: 1973-1979.* Normal: Center for the Study of Educational Finance, Illinois State University.
Johnson, G. E., and Stafford, F. 1973. Social returns to quantity and quality of schooling. *Journal of Human Resources* 8 (2): 139-55.
Knickman, J. R., and Reschovsky, A. 1980. The implementation of school finance reform. *Policy Sciences* 12 (Oct.): 301-315.
Levin, B.; Muller, T.; and Scanlon, W. F. 1972. *Public school finance: present disparities and fiscal alternatives*, II. Washington: Urban Institute.
McMahon, W. W. 1979. Measurement of non-monetary returns to education. Manuscript.
Mincer, J. 1974. *Schooling, experience, and earnings.* New York: National Bureau of Economic Research.
Murnane, R. J. 1975. *The impact of school resources on the learning of inner city children.* Cambridge: Ballinger.
Solomon, L. 1973. Schooling and subsequent success. In *Does college matter?*, ed. L. Solomon and P. Taubman. New York: Academic Press.
Summers, A. A., and Wolfe, B. J. 1975. Which school resources help learning? Efficiency and equity in Philadelphia public schools. *Federal Reserve Bank of Philadelphia Review* (February).
Thomas, J. A. 1971. *The productive school.* New York: John Wiley and Sons.
Wachtel, P. 1974. *The effect of school quality on achievement, attainment and earnings.* New York: New York University.
―――. 1975. The returns to investment in education: another view. In *Education, income, and human behavior*, ed. F. T. Juster. New York: McGraw-Hill.
Windham, Douglas M., ed. 1979. *Economic dimensions of education.* Washington: National Academy of Education.
Wirt, F. 1978. Does control follow the dollar? Value analysis, school policy, and state-local linkages. Paper presented at the American Political Science Association annual meeting, New York.
Wise, D. 1975. Academic achievement and job performance. *American Economic Review* 65 (3): 350-66.

Notes on Contributors

KERN ALEXANDER is Professor of Educational Administration and Director of the Institute for Educational Finance at the University of Florida at Gainesville. He served as Associate Director and Director of the National Education Finance Project from 1968-1974, and has been editor of the *Journal of Education Finance* since 1975. His major publications include: *Financing Education: Fiscal and Legal Alternatives* with R. L. Johns and K. F. Jordan (1972); *Constitutional Reform of School Finance* with K. F. Jordan (1973); *Educational Need in the Public Economy* with K. F. Jordan (1976); and *School Law* (1980).

CHARLES S. BENSON is Professor of Education at the University of California-Berkeley. He is a past president of the American Education Finance Association (1977-78). His distinguished career of research contributions continues to have a significant impact on public school finance. His books include: *Perspectives on the Economics of Education* (1963); *The Cheerful Prospect* (1965); *Planning for Educational Reform: Financial and Social Alternatives* with P. M. Goldfinger, E. G. Hoacklander, and J. S. Pers (1974); *Education Finance in the Coming Decade* (1975); and *The Economics of Public Education*, 3rd ed. (1978).

STEPHEN J. CARROLL is a Senior Staff Member in the Economics Department at the Rand Corporation. He is particularly noted for his work investigating the effects of school inputs and other factors on students' achievement, and the effects of school finance reform. His numerous articles and Rand reports include *How Effective is Schooling?* with H. A. Averch, T. S. Donaldson, H. J. Kiesling, and J. Pincus (1974), and "School District Expenditure Behavior," *Journal of Human Resources* (Summer 1976).

ELCHANAN COHN is Professor of Economics at the University of South Carolina. He also currently serves as editor of the *Economics of Education Review* and is engaged in research on the development of goal programming techniques as a potential tool with which to promote improved efficiency. His major books include: *Public Expenditure Analysis* (1972); *Economics of State Aid to Education* (1974); *Input-Output Analysis in Public Education*, with S. D. Millman (1975); and *The Economics of Education*, revised ed. (1979).

JOHN F. DUE is Professor of Economics at the University of Illinois at Urbana-Champaign. An acknowledged international and national expert on taxation, Professor Due has received a number of professional honors over the years, and is a past president of the Midwest Economics Association. He has published numerous books and articles including the widely used textbook, *Government Finance: Economics of the Public Sector*, with A. F. Friedlaender, 7th ed. (1981).

TERRY G. GESKE is Assistant Professor of Educational Administration with a joint appointment in the Bureau of Educational Research at the University of Illinois at Urbana-Champaign. His research is on the economics of education, public school finance, and cost-effectiveness analysis in education. His articles include: "Toward More Effective Use of School Resources," with R. A. Rossmiller, *Journal of Education Finance* (Spring 1977), and "Some Observations on Cost-Effectiveness Analysis in Education," *Journal of Education Finance* (Spring 1979).

FRANCES KEMMERER is Assistant Professor of Educational Administration at the State University of New York at Albany. Her primary research interest has been the allocation of time in the learning process. Her publications include "The Allocation of Student Time," *Administrator's Notebook* No. 8 (1978-79), and "Educational Administration: A Multi-Level Perspective," with J. A. Thomas and D. Monk, *Administrator's Notebook* No. 4 (1978-79).

WALTER W. McMAHON is Professor of Economics, Department of Economics, and Professor of Education, College of Education, at the University of Illinois at Urbana-Champaign. His research has been on the influences on investment in education, education and productivity, and the relation of human capital formation to supply-side effects in medium-term macroeconomic models. He is a member of the board of editors of the *Economics of Education Review*, and has served in various consulting roles. His publications include *Investment in Higher Education* (1974); "An Economic Analysis of the Major Determinants of Expenditures on Public Primary and Secondary Education," *Review of Economics and Statistics* (August 1970); "Investment by Blacks in Higher Education," *American Economic Review* (May 1976); "Measuring Cost of Living by States," *Industrial Relations* (October 1978); and "Expected Rates of Return to Education," *International Encyclopedia of Education* (1982).

ROBERT T. MICHAEL is Professor of Education and Director and Research Associate of the Economics Research Center of the National Opinion Research Center at the University of Chicago, following a period as director of the Palo Alto office of the National Bureau of Economic Research. He has conducted considerable research on the non-market behavior of households. His publications include: *The Effect of Education on Efficiency in Consumption* (1972); "Education and Consumption," in

Education, Income, and Human Behavior, by F. T. Juster (1975); "Family Size and the Distribution of Real Per Capita Income," with E. P. Lazear, *American Economic Review* (March 1980); and "Real Income Equivalence among One-Earner and Two-Earner Families," with E. P. Lazear, *American Economic Review* (May 1980).

DAVID H. MONK is Visiting Assistant Professor of Educational Administration at Cornell University. Professor Monk's major research interest is the economic analysis of resource allocation in classrooms. His publications include "Educational Administration: A Multi-level Perspective," with J. A. Thomas and F. Kemmerer, *Administrator's Notebook* No. 4 (1978-79), and "A Comprehensive View of Resource Allocation for Education," *Administrator's Notebook* No. 3 (1979-80).

SUSAN C. NELSON is Senior Staff Economist, Council of Economic Advisors, Washington, D.C. Recently she has focused on the financing of higher education, and in particular community colleges. Her publications include: "Financial Trends and Issues," in *Public Policy and Private Higher Education*, by D. W. Breneman and C. E. Finn, Jr. (1978); *The Equity of Public Subsidies for Higher Education: Some Thoughts on the Literature* (1978); and "Education and Training," with D. W. Breneman, in *Setting National Priorities: Issues for the 1980s*, by J. A. Pechman (1980).

ALLAN ODDEN is the Director of the Education Programs Division of the Education Commission of the States. He is a recent past president of the American Education Finance Association (1979-80) and has been actively involved in the development of school financing reforms in several states. His publications include: "Alternative Measures of School District Wealth," *Journal of Education Finance* (Winter 1977); *School Finance Reform in the States, 1978* (1978); and "Missouri's New School Finance Structure," *Journal of Education Finance* (Spring 1978).

RICHARD A. ROSSMILLER is Professor of Educational Administration at the University of Wisconsin-Madison. He is also a recent past president of the American Education Finance Association (1980-81), and currently serves as a member of the board of editors for both the *Economics of Education Review* and the *Journal of Education Finance*. He is particularly well known for his research on the pricing of educational programs for exceptional children. His recent publications include: *Resource Allocation and Time Utilization in IGE and Non-IGE Schools*, with T. G. Geske (1977), *Input-Output Relationships in IGE Schools* (1978), and *Expenditure and Funding Patterns in Idaho's Program for Exceptional Children*, with L. E. Frohreich (1979).

THEODORE W. SCHULTZ is Professor Emeritus of Economics at the University of Chicago. He received the highest honor the academic community can bestow, the Nobel Prize in Economics (1979), for his work on the importance of the development of human capital skills through education as a key means of raising productivity in agriculture in the poor countries, thereby reducing poverty and aiding growth. Professor Schultz has probably done more than any other person to inspire and aid basic research on the contribution of education to economic growth. He is also a past president of the American Economic Association (1960). His publications include *The Economic Value of Education* (1963); *Investment in Human Capital: The Role of Education and of Research* (1971); *Human Resources: Human Capital; Policy Issues and Research Opportunities* (1972); *Investment in Education: Equity-Efficiency Quandary* (1972); and *The New Family Economics* (1980).

J. ALAN THOMAS is the William C. Reavis Professor of Educational Administration at the University of Chicago, and past Dean of the Graduate School of Education. Among his extensive contributions, Professor Thomas is particularly noted for his book, *The Productive School* (1971). For the past several years, he has devoted considerable attention to problems of resource allocation in education, which has resulted in a recent book, *The Analysis of Educational Productivity, Volume I: Issues in Microanalysis*, with R. Dreeben (1980).

ALAN P. WAGNER is Assistant Professor, Department of Consumer Economics and Agricultural Experiment Station, Purdue University. Professor Wagner's major areas of research include the economics of education, human capital, and the financing of postsecondary educational and training programs. His publications include "Financing Postsecondary Learning Opportunities through Existing Student Aid Programs," *School Review* (May 1978), "Expected Returns to Investment in Higher Education," with W. W. McMahon, *Journal of Human Resources* (July 1981).

Index

Ability of student, and input substitution, 106-8
Achievement of pupils, and influence of teachers, 329
Allocation of resources: see Resources, allocation of
Allocative efficiency, 9-10
Asset management, and schooling, 130-31
Authority, effects of, shifts in, 43-47

Basic Educational Opportunity Grant program, 10, 337
Ben-Porath neutrality, 124
Benefits: consumption, 119-20, 122; educational, 20; non-monetary, 119-46
BEOG. See Basic Educational Opportunity Grant program
"Black box," 92-93
Bond issues, voter action on as evidence of dissatisfaction, 275

California, educational finance system in, 215-36, 238-45
Centralization of decisions, in educational finance, 41-42
Characteristics of students, as predictors of classroom structure, 114
Child equity, 14-16, 313-14, 326, 334-37
Children's Time Study Project, 59
Choice: and efficiency, 91-92; and equity, 91-92
Class-dominant model, and student achievement, 55-56
Classroom activities, structuring of, 104-9
Coleman Report (1966), 52, 81
Community colleges, and equity, 226-32
Commutative equity, 20, 196-97, 210-11
Competency testing, 344
Consumption behavior, and schooling, 131-35

Consumption benefits: see Benefits, consumption
Cost adjustment provision, of teachers in New Mexico, 254
Cost differences, for higher education institutions, 162-65
Cost effectiveness: analysis of, 10; as financing criterion, 78-97; indexes of, 13; studies of, 84-86; techniques, 90-91
Costs, educational: 303-5; as public policy issue, 32; of reform of educational finance system, 240-42. See also Opportunity costs; Social costs

Decisions, loci of, in education, 42-47
Differentials, of earnings: see Earnings differentials
Dissatisfaction with taxes, 275-85
Distribution of revenues, among rich and poor children, 256
District power equalizer formula, 15, 335
District revenue, growth in, by reform, 255
DPE: see District power equalizer formula

Earnings, actual, as element of humane growth, 2-3. See also Expected earnings
Earnings differentials, due to education, 138, 181-82
Economic efficiency, 8
Education; benefits to individual and society, research on, 31-32; local financing of, 267-72; and state control, 340-41; state financing of, 267-70
Educational finance: and Proposition 13, 283-85; reform movement in, 237-65, 312-19; and role of federal government, 319-22; sources of, 267-70

351

352 Financing Education

Educational opportunities, equality of, 226
Educational outcomes, and resource inputs, 86-89
Educational production function, 293-94
Efficiency, 38; and choice, 91-92; classroom perspective of, 100-116; and educational inputs, 325; and educational outputs, 325-26; and educational policy and programs, 287-88; and equity, tradeoffs of, 5-8, 24-25, 48, 91-92; role of, in higher education, 216; social, 2, 13-14, 327; and state allocation goal-programming model, 342; and student decisionmaking, 103-4; technical, 8-9, 330. *See also* Allocative efficiency; Economic efficiency; Exchange efficiency; Pareto efficiency; Production efficiency
Efficiency criteria, 8-14, 327-34; and equity criteria, 341-45; hierarchy of, 11-13; and educational finance system, 290-92, 300-307
Equality of Educational Opportunity (EEO) study: *see* Coleman Report
Equality, and equity, 195-98. *See also* Revenues, per-pupil
Equalization: fiscal, 200, 211-12, 251-52; of fiscal opportunity, among school districts, 238-39; of fiscal outcomes, among school districts, 238-39; of outputs, 306; of property tax rates, 255
Equity, 2-4; and choice, 91-92; and community colleges, 226-32; concepts of, 193-213; of costs and benefits, 223-24; distributive, 196-97; in educational finance, 189-90; model of, 335; present status of, 206-10; trends in, 312-22; and educational policy and programs, 287-88; and efficiency, 5-8, 24-25, 48, 91-92; in higher education, 215-33, 337-38; horizontal, 16-17, 326; legal, 198-206; and lifetime redistribution, 222-23; and litigation, 200-205; philosophical, 194-98; and student decisionmaking, 103-4; taxpayer, 314-15; types of, 16-20. *See also* Child equity; Commutative equity; Intergenerational equity; Tax equity
Equity criteria, 334-41; and educational finance system, 290-91; and efficiency criteria, 341-45; hierarchy, 20-22
Equity model for educational finance, requirements of, 205-6
Exchange efficiency, 4, 10

Expected earnings, of college graduates, 165
Expenditure, per-pupil, and humane growth, 342-43
Expenditure disparity text, 209
Expenditure inequalities: reduction of, 100-101
Externalities in education: *See* Benefits, Social

Family formation, and schooling, 136-37
Federal government, role in educational finance, 319-22
Fertility control behavior, and schooling, 133
Financial distress, of higher educational institutions, 177
Financial resources available for education, 7-10
Fiscal neutrality, 19-21, 207-8, 251-52, 335; as objective of reform, 238, 243-44
Fiscal opportunities, equalization of: *see* Equalization, of fiscal opportunities
Fiscal outcomes, equalization of: *see* Equalization, of fiscal outcomes
Flat grants, in California, 253
Florida, educational finance system in, 239-45
Foregone learning, 102-3
Formal schooling: *see* Schooling, formal
Foundation program, 207
Freeman, Richard, 47-48, 154-55
Fuel taxes, as source of revenue, 209

Goal-programming models, 295-300, 302-3
Goal-programming requirement, in state aid plans, 302
Government services, dissatisfaction with, as reason for taxpayers' revolt, 278-79
GTB. *See* Guaranteed Tax Base
Guaranteed Tax Base, 246, 249-50

Health, as benefit from schooling, 126-27
Home background factors, as predictors of student achievement, 81
Horizontal equity: *see* Equity, horizontal
Human capital: and education, attributes of, 39; and organization of education, 40; and schooling, 124-26
Human capital theory, 36
Humane growth; 2-3, 341-45; criteria of, 6-8, 22-25

Index

Incentive funds, in state aid plans, 301
Income, equitable distribution of, 2
Income tax, as source of revenue, 269, 272
Income tax rebate, in Kansas, 253
Inefficiency: see Efficiency
Inequality: see Equality
Inequity: see Equity
Inflation, as reason for taxpayers' revolt, 278
Instructional groups, 114
Intergenerational equity, 18-19, 338
Irrational behavior, and taxpayers' revolt, 281-82

Jointness in production, 111
Justice, and equity, 194-98

Kansas, educational finance system in, 239-45

Legal equity: see Equity, legal
Local spending, restrictions on, 275

Matching grants, by states, effect on school district spending, 256
Mathematical programming, and efficiency of resource allocation, 294-95
Michigan: educational finance system in, 239-45; budgetary behavior of school districts, 245-50
Migration, and effect from schooling, 127-28
Milieu, as resource input, 90
Minority rights, improvement as reason for taxpayers' revolt, 280
Money, as resource input, 89
Motor vehicle license fee tax, as source of revenue, 261
Municipal overburden provision, in Michigan, 253

Neighborhood dominant model, and student achievement, 54-55
Neighborhood effects, and learning, 328
Net benefits, and higher education, 217-18
Neutrality, Ben-Porath: see Ben-Porath neutrality
Neutrality, fiscal: see Fiscal neutrality
Neutrality theory (Hayek), 201
New Mexico, educational finance system in, 239-45
Non-instructional use of revenues, 242-43
Non-labor market productivity, 123-24
Non-monetary benefits. See Benefits, non-monetary

Non-wage dimensions of labor market remuneration, 121

Opportunity costs, 325
Optimization of internal efficiency, 302-6
Outcomes of schooling, 96-97
Output incentives, in state aid plans, 301
Outputs, and relation to efficiency, 292-94
Overtaking age, 157

Parent-dominant model, and student achievement, 53
Parental involvement, 45-47, 74-75, 327
Parents, reasons for reduction in authority of, 41-42, 44-47
Parents' schooling, and effect on earnings of offspring, 139-41
Pareto efficiency, 4, 327
Pell Grant: see Basic Educational Opportunity Grant program
Penalty factor, in state aid plans, 301
Per-pupil expenditure, 255, 291-92; differences in, 313
Per-pupil revenues, equality of, 242-43
Philosophical equity: see Equity, philosophical
Physical capital, and human capital, 39
Positivism (Rawlsian equity), 21-22, 197-98, 201, 212-13
Price efficiency, 8
Process of schooling, as resource input, 90
Process-product approach, and school productivity, 95-96
Production efficiency, 4, 8-10
Production function model, for school productivity, 94-96
Production function studies, 79-84
Production of learning, and equity and efficiency, 103-4
Productivity: in activities outside labor market, 122; as financing criterion, 78-97
Property tax, reliance on for education financing, 268, 270
Proportionality, 21
Proposition 13 (California), 275, 281-84
Public finance, and education, 38-39
Pupil achievement: see Achievement of pupils
Pupil weighting system, in Florida, 253
Putty-clay effect (capital theory), 109

Quality of education, and costs, 32

Rate of return: concept and method of, 152-54; to education, 37, 157-58, 160; to higher education, decline of, 154-55; internal, calculation of, 179-80; monetary: 153-54, by intended occupation, 169-76, to higher education, 150-85, 332-34, by type of institution, 161-69; private: 152-54, for higher education, 166, by intended occupation, 169-70; social, 152-54, 167-69, 170-76, 332-34
Rawls, John, 197-98
Redistribution, and other views of equity, 220-22
Regulatory policies, as reason for taxpayer revolt, 278-80
Resource allocation, in schools, 101-16, 292-95
Resource flows, to students, 110-13
Resource inputs, and educational outcomes, 86-89
Restitution, 212
Returns to education, non-monetary, 2-3, 331-32
Return, rate of: see Rate of return
Revenues, for non-instructional use: see Non-instructional use, of revenue
Revenues, per-pupil: see Per-pupil revenues
Revolt, of taxpayers: see Taxpayer revolt

Salaries: of college graduates, compared to high school graduates, 156-57; starting, trends in, 155-56, 177
Sales tax, as source of revenue, 269, 273-75
Scale of educational institutions, and effects, 43-47
School budget, and decisionmaking in educational finance, 101-2
School dominant model, and student achievement, 53-54
School finance: see Educational finance
School productivity; and educational finance reform, 318; studies of, 79-90
Schooling: formal, investment in, 31; technology of, 41
SES. See Socioeconomic status
Skilled labor, as attribute of human capital, 39
Social benefits: see Benefits, social
Social costs, for higher education, 165
Social efficiency: see Efficiency, social
Social reform, and schools as agents of, 41-42; programs, and effect on schools, 46-47

Social welfare function, 5-6
Socioeconomic status, and student achievement, 53-75
State aid for higher education, modifications of, 252-55
State aid plans, 300-306
State allocation goal-programming model, 342
State control of education: see Education, and state control
State spending, restrictions on, 275
Strayer-Haig-Mort Foundation Programs, 291
Structure, administrative and organizational, and humane growth, 344-45
Student ability: see Ability of student
Student achievement, and socioeconomic status, 53-75
Student-teacher interaction, 329
Student equity: see Child equity
Student involvement in learning, 113-15
Student's time: see Time, student's
Subsidies, in higher education, redistribution of, 218-20
Substitution of inputs, in classroom, 105-6

Target output levels, 303-4
Tax: see specific types, e.g., Income, Sales, Property, Fuel, Motor vehicle fee
Tax equity, 228, 336, 338-41; changes in, as result of education finance reform, 245
Tax increases, as reason for taxpayers' revolt, 276-78
Tax structure, changes in, 276-81
Taxpayer equity: see Equity, taxpayer
Taxpayers' revolt, 275-85
Teacher-student interaction, 329
Teacher time, allocation among students, 109-12, 114
Teachers: behavior and student achievement, 53-54; as consequence of shift in loci of decisionmaking, 43-44; as resource input, 90
Technical efficiency: see Efficiency, technical
Technology of schooling: see Schooling, technology of
Testing competency, 344
Time, student's, as valued resource, 102-3
Time, teacher's: see Teacher time
Time availability, and socioeconomic status, 60-74
Time budget studies, and student achievement, 56-57

Tuition, and enrollment at community colleges, 229-32

Utility, calculation of maximum, 143-44

Vertical equity, 17-22
Voucher system, 344-45

Wealth neutrality test, 209